Evaluation and Treatment of Neuropsychologically Compromised Children

Evaluation and Treatment of Neuropsychologically Compromised Children

Edited by

Darlyne G. Nemeth
Janna Glozman

ELSEVIER

ACADEMIC PRESS
An imprint of Elsevier

Academic Press is an imprint of Elsevier
125 London Wall, London EC2Y 5AS, United Kingdom
525 B Street, Suite 1650, San Diego, CA 92101, United States
50 Hampshire Street, 5th Floor, Cambridge, MA 02139, United States
The Boulevard, Langford Lane, Kidlington, Oxford OX5 1GB, United Kingdom

Notices
Knowledge and best practice in this field are constantly changing. As new research and experience broaden our understanding, changes in research methods, professional practices, or medical treatment may become necessary.

Practitioners and researchers must always rely on their own experience and knowledge in evaluating and using any information, methods, compounds, or experiments described herein. In using such information or methods they should be mindful of their own safety and the safety of others, including parties for whom they have a professional responsibility.

To the fullest extent of the law, neither the Publisher nor the authors, contributors, or editors, assume any liability for any injury and/or damage to persons or property as a matter of products liability, negligence or otherwise, or from any use or operation of any methods, products, instructions, or ideas contained in the material herein.

Library of Congress Cataloging-in-Publication Data
A catalog record for this book is available from the Library of Congress

British Library Cataloguing-in-Publication Data
A catalogue record for this book is available from the British Library

ISBN 978-0-12-819545-1

For information on all Academic Press publications
visit our website at https://www.elsevier.com/books-and-journals

Publisher: Nikki Levi
Editorial Project Manager: Pat Gonzalez
Production Project Manager: Kiruthika Govindaraju
Cover Designer: Matthew Limbert

Typeset by SPi Global, India

Contents

Contributors xiii
About the authors xv
About the editors xxiii
Foreword xxvii
Acknowledgments xxix
Prologue xxxi

1. The contributions of Luria and Reitan to developmental neuropsychology and to the understanding of neuropsychologically compromised children

Janna Glozman, Darlyne G. Nemeth

The contributions of Luria to developmental neuropsychology 1
Developmental neuropsychology in Russia 2
Developmental neuropsychology in America 4
The contributions of Reitan to developmental neuropsychology 5
Diagnostic case examples of neuropsychologically compromised children 6
An example of Reitan-Indiana Neuropsychological Test Battery scoring 7
Learning disabilities 12
Mathematics (dyscalculia) 16
Reading (dyslexia) 16
Written language (dysgraphia) 17
Attention deficit hyperactivity disorder (ADHD) 18
Agenesis of the corpus callosum (ACC) 20
Asperger's syndrome 20
Autism spectrum disorder 20
Cognitive disorder secondary to epilepsy and cerebral palsy 22
Global developmental delay with cognitive, affective, and behavioral dyscontrol 23
Bipolar disorder 23
Traumatic brain injury (TBI) 23
Summary 23
In conclusion 23
References 24
Further reading 26

2. Heritage of Reitan and Luria to 21st century developmental neuropsychology

Joaquim Quintino-Aires

Introduction 27
Ralph M. Reitan, pioneer of neuropsychological clinical practice. An ever-present teacher without even knowing it himself 28
Alexander Luria, A theory for neuropsychological clinical practice. An ever-present teacher without even knowing 32
Higher cortical functions in man and the regulatory role of language 34
Systemic organization of higher cortical functions 36
Dynamic organization of higher cortical functions 37
Bottom-up development 38
Luria's concept of three functional blocks 39
Lurian clinical-psychological investigation 41
Reitan and Luria in the new clinical practice in developmental neuropsychology in the 21st century 43
Neuropsychological habilitation 43
Case study 44
In conclusion 49
References 50

3. Integrating quantitative and qualitative measures with neuropsychological assessment and intervention

Janna Glozman

Introduction 53
Who needs neuropsychological assessment? 53
How to assess? 54
Case study 61
Combined neuropsychological evaluation 61
Conclusions 69
Acknowledgment 69
References 69
Further reading 72

4. Combining qualitative and quantitative measures in the evaluation of executive functions in ADHD

Irina Shevchenko

Introduction 73
Rationale for the choice of measures 74
Luria's qualitative methods of neuropsychological assessment 75
Conners' scale 78
Questionnaire of early child development 79
Quantitative assessment measures 79

Results of evaluation of executive functions in ADHD 83
Luria's approach 83
Quantitative methods 86
Conclusion 88
References 89
Further reading 91

5. Ralph M. Reitan and the clinical interpretation of neuropsychological test data

Arthur MacNeill Horton Jr.

Introduction 93
Research status 94
Methodological contributions 95
Test battery components 97
The Category Test 97
Tactual Performance Test 97
Speech Sounds Perception Test 98
Rhythm Test 98
Trail Making Test 98
Finger Tapping Test 98
Reitan-Indiana Aphasia Screening Test 99
Reitan-Klove Sensory-Perceptual Examination 99
Reitan-Klove Lateral Dominance Examination 99
Strength of Grip 99
Additional tests for the HRNB 99
Children's versions 100
General Neuropsychological Deficit Scale (GNDS) 100
Alternative Impairment Index 101
Children's version of the AII 101
Clinical interpretation of the HRNB 102
Screening for brain damage 103
Factor structure of the HRNB for older and younger children 103
Conclusion 104
References 104
Further reading 106

6. Executive functions defined

Darlyne G. Nemeth, Kayla Mckenzie Chustz

Background information 107
The value of play in executive functions 108
Learning emotional regulation via play 109
Defining executive functions—American style 109
Executive function questionnaires—An American perspective 111
Executive function dysregulation profile 113
Defining executive functions—Russian style 115
Measuring executive functions–An American perspective 115

Understanding executive functions from a Russian perspective 117
Luria's approach 117
In conclusion 118
References 119
Further reading 120

7. Understanding "hot and cold" executive functions in children and adolescents
Darlyne G. Nemeth, Kayla Mckenzie Chustz

Introduction 121
Defining "hot and cold" executive functions 122
The executive functioning dysregulation profile 123
IQ versus EQ 124
Anxiety and cognition 126
Case illustration 126
Depression and cognition 127
Case illustration 128
Conclusions 128
References 129
Further reading 130

8. Preparing children to learn through early intervention
Carla Anauate, Edna Maria Severino Peters Kahhale

Introduction 131
Alexander R. Luria 132
Ralph M. Reitan 133
Early intervention—Prenatal stage 134
Early intervention—Postnatal 138
Orientations to caregivers based on the spheres of SGSII 138
Attachment and brain development 142
Childhood interventions 146
Luria's functional system 148
Recent studies 150
Low birth weight 150
Early stimulation 151
Interactive activities 152
Extreme vulnerability 153
The importance of early intervention 153
Conclusion 153
References 155

9. The role of family in speech rehabilitation of children with learning disabilities: Clinical observations by Luria and Reitan
Natalyia Karpova, Elena Nikolaeva

Introduction 157
Genetic and psychophysiological courses of stuttering 158

Communication problems and stuttering 159
Methods and techniques of speech remediation in children and adolescents with learning disabilities based on theories by Luria and Reitan 161
System of family relations and speech disturbances 161
Family group logopsychotherapy by Nekrasova and Karpova 162
Neuropsychological, psychological, and psychophysiological study of participants in family logopsychotherapy 163
The results of a system inter- and multidisciplinary study of the brain mechanisms of stuttering in the context of logopsychotherapeutic rehabilitation 163
Lateral features in stutterers 164
Retention of the results in the 6th month 166
Using the Luria battery in assessment of communication in stuttering 167
Involvement of family members of individuals in active participation during the remediation of verbal communication in family group logopsychotherapy 168
Psychological mechanisms of the remediation process and general principles of social rehabilitation 171
Conclusion 173
Acknowledgments 174
References 174
Further reading 177

10. Formation of higher mental functions in children with special educational needs via social interaction

Vitaly Rubtsov, Andrey Konokotin

Introduction 179
Aim of research and methods 182
Analysis of the results 186
Some concluding remarks 193
Summary 194
References 195

11. Laying the framework for developing executive functions in tweens with learning disabilities

Fernando Pastrana, Patricia A. McElroy, Scott Johnson, Kayla Mckenzie Chustz, Darlyne G. Nemeth

Introduction 197
A historical perspective 198
Integrating the Luria and Reitan models of intervention 200
Program description 202
Measures/materials utilized 204
Program outline 205
Online math training software 210
Methods and results 210
Participant demographics 210

Methods 211
Results—Questionnaires 211
Results—Objective measures 212
Summary 216
Limitations 217
Acknowledgments 218
References 218

12. Rebuilding executive functions in environmentally traumatized children and adolescents
Judy Kuriansky, Darlyne G. Nemeth

Introduction 221
Conceptual and contextual framework 223
Executive functions 224
The context of a model of Russian neuropsychology 224
The context of a model of American neuropsychology 224
The anniversary wellness workshops in the wake of natural disaster: Association to the REHABIT system 225
The multisensory approach 227
Neurocognitive aspects of the workshop activities 227
Restoring trust 230
Insuring safety 230
Assuring attention 231
Moving energy 231
Boosting self-esteem 232
Storytelling 232
Different learning styles 232
Discussion 233
The value of acknowledgment 234
The value of processing anniversary reactions 234
The value of the group format 234
Long-lasting trauma 235
Posttraumatic growth 235
Neurocognition in a holistic view of disaster recovery interventions 235
Stages of recovery 236
Assessment 237
Applications of wellness workshops in various cultures and settings 237
Context of major policy agreements 238
Recommendations 238
Conclusions 239
Appendix 240
Acknowledgments 240
References 241

13. Neuropsychological evaluation of children with complex medical concerns

Traci W. Olivier

Pediatric neuropsychological evaluations 249
Referral source and reason for referral 249
Consider the setting 250
Essential components of a neuropsychological evaluation 251
Complex pediatric medical conditions 254
Complications associated with prematurity and/or low birth weight 254
Pediatric cancer 257
Acquired and traumatic brain injuries 260
Special considerations for pediatric neuropsychologists 261
Intellectual assessment batteries 261
Performance validity tests 262
Concluding comments 262
The role of the pediatric neuropsychologist in interdisciplinary care 262
Promoting resilience in children and families 263
References 263

14. When medication may be helpful

John A. Flatt, Darlyne G. Nemeth

Introduction 267
Neuroimaging studies and neurodiagnostic testing 268
The process 270
Frequently used measures 274
The IEP meeting 274
Are medications needed? 275
What medications for what symptoms? 275
Symptom-based approaches 276
Attention deficit and hyperactivity disorders 276
Sleep disorders 279
Seizures and epilepsy 281
Headaches 283
Tic disorders 286
Obsessive-compulsive disorders 287
Aggressive behavior 288
Drooling 289
Constipation 292
When pharmacogenomic studies help 293
Medicine versus behavior modification 294
References 295
Further reading 297

15. Implications for the future
Darlyne G. Nemeth, Janna Glozman

Let us summarize the recommendations for the future 302
Assessment 302
Intervention 303
Research 303
References 304
Further reading 304

Epilogue 305
Index 307

Contributors

Numbers in paranthesis indicate the pages on which the authors' contributions begin.

Carla Anauate (131), CINAPSI—Centro Integrado de Neuropsicologia e Psicologia, Integrated Center of Neuropsychology and Psychology; PUCSP—Pontifical Catholic University of São Paulo, Department of Psychology, São Paulo, Brazil; Department of Psychology, Emory University, Atlanta, GA, United States; CENSUPEG—College of Science, Education, Health, Research and Management, Joinville, Brazil

Kayla Mckenzie Chustz (107,121,197), The Neuropsychology Center of Louisiana, LLC, Baton Rouge, LA, United States

John A. Flatt (267), The Jason Foundation, Inc., Hendersonville, TN, United States

Janna Glozman (1,53,299), M. V. Lomonosov Moscow State University, Moscow, Russia

Arthur MacNeill Horton Jr. (93), Neuropsychology Section, Psych Associates of Maryland, Bethesda, MD, United States

Scott Johnson (197), Pediatric Development & Therapy Center, Our Lady of the Lake Children's Health, Baton Rouge, LA, United States

Edna Maria Severino Peters Kahhale (131), PUCSP—Pontifical Catholic University of São Paulo, Department of Psychology, São Paulo, Brazil

Natalyia Karpova (157), Psychological Institute of Russian Academy of Education, Moscow, Russia

Andrey Konokotin (179), Moscow State University of Psychology and Education, Moscow, Russian Federation

Judy Kuriansky (221), International Association of Applied Psychology, Indianapolis, IN; Teachers College, Columbia University, New York, NY, United States

Patricia A. McElroy (197), The Neuropsychology Center of Louisiana, LLC, Baton Rouge, LA, United States

Darlyne G. Nemeth (1,107,121,197,221,267,299), The Neuropsychology Center of Louisiana, LLC, Baton Rouge, LA, United States

Elena Nikolaeva (157), Herzen State Pedagogical University, Saint-Petersburg, Russia

Traci W. Olivier (249), Pediatric Development & Therapy Center, Our Lady of the Lake Children's Health; Neuropsychology Center of Louisiana, Baton Rouge, LA, United States

Fernando Pastrana (197), Neuropsychology Center of Louisiana at Gretna, LLC, Gretna; The Neuropsychology Center of Louisiana, LLC, Baton Rouge, LA, United States

Joaquim Quintino-Aires (27), Neuropsychology Department, Vygotsky Institute, Lisbon, Portugal

Vitaly Rubtsov (179), Moscow State University of Psychology and Education, Moscow, Russian Federation

Irina Shevchenko (73), Neuropsychological Remediation Center "Cortex", Krasnogorsk, Moscow Region, Russian Federation

About the authors

Carla Anauate, Ph.D., Director of CINAPSI: Integrated Center for Neuropsychology and Psychology, is a psychologist, psychotherapist, and neuropsychologist from São Paulo, Brazil. She received her doctorate in 2019 in clinical psychology from a combined program with Pontifícia Universidade Católica of São Paulo and Emory University. Her master's degree was obtained from Universidade de São Paulo in educational and developmental psychology in 2008. She focused on the inclusion of deaf and listening students in elementary school. She completed courses in neuropsychology, psychopedagogy, sociohistorical clinical psychology, the Rorschach test, and domestic violence. She was an undergraduate university professor in the psychology course at Universidade Nove de Julho and actually served as a graduate professor of courses regarding neuropsychopedagogy at CENSUPEG. Anauate has experience in judicial psychology, educational psychology (inclusion of children with deficiencies and disabilities), and health psychology (adolescence program) in BRAZIL. Anauate is a Member of International Society of Applied Neuropsychology.

Kayla Mckenzie Chustz, B.S., graduated from Louisiana State University in 2018 with a major in psychology. She is serving a clinical externship under Darlyne G. Nemeth, Ph.D., M.P., at the Neuropsychology Center of Louisiana. Chustz's primary emphasis has been on the evaluation and treatment of neuropsychologically compromised children. She has tested more than 200 children for brain-behavior, attentional, and affective dysfunction focusing on executive, school, and family issues. Chustz is skilled in working with children, families, and schools to assist in the pediatric developmental issues that cause the most disruption in a school setting. She has had presentations accepted at the following meetings: the American Academy of Pediatric Neuropsychology, the Louisiana Psychological Association, the National Academy of Neuropsychology, and the Neuroscience Education Institute. Chustz has coauthored two chapters in this volume, focusing on executive functions in children. She has been Dr. Nemeth's primary assistant in the research and preparation for this volume.

John Flatt, M.D., is originally from Hendersonville, Tennessee, and now resides just outside of New Orleans. He completed medical school in Memphis at the University of Tennessee Health Science Center, and he also completed his general pediatric training at Le Bonheur Children's Hospital in Memphis. He then matriculated at Vanderbilt University to complete his pediatric neurology training, including a chief resident year at the Vanderbilt Children's Hospital. After completion of training, he entered private practice in pediatric neurology in Louisiana. His clinical practice was unique as a pediatric neurologist in addressing a wide array of neurological conditions as well as psychological comorbidities or neuropsychiatric syndromes as the primary medical provider. Beyond clinical practice, he also serves as the chief medical officer of the Jason Foundation, a not-for-profit organization founded by his family for the awareness and prevention of youth suicide. Professionally, he has emphasized the importance of integrated care.

Arthur MacNeill Horton, Jr., received his Ed.D. from the University of Virginia in 1976. He also holds diplomates in both clinical psychology and behavioral psychology from the American Board of Professional Psychology; in neuropsychology from the American Board of Professional Neuropsychology; and in pediatric neuropsychology from the American Board of Pediatric Neuropsychology. Horton is the author/editor of 17 books, 47 book chapters, and more than 130 journal articles. He is a past president of ABN, the National Academy of Neuropsychology, and the Maryland Psychological Association. Previously, Horton was a program officer with the National Institute of Drug Abuse of the National Institutes of Health with responsibilities for neuropsychology and child development. He has taught at the University of Virginia and the Johns Hopkins University, among other universities. He is the current editor in chief of both APPLIED NEUROPSYCHOLOGY-ADULT and APPLIED NEUROPSYCHOLOGY-CHILD.

Scott Johnson, M.Ed., is a statistical and data analyst. He has consulted with failing schools to assist in the development of positive changes in regard to teaching and instruction adaptation. His expertise in Register Transfer Level has helped many Louisiana school districts improve to the Top 5 in student growth and development. Johnson has trained more than 2000 teachers and built interventions for more than 20,000 students. He led an assessment program that has assisted more than 300,000 students. Currently, Johnson is a clinical and research assistant at the Our Lady of the Lake Children's Health Clinic and the Neuropsychology Center of Louisiana in Baton Rouge. Johnson earned his master's in education at Louisiana State University and has accumulated more than 5 years of doctoral credits in school psychology. At NCLA, Johnson has directed the mathematics mentoring program for the Build-A-Brain program.

Edna Maria Severino Peters Kahhale, Ph.D., holds a degree in psychology from the Pontifical Catholic University of São Paulo, a master's in experimental psychology from the University of São Paulo, and a doctorate in experimental psychology from the University of São Paulo. She is currently a researcher, associate professor, and coordinator of LESSEX (Laboratory of Health and Sexuality Studies), linked to the Psychosomatic and Hospital Psychology Center of the Pontifical Catholic University of São Paulo. She is also leader of the research group registered at CNPq Psychosomatics and Hospital Psychology, and is university certified. She has experience in psychology, focusing on psychosomatic disorders, including adolescence, sociohistorical psychology and the extended clinic, sexuality, psychoprophylactic care, and women's health. She is the organizer and author of chapters in several books on sociohistorical psychology, including *The Diversity of Psychology: A Theoretical Construction; HIV/AIDS: Facing Psychological Suffering; Research in Clinical Psychology: Context and Challenges; Sexual Identity: Metamorphosis-Emancipation from Dialectical Materialism.*

Natalia Karpova, Ph.D., is a leading researcher at the Psychological Institute of the Russian Academy of Education, where she has been working since 1988. She is a doctor of psychological sciences and professor at Moscow State Psychology-Pedagogical University. She is a member of the Russian Academy of Natural Sciences, the Academy of Pedagogical and Social Sciences, the Russian Psychological Society, and the International Society for Quality-of-Life Studies. She directs the work of groups for family logopsychotherapy in different Russian cities, including Moscow, Samara, Taganrog, Vladivostok, and Saratov. Karpova is the author and/or editor of 12 books: (collective monographs and conference materials): *Psychology of Communication: Encyclopedic Dictionary* (2011, 2014), *Family Group Logopsychotherapy: The Study of Stuttering* (2011), *Bibliopsychology and Bibliotherapy* (2005, 2014), etc. She has more than 200 publications. A scientific documentary film "Man can do all-2" (SKIP film, 2000) was made about her work.

Andrey V. Konokotin is a doctoral student at the Moscow State University of Psychology and Education under the supervision of Professor V.V. Rubtsov. In 2015, he received a bachelor's degree in legal psychology. His research topic was "Social Representations of Mentally Ill Children in Secondary and High School." In 2017, he received a master's degree in psycho-pedagocial education. His thesis was "Individual Characteristics of Self-Esteem in Teenagers with Special Educational Needs in Interaction with Group-mates." He has published two papers: "A review of psychological studies on social interactions of students in inclusive classrooms" and "Inclusion of children with special educational needs and normally developing children in a joint solution of educational tasks" (e.g., solving tasks on the understanding of multiplicative relationships). His dissertation research focuses on the inclusion of children ages 6–9 with special educational needs in a joint-distributed learning activity. From 2014 to 2019, he worked as a school psychologist.

Judy Kuriansky, Ph.D., a noted international clinical psychologist, is on the faculty of Columbia University Teachers College. She is a United Nations NGO representative for the International Association of Applied Psychology and the World Council of Psychotherapy. She has advocated successfully for the inclusion of mental health and well-being in the UN 2030 Global Agenda, the Universal Health Coverage Political Declaration, the Sendai Framework, the Global Compact on Migration, and the Astana Declaration on Primary Health Care. In her humanitarian work, she has provided psychosocial support after natural disasters in China, Haiti, Iran, Japan, Sint Maarten, and the United States as well as with refugees in Jordan and during the Ebola outbreak in West Africa. She also codeveloped a girls' empowerment camp in Africa. Her many books address disaster recovery, the Middle East crisis, the Ebola epidemic, ecopsychology, sexuality education, children's self-esteem, and healthy relationships. She received the Humanitarian Award for Lifetime Achievement in Global Peace and Tolerance.

Patricia A. McElroy, Ed.S., NCED, has been in practice as an educational diagnostician for 46 years. McElroy received her bachelor's degree in special education and mental retardation from Oklahoma State University in 1973. She pursued a master's in education, focusing on learning disabilities, and received her education specialist degree from Louisiana State University. McElroy served as a member of the Livingston Parish, Louisiana, Pupil Appraisal team as an educational diagnostician. She was then affiliated with the Louisiana Department of Education as the state supervisor for educational diagnosticians. During her tenure at the Louisiana State Department of Education, McElroy was one of the authors of record for Bulletin 1508, a qualifying bulletin at the state level that complies with the United States' national Individualized Disabilities Education Act. Now, a valued member of the Neuropsychology Center of Louisiana, McElroy evaluates and treats children with educational needs.

Elena I. Nikolaeva, Ph.D., Sci.D., was born in 1953 in Abakan, USSR. She graduated from the Novosibirsk State University, then received her Ph.D. in 1981 and her Sci.D. in 1996. She has been a professor in the Department of Developmental Psychology and Family Pedagogics at Herzen State Pedagogical University in St. Petersburg, Russia, since 2002. She has been the supervisor of 14 Ph.D. dissertations. She has been a member of the Russian Psychological Society since 2003; the European Health Psychology Society since 2003; and the Interregional Association of Cognitive Researchers since 2007. Her research interests include psychophysiology, family psychology, child creativity; developmental psychology, and health psychology. Nikolaeva is a member of the editorial boards of the Psychology of Education in Polycultural Field (Russia, Eletz); Current Issues in Education (the publisher of which is Małopolska School of Economics, Poland); the Russian Humanitarian Journal; and Health Psychology and Behavioral Medicine. She is the author of more than 500 articles and books.

Traci W. Olivier, Psy.D., specializes in neurocognitive evaluations and rehabilitation for children/adolescents experiencing cognitive difficulties secondary to medical conditions, including developmental disorders, acquired or traumatic brain injuries, seizure-related disorders, central nervous system tumors, and other hematology/oncology diagnoses. Her latest publication, in the *Journal of Clinical Oncology*, focused on reading-related difficulties secondary to ototoxicity in children treated for embryonal brain tumors. Her doctorate in clinical psychology with an emphasis on neuropsychology was obtained from Nova Southeastern University. She completed her internship at the Kennedy Krieger Institute and Johns Hopkins University School of Medicine, which is a Leadership Education in Neurodevelopmental and Related Disabilities program. Olivier completed a postdoctoral clinical/research fellowship in pediatric neuropsychology at St. Jude Children's Research Hospital in Memphis. She heads the division of pediatric neuropsychology at Our Lady of the Lake Children's Health and practices at the Neuropsychology Center of Louisiana in Baton Rouge.

Fernando Pastrana, Jr., received his Ph.D. in clinical psychology from the Pacific Graduate School of Psychology at Palo Alto University in 2011 with a certificate in neuropsychological assessment proficiency. He completed an APA-approved internship at Wright State University and a 2-year postdoctoral fellowship in rehabilitation psychology at the Shepherd Center. He is licensed in Louisiana with specialties in clinical psychology and clinical neuropsychology. He has coauthored a book chapter in a two-volume anthology on the topic of ecopsychology. He has served as Executive Council Member, Diversity Committee Chair, and American Psychological Association Diversity Delegate of the Louisiana Psychological Association. Pastrana has presented nationally and internationally on a variety of topics in the field of psychology. He earned a master's degree in clinical psychopharmacology from Alliant International University. Pastrana is in private practice at the Baton Rouge and Gretna Offices of the Neuropsychology Center of Louisiana.

Antonio Puente, Ph.D., is professor of psychology at the University of North Carolina-Wilmington. Born in La Habana, Cuba, he immigrated to the United States in 1960. Puente received his Ph.D. from the University of Georgia. Since 1981, he has taught classes on brain and behavior, clinical neuropsychology, and the history of psychology. He is the founding director of UNCW's Centro Hispano and his research focuses on the interface between culture and neuropsychology. He has published scientific and professional articles in several languages. Puente has been president of the American Psychological Association, the North Carolina Psychological Association, the North Carolina Psychological Foundation, the Hispanic Neuropsychological Association, the National Academy of Neuropsychology, and the Society for Clinical Neuropsychology (Division 40 of APA). He received APA's Distinguished

Professional Contributions to Independent Practice in 2011. Puente has a private practice in clinical neuropsychology and provides behavioral health services for the poor and uninsured at Cape Fear Clinic, where he is the founder and director.

Joaquim Quintino-Aires, Ph.D. in psycholinguistics, graduated in clinical psychology from the University of Lisbon. He holds a professional title in neuropsychology and psychotherapy by Ordem dos Psicólogos Portugueses. He served in the neurosurgery department of the Military Hospital in Lisbon and as a professor of psychology, education, and sport at Lisbon Lusófona University. He founded the first neuropsychology laboratory in a Portuguese university and the first Portuguese postgraduate neuropsychology course. He has authored numerous books, book chapters, and articles. He has given conferences and courses in more than 50 countries. He has received many awards: In 2009, he received the honorary title of "professor emeritus" from Moscow State University; in 2012, the Copernicus Award from the Polish Society of Neuropsychology; and in 2017, the Luria award from Moscow State University. He continues to appear on weekly television programs regarding development and human behavior. He heads the Vygotsky Institute in Portugal, where he conducts clinical practice, teaching, and research activities.

Vitaly V. Rubtsov, Professor, doctor of psychology, honorary professor of the University of Wisconsin (1999, Wisconsin, United States). From 1997 to 2018 he was the Rector (leading person), from 2018 he is the President (Scientific Director) of Moscow State University of Psychology and Education (Moscow, Russia). Since 2004, Rubtsov has chaired the All-Russian Federation of Educational Psychologists. Rubtsov's scientific interests include age psychology, educational psychology, cultural-historical theory, and activity approach in education. He has focused on social interactions in learning and on the professional activities of educators, teacher-psychologists, social workers, and professional educators. Rubtsov has conducted fundamental research on psychological patterns, the mechanisms of organizing joint learning activities, and the genesis of cognitive actions in children. He expanded the social-genetic concept of joint learning activities and created a new type of genetic modeling method to study learning actions in children in the process of social interactions. Rubtsov has published more than 200 scientific works and fundamental monographs on age psychology and educational psychology.

Irina Shevchenko has a Ph.D. in medical psychology from Tomsk University (Tomsk City, Russia). She is a child neuropsychologist who specializes in neuropsychological assessment and remediation. For the past 8 years, Shevchenko has specialized in neuropsychological assessment and remediation of preschool and primary school children with delayed development. She has focused on neurological diagnoses (e.g., ADHD), birth injuries, and persistent learning and behavioral difficulties at school. In private practice, Shevchenko works with children individually, supporting a complex approach to neuropsychological remediation with children with developmental delays and learning disabilities. She also uses body-oriented techniques. Shevchenko has participated in many Russian and international conferences and congresses. She is the author and/or coauthor of 16 scientific articles and four book chapters dedicated to neuropsychological remediation. She has conducted training programs in neuropsychological remediation for psychologists and neuropsychologists in Brazil (São Paulo, Campinas, Foz do Iguaçu cities; 2017, 2019).

About the editors

Janna Glozman, Ph.D., D.Sc., was born in Moscow, Russia, in 1940. She is a neuropsychologist, neurolinguist, research scientist, specialist in neuropsychological assessment and rehabilitation, and a professor of neuropsychology, neurogeriatrics, developmental neuropsychology, and communication problems.

In 1963, Glozman graduated from Moscow Linguistic University with a master's degree in general linguistics (problems of word etymology). She then developed an interest in neurolinguistics and neuropsychology. In 1970, Glozman obtained a master's degree in psychology from Moscow State University. Her master's thesis on memory troubles in focal brain damage was supervised by A.R. Luria.

Since 1970, Glozman has worked as a research scientist at Moscow State University's Psychology Department. Currently, she is the leading researcher in that department. She combines neuropsychological research and assessment of brain-damaged patients. These efforts are conducted in the Laboratory of Neuropsychology at the Neurological Hospital of Moscow Medical University. This laboratory was founded by A.R. Luria in the 1920s. Her work, which includes using Luria's methods to evaluate and treat learning-disabled children, is conducted at Luria's Research Center of Developmental Neuropsychology.

In 1974, Glozman obtained her Ph.D. from Moscow State University. Her psychology dissertation focused on the neurolinguistics study of agrammatism in aphasia. In 1990, Glozman was a visiting scholar at the New Medico Rehabilitation Center, in Troy, New York, in the United States. In 1996, she was a visiting professor at the University of North Carolina at Wilmington, also in the United States. In 2000, she received a doctor of sciences degree in psychology, with a dissertation focusing on "Communication disorder and personality." In 2001, she was nominated as the Moscow State University Emerite Scientist. In 2002, she was elevated to a full professor at the Psychology Department.

Glozman has been a member of the Russian Psychological Association since 1991 and an honorary member of the Polish Neuropsychological Society since 2002. She was also a member of the New York Academy of Sciences from 1995 to 2010.

Glozman also serves on many editorial boards, including *Neuropsychology Review* (1996–2005); *Acta Neuropsychologica* (since 2005); the *International Journal of Contemporary NeuroScience* (since 2011); the *East European Journal of Psycholinguistics* (since 2015); and the Annales of the University of Maria Curie-Skłodowska in Lublin, *sec.* J, Pedagogia—Psychologia (since 2015).

Glozman is the author and editor of more than 500 publications and 45 books in Russian, English, German, Polish, Spanish, French, and Portuguese. She has given more than 100 presentations at various international congresses throughout the world. Every 5 years, Glozman is in charge of organizing the International Luria Memorial Congress, which has become a significant event for international neuropsychologists.

Glozman has been recognized for her outstanding contributions to the science and practice of neuropsychology in many ways: her biography was included in the 14th edition of *Who's Who in the World*, 1997; in the book *2000 Outstanding People of the 20th Century*, International Biographical Centre, Cambridge, 1998; in the book *Famous Russians*, Moscow, 1999; in the 6th and 9th editions of *Who's Who in Science and Engineering*, 2001 and 2006; in the book *2000 Outstanding People of the 21st Century*, Cambridge, 2004; in the biographical dictionary *Women of Moscow University*, 2004; and in the Encyclopedia of Moscow University, biographical dictionary, Moscow 2006. She has been decorated with the Medal of Academy of Reeducation, Krakow, Poland, 1994; medals for 850Years of Moscow, 1997, and 250Years of Moscow State University, 2005; the Prime of Vygotsky from the Association Portuguese "Lev Vygotsky in Education," 2010; the Medal of Chelpanov, 2014; the architect of Polish Neuropsychology, 2017; the Golden Psyche, 2018; and the National Prime "Harmony" from the Union of Mental Health, 2019.

Glozman has not only espoused the ideas of her mentor, A.R. Luria, throughout the world, but she has also creatively evolved those theories to meet today's needs. She founded a new branch of neuropsychology, the *Neuropsychology of Communication*, and published books on it in Russia, Great Britain, and the United States. The focus of her research has been to study the interrelations between communication and personality disturbances. Glozman has developed a system of scoring Luria's neuropsychological assessment data for both children and adults. This system has been published in Russian, English, and Portuguese. Glozman is currently serving as the editor in chief of the new international journal, the *Lurian Journal*. The purpose of this journal is to promote and develop Luria's theories in psychology throughout the world.

Darlyne Gaynor Nemeth, Ph.D., M.P., M.P.A.P., founded the Neuropsychology Center of Louisiana, where she has a broad-spectrum practice in the areas of clinical, medical, and neuropsychology. Her practice interests include working with adults and children with brain-behavior dysfunction, including head injuries, attention deficit disorder, learning disabilities, and/or individuals with special needs. Her academic interests include teaching and supervising graduate students as well as researching and developing intervention programs. One such program is NCLA's Build-A-Brain series, which is described in Chapter 11 of this volume.

In 2017, Dr. Nemeth, with her colleague Dr. Traci Olivier, coauthored *Innovative Approaches to Individual and Community Resilience: From Theory to Practice*. This volume won a Prose Award for (1) groundbreaking contributions to the scholarly community, (2) rigorously researching, editing, and fact checking the literature, (3) delivering an engaging and compelling narrative, (4) including supporting materials such as reviews and information about the authors, and (5) creating content that is impeccably produced with exceptional quality. Nemeth and Olivier presented a seminar on resilience at the 2018 Louisiana Book Festival.

Nemeth's first book, *Helping Your Angry Child*, coauthored with Kelly P. Ray, Ph.D., and Maydel M. Schexnayder, M.S., was published in 2003 and has since sold out. Other volumes have included *Living in an Environmentally Traumatized World: Healing Ourselves and Our Planet* (2012) and *Ecopsychology: Advances from the Intersection of Psychology and Environmental Protection* (2015), which was coedited by Robert Hamilton, Ph.D., and Judy Kuriansky, Ph.D.

Nemeth has published articles in the International Journal of Group Psychotherapy, Global Horizons, the Center for Policy and Resilience, and the Journal of Pediatric Neuropsychology. She has written several book chapters, including for Dr. George Kapalka's book, *Pediatricians and Psychopharmacologically Trained Psychologists—Practitioner's Guide to Collaborative Treatment* (2010), Springer, and for Dr. Katie Cherry's and Dr. Allison Gibson's forthcoming book, *The Intersection of Trauma and Disaster Behavioral Health.*

Nemeth was the 11th woman to be elected to a fellowship in the American Psychological Association's Division 40 (Clinical Neuropsychology). She has served the profession as a two-term member of APA's Council of Representatives; a cochair of the Louisiana State Board of Examiners of Psychologists, having been licensed to practice psychology since 1975; and president of both the Louisiana Group Psychotherapy Society and the Louisiana Psychological Association, wherein she was the recipient of the 2010 Distinguished Psychologist Award.

As cosecretary general of the World Council for Psychotherapy, Nemeth has presented in Austria, Argentina, China, Australia, France, and Russia as well as at the United Nations. While in Moscow, Nemeth was introduced to Dr. Janna Glozman, leading researcher and professor of psychology at Moscow

State University and Research Director of the Center of Developmental Neuropsychology, by Dr. Antonio Puente, clinical neuropsychologist and past president of the American Psychological Association. This meeting sparked an interest in comparing and contrasting the evolution of clinical/developmental neuropsychology in Russia and in America by tracing the contributions of the field's preeminent forefathers, A.R. Luria and R.M. Reitan.

Nemeth has been a trailblazer in the practice of medical psychology in America. As such, she graduated from the first postdoctoral master of science program in clinical psychopharmacology in the United States and, since 2007, she has developed the unique specialty of evaluating, treating, and prescribing medication for neuropsychologically compromised children. Nemeth also holds degrees from Indiana University (B.S., 1965), Oklahoma State University (M.S., 1968), and Louisiana State University (M.A., 1971 and Ph.D., 1973).

Nemeth was introduced to Reitan's work while in graduate school and has pursued knowledge in neuropsychology ever since. She has presented hundreds of papers, posters, and symposia in this area. Nemeth has lead the advancement of the practice of clinical neuropsychology by being the first to establish a private practice neuropsychology laboratory in Louisiana (1977) and the first to use the Reitan REHABIT system (1980). Her symposium on the *Neurologically Dysfunctional Child: An Introduction to Concepts and Intervention Techniques with Brain Damaged, Learning Disabled and Attention Deficit Disorder Children* (Nemeth & Davis, 1994) helped to solidify her interest in child neuropsychology. Lastly, Nemeth sought out supervision and training opportunities from Reitan for many years. Her respect for Reitan's legacy has been unwavering.

Foreword

The specialty of clinical neuropsychology has proven to be the fastest growing and most exciting branch of psychology. The promises of understanding behavior, cognition, and emotion from a fundamental interfacing of underlying neurological processes were first realized by three prominent scientists on two continents more than 125 years ago. These pioneers were William James in Cambridge, Massachusetts (Harvard University), Wilhelm Wundt (Leipzig University), and Ivan Pavlov (Military Medical Academy, St. Petersburg). Via the interfacing of the emerging science of physiology with the age-old questions of philosophy, the promising science of psychology began. The strong presence of physiology with the demanding questions of philosophy resulted in the anchoring of this physiological approach to brain processes. These questions were so powerful that the only organ that seemed reasonably poised to help answer these uncertainties was the brain.

This initial trajectory was lost in psychology during most of the 20th century to the focus on behaviorism as a means to solidify the science of psychology. Whereas behaviorism provided the necessary foundation and support for the creation of psychology as a scientific enterprise, the cofounding of experimental psychology with behaviorism resulted in a clouding of the historical roots of psychology, especially the role of brain processes in the explanation of the human mind.

The emergence of the ideas of Alexander R. Luria in Russia and Roger W. Sperry in the United States provided glimmers of hope that the critical foundations of psychology and the importance of the brain in psychology would indeed not be lost to behaviorism. In the east, Luria provided an understanding of behavior inside what he called a "romantic" science that placed the mind inside a complex sociohistorical context. Without understanding the gestalt of the individual, brain processes would exist in a vacuum. And, indeed, the whole, namely the person, could only be understood as much more than the sum of the parts, including the corresponding behavioral and neural concomitants. Sperry, in contrast, won the Nobel Prize in 1981 in Medicine and Physiology for his pioneering work on understanding the role of the cerebral hemispheres. Much like Luria, the brain, according to Sperry, could only be understood within the context of a much larger consciousness. Using the idea of downward and upward causation, the brain exerted its force to produce behavior, cognition, and emotion; those, in turn, produced consciousness. It is that consciousness that should be understood and focused upon, but not until the underlying brain processes that produce that consciousness are considered. In essence, both emphasized the role and critical importance of the brain. But both similarly emphasized the unwavering need to place brain processes in much larger contexts. Subsequent to these experimental efforts, Ralph M. Reitan provided the first viable psychometric approach with the Halstead-Reitan Neuropsychological Battery for clinically measuring brain impairments across cerebral domains.

Unfortunately, the works of Luria, Sperry, and Reitan have resided in two geographically and intellectually disconnected cultures for too many years. Whereas these ideas have been acknowledged in both Russia and the United States for many years, the merging of the east and west has left much to be desired. As Sperry discovered with his riveting work on the disconnection syndrome of the cerebral hemispheres, one hemisphere alone is insufficient to give rise to a complete consciousness. Similarly, the ideas of Russian and American neuropsychology alone are insufficient to give rise to a much-needed comprehensive neuropsychology.

The interface of Russian and American neuropsychology holds much promise for a more robust and powerful neuropsychology. The hard science of the west, as illustrated by Sperry and Reitan, with the romantic cultural-historical science of the east, as best espoused by Luria, is the only viable solution that psychology has to loosen the century-long grip of behaviorism on psychology. The birth of a unified neuropsychology opens endless possibilities for the future.

This volume is one of the most promising illustrations of how Eastern neuropsychology can merge with Western neuropsychology to make a unified and universal neuropsychology. The spirit of the early pioneers in psychology is found in each and every one of the chapters. With its focus on the development of the mind, this book, much like the emergence of a new neuropsychology, focuses on the future. The future of the person, by focusing on its early development, brings promise and hope that psychology will again find its way back to the fundamental and critical understanding that behavior, cognition, and emotion should only and can only be understood within the context of the brain and its place in a greater sociocultural and consciousness perspective.

Antonio E. Puente, Ph.D.
President of the American Psychological Association, Clinical Neuropsychologist, Professor of Psychology, University of North Carolina Wilmington, Wilmington, NC, United States

Acknowledgments

Alexander R. Luria and Ralph M. Reitan were two of the most resilient psychologists of the 20th century. They built vast pyramids of knowledge at different times in different places. Their brilliant ideas and generous collaborations have inspired others. These two amazing pioneers forged a new area of research. They were firmly grounded in their scientific studies and clinical practices. By learning from their mentors, Lev Vygotsky and Ward Halstead, they created a new field of psychology, now referred to as neuropsychology. They willingly invested in others. We, Janna Glozman and Darlyne G. Nemeth, were among the many neuropsychologists who were fortunate enough to benefit from their mentorship and/or direction. In this regard, others who have invested in us must now be acknowledged.

Janna Glozman, Ph.D., D.Sc.

I wish to thank Dr. Darlyne Nemeth, first for her great idea to combine in one book clinical applications post-Luria and Reitan—two fathers of neuropsychology and fortunately our great teachers—in the evaluation and treatment of neuropsychologically compromised children. Representative of different times and cultures, both Luria and Reitan would change the world of neuropsychology in both America and Russia. All chapters of this book prove it and I wish to acknowledge all chapter authors for sharing our idea as well as for their dedication, perseverance, and great effort to finish this book in time.

Nemeth is a wonderful coeditor. Her energy and resilience together with a very warm attitude and readiness to help all contributors of this international book permitted us to offer this tribute to our mentors.

I wish to thank Pat Gonzales for being a wonderful editorial project manager.

To my mentor in neuropsychology, Alexander Luria, thank you for teaching me and having supervised my work in adult and child clinical neuropsychology for about 10 years.

Darlyne G. Nemeth, Ph.D., M.P., M.P.A.P.

I wish to thank Antonio Puente, Ph.D., for introducing me to Janna Glozman, Ph.D., D.Sc., during my 2016 trip to Moscow, Russia. At that time, I was serving as the cosecretary general for the World Council for Psychotherapy, which was participating in the First World Congress on Mental Health. As I had volunteered to serve on Puente's election committee for his 2015 American Psychological

Association (APA) presidential campaign, I became well acquainted with his work in international neuropsychology. He had spoken so highly about Glozman's work at what he referred to as "the Luria Lab" at Moscow State University. Both Puente and Glozman had shared postdoctoral students. I was amazed at the quality and dedication of these professionals who served in this lab. When I was invited for tea, Glozman and her colleagues brought out some of Luria's original clinical findings. These included his hand-drawn pictures of patients' brain functions and problem areas. Over tea and cookies, Janna and her colleagues Tatyana Akhutina and Andrey Kiselnikov translated Luria's amazing findings from Russian to English. Touching history had a profound effect on me.

In 2017, Glozman and her colleague, Yulia Babayeva, docked in New Orleans on their Caribbean cruise. After spending the day with Janna and speaking about our amazing mentors, I invited Janna to collaborate with me on this wonderful tribute to them; she agreed. Then, I sought out Emily Elke from Elsevier/Academic Press. She had been an effective editor on my previous book, *Innovative Approaches to Individual and Community Resilience: From Theory to Practice*, which was coauthored by Traci Olivier, Psy.D. As Emily was in the process of leaving Elsevier to take a position with APA, she introduced me to Nikki Levy, an Elsevier/Academic Press publisher, who made publishing the book a reality. Levy then arranged for Pat Gonzales to be our editorial project manager. Pat has been amazing. She has kept us on track. Working with her has been a pleasure.

Glozman is a wonderful coeditor. She is warm, supportive, and inspiring. Her ideas have truly taken Luria's work to the next level. I am so humbled and proud to be sharing this experience with her. As Janna previously stated, working with Pat Gonzales at Elsevier/Academic Press has been a joy. Kayla Mckenzie Chustz is specially recognized for her incredible efforts to coordinate research and compile all phases of the development of this book. She is a superb clinical and research assistant. Her dedication, perseverance, computer and editing skills, and pleasant personality have made this journey a joy.

On a personal level, I wish to acknowledge my wonderful husband of 50 years, Donald Franklin Nemeth, Ph.D., geologist, who has always been there for me. He has created a wonderful world for us, which I truly cherish. My brother, Richard Gene Gaynor, M.D., internist, is acknowledged for his support and encouragement. Richard is a true example of a Renaissance man who has many talents and skills. His generosity to me as well as others is heartfelt. To my elegant sister-in-law, Susanne Maria Jensen, Ph.D., clinical psychologist, who was directly responsible for my having received my doctorate, thank you for being a wonderful mentor and friend. To my busy family, Madeline and Dave Simmons, and their two children, Collin and Leo, thank you for being happy and productive. To my mentors in neuropsychology, Ralph M. Reitan, Ph.D., and James C. Reed, Ph.D., thank you for having supervised my work in adult and child clinical neuropsychology for so many years.

Lastly, for all those who I have mentored and/or supervised over the years, thank you for spreading the joy.

Prologue

Darlyne G. Nemeth, and Janna Glozman

Life is about relationships … relationships with ourselves, our teachers, our people and pets, and our world. Two outstanding individuals, Alexander R. Luria in Russia and Ralph M. Reitan in America, with their creative ideas, changed the world of neuropsychology and our relationship to the field of neuropsychology forever.

Just like the building of the great pyramids in Egypt and Central America, these two pioneers built the science and practice of neuropsychology in different ways, in different places, and at different times. Furthermore, just like the pyramids, their contributions have stood the test of time. After all these years, neuropsychologists are still using the Lurian and Reitan approaches to evaluation and intervention. We are happy and proud to have such teachers. I was Luria's ardent disciple during the last 10 years of his life, from 1967 to 1977 (see Appendix A).

Luria was the first to build a new world of neuropsychology. Born in 1902, he started early to make a difference. In fact, Luria wrote his first book, *Principles of Real Psychology*, in 1921, at age 19. The main ideas of cultural-historical psychology were offered in this book. Luria described his journey in psychology thusly:

> *I began my career in the first years of the great Russian Revolution. This single, momentous event decisively influenced my life and that of everyone I knew.*
>
> *In comparing my experiences with those of Western and American psychologists, there is one important difference. Many European and American psychologists … have spent their lives in a comparatively quiet, slow-moving environment. Their cv reflect the course of their work as well as the people and events that have shaped them: their parents, teachers, colleagues and the intellectual issues in which they have participated. Their work as scholars consists of doing research and sometimes moving from University to University.*
>
> *The difference between us lies in the social and historical factors that influenced us. From the outset it was apparent, that I would have little opportunity to pursue the kind of well-ordered, systematic education that serves as the cornerstone for most scientific careers. In its place life offered me the* ***fantastically stimulating***

atmosphere of an active, rapidly changing society. *My entire generation was infused with* ***the energy of revolutionary change****—the liberating energy people feel when they are part of a society that is able to make tremendous progress in a very short time.*

Luria (*The Making of Mind*, 1979, p. 17)

Along the way, Luria earned doctor of science (D.Sc.) degrees in psychology and medicine. For 30 years, Luria directed the department of neuro- and patho-psychology at Moscow State University, and also became an Emerite member of many universities and academies all over the world (see Fig. 1).

FIG. 1 Luria, Emerite Member of Harvard University.

When he died in 1977, Luria had truly built a unique pyramid of neuropsychological knowledge in Russia and the world beyond. It included neuropsychological assessment with the well-known Luria battery; principles and methods of neuropsychological rehabilitation; the nature of human conflicts; the understanding of cerebral functions, functional systems, and syndrome analysis; the theory of three functional units of the brain; the classification of forms of aphasia, agnosia, amnesia, and apraxia; and the determining of the regulation and selectivity of human behavior. Luria determined the role of speech in the regulation of normal and abnormal behavior and also described the higher neural activity in normal and abnormal children. Both Luria and Reitan created a large international school of disciples and followers throughout the world (see Figs. 2 and 3).

FIG. 2 Luria's disciples.

... He is indeed one of the modern giants in the field ...

N. Geschwind (Harvard Medical School//Language, v. 48, # 3, p. 755, 1972)

FIG. 3 Ralph Reitan's colleagues and disciples.

> *It has been said with good reason that Reitan is the founder of clinical neuropsychology ... When he began [his] career, there was no field called clinical neuropsychology.*
>
> Hom and Goldstein (2015, p. 721)

Reitan was born in 1922, 20 years after Luria was born, and died in 2014, 37 years after Luria died. Reitan studied under and collaborated with Ward Halstead at the University of Chicago. Together, they developed a quantitative approach to neuropsychological assessment that became the "gold standard" in America.

Most unique about Reitan was his desire to share this knowledge with practicing psychologists. At that time, in the early 1970s, there were few postdoctoral fellowships available in neuropsychology. Reitan understood the need to bring this knowledge to the people. He wanted to move these procedures from the academic science to the clinical practice of neuropsychology. From the 1970s to shortly before his death, Reitan carried his message to practicing psychologists. He spent years traversing America, inviting psychologists to join in his love for neuropsychology and to adopt his quantitative approach to evaluation and treatment of brain-behavior functions in adults, older children, and younger children. He accepted all comers.

I was one such individual. I became an ardent disciple (see Fig. 3) of the Reitan method and attended many of his seminars from 1970 to 2010 (see Appendix B). I purchased Reitan's evaluation and intervention equipment (see Appendix B) and consulted with him on a regular basis. In fact, Reitan personally supervised my work for more than 10 years (see Appendix C).

For the majority of their careers, Reitan and Luria made themselves and their ideas easily accessible to those of us who thirsted for this knowledge. We will never forget their generosity of spirit. In doing so, Reitan and Luria built lasting pyramids of neuropsychological knowledge in America, Russia, and beyond that are still alive and well today. Their legacies live on.

**PEOPLE COME AND GO,
BUT THE CREATIVE SOURCES OF GREAT HISTORICAL EVENTS
AND THE IMPORTANT IDEAS AND DEEDS REMAIN.**

A.R. Luria

This volume is dedicated to the legacies of Luria and Reitan.
Darlyne G. Nemeth, Janna Glozman

Appendix A

The subcover of the 1971 Russian edition of Luria's book *The Man with a Shattered World: The History of a Brain Wound,* gift from Luria to Janna Glozman

At left: Luria with Lev Zasetsky, a Soviet soldier who was severely wounded in the head in World War II and who is described in this book

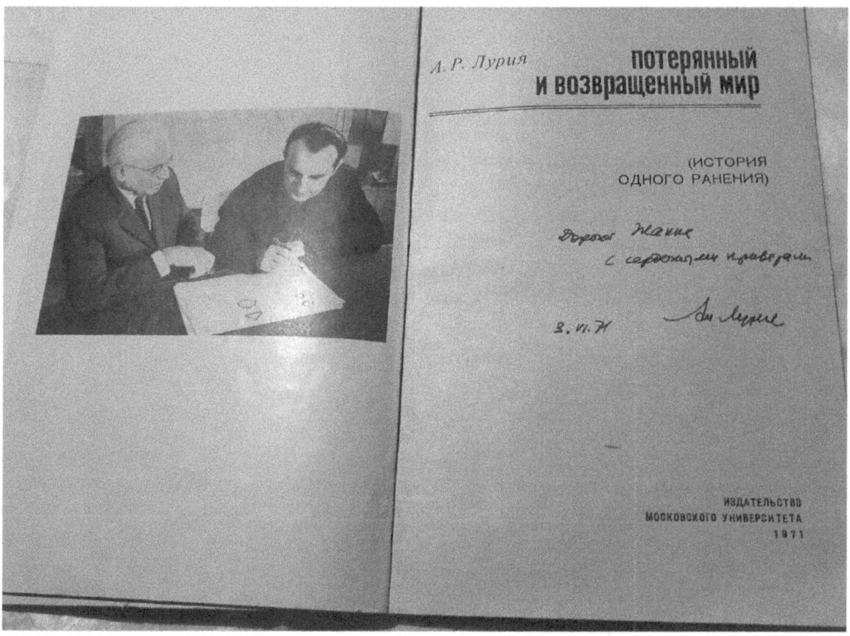

Translation of the inscription:
To dear Janna with my kind regards

Al. Luria, 3.VI.71

Appendix B

Clinical Neuropsychology Workshop Certificate

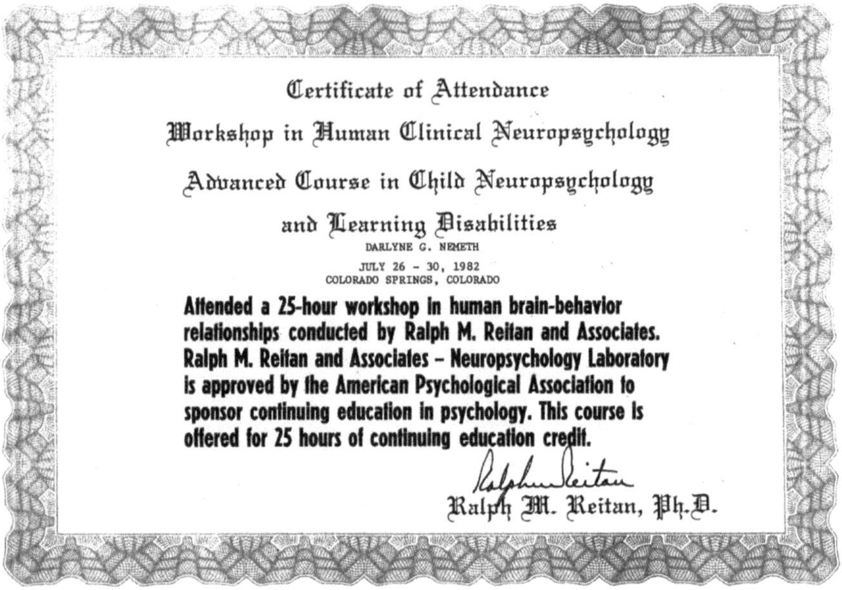

Certificate of Attendance

Workshop in Human Clinical Neuropsychology

Advanced Course in Child Neuropsychology

and Learning Disabilities

DARLYNE G. NEMETH

JULY 26 - 30, 1982

COLORADO SPRINGS, COLORADO

Attended a 25-hour workshop in human brain-behavior relationships conducted by Ralph M. Reitan and Associates. Ralph M. Reitan and Associates – Neuropsychology Laboratory is approved by the American Psychological Association to sponsor continuing education in psychology. This course is offered for 25 hours of continuing education credit.

Ralph M. Reitan

Ralph M. Reitan, Ph.D.

Reitan hosted many seminars to share his knowledge with psychologists.

Appendix C

Correspondence with Reitan

THE UNIVERSITY OF ARIZONA
TUCSON, ARIZONA 85721

COLLEGE OF LIBERAL ARTS
DEPARTMENT OF PSYCHOLOGY

August 21, 1980

Dr. Darlyne G. Nemeth
The Psychology Group
707 South Acadian Thruway
Baton Rouge, Louisiana 70806

Dear Darlyne:

It certainly seems that you have an exciting prospect coming in forming your own Clinic. I certainly wish you the best of success.

You are the first person to plan to proceed with use of the REHABIT program. I have been talking with some of my students here about a possible research project, but we do not yet have a solution to many of the practical problems. I feel sure that the program will be very helpful, and in the long run, could well be an extremely exciting addition, adding a significant treatment element to the area of Clinical Neuropsychology. I do believe that documented research results will be necessary in order to develop and sustain interest in clinical application. I don't have any final ideas with respect to a research design, but I have been doing a fair amount of thinking about how such a research program may be organized. If I make more progress in developing the design I should be pleased to send you a copy of it. In any case, I certainly wish you the best of success in any work that you undertake with respect to REHABIT.

I really enjoyed seeing you and your family in Santa Fe.

Sincerely,

Ralph

Ralph M. Reitan, Ph.D.
Professor

RMR:jya

We have entered your order for the tests and should be able to ship it by Sept 15-30. I presume you want it sent to the above address. Ralph

Reitan's personalized letter to Darlyne G. Nemeth, Ph.D., regarding her purchase of the REHABIT system.

Appendix D

Consultation with Reitan

From the Desk of:

RALPH M. REITAN, Ph.D.

1/28/98

Dear Darlyne -

Deborah and I have been giving a lot of thought and discussion about your letter. Your new situation sounds like a great opportunity not only to add a new dimension to neuropsychology in your area but to be of significant help to brain-injured persons.

In our experience, a major clue to success in neuropsychological rehabilitation lies in careful and complete identification of the deficits, in the individual case, that need to be dealt with. Only when the problems are known can they be rehabilitated.

We are trying to organize our thoughts further, and will be back in touch.

Best regards -

Ralph

In his correspondence with Nemeth, Reitan stressed the importance of carefully and completely identifying deficits before attempting intervention.

Chapter 1

The contributions of Luria and Reitan to developmental neuropsychology and to the understanding of neuropsychologically compromised children

Janna Glozman[a], Darlyne G. Nemeth[b]
[a]*M. V. Lomonosov Moscow State University, Moscow, Russia,* [b]*The Neuropsychology Center of Louisiana, LLC, Baton Rouge, LA, United States*

The contributions of Luria to developmental neuropsychology

Portions of this section were drawn from Glozman (2013).

The theoretical basis of developmental neuropsychology in Russia as well as of general neuropsychology has been based on three principles, proposed by L.S. Vygotsky and A.R. Luria: (1) the principle of social genesis of higher mental functions (HMFs); (2) the principle of system organization of HMFs; and (3) the principles of dynamic organization and localization of HMFs (Luria, 1958, 1959). These principles derived from the *cultural-historical* approach to the analysis of development of HMFs and of their difficulties. The focus was on orientation, not at the disease or the defect level but at the developmental level, looking at the history of culture for the reasons of mental phenomena and for the means of their remediation. Vygotsky concluded that a defect interferes with the child's cultural development, but that culture helps the child to overcome the

Evaluation and Treatment of Neuropsychologically Compromised Children.
https://doi.org/10.1016/B978-0-12-819545-1.00001-1

defect. By this, the cultural-historical approach has become and still is a methodological basis for remediating education.

One of the first studies based upon this approach was a comparative exploration of mental functions in urban, rural, and homeless children. This study confirmed the influence of social and cultural factors on child cognitive development (Luria, 1928, 1930).

Developmental neuropsychology in Russia

A review of Russian developmental neuropsychology highlighted the importance of the psychogenic studies in the 20th century in the Eugenics Office of the Academy of Sciences in St. Petersburg, created in 1921, and in the Laboratory of Heredity and Human Constitution at the Moscow Medico-biological Institute, created in 1928. The first institution used the genealogical method while the second used a more informative (as was proved later) twins method (Ravich-Scherbo & Sigal, 2003). The last compared the input of genetic and environmental factors in the individual variability of child psychological and neurophysiological features.

Luria began his work at the Medico-biological Institute in 1932. By this time, Lebedinsky's paper, "The problem of heredity in psychology and twins method," had already been published. This paper analyzed the method as well as the results of the assessment of different mental features (reasoning, mediation capacities, temper) in twins at different ages. It revealed both the greater genetic similarity of most features in monozygotic twins (genetically similar) as compared with dizygotic twins (genetically different), and also a dependence of similarity on the age of the twins and the function assessed. From 1932 until 1937 (when the Medico-biological Institute was closed as the genetic studies were prohibited), Luria directed studies of genotype/environment relations through cultural-historical theory (Fig. 1).

The group included Lebedinsky, Mironova, Morozova, and Yudovich. They were the first in Russia to use the "twins model" in experimental studies of genetic mechanisms of mind. The difference with similar studies in occidental countries consists of special tests, addressing predominantly the "natural" (genetic) or "cultural" (environmental) factors instead of standardized batteries measuring IQ. For instance, in nonverbal tasks, which better reveal "natural" factors, the results were more similar in monozygotic twins than in dizygotic ones.

Their program for the study of genotype/environment relations was based upon Vygotsky-Luria's theory of mental development. This research revealed changes in the relative input of heredity and environment due to modifications in mental functioning in answer to different educative procedures and to the role of speech acquisition in mental development (Lebedinsky, 1932; Luria, 1936, 1948, 1963, 2002; Mironova & Kolbanovsky, 1934; Ravich-Scherbo & Sigal, 2003). A study of 130 twin pairs, ages 6–11, revealed, for instance, that the

FIG. 1 Some of the twins that participated in the psychogenic studies by Luria. *(From Luria's archive courtesy of Luria's granddaughter, Helene Radkovskaya).*

elementary memory is determined by genetic features in all age groups while mediated remembering using pictograms was revealed dependent from genetic features only in preschoolers. To generalize, the influence of natural factors on a child's cognitive functions decreases with age, but the influence of cultural factors increases. This evidence indicates that, during ontogenic development, not only the psychological structure of the mental processes but also their internal nature dramatically changes (Luria, Symernitskaya, & Tybulevich, 1973, p. 112).

The research work in the Medico-biological Institute allowed Luria to develop the main ideas of developmental neuropsychology: "mental development in childhood is first of all a modification in his forms of activity, complication of the structure of this activity and enrichment of mental processes, developing inside this activity" (Luria, 1948, p. 34). In the process of development, a mental function "does not rest the same; … it changes significantly own structure, it solves the same task using different operations" (Luria, 2002, p. 17). With this, "the genotype influences to a great degree the speed of appropriation of these 'cultural' forms of mental activity …" (Luria, 2002, p. 18).

The psychogenetic studies first confirmed the formative effect of speech and language on mental processes, and then these studies revealed that twins form "a group of risk" for mental development. For instance, Luria, together with Yudovich, assessed a pair of 5-year-old twins with speech retardation combined with a retardation in general mental development. The authors hypothesized that the cause was in the "twins situation," not stimulating verbal activity but replacing it by some more primitive forms of communication. The researchers modified this situation; each twin was placed in a different kindergarten group, that is, an objective need to acquire speech as a means of communication was created (Luria, 1960; Luria & Yudovich, 1959). Besides, special lessons developing speech were done with one from the pair, with the second becoming a control twin. In 3 months, the verbal abilities of children (both vocabulary and grammar) changed significantly. The general mental development improved to a greater degree in the child who had speech therapy. So, when the objective need for verbal communication was created, both children acquired new verbal means of communication. Based upon verbal speech (Luria, 1960; Luria & Yudovich, 1959), it also provoked significant modifications in the structure of their conscious activity.

Luria's psychogenetic studies also formed the basis of neuropsychological remediation, namely the principles of developing games with small children and the role of the zone of proximal development in the differentiation of mental retardation from delayed development (Luria, 1963).

For example, in the pair of monozygotic 6-year-old twins, one approached the construction activity with cubes using a "step-by-step" method (that is, copying the teacher's actions). However, the second child followed the "model" method, when he saw only the general shape of the construction and he had to self-select the elements fitting this shape. The second version of the game, aimed to develop visual reasoning and the abilities of constructive analysis and synthesis, was much more efficient. The developing effect also included some other forms of creative activity and was stable, which was revealed 1–5 years after the program (Luria, 1948).

Developmental neuropsychology in America

In America, developmental (also called pediatric) neuropsychology became a major area of research and practice during the second half of the 20th century. "It was in 1960 that the clinical picture of the 'clumsy child' (renamed *developmental dysgnosia and dyspraxia*) was described, specific reading disability (renamed *developmental dyslexia*) was investigated from a neuropsychological standpoint, and the concept of *minimal brain dysfunction (MBD)* was formulated to account for these and a myriad of other behavioral disabilities in children. Since this time, pediatric neuropsychology has become a flourishing area of research and practice, generating new knowledge and deeper understanding. Today, the evaluation and management of children with documented or suspected brain dysfunction by well-informed neuropsychologists are incomparably more insightful and effective than was the case 20 years ago" (Benton, 2000, p. XV).

The progress of developmental neuropsychology follows the general tendency all over the world to replace the "*static neuropsychology*" relating subjects' behavior to definite brain areas with "*dynamic neuropsychology.*" This requires analyzing the dynamics of brain/mental functioning interaction through the social conditions of the subject's life; that is, viewing childhood disorders within a developmental context (Glozman, 2002, 2013; Rourke, 1985; Tupper & Cicerone, 1991). Such an approach surmounts the "biologizing" tendencies of the psychology of the 19th to 20th centuries. Analogously, Vygotsky (1925) represented the psychology of the future, like a study of "biosocial synthesis," a union of natural and human sciences.

It is likely that the main cause of delayed development (immaturity) of a child's functional mental systems is an unfavorable environment during the child's formative years (e.g., complicated intrafamily relations, bad conditions of everyday living, harmful ecological factors, lack of socialization and of inclusion into educative and upbringing programs) (Korsakova, Mikadze, & Balashova, 2001).

This explains the predominant importance of *functional diagnostics* (i.e., to compare with *topical diagnostics* of immature or impaired brain structures) or defects preventing the child from acquiring knowledge and abilities, adjusting into society (school or family), and developing to a greater degree his/her own potential and personality.

The actual task in the progress of developmental neuropsychology consists of a need to pass from a phenomenological description of abnormal child development to the study of the interactions between the brain, genetics, sociology, and personality in the formation of different kinds of abnormal or nontypical development (Glozman, 2013). In other words, developmental neuropsychology should now be based on an integrative multidisciplinary approach, founded by Lenneberg (1967).

The contributions of Reitan to developmental neuropsychology

The following information was primarily taken from Reitan and Wolfson (1992b).

Reitan began his scientific career in 1945 under the direction of Ward Halstead at the University of Chicago. Much of their work had been influenced by wounded World War II veterans. During many years of study and collaboration, the Halstead Reitan Neuropsychological Test Battery was developed. (Reitan's published works have been compiled by Hom & Nici, 2015.)

"In 1951, at the Indiana University Medical Center, Reitan started his laboratory for the study of brain-behavior relationships in both adults and children" (Reitan & Wolfson, 1992a, 1992b, p. 20). During his time at Indiana University Medical Center, Reitan concluded that brain functions in adults and children were vastly different. As Reitan stated, "in adult neuropsychology the major emphasis has centered on impairment of previously developed neuropsychological functions. In child neuropsychology, impairment of brain functions occurs during the developmental years, and a major additional factor involves the limiting effect of brain damage on the potential for normal development of brain-behavior relationships" (p. 238). Furthermore, Reitan noted that, "Among older children there is both a loss of previously acquired abilities and an impairment in the ability to normally acquire future neuropsychological skills. However, the older child suffers less in this latter respect because he/she had the opportunity for normal development during the earlier years" (p. 44).

In 1967, after a conversation with Luria, Reitan became even more committed to the importance of quantitative data analysis. While Luria "believed that it was necessary to observe the performance style of the brain-damaged individual in order to understand that person's limitations" (p. 233), Reitan came to the conclusion that a qualitative analysis must also be included. Reitan decided that "quantitative deficits (limitations in degree) and qualitative deficits (limitations in the type of process used) might both be significant in the assessment process" (p. 234). Therefore, as a part of the HRNB, the Aphasia Screening Test and the Sensory Perceptual Examination represent Reitan's efforts to include this evaluation of qualitative data. As Reitan concluded, "Many neuropsychologists would believe that both quantitative results and observations of performance deficits are relevant to clinical assessments" (p. 233). Furthermore, Goldstein and Kaplan strongly supported the inclusion of a process analysis in the evaluation of brain-behavior functions (p. 225).

As Reitan was not satisfied with the current methodology used for evaluating children's brain-behavior functions, he created the HRNB-OC and the RINB.

The issue of plasticity was critically important, especially in children. In 1974, Reitan noted that "early brain lesions interfere with normal acquisition of skills during the developmental years, and lesions sustained by adults tend to result in the loss of previously acquired skills" (as cited in Reitan & Wolfson, 1992b, p. 27). Reitan was especially concerned about the potential for a child's ability to adapt after a brain insult (p. 31). He concluded that "It appears that the long-term outcome in young brain-damaged children relates principally to their ability (or lack of ability) to acquire future neuropsychological functions" (p. 44). Thus, examples of neuropsychologically compromised children are included in this chapter.

Diagnostic case examples of neuropsychologically compromised children

The difference between normal and neuropsychologically compromised children is often undetectable in the early years. Once children start school, however, it becomes quite obvious. Problems in learning, emotion, and behavior abound.

Nevertheless, the Lurian assessment methods for preschoolers ages 2–3 can reveal and timely remediate a risk of future learning disabilities (LD) (Glozman, Soboleva, & Titova, 2020). For example, poor drawing abilities in a preschooler can often predict his/her dysgraphia at school; likewise, undeveloped self-regulation provokes behavior problems, and bad communication skills cause primary school maladjustment.

Children with normal neuropsychological functions usually adapt quite well to the educational environment. They are able to perform tasks commensurate with their abilities. For example, children with normal neuropsychological functions with an intellectual quotient (IQ) of 100 can usually perform at the average to above average level in school. However, neuropsychologically compromised children with similar intellectual skills may not be able to do so. These children may have learning, emotional, and/or behavioral difficulties that often impair their performances. Because their brains do not process information effectively, problems emerge.

Reitan's most significant quantitative contribution to developmental neuropsychology was the Reitan-Indiana Neuropsychological Test Battery (RINB) for children ages 5–8 (Reitan & Wolfson, 1992a, 1992b). Table 1 offers a comparison of the RINB to Reitan's Adult (ages 15 and above) and Older Children's (ages 9–14) Batteries.

The following quantitative analyses allow a comparison of a child's RINB scores on four variables: (1) level of performance, (2) right-left differences, (3) dysphasia and related variables, and (4) total Neurological Deficit Scale. These age-related variables are listed in Tables 2 and 3.

An example of Reitan-Indiana Neuropsychological Test Battery scoring

Oftentimes, without comprehensive neuropsychological evaluations, symptoms become the focus of the intervention. Without a clear understanding of their etiology, interventions frequently fail. Because such interventions are often too narrow or specific in focus (e.g., cognitive behavior therapy), they leave the core issues yet to be discovered. This typically results in frustration. Families tend to give up rather than investigate further. Especially with boys, the neuropsychologist frequently has only one chance to "get it right," so to speak. That is why a thorough investigation into and understanding of the child's presenting problems is so important.

Reitan's work on the norms for the 5–8 year olds for the RINB is so valuable in this regard (see Tables 2 and 3). One such example is of an 8-year-old child who was having severe learning problems in second grade. Alcohol-Related Neurodevelopmental Disorder (ARND) was suspected by his pediatrician, but because of the parents' denial, it was not diagnosed. Results of his RINB summary (see below) were as follows (Table 4).

This 8-year-old's scores are not within normal limits in all of the above categories. Therefore, information from the Selz-Reitan study is graphed below. As can be seen from the graph, his scores fall into the middle area, suggesting performances more similar to those of learning-disabled children with brain-behavior dysfunction than those of normal children (Fig. 2).

TABLE 1 This table presents a description of the Halstead Reitan Neuropsychological Test Battery (HRNB), the Halstead Reitan Neuropsychological Test Battery for Older Children (HRNB-OC), and the Reitan-Indiana Neuropsychological Test Battery for Children (RINB).

Test	Battery	Cognitive functions assessed
Seashore rhythm test	HRNB, HRNB-OC	Alertness, sustained attention, auditory perception, sequencing
Speech-sounds perception test	HRNB, HRNB-OC	Attention, concentration, auditory perception, visual integration, judgment
Trail making test (parts A and B)	HRNB, HRNB-OC	Flexibility, sequencing, scanning ability, symbolic appreciation
Sensory perception	HRNB, HRNB-OC, RINB	Sensory perception, attention
Strength of grip	HRNB, HRNB-OC, RINB	Motor strength of upper extremities
Lateral dominance	HRNB, HRNB-OC, RINB	Left-right preference
Category test	HRNB, HRNB-OC, RINB	Concept formation, intelligence, problem solving, new learning, flexibility
Tactual performance test	HRNB, HRNB-OC, RINB	Somatosensory and sensorimotor ability, organization, problem solving
Finger tapping test	HRNB, HRNB-OC, RINB	Fine motor speed
Aphasia Screening Test	HRNB, HRNB-OC, RINB	Expressive and receptive language, spatial abilities, reading, writing
Matching pictures test	RINB (optional)	Perceptual recognition, attention
Individual performance tests	RINB (optional)	Visual perception, visual-motor ability
Marching test	RINB (optional)	Gross motor control
Progressive figures test	RINB (optional)	Flexibility, abstraction, attention
Color form test	RINB (optional)	Flexibility, abstraction, language comprehension
Target test	RINB (optional)	Memory for figures, attention, concentration, sequencing

TABLE 2 Comparisons of normal and brain-damaged children on the Neuropsychological Deficit Scale for ages 5–8.

Groups	N	Level of performance (21 variables)	Right-left comparisons (9 variables)	Aphasia Screening Test (22 variables)	Total Neuropsychological Deficit Scale (52 variables)
Normal	29	$M=19.55$ SD=9.92	$M=7.21$ SD=2.87	$M=5.79$ SD=6.40	$M=32.55$ SD=16.12
Brain-damaged	29	$M=42.24$ SD=9.41	$M=17.21$ SD=4.44	$M=19.83$ SD=10.07	$M=79.28$ SD=19.28
		$t=8.76$ $P<0.001$	$t=10.04$ $P<0.001$	$t=6.24$ $P<0.001$	$t=9.84$ $P<0.001$
		Cutoff score: 31/32	Cutoff score: 11/12	Cutoff score: 10/11	Cutoff score: 54/55
Estimated misclassification	BD Control	14% 17%	7% 7%	21% 24%	10% 14%

TABLE 3 Developmental data on the Neuropsychological Deficit Scale for normal children aged 5–8 years.

Groups	*N*	Level of performance (21 variables)	Right-left comparisons (9 variables)	Aphasia Screening Test (22 variables)	Total Neuropsychological Deficit Scale (52 variables)
5 years	15	*M*=29.80 SD=7.93	*M*=6.93 SD=3.30	*M*=15.27 SD=5.50	*M*=52.00 SD=11.74
6 years	30	*M*=18.83 SD=9.01	*M*=7.30 SD=2.98	*M*=5.70 SD=4.50	*M*=31.83 SD=13.30
7 years	34	*M*=12.29 SD=6.93	*M*=7.26 SD=2.73	*M*=2.06 SD=2.06	*M*=21.61 SD=8.86
8 years	31	*M*=6.42 SD=3.78	*M*=5.97 SD=2.65	*M*=0.65 SD=0.82	*M*=13.04 SD=5.76
Comparisons of adjacent age groups					
5 vs. 6 years	*t* *P*<	3.92 0.001	0.37 0.80	6.10 0.001	4.87 0.001
6 vs. 7 years	*t* *P*<	3.22 0.005	0.06 0.90	4.18 0.001	3.60 0.001
7 vs. 8 years	*t* *P*<	4.11 0.001	1.90 0.10	3.52 0.001	4.47 0.001

TABLE 4 Summary of Reitan-Indiana Neuropsychological Test Battery scores.

Category total	Child's scores	Mean for control 8 year olds	Standard deviations of the mean for control
Level of performance total	10	6.42	3.78
Right-left differences total	11	5.97	2.65
Dysphasia and related variables total	4	0.65	0.82
Total Neurological Deficit Scale score (NDS)	25	13.04	5.76

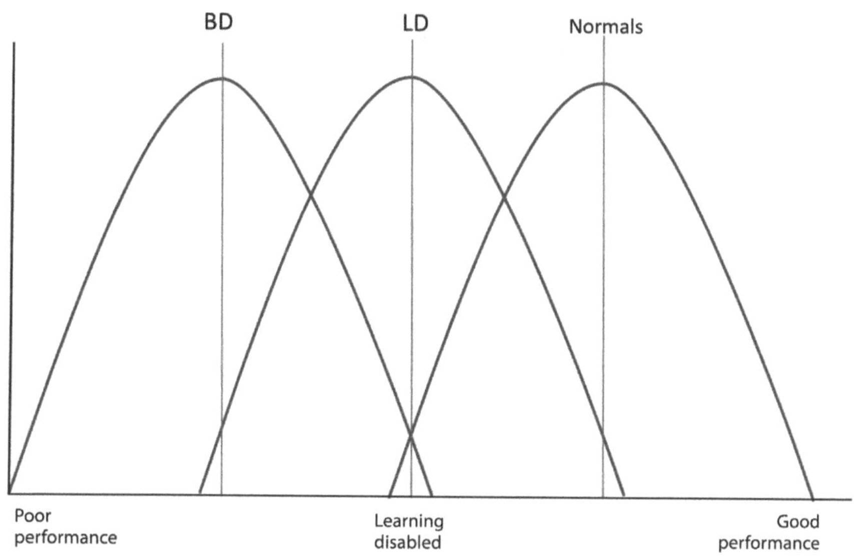

FIG. 2 "Children with learning disabilities tended to resemble the brain-damaged group much more than the control group" (Reitan & Wolfson, 1992a, 1992b, p. 260).

For example, this child's profile was consistent with other ARND findings. An ARND profile often included but was not limited to the following: (1) problems with learning (math and reading) and adaptability, (2) affective and behavioral difficulties, (3) inattention and executive dysfunction, and (4) average IQ with working memory problems. At the feedback session with both the child's parents and grandparents, the Reitan-Selz graph, shown above, was used to further explain these findings.

In *summary*, it is important to understand that children with LD can look completely normal and relatively free from brain-behavior dysfunction. From a neuropsychological perspective, however, they are not. They struggle in school, especially with math and reading, and they exhibit emotional and behavioral difficulties. Oftentimes, these difficulties are so severe that they perform more like brain-injured children than normally functioning children. Yet, as in the aforementioned case, these problems are often dealt with superficially. Seldom is intervention, other than medication, conducted. This lack of follow-through by the family typically results in more school and behavioral problems, even on medication. As Reitan stated, "behavioral diagnoses almost invariably oversimplify a complex range of neuropsychological deficits and lead to a situation in which rehabilitation attempts are oriented toward changing or modifying a limited and circumscribed behavior" (p. 273).

The following discussions of neuropsychologically compromised children's primary diagnoses are now offered.

Learning disabilities

Recently, there has been a significant increase in the number of learning-disabled pupils. Thus, according to various estimates, their number exceeds 30% of students, ranging from 15% to 40% in primary school (Glozman, 2013). Less than 50% of children who reach age 6 are ready for school (Korsakova et al., 2001). A lack of readiness to learn can provoke an imbalance in the subsequent development of the child included in educational activities. When the level of school demands may be ahead of age readiness to implement them, a child who does not "fit" the class and has not kept pace with his peers may be labeled "retarded" or "stupid." This label may then negatively impact the child's self-esteem. Readiness for school involves the formation of voluntary behavior and mastering standards and cognitive work. It also necessitates movement from egocentrism to decentration (Obukhova, 1997). Also important is the maturity of skills to work independently, to maintain control and self-control, and to coordinate and subordinate one's own actions.

The aforementioned difficulties at school reflect deficient morphological and functional genesis. A thorough neurological examination of children unready for school or unsuccessful therein reveals soft signs of disturbance, usually classified as "minimal brain dysfunction" (Clements, 1973). These symptoms are often disregarded by parents and pediatricians until the child starts school, when heightened physical and emotional changes increase symptoms of brain dysfunction. At the behavioral level, they may prevent the child from meeting the requirements of school and provoke school maladjustment.

Pylaeva (1995) suggests the following hierarchy of immaturity of mental functions that leads to school failure:

1. Reduced working capacity, fluctuations in attention, weak mnestic processes, lack of speech maturity.
2. Underdevelopment of programming and monitoring functions.
3. Visual-spatial and quasispatial constraints.

Two further factors entail difficulties in processing auditory and visual information.

This hierarchy matches Luria's theory of three functional units of the brain (Table 5) and the data from our assessment of children with difficulties at school, using Luria's battery and Lurian qualitative analysis (Table 6).

A number of defects such as difficulties of orientation in time; excitability; anxiety; failures in reciprocal coordination; in digital praxis; defects of phonemic hearing; guessing reading; misunderstanding of logical-grammatical relations; insufficient productivity of remembering; semantic and perceptive substitutions in remembering; impulsivity; when analyzing a picture or a story; the inability to make a program for problem solution; and counting problems are *specific for learning-disabled children*. They did not occur in the control group of children. Other defects (instability of mental activity, echo-responses in selection test, impulsive and stereotyped movements, lack of attention to acoustic perception, increased inhibition of memory traces, dysgraphia, and dyslexia) were very frequent in the LD group and significantly rarer in the control group. Some defects (low mental ability and exhaustibility, rare words search, inertia and program simplification in dynamic praxis, and spatial errors in praxis and drawing) were frequent enough in both groups of children; that is, they can be considered normative for the functional development of primary school students. However, their presence in the experimental group was higher than in the control one.

As is apparent, differences between LD and control groups are not only in quantitative scores, but also in the frequency of the defects and their specificity. Most of the defects were specific for children experiencing learning difficulties in elementary school.

Neuropsychological differential functional diagnosis uses Luria's efficient theory of three functional units of the brain (Luria, 1973).[a] Almost all children with problems at school reveal, upon neuropsychological assessment, a weakness in the functioning of the first unit—brain activation provided by the stem and diencephalic structures of the brain. The prevalence of immaturity of subcortical structures, when compared with the cortical functioning in 7–8-year-old children with problems in primary education, can be seen as a distortion in their cerebral organization of HMFs. The energy deficit means that the child lacks the resources to perform many operations provided mostly by the second unit (a unit of information processing and storage), even when it is mature to perform this operation. Therefore, periods of success both in learning activities and in the process of testing alternate in such pupils with periods of complete failure, and only neuropsychological analysis allows them to be differentiated from children with mental retardation.

In Reitan's research, "Children with learning disabilities usually have no positive neurological findings, but upon complete examination demonstrate neuropsychological deficits that extend far beyond academic learning problems" (p. 272). He found that "the most striking finding of this study was represented by the severe degree of deficit shown by children with learning disabilities in

a. See more details about this theory in Chapter 2, by J. Quintino-Aires.

TABLE 5 Test battery for the assessment of children 6–9 years old (based on Luria's neuropsychological tests) (Mikadze, Ardila, & Akhutina, 2019, p. 798).

	Unit III. Programming, regulation, and control
Serial organization of movements and speech	Palm-first-edge test Reciprocal coordination Graphomotor sequences test Reproduction of rhythms (after instruction) Sentence completion Creating a story based on the series of pictures
Programming and control voluntary actions (executive functions)	Go-no-go tasks (reciprocal motor program) of Schulte's tables Counting Problem solving Verbal fluency tests "Odd one out" Arranging series of pictures
	Unit II. Information perception, processing, and storage
Processing of kinesthetic information	Finger position test Information Oral praxis
Processing of auditory information	Rhythm reproduction and evaluation Understanding of similar sounding words Understanding of words similar in meaning Verbal memory test
Processing of visual information	Perception of superimposed, crossed out, and unfinished images Design fluency tests (free drawings, drawings of plants)
Processing of visual-spatial information	Head's test (reproduction of hand position) Constructional test (mental rotation) Three-dimensional drawings Block design test Visual-spatial memory Understanding of logical-grammatical structures
	Unit I. Energy unit and subcortical-brainstem structures
	The functions of this unit can be assessed in the process of completing the whole test battery, in particular movement trials and Schulte's tables. The fluctuations of attention, exhaustion, micro- and macrography, muscle hypo- and hypertension, speed, and pauses are considered

TABLE 6 Qualitative analysis of frequent errors in neuropsychological tests in LD and control groups of children (% of total number of children in the group) (Glozman, 2013, p. 113).

Defects	LD group (*N*=102)	Control group (*N*=52)
General characteristics of the child		
Low mental activity level	100%	53%*
Exhaustibility	82%	20%*
Instability of mental activity	39%	7%*
Difficulties of orientation in time	19%	0**
Anxiety	12%	0**
Excitability	10%	0
Motor functions		
Inertia in dynamic praxis	100%	61%*
Echo-responses in selection test	80%	7%*
Spatial errors in praxis and drawing	40%	28%
Program simplification in dynamic praxis	38%	11%*
Impulsive movements	32%	4%**
Stereotyped movements	24%	8%*
Failures in reciprocal coordination	17%	0**
Failures in digital praxis	42%	0%*
Memory		
Increased inhibition of memory traces	35%	5%
Semantic substitutions in remembering	33%	0
Perceptive substitutions in remembering	28%	0
Insufficient productivity of remembering	21%	0**
Gnosis		
Lack of attention to acoustic perception	19%	7%*
Reasoning		
Impulsivity, when analyzing a picture or story	17%	0**
Inability to make a program for problem solution	14%	0**
Counting problems	12%	0**

Continued

TABLE 6 Qualitative analysis of frequent errors in neuropsychological tests in LD and control groups of children (% of total number of children in the group) (Glozman, 2013, p. 113)—cont'd

Defects	LD group ($N=102$)	Control group ($N=52$)
Speech		
Words search	38%	21%
Guessing reading	16%	0**
Defects of phonemic hearing	15%	0**
Misunderstanding of logical-grammatical relations	15%	0**

*$P<0.05$. **$P<0.01$.

the area of alertness and concentration. These children have great difficulty in paying attention to specific stimulus material and registering incoming information in a way that would make it possible for the brain to deal with it in terms of central processing" (p. 287).

The most frequent manifestations of LD are as follows.

Mathematics (dyscalculia)

Deficient spatial concepts is one of the most common causes of a child's learning difficulties in the elementary school, especially in mathematics and native language. In studying these subjects, a child requires spatial representation for:

- Understanding the meaning of numbers (for example, 17 and 71 differ only by "place" of included numbers);
- Correcting writing and perception of spatially similar numbers and letters (for example, 6 and 9);
- Understanding the direction of counting operations (addition, subtraction, division, multiplication);
- Understanding instructions: often an arithmetic problem is not solved because of difficult grammatical wording of its tasks (e.g., "so many more" or "so many times more"); and
- Working with multivalue numbers, where each digit is determined by its range (e.g., 107 and 1007).

Another important cause of dyscalculia is executive disturbances, which provoke impulsivity in mathematics.

Reading (dyslexia)

The road to literacy is "a journey from the city 'Speech-Language' to the city 'Writing-Reading'" (Inshakova, 2001, p. 4). Most children are moving on this journey through the fast track, but some are in a difficult situation and are moving by a long alternative track (Inshakova, 2001).

The phonological theory of dyslexia has been strongly supported by Ramus and Szenkovits (2008) and confirmed by positron-emission tomography data (Paulesu, McCroy, Fazio, et al., 2000). This approach focused on the presence of optical and optical-spatial disturbances in students with specific disorders of writing and reading and preserved oral communication. Defects of visuospatial attention were also typical for dyslexic pupils (Facoetti, Zorzi, Cestnick, et al., 2006).

Luria developed a neuropsychological approach to writing as a complex functional system consisting of many structural components that are dynamically developing in the process of ontogenesis and carry out joint and integrated activities of various brain regions. The immaturity of each of these provokes specific forms of dyslexia and dysgraphia (Luria, 1950). This approach primarily emphasizes a systemic immaturity of this and other HMFs while also differentiating primary defects, their secondary effects, and compensatory adjustment. This means that the difficulties of mastering writing and reading are never isolated defects. A primary defect (immaturity) of a functional component, which caused difficulties of writing or reading, necessarily has an impact on other mental functions to which this structure belongs. In other words, there is an inherent systemic relationship between the type of specific disturbances of the children's writing and the features of their spoken language and other mental functions, the latter of which is defined by a lack of certain structural components of a functional system of writing, composing other HMFs. The neuropsychological mechanisms of disturbances differ at different stages of learning, writing, and reading.

As with dyscalculic children, reducing anxiety and shame is crucial to learning. These children usually do not learn to read using traditional approaches. Devising new methods to encourage effort and motivation are crucial. Seldom is medication helpful.

The neuropsychological mechanisms of dyslexia associated with a lack of certain components of mental functions should be differentiated from neuroophthalmological pathology, such as troubles of binocular eye movements.

Written language (dysgraphia)

Neuropsychological assessment methods reveal the relations of specific disturbances of writing with defects of other mental functions. For example, spatial errors in writing always coincide with similar defects in gnosis, praxis, and drawing. Moreover, the undeveloped drawing in preschool children and the insufficient attention of parents and caregivers to drawing can be signals predicting dysgraphia in primary school age. The timely correction of drawing defects at the preschool age can prepare the child for nonverbal learning and prevent the appearance of dysgraphia.

Underdeveloped regulatory functions as well as the general orientation activity, selection, and concentration of attention difficulties mean that the child cannot distribute attention between the technical side of writing and the need to express one's own ideas, resulting in a disturbance of sentence boundaries, such as a period and a capital letter. Sometimes, children have finished writing the text, but after the teacher's instruction to "check it," start placing periods at the end of each sentence and replacing lowercase letters with capital ones. Even after learning the orthographic rules, some children have difficulties in applying them (unstressed vowels, voiced or voiceless consonants, etc.). Other typical symptoms of regulatory dysgraphia are perseverations and anticipations of letters in the word.

Several forms of dysgraphia can be ameliorated with occupational therapy (OT) intervention; however, ideomotor dysgraphia cannot. In the latter case, technical assistance (e.g., voice-activated writing) can be helpful.

Neurophysiologic data indicate the presence of dysgraphia in children with functional disorders in projective and associative posterior cortical areas of the right hemisphere involved in sensory-specific analysis of visual images, and disturbances of interhemispheric interaction of these areas in the process of remembering the visual information and deficiency of processes of senso-motor integration.

An analysis of dysgraphia and dyslexia, in terms of Luria's theory of brain functional units, can be found in Glozman (2013).

Attention deficit hyperactivity disorder (ADHD)

Voluntary attention is a critical mental process. Its main function is to control and organize behavior and cognitive flexibility (Luria, 1973; Vygotsky, 1956). "Voluntary attention has complex organization, including at least three components. These are wakefulness (activation component), maintaining the required level of activity (motivational component), and selective processing of the relevant signal (information component)" (Machinskaya & Dubrovinskaya, 2003, p. 310). The overall level of activation depends upon the reticular formation of the brain stem, the motivational aspect of the attention occurs within the structures of the limbic system, and the informational one within the frontothalamic regulatory system (Machinskaya & Dubrovinskaya, 2003).

Hyperactive adolescents and adults also have various forms of oppositional and deviant behavior, including aggression as well as alcohol and drug abuse. Often, children with ADHD engage in criminal behaviors in their teens. One of the mechanisms of this is a *reduced sensitivity to weak stimuli*, including signals of danger. It is important to note that the human brain is not only a reactive system, but also a system anticipating and controlling the future behavior of the individual. Children with ADHD have difficulties distinguishing and reproducing time intervals.

Studies of hyperactive children show frequent (up to 50%) *family hyperactivity*, i.e., hyperkinetic symptoms and disorders of attention both in children and in adults.

Since 1987, this disorder has been highlighted as a separate neurological unit and included in the Diagnostic and Statistical Manual of Mental Disorders (DSM-IV-TR) of the American Psychiatric Association (2000), and the International Classification of Diseases, Tenth Revision, Clinical Modification (ICD-10-CM), a system used by physicians and other healthcare providers to classify and code all diagnoses, symptoms, and procedures recorded in conjunction with hospital care in the United States. Quite often, however, hyperactive disorders accompany various anomalies of mental ontogenesis, such as mental retardation, early infantile autism, etc. In recent years, according to many Russian and American researchers, the presence of ADHD in pediatric populations has risen to threatening dimensions (up to 43% of the total population of children and up to 81% of LD children).

The primary symptoms of this disorder are *disturbances of attention concentration* (i.e., instability, low selectivity, distractibility with frequent switches of attention) and *increased unstructured activity*. The latter is expressed in agitation, fussiness, many movements not adequate for the situation (i.e., without purpose and functional significance), an inability to sit still in one place, and talkativeness. During a diagnostic assessment, children with ADHD often start talking on abstract themes, refuse to perform tasks, rise from the seat, and touch everything that can be seen. In class, they often interrupt teachers, cannot sit still at their desk for a long time, often drop their belongings to move under the desk, and can suddenly get up and go out of the class, etc.

Usually, the first symptoms of ADHD appear in the first 5 years of life, but deviations are especially evident in primary school age. This is due to the transition from external regulation in the nursery to self-regulation in school. The existence of ADHD is a risk factor for disturbances of child-parent relations and communication with peers, dissatisfactory school achievement, and school maladjustment.

Neuroimaging (MRI) techniques identify, in ADHD children, a brain volume decrease in frontal areas, caudate basal ganglia, and the cerebellum. Functional magnetic resonance imaging (fMRI) shows the relation of emotion regulation processes with the balance between the amygdala and the premotor cortex. The amygdala is formed first and is responsible for the initial reaction of the child; its imbalance causes impulsivity. Both provide regulation and inhibition of reactions. The psychopathic reactions are also related to reduced activity of the amygdala and increased activity of the premotor structures on fMRI. The impulsiveness reflects an increase in the activity of the amygdala and a decrease of frontal activity. Thus, ADHD is explained by immaturity of frontal-subcortical relationships.

Thus, ADHD is a neurodevelopmental, not a behavioral, disorder that interferes with learning. Focusing difficulties disrupt a child's working memory. Thus, encoding, retention, and decoding are often impaired. If a child cannot pay attention for the first 3 s of an exercise, he has not learned the first step (e.g., in mathematics) in order to move on to the next step. For girls, the problem is often less obvious than for boys, who are typically more disruptive in the classroom. Medication and behavioral intervention are often very helpful, if the medicines do not inhibit the ADHD child's already poor mental activity. The neuropsychological approach to ADHD problems is one of the most productive and informative. The use of medication alone is not enough; rather, a comprehensive intervention plan is needed.

Agenesis of the corpus callosum (ACC)

ACC is a birth defect that occurs when the corpus callosum fails to develop properly; however, many children with ACC have normal development due to the plasticity of the young brain. One very bright 9-year-old boy with ACC began having problems when he entered school. He would speak very loudly and overreact emotionally and behaviorally. Interventions including medication for affective balance, teaching quieting strategies, and classroom management to cue both sides of his brain to elicit the correct response were effective.

Asperger's syndrome

This mild form of autism can be both academically and socially disruptive. These children are usually very pedantic and miss important social cues. Assisting them to develop a better understanding of peer language often helps them to mainstream successfully.

This now young adult has been followed for the past 10 years. She was first seen at age 10. Although quite bright, but learning disabled, this musical genius lacked social skills. In fact, her social skills were so deficient that thriving in school became impossible. Furthermore, neither medication nor cognitive behavior therapies have been effective. She has struggled to complete the last two courses required for a high school diploma. She hopes to major in music at a college level.

Autism spectrum disorder

Autism is a complex mental disorder that develops in early childhood, usually during the first 3 years of life. Autism symptoms tend to be life-long. Autism is characterized by significantly underdeveloped social interactions, often accompanied by delayed speech and intellectual development, and stereotypical behavior. This is an extremely serious illness that becomes a heavy burden not only for the child, but also for the entire family. In the *etiology* of autism, around 0.5%–1% of cases are idiopathic, which cannot be explained by other known mechanisms. However, 10%–25% of patients have the syndrome of an X-chromosome break in conjunction with other chromosomal abnormalities (Maestrini, Paul, Monaco, & Bailey, 2000).

The *brain basis of autism*, according to autopsy and CT findings, involves diffuse damage to brain structures and their connections, including an aborted development of dendritic structures of the limbic systems. Also present are a reduction in the number of neurons, an increase in the number of abnormal cells in the cerebellum, excessive growth of rear cortical areas, and signs of diffuse disturbances of cortical relations (Joseph, 1999). Electrophysiological studies with autistic children found an increase of beta activity on EEG. The *neuropsychological model* in principle can give a single explanation for a wide range of behavioral reactions and symptoms that seem to be completely independent and not linked (Joseph, 1999, p. 309). Three complimentary *neuropsychological theories of autism* are described as follows:

1. *Regulatory Dysfunction* (Executive Dysfunction)—Disturbances of planning, processing of information in short-term memory, switching, mobility of reasoning, ability to deal with atypical problem tasks, and selective reactions. According to the Wisconsin Cards Sorting Test, many symptoms are common to autism and frontal injuries (Rumsey, 1985, as cited by Joseph, 1999). To perform this test for a better understanding of social behavior, an integration and incorporation of many features of the situation, a selective attention to important aspects of the environment, and the preservation of inductive logic are necessary. Disturbances of programming and monitoring in abnormal development can not only be caused by pathology of the frontal lobes, but also because of the weakness of interaction of cortical and subcortical structures. Although an autistic child is able to conceptualize, he/she has compromised abilities to change his/her own cognitive strategy. There are also perseverations at the program level (i.e., system preservations).

   The main symptom of distorted development in autism is the weakness or absence of the capacity to participate in social communications (i.e., social maladjustment). This is due to difficult operational evaluation and the selection of suitable responses to constantly changing information (rigidity of cognitive attitudes) as well as to an inability to understand the feelings of others (disturbances of social perception) (Nikolskaya, Baenskaya, Libling, et al., 2005).
2. *Weakness of Central Link*—A destruction of gestalts, the fragmented strategies of information processing at the level of images and meanings. The result is a fragmentation of interests. Children with autism are characterized by an uneven degree of disturbances of different mental functions. This phenomenon is known in the literature as "islands of outstanding abilities." Autistic children have good results on the Block Design subtest from the Wechsler series, compared to other subtests from this battery. Perhaps this is due to the ability to perform this test using the strategy of dissecting into parts without the need for a holistic, gestalt perception. Characteristically, autistic children are less prone to illusions in special tests for visual illusions than other children of the same age. Information processing occurs in autistic individuals regardless of the broader context. This is confirmed by the fact that semantic and categorical organization of material does not improve memorization by autistic individuals, unlike in mentally retarded children.

3. *Limbic Dysfunction*—(Basal frontal areas, medial temporal areas, and the hippocampus). This theory is confirmed by the cases of autism in monkeys after removal of the medial temporal zone, including the hippocampus and the amygdala. The relationship of these areas with emotional and mnestic functions is widely known. Adherents of this theory consider autism as a "dysontogenic form of amnesic syndrome" (Boucher & Warrington, 1986, as cited by Joseph, 1999). Autistic children have a weak ability for delayed reproduction, similar to adult patients after hippocampal lesions. An alternative hypothesis is that a weak memory is due to difficulties of material organization (i.e., regulatory constraints).

Children with autism are frequently viewed by their peers as "different." As such, when mainstreamed, they are either embraced or avoided. As this young boy was very likeable, he was embraced and had many educational and social opportunities along the way. Although still exhibiting limited intellectual skills, he managed to obtain a high school diploma and is attempting remedial courses at a local community college. Medication and intervention have been helpful.

Cognitive disorder secondary to epilepsy and cerebral palsy

Infantile cerebral palsy is a progressive disease of the nervous system, characterized not only by a severe disabling motor disorder (inability to walk, sit, stand, keep own head up, manipulate with hands), but it also provokes a retardation of general mental development.

It is caused by different pathological effects on the brain in the last weeks of gestation, at the time of birth, and in the first weeks of life. In the first 6 months (sometimes up to 4 years), movement disturbances include muscle weakness and a loss of tone. Muscle weakness then gives way to the growing spasticity, which leads to disturbances of swallowing, chewing, and speech. Spastic muscles of the legs block walking. The disturbances of HMFs in children with cerebral palsy show the system is bilateral and has multilevel effects on brain structures. There are, however, limited opportunities for socialization and education, which depend not only on the severity of movement disturbances, but also on the state of the HMF.

This 15-year-old adolescent female exhibited severe cognitive, attentive, working memory, and learning difficulties secondary to her medical diagnosis. Although she was not retarded, these difficulties impeded her academic performance. Medication management, individual and family therapy, placement in a therapeutic school setting, and participation in equine therapy allowed her to thrive. She was able to complete high school and has begun to train as an equine therapist.

Global developmental delay with cognitive, affective, and behavioral dyscontrol

This 12-year-old boy presents with inattention and autistic qualities. His memory is adequate and he can be comforted by songs. As his deficits in math are quite severe, participation in a small (four boys) group-oriented program has been effective. Via medication management and individual therapy, he became less agitated and more cooperative. Currently, these interventions are generalizing to the school setting.

Bipolar disorder

This 9-year-old girl was presented by her mother due to her oppositional and hyperactive behaviors. After a comprehensive neuropsychological assessment, the issue of bipolarity emerged. During the feedback session, the mother revealed that she was bipolar. As bipolar disorder has a genetic component, this information helped to better understand the etiology of her difficulties. Appropriate medication management and behavior therapy were initiated. By age 14, the girl was stabilized and doing well at home and school.

Traumatic brain injury (TBI)

At 2.5 years old, this child received a severe TBI due to a motor vehicle accident. At age 5, he was referred by his pediatrician for neuropsychological evaluation and intervention. The latter included physical therapy and educational consultation and intervention to allow academic success. He finished high school and was endeavoring to qualify for a driver's license. Intervention for the latter was being conducted by an occupational therapist. When concluded, a follow-up neuropsychological evaluation will then be administered so that his pediatrician will have the information upon which to make an appropriate recommendation regarding driving.

Summary

In *summary*, when reviewing the aforementioned examples, it is obvious that all these individuals had more than one diagnosis. All these cases were quite complicated and involved a multifaceted approach to intervention. The primary diagnosis, however, had to be identified via neuropsychological evaluation and addressed before any additional diagnoses could be managed.

In conclusion

Combining Luria's qualitative approach with Reitan's quantitative approach to evaluation and intervention allows the neuropsychologist to enhance his/her understanding of the child's brain-behavior functions in a cultural-historical context. This combined approach is especially valuable when it comes to intervention. Without this understanding, children may receive inappropriate interventions. What may appear to be a useful intervention in one setting may not be useful in a different setting. For example, if a child is taught to play the piano to enhance motor skills, but has no access to a piano, how is this helpful? Likewise, if a child is taught a skill to enhance math, but has no need for this skill, how is this helpful?

The interventions that are taught must be child-specific within his/her world. They must not only be meaningful, but applicable and enjoyable. For example, if the child does have access to a piano, are the exercises/interventions fun? If the interventions are not meaningful and fun, children will resist. Play with a purpose is the best form of intervention for young children. By making it meaningful and fun, the outcome of combining both the Lurian and Reitan approaches to evaluation and intervention will lead to a more productive outcome.

References

Benton, A. (2000). Foreword. In K. Yeates, M. Ris, & H. Taylor (Eds.), *Pediatric neuropsychology. Research, theory and practice* (p. XV). New York/London: The Guilford Press.

Clements, S. D. (1973). Minimal brain dysfunction in children. In S. Sapir & A. Nitzburg (Eds.), *Children with learning problems*. New York: Brunner/Mazel.

Facoetti, A., Zorzi, M., Cestnick, R., et al. (2006). The relationship between visuospatial attention and non-word reading in developmental dyslexia. *Cognitive Neuropsychology*, *23*, 841–855.

Glozman, J. M. (2002). The cultural-historical approach as a basis of the neuropsychology of the XXI century. *Voprosy Psikhologii*, *4*, 62–68 [in Russian].

Glozman, J. M. (2013). *Developmental neuropsychology*. London/New York: Psychology Press/ Taylor and Francis Group.

Glozman, J., Soboleva, A. Y., & Titova, Yu. O. (2020). *Neuropsychological assessment of preschool children*. Moscow: Airis Press [in Russian].

Hom, J., & Nici, J. (2015). Ralph M. Reitan's bibliography. *Archives of Clinical Neuropsychology*, *30*, 774–783.

Inshakova, O. B. (Ed.), (2001). *Writing and reading: Learning problems and remediation*. Modek: Moscow/Voronezh [in Russian].

Joseph, R. M. (1999). Neuropsychological frameworks for understanding autism. *International Representation of Psychiatry*, *11*, 309–325.

Korsakova, N. K., Mikadze, Y. V., & Balashova, E. Y. (2001). *Unsuccessful children: Neuropsychological assessment of learning difficulties*. Moscow: Russian Psychological Agency [in Russian].

Lebedinsky, M. S. (1932). Problem of heredity in psychology and twins method. *Psychology*, *1–2*, 163–204 [in Russian].

Lenneberg, E. (1967). *Biological foundations of language*. New York: Wiley.

Luria, A. R. (1928). The problem of the cultural behavior of the child. *Journal of Genetic Psychology*, *35*(3), 493–506.

Luria, A. R. (1930). *Speech and intelligence of urban, rural and homeless child*. Moscow/Leningrad: Gosizdat [in Russian].

Luria, A. R. (1936). The development of mental functions in twins. *Character and Personality*, *5*, 35–47.

Luria, A. R. (1948). Development of constructive activity in preschoolers. In A. N. Leontiev & A. V. Zaporozhets (Eds.), *Psychology of preschoolers* (pp. 34–64). Moscow: Russian Pedagogical Academy Press [in Russian].

Luria, A. R. (1950). *Essays in the psychophysiology of writing*. Moscow: Russian Pedagogical Academy Press [in Russian].

Luria, A. R. (1958). Dynamic approach to the mental development of the abnormal child. *Journal of Mental Deficiency Research*, *2*, 27–52.

Luria, A. R. (1959). Experimental study of the higher nervous activity of the abnormal child. *Journal of Mental Deficiency Research*, *3*, 1–22.

Luria, A. R. (1960). Verbal regulation of behavior. In M. Brazier (Ed.), *The central nervous system and behavior: Transactions of the third Macy conference* (pp. 359–421). New York: Josiah Macy Jr. Foundation.

Luria, A. R. (Ed.), (1963). *The mentally retarded child: Essays based on a study of the peculiarities of the higher nervous functioning of child-oligophrenics*. New York: Macmillan/Pergamon.

Luria, A. R. (1973). *The working brain. An introduction to neuropsychology*. London: Penguin Books.

Luria, A. R. (2002). On nature of mental functions and its variations through genetic analysis. *Voprosy Psikhologii*, *4*, 4–18 [in Russian].

Luria, A. R., Symernitskaya, E. G., & Tybulevich, B. (1973). On changes in cerebral organization of mental processes during their functional development. In A. N. Leontiev, A. R. Luria, & E. D. Khomskaya (Eds.), Vol. 4. *Psychological studies* (pp. 111–119). Moscow: Moscow University Press [in Russian].

Luria, A. R., & Yudovich, F. I. (1959). *Speech and the development of mental processes in the child*. London: Staples Press.

Machinskaya, R. I., & Dubrovinskaya, N. V. (2003). Brain basis of informative and motivative components of voluntary attention in primary school pupils. In T. V. Akhutina & J. M. Glozman (Eds.), *A.R. Luria and psychology of 21 century. Proceedings of the 2nd international conference devoted to 100 years from Luria birth* (pp. 309–317). Moscow: Smysl [in Russian].

Maestrini, E., Paul, A., Monaco, A. P., & Bailey, A. (2000). Identifying autism susceptibility genes. *Neuron*, *28*, 19–24.

Mikadze, Y. V., Ardila, A., & Akhutina, T. V. (2019). A.R. Luria's approach to neuropsychological assessment and rehabilitation. *Archives of Clinical Neuropsychology*, *34*, 795–802.

Mironova, A. N., & Kolbanovsky, V. N. (1934). Comparative study of combination abilities development. Experiences with monozygotic twins. *Papers of the Medicobiological Institute*, *3*, 104–118 [in Russian].

Nikolskaya, O. S., Baenskaya, E. P., Libling, M. M., et al. (2005). *Children and teenagers with autism. Psychological help*. Moscow: Terevinf [in Russian].

Obukhova, L. F. (1997). *Developmental psychology: Theories, facts, problems*. Moscow: Trivolla [in Russian].

Paulesu, E., McCroy, E., Fazio, F., et al. (2000). A cultural effect of brain function. *Nature Neuroscience*, *3*, 91–96.

Pylaeva, N.M. (1995). Practice of neuropsychological assessment of 5-6 years old mentally retarded children. *Vestnik of Moscow University Series 14, Psychology*, *3*, 37–45 [in Russian].

Ramus, F., & Szenkovits, G. (2008). What phonological deficit? *The Quarterly Journal of Experimental Psychology*, *61*, 129–141.

Ravich-Scherbo I.V. & Sigal N.L. (2003). Alexander Romanovich Luria and national psychogenetics. In A.R. Luria and psychology of 21 century, Proceedings of the 2nd International Conference devoted to 100 years from Luria birth. Ed. by T.V. Akhutina and J.M. Glozman. Moscow: Smysl p. 324–328 (in Russian).

Reitan, R. M., & Wolfson, D. (1992a). *Neuropsychological evaluation of younger children*. Tucson, AZ: Neuropsychology Press.

Reitan, R. M., & Wolfson, D. (1992b). *Neuropsychological evaluation of older children*. Tucson, AZ: Neuropsychology Press.

Rourke, B. P. (Ed.), (1985). *Neuropsychology of learning disabilities*. New York: Guilford Press.

D. Tupper & K. Cicerone (Eds.), (1991). Preface. In *The neuropsychology of everyday life. Issues in development and rehabilitation* (pp. XIII–XIV). Boston: Kluwer Academic Publishers.

Vygotsky, L. S. (1925). *Introduction to the book by Lazursky A.F. General and experimental psychology*. Leningrad: Pedagogica [in Russian].

Vygotsky, L. S. (1956). *Selected psychological writings*. Moscow: Pedagogica [in Russian].

Further reading

Reitan, R. M., & Wolfson, D. (1994). *Neuropsychological evaluation of young children*. Unpublished manuscript.

Selz, M., & Reitan, R. M. (1979). Comparative test performance of normal, learning disabled, and brain-damaged older children. *Journal of Nervous and Mental Diseases*, *167*, 298–302.

Vygotsky, L., & Luria, A. (1993). *Studies on the history of behavior: Ape, primitive, and child*. Hillsdale, NJ, USA: Lawrence Erlbaum Associates, Inc.

Chapter 2

Heritage of Reitan and Luria to 21st century developmental neuropsychology

Joaquim Quintino-Aires
Neuropsychology Department, Vygotsky Institute, Lisbon, Portugal

Introduction

The clinical practice of neuropsychology in Portugal began in the late 1980s. At that time, Ralph M. Reitan's work served as a guide to the work of young psychologists who sought to improve what they were still learning. Even today, we find his influence in the presence of ideas such as "blind approach" examination, attention to the nature of the lesion (e.g., acute versus static or progressive versus chronic) and its impact on the psychological test results, the look for pathognomonic signs of brain dysfunction, attention to qualitative and quantitative aspects, and the need for special care in the evaluation of children, including in the materials used in the examination. All these aspects continue to mark the clinical neuropsychological practice in Portugal, a mark of Reitan's influence. By the 1990s, the first neuropsychology laboratory in a psychology department was established at the Universidade Lusófona de Humanidades e Tecnologias in Lisbon. It was there that a more systematized study began on the part of students of psychology, particularly the study of neuroanatomy and neuropathology, also guided by his work.

Many questions from Reitan led to a study of the work of A.R. Luria, beginning in Portugal in the 1990s. With the guidance of professors from Moscow State University, it was possible to bring to clinical practice new methods of assessment and therapy, maintaining and developing the guidelines of Reitan, mentioned earlier.

At the beginning of the 21st century, neuropsychology went beyond the field of neurosurgery and neurology, and is widely used in schools, particularly in the area of learning disabilities. It is applied in new areas, such as professional reorientation of the long-term unemployed. In the field of psychiatry, it gives an almost unique answer today in the treatment of various categories of personality

Evaluation and Treatment of Neuropsychologically Compromised Children
https://doi.org/10.1016/B978-0-12-819545-1.00002-3

disorders. In the daily work of many neuropsychologists, despite all these new applications, it is possible to easily recognize the heritage left by Reitan and Luria.

The integration of the contributions of these two great names in the history of neuropsychology produced a more consistent practice and motivated the greater interest of more professionals. Today, this is one of the professional specialties recognized by the Ordem dos Psicólogos Portugueses, the institution that regulates the practice of the profession in Portugal.

Ralph M. Reitan, pioneer of neuropsychological clinical practice. An ever-present teacher without even knowing it himself

One of the first places where the clinical practice of neuropsychology in Portugal emerged was in the neuropsychology laboratory of the neurosurgery service at Hospital Militar Principal (Lisbon). I had the pleasure of starting my professional career in 1989 with the guidance of Dr. Ana Paula Cerejo.

It was early on in that job, and thanks to the support of the director of the service, the neurosurgeon Dr. António Pereira Gonsalves, it was possible to provide the maximum resources to prepare the psychologists who worked there. It is important to say that none of us had received university education or training in this field of psychology. So, the challenge was great and difficult, and the need for masters and mentors became critical. It is in this effort that the team would find in the work of Reitan a theoretical and practical guide so that we could start the journey. The extensive work and the consistency of its contents were the confirmations that we had found the right "teacher" to learning the path we had chosen. What have we learned from Reitan?

I wanted to start with something with which we, early psychologists and our neurological colleagues, have been absolutely fascinated: the blind interpretation approach. Reitan proposed the complete separation of criterion information from the psychological test data. The psychologist should start by only using test data, focusing on the data and the patient observations as well as elaborate detailed written conclusions. The conclusions are then compared with the criterion information. Although we were aware that this approach was possible for Reitan as a result of many years of work, we were just getting started. For us, this proposal would be quite difficult. Nevertheless, the possibility of this approach was clearly a deep motivation, for its seriousness and for a dedicated study that we knew would be extremely demanding. We knew our way would be long. But if it was possible to get there, if someone had already done it, we wanted it too. We wanted to do it.

Our main task at the neuropsychology laboratory at the Military Hospital was to evaluate candidates for the army immediately before joining the company. At that time, all males were previously assessed when they were 18 years old. However, they would only be incorporated into one of the three branches of the armed forces (Army, Navy, or Air Force) the year they turned 21. There were sometimes traffic accidents within that period. In most cases, traffic accidents with motorized vehicles caused eventual brain injury. It was necessary to ensure the security of their integration into the army. On the other hand, it was often the case that the traffic accident consequences were used as an argument to be exempted from military service, which was then mandatory because not everyone wished to have this obligation. Our work therefore was a huge responsibility, and it was necessary to ensure enormous seriousness in clinical reports.

So, what tests to use to ensure the best quality of our technical response? The answer was the psychological tests that we had studied and trained on at the university. Some could be useful to distinguish the presence or absence of defects after traumatic brain injury. But not all. And even if the designation of the test refers to this goal of discriminating between committed or not compromised by brain injury, not all would be good tools.

In Reitan's investigations, we found that the Rorschach test could be a good instrument, through the 10 signs of Piotrowski and others that he himself identified (Aita, Reitan, & Ruth, 1947). The Wechsler scales also showed good diagnostic quality. But others, such as the Hunt-Minnesota Test for Organic Brain Damage, showed little value in differentiating brain damage from the control group (Aita, Armitage, Reitan, & Rabinovitz, 1947). These data alerted us to the need to look for more studies, such as those carried out and presented by Reitan. This information shows that self-taught practice is risky. We wanted to do our job well. We needed to follow the line of thought of a "mentor," and it seemed to us that Reitan could be our "mentor."

For him, theory and practice need to unite. It is not because the academic scientific community says that a test is meant to measure organic brain damage that we are going to use it. You need to test it over and over on real patients, and Reitan did that. About his work, he wrote: "... a wonderful procedure for generating research hypotheses. We were able to conduct and publish a large number of individual studies quite efficiently, mainly because our hypotheses for investigation had already been strongly supported by our findings on individual subjects. Thus, we did not have to pick hypotheses for research either out of the blue sky or from some type of theoretical formulation. Instead, our research hypotheses were based on observations of natural (phenomena). We dug very few dry holes, with nearly every research study producing publishable findings" (Reitan as cited in: Stringer, Cooley, & Christensen, 2002, p. 232). According to J. Hom and J. Nici (Hom & Nici, 2015), this attitude was not always accepted. Nevertheless, as we all understand, it is the right attitude, even if infrequent in psychology. That is why it brought us confidence.

We could integrate this knowledge more quickly in our practice because it was simpler and meant we would be using an instrument that we already knew. The Weschler Scale showed the association between injury in the left cerebral hemisphere and a significantly lower result in verbal IQ in relation to IQ of achievement, and the inverse was true in the injury of the right cerebral hemisphere. This ability of psychological tests to reflect the lateralization of the injury had already been studied by Reitan (Reitan, 1955). But for us, beginning psychologists working on a team of neurosurgeons and neurologists, in hindsight, it gave meaning to our efforts to understand clinical neuropsychology.

During his professional career, Reitan identified several other specificities of the psychological tests that were related to the effect of different localizations of the lesions. For example, the altered result X in test A was associated with injury in the region α. And the result Y changed in test B was associated with injury in region β. The systematization of this information has become a priority for us. The more complete our collection, analysis, and systematization of this type of information, the more complex our dissections of the test data became and the more correct our reports would be.

Reitan identified other factors important to the understanding of the effects of brain lesions on psychological function. For example, he found that the nature of the lesion (e.g., acute versus static or progressive versus chronic) impacted the psychological test results (Fitzhugh, Fitzhugh, & Reitan, 1961). At this point, our neuropsychological assessments also integrated neurological patients. We began to evaluate patients with cerebrovascular and dementia pathology, and therefore this orientation about the nature of the lesions was crucial for us. Not only in the reports we produced, but also in the interventions we recommended in the department's clinical meetings could our work become more frequent and more valued by the other team members.

Neuropathology is also a topic we studied with the guidance of the physicians on the team, specifically Dr. Manuel Machado, the then-coordinator of neurology. Concepts such as tumors, epilepsy, strokes, dementia processes, or head injuries must be part of our understanding and deserve our attention when interpreting the results of neuropsychological evaluations. This necessitated a greater study, not only of neuropathology but also of clinical neuropsychology, in order to function effectively on a team with neurology and neurosurgery.

In addition, the study of thousands of clinical cases in a case-by-case approach has impressed us. It is evident that we also found this form of study in the then-emerging cognitive neuropsychology field (Ellis & Young, 1988; Seron, 1993). However, cognitive neuropsychology was a proposal of the late 20th century, when Reitan's proposal for a case-by-case approach had come at a time when "numerology" dominated psychology. Reitan defended this approach as specific to neuropsychology, and this was his way of working and building his knowledge in neuropsychology, by showing attention to the clinical practice that guided his work. The analysis of individual test protocols on a case-by-case basis allowed Reitan to discover and identify what "big numbers" studies would never reveal. After many years, cognitive neuropsychology has shown the value of case studies (Ellis & Young, 1988).

In Reitan's lectures, we also found a method for working with the data resulting from each neuropsychological evaluation. In his clinical case analysis, Reitan did not merely record the level of patient performance. His method of inference for the individual patient was to: (1) consider the level of performance, (2) evaluate the patterns of test performances among various areas of neurocognitive function, (3) compare the function of the left and right sides of the body, and (4) look for pathognomonic signs of brain dysfunction. These are the four basic methods of inference that have been employed by Reitan to draw valid conclusions concerning the biological condition of an individual's brain as well as the neuropsychological implications of these results. These methods allowed Reitan to determine whether brain damage was present, the nature of the damage (chronic or acute), whether it was lateralized or diffuse, and the type of brain injury.

All his ideas and methods have been incorporated into the neuropsychological assessment battery he and Ward Halstead composed, which has also become a working tool for us. Specifically, Reitan considered that the Halstead-Reitan Neuropsychological Test Battery (HRNB) (Reitan & Wolfson, 1985a), while extensive, was a bare-bones battery (Hom & Nici, 2015). The component tests were selected on an empirical basis rather than a theoretical basis, and they were chosen as important sample areas of human ability and to allow inferences regarding the individual patient. The findings are looked at in a qualitative and quantitative way, and these required new approaches in interpretation.

At some point in our work at the Military Hospital, and thanks to the good reputation our work received with other clinical services, we were also asked to develop neuropsychological evaluations for children, relatives of military personnel. They also had medical services at the hospital. This would be a new task for the team. Therefore, it was necessary to look to "our advisor," Reitan, for the necessary support for our preparation.

Reitan realized that adult neuropsychological practice knowledge could not be directly applied to working with children. In order to evaluate children, either in the context of a neurological or neurosurgical clinic or in a school context for children with learning disabilities, further studies were needed. A first study (Reed, Reitan, & Klove, 1965) was focused on the preparation of the neuropsychological battery for children between 9 and 14 years old. Several adaptations were performed with the tests, which were also shortened in the number of items due to children's attention span limitations.

In order to test even younger children, Reitan made some additional modifications to the test procedures and developed some new tasks that would be developmentally appropriate for children in the age range of 5–8. He called this battery the Reitan-Indiana Neuropsychological Test Battery (RINB). As an example of one of the additional modifications that he made, the Category Test was changed so that the answers were based on color rather than number. One of the new tasks, called Color Form, involved a cognitive switching task (as in Trails B) but with the child switching between shape and color (Reitan, 1974).

Concluding this brief presentation of Reitan's contribution to the beginning of clinical neuropsychology in Portugal, I would like to refer to his "presence" at the Neuropsychology Laboratory of the Department of Psychology at the

Universidade Lusófona de Humanidades e Tecnologias in Lisbon. This was the first neuropsychology laboratory in a psychology department in our country. Among other things, the lab had the task of training and preparing those students who showed interest in neuropsychology. And in this motive, the study of some fundamental subjects became essential. This is when Reitan's book *Neuroanatomy and Neuropathology: A Clinical Guide for Neuropsychologists*, written in conjunction with his colleague D. Wolfson in 1985 (Reitan & Wolfson, 1985b), became a guide for every student.

To summarize, Reitan had, without even knowing it himself, a very marked presence at the beginning of clinical neuropsychology in Portugal. After him, many neuropsychologists have come to practice concepts or ideas such as the "blind interpretation approach," forming hypotheses based on observations of natural phenomena, attention to the nature of the lesion, a case-by-case approach, not just to record the level of performance, looking at the data in a qualitative and quantitative way, the understanding that adult neuropsychological practice could not apply directly to work with children, and therefore neuropsychological work with children required its own approach. But also, the idea that theory and practice need to come together. And the academic scientific community, if not involved in the practice, should be looked upon with some reserve. All these concepts are clearly a heritage that Reitan left in clinical neuropsychology in Portugal.

Alexander Luria, A theory for neuropsychological clinical practice. An ever-present teacher without even knowing

My contact with the work of A.R. Luria began about 30 years ago. A colleague handed me a book, *Working Brain*, in a Portuguese translation published in Brazil in 1981. Reading and then studying this book made me feel fascinated and curious. My knowledge of neuropsychology, which was somewhat scattered, seemed as systematized and consistent as I had ever seen.

At the same time, I had the opportunity to visit Professor Jordi Peña-Casanova's department at the Hospital del Mar in Barcelona. It was in Barcelona that I discovered that Peña-Casanova studied Luria's work. He translated one of Luria's books into Spanish, *Fundamentos de neurolingüística* (Luria, 1980). He even directly corresponded with the father of neuropsychology, Alexander Romanovich Luria. From this visit came the possibility of a guided study, which was why many more trips to Barcelona followed.

Then I began to study the work of Luria (1902–1977), and of those with whom he worked and developed his theory, namely L.S. Vygotsky (1896–1937) and A. N. Leontiev (1903–1979). I quickly realized that from a theoretical point of view, the scientific approach was quite different from what I had studied at the University of Lisbon. Guidance was required for the study of these authors. In 1996, I met Professor Janna Glozman in Canada, and through her intermediary, I received the first invitation to visit Moscow State University. Naturally, many other trips to Moscow followed, with the possibility of learning and receiving guidance for the study of Luria, Vygotsky, and Leontiev, but also of A.V. Zaporozhets, P. Galperin, and others, including a completely new understanding of I. Pavlov's work.

It is very important to note that understanding Luria's work is not possible without the joint study of Vygotsky and Leontiev. The three together are considered the founders of cultural-historical psychology, which is at the same time a neuropsychological theory. Without studying the work of the three psychologists, their individual work is impossible to understand in its entirety. I think it is impossible to penetrate the neuropsychological approach that Luria practiced and taught, either in neuropsychological assessment or in rehabilitation, without first knowing the cultural-historical theory.

The many references to Luria in the last 50 years include many misinterpretations of what he proposed. Perhaps the strongest example is the Luria-Nebraska Neuropsychological Battery (Golden, Purisch, & Hammeke, 1979). About it, J. Peña-Casanova wrote that it is something like "Luria since Luria" (Peña-Casanova, 1989, p. 164), that is, Luria in name but not in conception. Also T. Akhutina and L. Tsvetkova wrote that "it seems to us that the battery is not fully effective in fulfilling the tasks of topical diagnosis and the construction of rehabilitation and teaching programs, as it does not consistently follow Luria's principle of qualitative analysis…" (Akhutina & Tsvetkova, 1983, p. 133).

Many other bad examples followed, and not just in the case of neuropsychological assessment. It is also strange that in today's world, so many neuropsychological rehabilitation centers work on a repetition training methodology, with poor results, when Luria's proposal for neuropsychological rehabilitation, the theory of reorganization of functional systems, has been proven effective for more than 70 years (Luria, 1948/1963).

I think it is the attempt to study Luria without first knowing the cultural-historical theory that justifies such statements as: "The power of this book is that it brings Luria to those of us who know they should, but have never developed the patience and perspective needed to read it comprehensively," written by A.L. Holland in the preface to Kagan and M. Saling's book, *An Introduction to Luria's Aphasiology: Theory and Application* (Kagan & Saling, 1988). When he writes about those who have never developed the patience and perspective necessary to read it comprehensively, which in my view portrays reality very well, it follows that once one begins to study Luria, we quickly come across a different science of which we are unaware and which we do not know, and the reading quickly becomes confusing and the reader gives up.

For this reason, I chose first to present a brief summary of cultural-historical psychology to facilitate an effective understanding of Luria's proposals for neuropsychological clinical practice. Because, and remembering his words: "There is no better theory than a good practice; there is no better practice than a good theory." Luria's work is very extensive. What I present are those core ideas that are fundamental to understand the work we do today in developmental neuropsychology on the path of this legacy.

The novelty that we can consider truly revolutionary in cultural-historical psychology is its understanding of the relationship between the biological and the social, in the genesis of the human psyche. The existence of specifically human brain areas, such as the prefrontal region and the parieto-temporo-occipital intersection, and the fact that these regions exhibit "double experience" functioning when speech takes place, require an understanding of human brain development and functioning completely different from the brain functioning of animals. Thus, even though animal studies bring so much knowledge to neurobiology, they do little or nothing to teach us about neuropsychology.

Higher cortical functions in man and the regulatory role of language

In humans, the frontal lobe has a longer extension toward the front pole. It has arrangements of neurons making connections with virtually every other brain region. Such a large rate of connection between regions is not observed in the brain of any other species. Similarly, at the intersection of the parietal, temporal, and occipital lobes in the posterior region of the cerebral hemispheres, we once again find a unique anatomic-physiological organization in humans. These brain regions (i.e., tertiary zones of the cerebral cortex) are especially involved in the processing of higher cortical functions, such as voluntary attention, logical memory, verbal thinking, and particularly adult language. In addition, these regions have a maximum level of plasticity, starting up and structuring only as they are used. These understandings require a different, new approach when we study and work on higher cortical functions.

When we study the higher cortical functions in the child, we find that each higher form of behavior comes into play twice in development. "First as a collective form of behavior, as an interpsychological function. It is a reciprocal psychological process. One process takes place in my brain, the other process in the brain of another with whom I have an argument" (Vygotsky, 1930/1996, p. 126). Vygotsky wrote: "Each higher cortical function is originally shared between two people. Later, when the resulting development of learning has occurred, then the process takes place as an intrapsychological function" (Vygotsky, 1930/1996, p. 126). The interpsychological process and the intrapsychological process for the same higher nerve activity naturally have different brain neurodynamics.

This understanding of brain development in humans is known as the Double Development Law. And according to many psychologists, myself included, it expresses the General Law of Psychology, or the Dogma of Psychology. The developmental process stems from a relationship with a "competent veteran," giving rise to the concept of the zone of proximal development (ZPD), a dynamic process whereby what was interpsychological (social) becomes intrapsychological (psychological). As Dorothy Robbins wrote, quoting Newman and Holzman (1996), "the particular relational activity that is simultaneously and makes possible the transformation of rigid behavior (forms of life that have become alienated and fossilized) into new forms of life" (Robbins, 2003, p. 40).

Essential in the process of development is the individual's own activity upon the world, an activity mediated by instruments of culture. It is this instrumental activity that gives rise to the structuring of higher cortical functions (Zaporozhets, 1971/2002). It underpins the development process described in the Double Development Law. A relationship with an "other veteran" is necessary for the presentation of the behavioral activity model and, fundamentally, for the orientation of the "other veteran" during the interpsychological phase.

The human brain differs from the brain in other animal species by functioning in "double experience." The animal, devoid of its nervous activity and relying only on innate reflexes, would lead a disabled life and be condemned to die upon being abandoned. Everyday life requires more flexible and more specialized relationships between the animal and the outside world. These higher-order relationships are established in the cerebral hemispheres. Here, a multitude of agents from the outside world are signaled, all of them extremely variable. Only in this way can an accurate and subtle balance be achieved between the body and the environment. The activity of the cerebral hemispheres in humans, which also results from verbal stimuli, is based on everyone's semantic system.

From here comes an important line of research adopted by Luria. He studied with great interest the psychophysiological mechanisms involved in the voluntary regulation of motor behavior and investigated the regulating role of language on behavior. Luria's work on this topic began in the 1950s. A summary of his conclusions, published in English, followed three lectures that Luria gave in 1958 at London University College, in his book *The Role of Speech in the Regulation of Normal and Abnormal Behavior* (Luria, 1961). I must say that this is one of Luria's books that fascinated me. Within Vygotsky's theory, Luria studied the gradual formation of complex models of verbally controlled motor behavior programs. He documented the distinction between organized behavior based on higher language-mediated processes and behavior based on natural processes. Together with his collaborators, Luria presented the different neurodynamic mechanisms involved in each form of behavior.

Much of his work increasingly brings this aspect of the regulative function of language. It becomes impossible to understand Luria's neuropsychology without integrating the mediating role of language in brain organization. The enormous value given to language, when we study the state of the human brain in relation to voluntary and oriented behavior, can be seen when he was writing with his collaborator E. Homskaya. They note that the regulation of the orientation reflex through language is a characteristic so fundamental to healthy human mental functioning that it "may serve as an important indicator of the normal functioning of the brain" (Luria & Homskaya, 1970, p. 305).

Systemic organization of higher cortical functions

In addition to the Law of Double Development (the Dogma of Psychology), its corollary of the extracortical origin of higher cortical functions, and the mediating role of language in brain organization, Luria undertook a thorough review of the concepts of function, localization, and symptom. We find the basis of this extensive and very profound review by Luria in the text of *Psychology and the Theory of Psychic Function Localization* (Vygotsky, 1934/1996). From the result of this review and the repercussion it had on his work emerges the name with which his neuropsychology often is referred: Systemic and Dynamic Neuropsychology. This name was chosen precisely because it has at its center the issue of systemic and dynamic organization and the external origin of the higher cortical functions (HCFs).

The systemic organization of HCFs was first presented on Oct. 9, 1930, at a conference held at the Moscow Clinic of Neurological Diseases. Vygotsky defended the thesis that the HCFs of the human brain have a systemic organization. As with other functional systems in the human body, HCFs are not unitary in nature, not a function, as in classical neurology. On the contrary, they have a systemic organization.

The Russian physiologist P.K. Anokhin (Anokhin, 1935/1974) developed the concept of a "functional system" to underlie the understanding of higher psychic processes as complex functions. The functional system is characterized by its complex structure, which includes a series of differentiated components, often with distant brain localizations, and acting together. The functional system presupposes the existence of an invariant task or goal, which can be obtained through variable mechanisms. It is also important to say that the functional system is endowed with self-regulation, obtained through a complex interaction between central and peripheral formations. From the interaction between the central and peripheral formations results the possibility of brain reorganization of the "programs" of activity (P. Anokhin's theory of system genesis, Anokhin, 1974).

Just as, for example, digestion is a complex functional system that recruits various structures (such as the mouth, tongue, salivary glands, esophagus, stomach, intestines, etc.), so does each HCF. Speech, logical memory, perception, voluntary attention, etc., depend on a complex functional system, operating in an orchestrated manner and recruiting the processing of different brain regions. Thus, speaking of a function, for example speech, introduced an error that was repeated when we tried to understand the localization of that function. What is located in brain are components of functional systems and not functions that, moreover, exist only as categories, as study material or clinical work.

This systemic functioning can be demonstrated by the fact that patients with lesions in different brain areas may have the same behavioral defect. The patient with an injury at localization A cannot perform behavior X because he does not have the component α that would be located at A, which is necessary for this behavior. The patient with a lesion in B also cannot perform the same behavior X, for not having the component β, also necessary for this behavior, but with localization in B.

Using a classical psychological assessment task block design (Kohs's cubes), Tsvetkova (2002) showed that both patients with prefrontal lesions and patients with right parietal lesions are unsuccessful in performing the task. However, while patients with prefrontal lesions failed due to impulsivity (failure to inhibit) in the arrangement of the cubes, patients with right parietal lesions failed due to difficulty in the spatial analysis of the presented stimulus card. An analysis of how patients with parietal injury and patients with frontal injury perform the task immediately made this difference evident. Both the frontal and right parietal regions as well as others are required for successful block design tasks.

Dynamic organization of higher cortical functions

Switching from the theoretical conception of function as a unit to the theory of functional system requires rethinking the concept of brain localization. First, it is important to note that functional systems are developed in ontogenesis, and that different functional systems develop at different times of development (Filimonov's chronogenetic principle). There is the possibility of recruiting different groupings of components for the realization of the same behavioral product as well as the possibility of the same component integrating different functional systems (Filimonov's principle of multivalence). So, the cerebral representation of the functional system is not static but dynamic, therefore leading to the need to know the dynamics of localization in different ages and different cultures. This is the **principle of dynamic localization of higher cortical functions**. Vygotsky spoke of dynamic localization at the Moscow Institute of Experimental Medicine on April 28, 1934 (just two months before his death). This idea, first presented by Filimonov,[a] is known as the chronogenetic principle of function localization, and explains the dynamic nature of brain localization in ontogenesis.

For example, in the first years of life (from birth to around 5–7 years), the attention system results from an activation created at the level of the first brain block (brainstem and thalamus). The child's attention is scattered, constantly responding to changes in the environment, which does not allow him to perform focused attention activities. Around 5–7 years of age, in a child with a common life history, the descending reticular activator system begins to structure (connecting the frontal lobe with the first block). This is a neurophysiological system consisting of nerve fibers located between the prefrontal region and the brainstem. The structuring of these long association fibers allows the child to

---

a. The reference to Filimonov's scientific ideas is found several times in the works of Luria and Leontiev. Unfortunately, his texts are not easily accessible.

inhibit responses to each new random stimulus in the environment (blocking his distracted behavior) and to attend, for instance, to the various explanations the teacher presents to him in the classroom.

Bottom-up development

This alteration in the cognitive structure of attention presupposes, of course, changes in the cerebral localization of the cerebral attention system. The new attention system is no longer located only in the brainstem and base nuclei, but is significantly dependent on structures located in the frontal lobe and its connections with subcortical structures. As Vygotsky wrote, "It is possible to observe an analogous symptomatic picture in children and adults when the localization of the lesions is different and, on the contrary, lesions with the same localization in the child and adult may give rise to completely different symptomatic pictures" (Vygotsky, 1934/1996, p. 197). **As a general principle, development goes from the bottom up**. That is, the subcortical structures involved in certain functional systems can then be controlled by cortical structures, which means different neurodynamics for the same functional system. And, of course, with differences in behavior.

Functions can have different processing and characteristics, and these differences are realized in different brain regions. Vygotsky enunciated this principle as the "dynamic localization" of the higher cortical functions, which finally allowed us to interpret the fact that often in different people, a different localization is found for the "same function," and even in the same person at different stages of ontogenesis. Russian physiologist N. Bernstein (1967) systematically studied and demonstrated the **principle of dynamic localization**, a principle that revolutionized our understanding of brain organization.

At the conference of October 9, 1930, cited earlier, Vygotsky also presented the most revolutionary of his theses: that the HCFs have a relational (social) origin. Typically, human functions such as voluntary attention, logical memory, language, consciousness, will, etc., are not innate, not the result of a biology with millions of years of phylogenetic evolution. They are structured in the human brain in a process of acting with tools in a relationship with another human. This is the **principle of relational (extracortical) origin of higher cortical functions.**[b]

His idea was initially verified experimentally in works on the organization of motor activity with patients suffering from Parkinson's disease. With Luria, he used external signs as auxiliaries (pieces of paper scattered on the floor). The placement of sheets clearly facilitated walking in Parkinsonian patients, as was already known in clinical neurology. Vygotsky then hypothesized that patients' brains make a connection between different points through this external sign (the sheet of paper), influencing brain organization from the outside. Thus, in

---

b. See experimental confirmation of this idea in Chapter 9 of this book.

structuring psychological systems, Vygotsky stressed the importance of "extra-cerebral" links and justified the possibility of formation of "new brain organs," structural changes induced in the body from the outside.

This is a new form of (ontogenetic) evolution, which is observed only in humans. Human brains contain the conditions and possibilities for combining functional components into a new synthesis, forming new functional systems that had not previously been structured in phylogenesis. Studies to demonstrate this idea were, for political reasons, continued at the Kharkov (Ukraine) Psychoneurological Institute. Leontiev, Zaporozhets, and Bozhovich conducted experiments that allowed them to demonstrate this principle of formation of cerebral "new functional organs" (Ukhtomsky's term 1934; in: Leontiev, 1981), or brain neoformations that serve voluntary attention, semantic memory, language, and reasoning (Leontiev, 1981, 2004).

Summarizing at each stage of development and in the history of development as a result of the individual's objective activity in relation to other humans (ontogenesis), the links between the components of brain functional systems change, and new constellations, which were absent at the previous stage, emerge. The development of these new and flexible relationships between brain functional components gives rise to a psychological system (Vygotsky, 1930/1996; 1934/1996). The brain substrate of mental processes is organized into complex systems distributed throughout the brain (neoformations), which represent intricate cooperation between different zones.

Luria's concept of three functional blocks

So far it seems that Luria "only" has organized the thinking of different scientists into a unitary and consistent formulation, what would already be a work of genius. But he also added to the theory something extremely useful and important to the work of the practical neuropsychologist: the brain organization into three functional blocks.

We know from neurology that the brain has motor and sensory areas, primary projection areas, and areas of association. The functional activity of the great cerebral hemispheres is organized in various analyzers, distributed in different cortical regions, and involved with vision, hearing, tactile and kinesthetic, and motor activity. In each analyzer, it is possible to distinguish nuclear zones, regions of primary projection of lobes of the cerebral hemispheres, and cortical extensors, corresponding to areas of association. These are further divided into secondary and tertiary areas, the latter corresponding to overlapping areas where the sensory mode of access (vision, hearing, tactile kinesthetic, or motor) is no longer represented.

In a simplified way perhaps, we can say that the visual analyzer corresponds to the occipital lobe, the temporal lobe auditory analyzer as well as the tactile and kinesthetic analyzer to the parietal lobe, and the motor analyzer to the frontal lobe. In fact, this is a simplification, as the tertiary areas of the three posterior analyzers overlap in the parieto-temporo-occipital region. Even the analyzers' nuclear zones have arrangements that suggest many, many cortical, subcortical, and bilateral connections.

Naturally, this systematized way of looking at brain function helped to integrate our knowledge of the systemic functioning of different brain areas. Yet, Luria did more. In his new work on brain functioning, Luria recognized the existence of three units that integrate with each other to perform any mental activity, such as voluntary attention, perception, logical memory, language, etc., each giving a specific contribution.

It is extremely interesting to know the organization, phylogenetic and ontogenetic origin, and participation of each of these three functional units or blocks. I suggest reading *Higher Cortical Functions in Man* (Luria, 1962/1966) or *The Working Brain: An Introduction to Neuropsychology* (Luria, 1973). Below, I briefly present the characteristics of each of the three functional blocks.

First Block: Unit to regulate tone, wakefulness, and brain activity. The first unit, or first brain block, is in the **brainstem**, nonspecific thalamus nuclei, and base nuclei. Its main contribution is to promote an optimal level of cortical tone. Below this activation level, the cortex is unable to process information well. Above this level, it becomes dysfunctional.

Second Block: Unit to receive, analyze, and store information. The second brain block has a **post-Rolandic localization**; that is, it extends from Rolando's fissure to the occipital pole. Each of its component brain lobes receives projections of a sensory modality. Thus, visual information is projected into the occipital, auditory information into the temporal, and tactile kinesthetic information into the parietal. Each of these three subblocks in the second block has the same organization: primary areas, peripherally located receiving sensory projections; secondary areas, where primary area neurons send information, but secondary areas can directly receive it via thalamus and base nuclei, thus without passing through the corresponding projection area; and tertiary areas, centrally located at the parieto-temporo-occipital intersection, perform a second and more complex integration of information.

In the second brain block, the neuronal networks are organized, giving rise to three general laws. The **first law refers to the hierarchical structure** of the areas of each subblock. According to H. Jackson's theory (1884: cited in Luria, 1973), the functioning of the primary areas is under the control of the secondary areas as soon as the secondary areas are structured, as is the latter between the secondary and tertiary areas. The **second is the law of decreasing specificity**. From primary to tertiary areas, the commitment to a sensory modality is decreasing. The **third is the law of progressive lateralization**. From the periphery to the center of the second brain block, differences in neuronal organization are accentuated and, as a result, the type of processing performed in the left and right TPO regions has a maximum lateralization. As a result, the processing modes are different, which justifies the possibility of holistic simultaneous treatment in the right hemisphere and analytical sequential treatment in the left hemisphere (Quintino-Aires, 2010).

Third Block: Unit to program, regulate, and verify the activity. The localization of this block corresponds to the **frontal lobe**. It is common to distinguish a posterior region, corresponding to the motor and premotor areas, and an anterior region of the frontal lobe, corresponding to the prefrontal. It is an apparatus that forms stable plans and intentions capable of controlling behavior. The frontal region checks each production to see if the planned behavior matches the behavior performed. It has a fundamental role in inhibition mechanisms.

In summary, Luria recognized in the active brain an organization of three functional blocks, each making a specific contribution and highlighting its own organization. High nervous activity always results from the integrated functioning of the three blocks. It is possible to describe the contribution of each region of each block to each complex functional system (as it is proposed for functional systems of writing and reading in Glozman, 2013, p. 85).

Contemporary psychology thus gives a different idea of how personality is structured and how it can be transformed. We agree with Vygotsky when he says that "The brain has enormous possibilities for the emergence of new [neuropsychological] systems" (Vygotsky, 1930/1996, p. 115). Of course, such a perspective places greater responsibility on the work of psychologists and therapists, but it also opens a wide window for intervention and rehabilitation.

Lurian clinical-psychological investigation

Concluding this brief presentation of Luria's systemic and dynamic neuropsychology, it is important to mention some concepts such as qualitative and quantitative, symptom and syndrome analysis, and organization and reorganization of HCFs. A review of the concepts of function and localization also requires a review of the symptom concept. In Luria's systemic and dynamic neuropsychology, the symptom of a brain injury, understood simply as the loss of a function, may indicate the localization of the lesion only in relation to the most elemental functions. When we talk about the most complex activities, the simple loss of function says nothing about the localization of the injury, nor does it allow us to think of a rehabilitation plan for that specific person.

The symptom no longer corresponds to the simple indication of defect or its absence, and even its quantification. It now requires an analysis of the psychological structure that can be understood by the way the patient performs the proposed activity in the exam. Thus, the qualification of the symptom is made, and this is **syndromic analysis**. HCFs have many elements and rely on the joint work of many areas of the cerebral cortex, each of which has its own role in the functional system as a whole. The analysis of the specific character of the alteration of the higher cortical functions allows us to identify the primary defect that underlies the disturbance, and this is, for Luria, the fundamental purpose of the neuropsychological assessment, which he calls the **clinical-psychological investigation**. The need to qualify the observed symptom requires a qualitative analysis of the symptom, the study of the psychological structure of the disorder, and the identification of the factor (primary symptom) that causes the observed symptom.

To achieve this goal, Luria created his own neuropsychological assessment "battery." This was first published in 1947 as a result of his work during World War II and the following years at the Kisegatch hospital in the Urals in the Soviet Union (Luria, 1947/1970). Later, in 1962, as a result of his work at the Burdenko Institute of Neurosurgery in Moscow, Luria published his neuropsychological assessment methodology in his book *Higher Cortical Functions in Man* (Luria, 1962/1966).

In 1975, at the suggestion of Luria himself, the Danish neuropsychologist Anne-Lise Christensen published, in English, the book *Luria's Neuropsychological Investigation* (Christensen, 1975). Already in the title is Luria's main idea regarding the neuropsychological assessment: "Investigation" ... a job the neuropsychologist does the way a criminal investigator does. The investigator takes a clue, forms a hypothesis, and always goes on looking for new clues and formulating new hypotheses until he reaches a final diagnosis. Adaptations to children's neuropsychological assessment have also been proposed by Lurian-trained neuropsychologists, such as Mikadze (Mikadze, 2008) and Glozman (Glozman, 2013).

Such a specific approach to neuropsychology would naturally have to bring with it a rehabilitation proposal based on the same theory. The first publication on the theory and practice of functional system reorganization (rehabilitation) appears in his 1947 work, Traumatic Aphasia–Its Syndromes, Psychology, and Treatment. The following year, in 1948, he published a specifically rehabilitation-oriented book, *Restoration of Function after Brain Injury* (Luria, 1948/1963). Specifically about the reorganization of the functional systems, that is, in the pedagogical intervention in thc lcarning disabilities, Luria published in 1972 with L. Tsvetkova the work *Reeducation of the Basic Abilities: Neuropsychology and Pedagogy* (Luria & Tsvetkova, 1972/1987). In this type of work, it is not a reorganization of functional systems after brain injury, but rather the organization of complex brain functional systems that were not yet prepared in that child to be able to respond to school demand.

Summarizing, like Reitan, Luria also had, without even knowing it himself, a very marked presence on the beginning of clinical neuropsychology in Portugal. His work has been systematically studied by various groups of psychologists working under the same coordination in cities such as Lisbon, Oporto, Coimbra, Faro, Funchal, and Ponta Delgada. Many neuropsychologists have come into the practice of concepts or ideas such as the law of double development, recognition of the role of language in brain organization, systemic and dynamic nature and extracortical origin of higher cortical functions, brain activity divided into three functional blocks, and neuropsychological investigation (assessment). Special attention was given to concepts such as qualitative and quantitative, symptom and syndromic analysis, and organization and reorganization of higher cortical functions.

Reitan and Luria in the new clinical practice in developmental neuropsychology in the 21st century

Today, there are many Portuguese psychologists with the official title of neuropsychologist. Many work in exactly the tradition that we present. As in the early years, they work in connection with neurosurgery and neurology. However, today they also work in schools in the area of learning disabilities, or with psychiatry and in personal development programs.

The richness of the principles pointed out by Reitan and the theoretical support to neuropsychological practice brought by Luria allow us today to find the practice of developmental neuropsychology in different areas. Much of the daily work done is quite like what they did. Although based on their theories, a broad discussion for the introduction of new methodologies, used by many professionals, is needed. Even in this case, observing clinical practice in developmental neuropsychology allows us to quickly "find" Reitan and Luria.

Neuropsychological habilitation

The area of developmental neuropsychology that has evolved the most in the last 20 years in Portugal has been its application in connection with psychiatry and personal development. In these cases, most clients do not have a local brain injury or neurological degenerative process. In this practice, psychologists work with patients whose life histories have led to different organizations of functional systems, making them less suited to the demands of society and psychosocial functioning. That is why what is being addressed here is the formation of abilities (skills) by the (re)formation of complex functional systems. And more than rehabilitation, we use the designation "neuropsychological education (habilitation)" to refer to this work.

The study of other scientists who worked together with Luria, Vygostsky, and Leontiev was very interesting. In organizing the clinical practice of neuropsychological habilitation, P. Galperin (1902–1988) was especially important. Galperin tried to explain how the process of formation of internal mental actions in development takes place, that is, the stages through which the action goes through the process of appropriation by the individual in the (successful) attempt to orient the pedagogical process toward a more effective outcome. Galperin worked within Vygotsky's theory, and very close with Leontiev's theory of activity, and developed a theory about the stages of transformation from interpsychic to intrapsychic.

Galperin elaborated "a theory to explain the ontogenetic development of psychic reality, namely the assimilation by man of the historical-social experience and culture" (Núñez & Ramalho, 2018, p. 11). This theory explains how the mental processes and the laws of their formation (theoretical contribution) are formed and presents methodological principles to effectively organize the teaching and learning processes (methodological and practical contribution), which we adopt in the work of neuropsychological education (habilitation).

Abilities training and development are processes that go through different and increasingly complex levels, leading one to broaden the possibilities of using these abilities and to make them an element of one's personality (Núñez, Ramalho, & Oliveira, 2018). At first, the learner is not autonomous because the ability is not yet formed. Once the sessions have begun, no significant progress can be seen immediately. Therefore, the therapist must plan and organize the process of abilities formation. This responsibility cannot be left to the person. It is up to the therapist to guide and control the action.

In Galperin's theory, the formation of new mental actions takes place in stages, which are designed to allow the passage from social to individual experience. In the words of Vygotsky, the passage from the interpsychological plane to the intrapsychological plane, which is always an expression of the construction of brain neoformations, forms new functional (psychological) systems. In abilities formation, it is first necessary to find a system of operations (action model), to represent it in materialized form, and finally to organize and develop training that leads to the realm of execution and its control.

The activities that will consist of the materialization of the activity, in this case, the rehabilitating activity, are not a prebuilt and edited kit, not even a set of tasks or activities where the therapist should continue reading the instruction manual. On the contrary, the therapist must have the necessary preparation to begin by conducting a client's psychological laboratory investigation (assessment), to be able to interpret the data and relate it to the complaint, and to design a neuropsychological education (habilitation) work plan. The therapist should be prepared to do the syndromic analysis and identify the factors that may justify the complaint. He must have enough knowledge of systemic-dynamic neuropsychology, be able to analyze the psychological structure of his client's difficulty, and understand the neurodynamics involved. This means that it is up to the therapist to design the specific work plan for that specific client.

The rationale of this work and the methodologies used are described in other works (Quintino-Aires, 2016). The following is a case that I think illustrates this type of practice, the methodological novelty in an area of psychological intervention that in the past was not associated with neuropsychology, and the results achieved.

Case study

Case André: Syndrome of frontal lobe action control disorder

Developmental neuropsychology today is not just a discipline that deals with brain damage and the resulting behavioral changes. Much of the work of psychologists has focused on enhancing children and young people, and even adults, so that they can more truly achieve their status as a person or citizen, and of course also deal with complaints that, in the past, led to scheduled appointments with clinical psychologists and psychiatrists.

After severe frontal lobe injuries, the patient may develop disorders that are often barely noticeable at the level of movement, sensation, gnosis, praxis, and speech, and usually not of his "formal intelligence" appears to be compromised. But his goal-directed behavior is deeply disturbed. In 1907, Bekhterev called this syndrome a disturbance of "psychoregulatory activity" (Luria, 1963/1966). Individuals do not evaluate the outcome of their actions as they should, do not correlate the new external impressions with the past experience result, and do not direct their movements and actions for their own good.

Any animal or human activity, complex in its organization, is determined by a program that ensures not only that the subject reacts to real stimuli, but within certain limits predicts the future. In humans, the creation of these action programs is incomparably more complex in structure because it is the result of historical-social experience, occurs with the participation of abstraction and generalization, and is mediated by language (Luria, 1962/1966, 1963/1966, 1973; Vygotsky, 1934/1996; Vygotsky & Luria, 1993). In 1963, Luria designated this condition in humans as ***Syndrome of Frontal Lobe Action Control Disorder*** (Luria, 1963/1966).

André is a 12-year-old boy, the first of two brothers, with the second being 8 years old. He lives with his parents, who both have college degrees. He is brought to the clinical department of neuropsychology at Instituto Vegotsky by his parents. He has impulsive problems, an inability to be in the classroom for the required 50 min, cigarette smoking habits, and sexual behavior with other pupils at school as well as with his younger brother at home. Parents of the other children at school demand that he be expelled because they do not want their children with him in school.

He has been followed in child psychiatry for the past 5 years and has been diagnosed with affective psychotic disorder. When we first saw him at the clinic, he was taking DIPLEXIL-R 250 mg (Divalproex Sodium) and ZYPREXA 5 mg (Olanzapine). At an earlier stage, his parents had already sought psychotherapy. He spent 2 years in psychoanalysis, but without success, and 2 years in cognitive behavioral therapy, also unsuccessfully. As their condition at school is quite complicated, the parents decided to continue the medication as prescribed by the child psychiatrist, and to do one more attempt at psychological work. So, they went to the Instituto Vegotsky clinic. What they were looking for was not exactly another approach to psychotherapeutic intervention, but a professional who could eventually work with their son.

After the parental interview, a laboratory psychological investigation exam was performed using Luria's Neuropsychological Investigation (Luria, 1962/1966) and Rorschach-Exner (Exner, 2007) methodologies. Syndromic analysis data on neuropsychological assessment revealed impulsiveness as the main factor, present in the following tests: Pierón-Ruzer, Schültz, Analogies, Verbal Simple Analogies, Visual Image and Geometric, Simple Analogies, Highlighted Two key indices, Spatial configuration of objects, Visual and Verbal and Temporal Bert Test. Syndromic analysis also showed low verbal regulation, observed in selective motor reaction tests by verbalized conventional verbal instruction and selective motor reaction in the conflict between direct input and conditioned meaning of stimulus [Method of E.D. Homskaya, 1956, described in (Luria, 1962/1966)]. We also verified exhaustion and decreased volume in the Pierón-Ruzer.

The Rorschach-Exner examination data were compatible with the neuropsychological data. Difficulty in controlling one's own behavior (FC: CF+C=1: 1), difficulty in affective sharing (Afr=0.32), immaturity expressed in adult dependence on decision-making (Fd=3), opposition to interpersonal relationships (S=4), and the presence of cognitive distortion in opposition (S-%=0.50). From the analysis of the clinical interview and the psychology laboratory data, we diagnosed a ***Syndrome of Frontal Lobe Action Control Disorder*** (Luria, 1963/1966).

The neuropsychological habilitation plan included the tasks we call Color Piano, 10-Finger Attention, and Speech Unfolding. In our working method, all plans are scheduled for 12 weeks, after which the client is reevaluated and the intervention plan retrofitted if necessary. André performed two of these series, that is, his neuropsychological habilitation program lasted 6 months.

The activity we call *Color Piano* is the use of an A4-sized card that is presented horizontally to the client. On this card are small squares of 2 cm × 2 cm, printed in five different colors—green, red, yellow, blue, and black—distributed at random. Each case is different from the others, and it is up to the therapist to design the way he will work with each client, always reevaluating and reorganizing the plan according to the client's activity. Usually, the first activity is simply naming the colors of each square. Depending on the trainee, he may be asked to put the nondominant hand under pressure on the table and to point out each square he is naming with the other. Or the nondominant hand may serve to indicate the line of squares being named. The rhythm must be imposed by the therapist, who signals, blocking the continuation of the activity whenever the client misses the color name of a square.

At least six consecutive turns are usually required, and the trainee's actual performance level can only be realized after the third. So, we say that only from the fourth lap are we really working on the transformation. The therapist records the number of the lap at which fatigue (slowing processing speed) begins to appear and the appearance of errors (precision) as well as the type of errors. The most typical mistake is naming the color of the square next to the one being pointed.

On a second level, the therapist indicates that the learner should inhibit saying the name of one of the colors, usually the black one. The task is like the previous level, except that when he touches his finger on the black square for a second and says nothing. Then continue. What has been said about the number of turns, speed, and accuracy is similar, adding of course the inhibition of verbalization when the square is black.

At level three, the learner is oriented to exchange two colors. For example, where it is red should say green, and vice versa; or where it is yellow it should say blue, and vice versa. There is no strict order about which colors to change. Usually, I use these because, in Portuguese language, phonologically they start similarly (/ ver /, for green [*ver*de] and red [*ver*melho]; / a /, for yellow [*a*marelo] and blue [*a*zul]. Upon reaching level four, the learner can make either one or both of these exchanges and inhibit the black square. If the therapist wants to go to level five, he can do both exchanges and inhibit black verbalization.

The *10 Finger Attention* activity has many different forms. In the simplest, it is indicated for the learner to count aloud from 1 to 100. The therapist records omissions, speed, and fatigue (where numbers begin to slow down or errors increase). This form is considered too simple and is only used for trainees with greater difficulty. For most trainees, the therapist begins work on this activity at the next level.

At level two, the learner is advised to count from 1 to 100, saying one number aloud and the next number quietly. He is explained that when he says in a low voice he should do so as a whisper, but still the therapist must be able to hear what number is said. He is also told that the correct procedure requires switching the focus of sound production between the mouth and throat. That is, when saying out loud think the sound coming out of your mouth; when saying quietly, think of the sound coming out of your throat. In guidance, the therapist can help by pointing to the mouth or throat in one's own body, depending on whether the trainee should say it out loud or in a low voice. You can also use your own hands and forearms to make upward or downward movements for the same purpose. These external mediators are especially important in the early stages of the activity.

When we start, it is common for the trainee's tone of voice to be too loud, giving the feeling that his voice comes out "raw" straight from the rib cage. It is also common for your trunk and head to accompany the tone of voice alternations. It is up to the therapist not only to guide but also to control the exercise from the beginning. But this requirement must keep pace with the client's ability to perform.

At level three, the therapist indicates that he should say one number in a loud voice and two in a low voice, or vice versa. And he should use one finger on one hand and two on the other to track the count with flexion movements of one finger for each number (hence the name of the task). Here, the therapist must also impose speed, lock on each error, and record fatigue (where speed or accuracy decreases) and the type of errors, such as using the wrong tone or skipping numbers.

At level four, the therapist indicates that the trainee should say two numbers in a high tone and three in a low tone, or vice versa. Using two fingers of one hand (when saying in a high tone) and three fingers of the other (when saying in a low tone), which should follow the counts with a bending movement. The records at this level are similar to the previous levels.

Hereafter, the therapist can indicate the levels and formats he decides, depending on the learner and his achievement. When there is no fatigue in counting to number 100, the therapist should change to counts up to number 150 and if necessary up to number 200. It is critical that the therapist orient and control the accomplishment of the task with the trainee looking into the eyes of the therapist. In addition, in relation to this requirement, it must accompany the evolution of the trainee's capacity for achievement.

Direct order counts are used for low-activated clients. If the problem is the opposite, that is, with the greatest need for inhibition, the counts should be performed in reverse order. Also, here at the beginning should work between 100 and number 1. If necessary, increase to start at 150 or number 200.

The Speech Unfolding task[c] is related to the passage from internal (predicative) speech to external (discursive) speech, one of the most important mental health abilities. However, for several reasons, it is common to find people with poorly structured ability to unfold speech. Active flow of thought is related to the ability to engineer certain internal dynamic patterns that lead to the production of smooth flows, or "kinetic melodies" that together with internal speech are essential for thought (Vygotsky, 1934/1986). The challenge is to develop the smooth and spontaneous flow of thought through the reorganization of the cerebral functional system, as worked by Luria since 1948. The methodology is based on the passage from the internal synthesis of the psychological process to the regulation of this process during speech. Particular attention is paid in the beginning to the learner's ability to "see" every detail in the image, and the therapist works permanently so that the learner will use an action guiding basis that will allow him to have a planned look at the entire drawing.

For this activity, we used a set of 20 cards with simple designs. It is suitable for the trainee to describe ALL that they see, and in greater detail. In counseling, the therapist should present an action guiding basis, "a system of conditions on which the person relies while performing the action" (Talizina, 1984/2000, p. 57). It helps the learner make a proper "sweep" of the figure to meet all the details. In controlling the activity, the therapist should ask for correction of all expressions such as "thing," descriptions using body movements or limbs in place of words. When the learner cannot find a word, it can be said by the therapist, but then repeated by the learner. Each card should be worked as many times as necessary for the activity to be performed smoothly and quickly. Many colleagues, after a first realization, cover the drawing and ask the client to do the activity based on memory. Here, the goal is not to work on memory, but to make the trainee more attentive to detail next time.

When the learner begins to show some ease in performing the activity, which will indicate that the ability is forming, the learner should then be oriented to say what is happening in the drawing. In the next step, he is also asked to say what happened before and what will happen next, depending on what is going on in the drawing. This change is sometimes very difficult for the client. It is

---

c. As if unfolding an idea by saying something using as many words as possible, so that it is explicit to the listener. In this case, based on an image that is displayed on a card.

then possible to use Luria's method, which consists of providing cards with words such as "However...", "Despite...", "After...", "Since...", etc., and what he called the Phraseological Transition Formula. The effect of using the transition formula is to be able to create intentions and make comparably more connected and more developed narratives, both grammatically and logically. The use of the transition formula is external. With the exercises, narrative speech becomes more fluent and spontaneous.

At the end of the 6 months of work with André, the data from Luria's neuropsychological investigation and Rorschach-Exner did not show the previous pathological signs. In the interview with André's parents, they say that the situation at school was normalized. There were no problems with the teachers, the other children, or the parents of these other children. André's behavior was like that of any other boy of his age. Child psychiatry discontinued the medication. The work with André was carried out between November 2011 and June 2012.

Recently, in 2019, André visited the clinic. Today, he is a student at the University of Lisbon with good academic results, is involved in academic and social activities, is a federated sportsman, and has a girlfriend.

In conclusion

We thank Reitan and Luria for what we have learned from them over the course of these many years, which has given us, today, the opportunity to do this kind of work with hundreds of other clients.

The practice of neuropsychology is very beautiful work, not just very useful. But it cannot be just an application of a set of tests that have been studied in a manual. Much less, does neuropsychological rehabilitation achieve any results by offering patients simple repetitions of various exercises? The ability not only to do a job well, but also to be able to plan new applications in different clinical settings, as I have shown here, results from the use of concepts and ideas such as those by Reitan and Luria.

Concepts as "blind interpretation approach," forming hypotheses based on observations of natural phenomenon, attention to the nature of the lesion, a case-by-case approach, not just to record the level of performance, looking at the data in a qualitative and quantitative way, the understanding that adult neuropsychological practice could not apply directly to work with children, and therefore neuropsychological work with children are required its own approach. Proposal and practice need to come together, and the academic scientific community, if not involved in the practice, should be looked upon with some reserve. All these concepts are clearly a heritage that Reitan left in clinical neuropsychology in Portugal.

The concepts or ideas of Luria, such as the law of double development; recognition of the role of language in brain organization; the systemic and dynamic nature and extracortical origin of higher cortical functions; brain activity divided into three functional blocks; neuropsychological investigation (assessment);

and attention to concepts such as qualitative and quantitative, symptom and syndromic analysis, and organization and reorganization of higher cortical functions are now everyday thoughts in the clinical and scientific reasoning of many psychologists involved in this type of work.

What we do today did not come out of nowhere. It has its origin in and development from the legacy of Reitan and Luria.

References

Aita, J., Reitan, R. M., & Ruth, J. M. (1947). Rorschach's test as a diagnostic aid in brain injury. *American Journal of Psychiatry*, *103*, 770–779.

Aita, J. A., Armitage, S. G., Reitan, R. M., & Rabinovitz, A. (1947). The use of certain psychological tests in the evaluation of brain injury. *Journal of General Psychology*, *37*, 25–44.

Akhutina, T., & Tsvetkova, L. (1983). Comments on a standardized version of Luria's tests. *Brain and Cognition*, *2*, 129–134.

Anokhin, P. K. (1935/1974). *Biology and neurophysiology of the conditioned reflex and its role in adaptive behavior* (English ed.). (J. E. R. Dartau, Trad.). New York: Pergamon Press.

Bernstein, N. (1967). *The co-ordenation and regulation of movements*. Oxford: Pergamon Press.

Christensen, A.-L. (1975). *Luria's neuropsychological investigation*. New York: Spectrum.

Ellis, A. W., & Young, A. W. (1988). *Human cognitive neuropsychology*. Hove and London: Lawrence Erlbaum.

Exner, J. E. (2007). *A Rorschach workbook for the comprehensive system* (Fifth ed.). Asheville, North Carolina: Rorschach Workshops.

Fitzhugh, K. B., Fitzhugh, L. C., & Reitan, R. M. (1961). Psychological deficits in relation to acuteness of brain dysfunction. *Journal of Consulting Psychology*, *25*, 61–66.

Glozman, J. (2013). *Developmental neuropsychology*. London: Routledge.

Golden, C. J., Purisch, A., & Hammeke, T. (1979). *The Luria-Nebraska neuropsychological battery: A manual for clinical and experimental uses*. Lincoln, Nebraska: University of Nebraska Press.

Hom, J., & Nici, J. (2015). Ralph M. Reitan: The pioneer of clinical neuropsychology. *Archives of Clinical Neuropsychology*, *30*, 724–732.

Kagan, A., & Saling, M. (1988). *An introduction to Luria's Aphasiology: Theory and application*. Johannesburg, South Africa: Witwatersrand U.

Leontiev, A. *Probleme Razvitiia Psikhiki* [The problem of psychic development]. (1981). Moscow: Moscow Univ. Press [in Russian].

Leontiev, A. N. *Deiatel'nost, Saznanie i Litchnost* [Activity, consciousness and personality]. (2004). Moscow: Akademia [in Russian].

Luria, A. (1947/1970). *Traumatic Aphasia – Its syndromes, psychology and treatment* (English ed.). (D. Bowden, Trad.). The Hague, Netherlands: Mounton & Co. N.V, Publishers.

Luria, A. (1962/1966). *Higher cortical functions in man* (English ed.). (B. Haigh, Trad.). New York: Basic Books, Inc., Publishers.

Luria, A., & Homskaya, E. (1970). Frontal lobes and the regulation of activation processes. In D. Mostofsky (Ed.), *Attention: Contemporary theory and analysis* (pp. 303–330). New York: Appleton-Century-Crofts.

Luria, A., & Tsvetkova, L. (1972/1987). *Recuperación de los Aprendizajes Básicos: Neuropsicología y Pedagogía* (A. V. Gutiérrez, Trad.). Madrid, Spain: G. Núñez Editor, S.A. (in Spanish).

Luria, A. R. (1948/1963). *Restauration of function after brain injury* (English ed.). (B. Haihg, Trad.). New York: The MacMillan Company.

Luria, A. R. (1961). *The role of speech in the regulation of normal and abnormal behavior*. New York: Liveright.

Luria, A. R. (1963/1966). *Human brain and psychological processes* (English ed.). (B. Haigh, Trad.). New York: Harper & Row, Publishers.

Luria, A. R. (1973). *The working brain: An introduction to neuropsychology* (B. Haigh, Trad.). London: Basic Books.

Luria, A. R. (1980). *Fundamentos de Neurolingüística* (Spanish ed.). (J. Peña-Casanova, Trad.). Barcelona: Toray-Masson. (in Spanish).

Mikadze, I. *Neyropsikhologiya Detskogo Vozrasta* [Childhood neuropsychology]. (2008). Moscow: Piter [in Russian].

Núñez, I., & Ramalho, B. (2018). *Galperin e a Teoria da Formação Planejada por Etapas das Ações Mentais e dos Conceitos*. Campinas, Brazil: Mercado das letras.

Núñez, I. B., Ramalho, B. L., & Oliveira, M. (2018). A Formação de Habilidades Gerais no Contexto Escolar: Contribuições da Teoria de Galperin. In I. B. Núñez & B. L. Ramalho (Eds.), *Galperin e a Teoria da Formação Planejada por Etapas das Ações Mentais e dos Conceitos* (pp. 23–78). Campinas, Brazil: Mercado das Letras [in Portuguese].

Peña-Casanova, J. (1989). A.R. Luria today: Some notes on "Lurianism" and the fundamental bibliography of A.R. Luria. *Journal of Neurolinguistics*, *4*(1), 161–178.

Quintino-Aires, J. (2010). *Neurogénese da Linguagem*. São Paulo, Brazil: IPAF Editora [in Portuguese].

Quintino-Aires, J. (2016). Vigotsky-Luria na Psicologia Clínica no século XXI. In D. Marques & Á.-T. José Hernando (Eds.), *De las neurociencias a la Neuropsicologia* (pp. 302–385). Barranquila, Colombia: Ediciones Corporación Universitaria Reformada [in Portuguese].

Reed, H. B., Reitan, R. M., & Klove, H. (1965). The influence of cerebral lesions on psychological test performances of older children. *Journal of Consulting Psychology*, *29*, 247–251.

Reitan, R. M. (1955). Certain differential effects of left and right cerebral lesions in human adults. *Journal of Comparative and Physiological Psychology*, *48*, 474–477.

Reitan, R. M. (1974). Psychological effects of cerebral lesions in children of early school age. In R. M. Reitan & D. Wolfson (Eds.), *Clinical neuropsychology: Current status and applications (pp. 19–46)* (pp. 53–90). Washington, DC: Hemisphere.

Reitan, R. M., & Wolfson, D. (1985a). *The Halstead-Reitan neuropsychological test battery: Theory and clinical interpretation*. Tucson, AZ: Neuropsychology Press.

Reitan, R. M., & Wolfson, D. (1985b). *Neuroanatomy and neuropathology: A clinical guide for neuropsychologists*. Tucson, AZ: Neuropsychology Press.

Robbins, D. (2003). *Vygotsky's and A.A. Leontiev's semiotics and psycholinguistics*. Westport, USA: Praeger Publishers.

Seron, X. (1993). *La Neuropsychologie Cognitive*. Paris: Presses Universitaires de France [in French].

Stringer, A. Y., Cooley, E. L., & Christensen, A.-L. (2002). *Pathways to prominence in neuropsychology: Reflections of twentieth century pioneers*. New York: Psychology Press.

Talizina, N. F. (1984/2000). *Manual de Psicología Pedagógica*. Potosí, México: Editora da Universidad Autónoma de San Luis.

Tsvetkova, L. S. *Afaziologia: savremennie probleme i puti ikh reschenia* [Aphasiology: Current problems and their resolution pathways]. (2002). Moscow: Psychological Social Institute Press [in Russian].

Vygotsky, L. (1930/1996). *Sobre os Sistemas Psicológicos* (Portuguese ed.). (C. Berliner, Trad.). São Paulo, Brasil: Martins Fontes. (in Portuguese).

Vygotsky, L. (1934/1986). *Thought and language* (A. Kozulin, Trad.). Cambridge, Massachusetts: The MIT Press.

Vygotsky, L. (1934/1996). A Psicologia e a Teoria da Localização das Funções Psíquicas. Em L. Vygotsky, *Teoria e Método em Psicologia* (C. Berliner, Trad., pp. 191–200). São Paulo: Martins Fontes. (in Portuguese).

Vygotsky, L., & Luria, A. (1993). *Studies on the history of behavior: Ape, primitive, and child*. Hillsdale, NJ, USA: Lawrence Erlbaum Associates, Inc.

Zaporozhets, A. V. (1971/2002). Toward the question of the genesis, function, and structure of emotional processes in the child. *Journal of Russian and East European Psychology, 40*(2), 45–66.

Chapter 3

Integrating quantitative and qualitative measures with neuropsychological assessment and intervention

Janna Glozman
M. V. Lomonosov Moscow State University, Moscow, Russia

Portions of this chapter were drawn from Chapter 18 in Glozman, J. M., & Tupper, D. E. (2005). Converging impressions in Russian and American neuropsychology. In T. V. Ahutina, J. M. Glozman, L. I. Moskovich, D. Robbins (Eds.), *A.R. Luria and Contemporary Psychology: Festschriftcelebrating the centennial of his birth* (pp. 187–195). NY: Nova science.

Introduction

Who needs neuropsychological assessment?

Neuropsychological assessment in theoretical and applied psychology can meet many of the following *purposes* (Glozman, 1999, 2012; Homskaya, 2005; Luria, 1965, 1969, 1973; Reitan, 1964):

- Neuropsychological study of normal and abnormal mental functioning.
- The focal diagnosis of the brain damage underlying observed defects of mental functioning.
- A differential diagnosis between organic and psychological etiologies of disturbances.
- A comprehensive description of impairments of higher mental functions and the identification of the factors underlying such impairments.
- Prediction and prevention of social manifestations and consequences of higher mental function disturbances.
- Neuropsychological study of individual differences.
- Development of individual treatment plans and strategies for the remediation of cognitive disorders.

Evaluation and Treatment of Neuropsychologically Compromised Children
https://doi.org/10.1016/B978-0-12-819545-1.00003-5

- Evaluation of the outcome of different kinds of treatment: surgical, pharmacological, psychological, and others.
- Determination of the best methods of treatment for different cases (both children and adults).

This list can be continued.

The field of neuropsychology shows both intensive and extensive development, as proved by the increased number of neuropsychological techniques and by the extended sphere of their application, not only in neurosurgery and neurology but also in psychiatry, gerontology, the somatic clinic, in normal and special education, etc. "Neuropsychology can provide valuable understanding in the treatment of such chronic diseases as lupus, chronic obstructive lung diseases (emphysema), cardiovascular disorders, and certain types of oncological disorders. ... In this respect, any medical complication or treatment having a direct or indirect impact on neural integrity should be considered within the scope of neuropsychology" (Horton & Puente, 1986, p. 18). Neuropsychological consequences appear after different diseases or deviated development. It makes neuropsychology the important part of the psychology of health (Ryan, Vega, Longstreet, & Drash, 1984).

The development of neuroimaging techniques does not decrease the diagnostic value of neuropsychological assessment in neurology and neurosurgery. "As exciting as these new diagnostic techniques are, they still fail (because of (the) inherent aspects of the technology) to provide an adequate presentation of human behavior. Because the neuropsychologist is beginning to use these methods as adjuncts to both research and clinical activities, further developments hinge on a close relationship between these two approaches (e.g., Swiercinsky & Leigh, 1979; Wedding, 1980)" (Horton & Puente, 1986, p. 18).

An important diagnostic task is to reveal mental disorders in cases where cerebral organic disturbances are not seen (for instance, after toxic injuries or vascular dysfunctions, or mental delay in children). Early neuropsychological diagnosis of mental dysfunctions helps to prevent an aggravation of defects and to select the most efficient methods of surmounting defects. It was proven that a remediation of learning-disabled children is more effective when it is based on neuropsychological assessment data (Akhutina & Pylayeva, 2008; Glozman, 2013; Harlage, 1975).

Therefore, the neuropsychological assessment has differential diagnostic, remediative, preventive, and prognostic aspects.

How to assess?

From description to measurement

Neuropsychology started by descriptions of individual cases with mental function disturbances (predominantly speech and memory) with attempts to relate them to an injury of definite brain areas. Such first attempts date as far back as

3000–2550 BCE (Walsh, 1978). At the end of the 16th and the beginning of the 17th centuries, some observations on localization of mental functions appeared in the works of René Descartes, but a real explosion of such observations in all countries was due to autopsy appearances in the 19th century: P. Broca, 1861; C. Wernicke, 1874; A.Ya. Kojevnikov, 1874; S.S. Korsakov, 1887; K. Goldstein, 1925; K. Lasley, 1929; M.B. Krol, 1934; A.R. Luria, 1947; R. Reitan, 1955; R. Sperry, 1961; M. Gazzaniga, 1970—see details in Glozman (2007).

In America, psychology was more oriented to diagnostic tasks than in other countries. This explained why the first *psychometric methods* appeared in the United States. The first version of the Wechsler scale was proposed in 1939 and was first used for pedagogical practice. Then, later in neuropsychology (Wechsler, 1974), this scale was severely criticized, denying the logic of intelligence measurement (Comrey, 1951) and even accusing it of being a "racist method" (Gould, 1981).

"It is completely unknown, what aspects of mental activity are studied and measured by these tests" (Leontiev, Luria, & Smirnov, 1968, p. 69). "The child as a whole disappears behind these numeric values and levels of development" (Semago & Semago, 2010, p.11).

Nevertheless, the psychometric methods developed quickly in America, first as isolated techniques; many of these are still used, such as the Stroop Test, proposed in 1935 (Groth-Marnat, 2009), and the Trail Making Test (Partington & Leiter, 1949). These tests measured specific mental functions such as selectivity or successive organization of behavior.

Clinical psychometric tests differ in specificity and sensitivity. Highly specific tests help to make a diagnosis, whereas highly sensitive tests can refute a diagnosis (Smith, Ivnik, & Lucas, 2008).

The next step in the development of clinical psychometric methods that assess human brain-behavior relationships was the creation of *neuropsychological batteries* of standardized methods "able to measure the full range of behavioral functions subserved by the brain" (Reitan & Wolfson, 1986, p. 134). W. Halstead proposed the first battery in 1947; later, with his disciple R. Reitan, he developed the Halstead-Reitan Neuropsychological Test Battery (Reitan, 1955; Reitan & Wolfson, 1986, 1993). The first task was to develop a comprehensive series of tests necessary to compare the damaged and normal brains. The researchers faced a very complicated situation and recognized that "normal brains vary considerably… two brains sustaining similar damage might not demonstrate exactly the same behavioral deficits… brain lesions showed a great deal of variability," (Reitan & Wolfson, 1986, p. 135), depending on the patient's age, education, socioeconomic status, personality, medical history, location and time of lesion, etc. The solution to these problems by the authors was a standardization of the assessment procedure "so that the independent variables (brain lesions) could be varied while the dependent variables (neuropsychological test results) were held constant" (Ibid.).

A three-step procedure permitted Reitan to determine tests that were helpful for brain damage diagnostics: (1) administering a comprehensive battery of neuropsychological tests to the patient without knowing his neurological findings; (2) predicting the patient's neurological status based on neuropsychological test results; and (3) comparing the neurological diagnosis with the neuropsychological test results. Other tests were used to localize and lateralize the damage and to differentiate acute and chronic lesions. This was due to the development of measurement strategies for valid interpretation.

The significant clinical value of the Halstead-Reitan Neuropsychological Test Battery (HRNB) and a large number of tests for different cognitive functions for both adults and children explains why this battery has been so popular in America and abroad for more than 70 years. Many tests are included in other authors' batteries created later, and these correspond to Reitan's approach because he did not consider it mandatory to use all subtests for each subject. A reduced version of HRNB was created for the elderly population (Tuokko & Hadjistavropoulos, 1998). Special versions of the battery assess children from 5 years old (Reitan-Indiana Neuropsychological Test Battery for Children, Williams & Boll, 1997).

Nevertheless, the authors themselves stated: "more investigation of the significance of deficits for everyday behavior is needed" (Reitan & Wolfson, 1986, p. 156). I would say that this task could not be achieved by the psychometric methods, nor could the development of individual treatment plans and strategies for the remediation of cognitive disorders in both children and adults.

Contemporary neuropsychology has in its possession a very large number of standardized methods to assess cognitive functions, and these methods permit a comprehensive description of impaired higher mental functions (e.g., Christensen, 1979; Golden et al., 1982; Golden, Purisch, & Hammeke, 1985; Reitan & Wolfson, 1993). Nevertheless, psychometric evaluation without a qualitative analysis of individual cases is not sufficient to define the mechanisms, or the (physiologically based) factors, to use Luria's term, that underlie these impairments.

From measurement to analysis

In order to achieve these purposes, a "neuropsychological investigation must not be limited to a simple statement that one or another form of mental activity is 'below level.' The investigation must be always a qualitative (structural) analysis of the symptom under study, specifying the observed defect, its possible character, and the factors causing it" (Luria, 1969, p. 306). "For example, it is well known that most patients with brain damage (both organic and functional) complain of 'memory troubles.' But, this 'memory trouble' can be provoked by different causes. We should precise (using special methods of neuropsychological assessment) the structure and the origin of this symptom, that is to qualify it and the underlying factors" (Ibid., p. 303). A.R. Luria named such an approach the *syndrome analysis*.

The theoretical basis of syndrome analysis is the understanding that each mental function is a functional system, including many components (factors) distributed in the brain (Ananiev, 1973). Each factor plays a specific role in function realization and creates a specific pattern of this function disturbance after brain damage or under development.

Qualitative syndrome analysis presupposes the analysis and comparison of primary disorders immediately connected with the impaired factor and related to definite brain areas, with secondary disorders that emerge in accordance with the systemic organization of the higher mental functions. This also includes an analysis of the intact functions (Luria, 1965, 1973; Homskaya, 2005). This last point is especially important for the neuropsychological assessment and remediation of children with abnormal (delayed) development as well as of brain-injured patients in a rehabilitation unit. The emphasis is on identifying the patient's strengths ("*positive symptoms*" of the injury) and potential compensatory strategies as well as the patient's ability to profit from instructional assistance or optimal conditions of task fulfillment, or, in other words, the "learning or rehabilitation potential" of the patient (Cicerone & Tupper, 1986; Glozman, 2013).

This is uniquely possible when an assessment becomes a *dialogue interaction,* a communication about the testing tasks, and an "experimental education" of the patient.

Syndrome analysis also presupposes the *task analysis* and reveals the psychological structure of each task or test, "addressing" different cognitive factors, both disturbed and intact. For instance in the Tactual Performance Test, included both in the Reitan-Indiana Neuropsychological Battery for Children and in the Luria battery, a failure may be caused by perceptive (parietal) disturbances as well as by inactivity of touching-executive (frontal) disturbances. In the Kaufman Brief Intelligence Test (K-BIT) (Kaufman & Kaufman, 1990), the task analysis differentiates seven types of cognitive behavior (Glozman, 2012):

1. Syntagmatic analysis (like: matches-fire).
2. Paradigmatic (categorical) relations (different flowers).
3. Perceptive matching (different configurations of points).
4. Perceptive matching with simultaneous synthesis (oval form with vertical line).
5. Perceptive comparison with spatial analysis (rotated figures).
6. Formation of abstract logical concepts (two equals and one double quantity).
7. Formation of abstract logical concepts with spatial analysis (arrow directions).

Syndrome analysis secures the validity of the testing performed. A comparative study of different test results, aimed to reveal common factors forming a syndrome proves the validity of assessment. For instance, if the hypothesis was that the subject has problems in space orientation after a lesion of the parietal brain areas, we expect defects in Head's motor test, in spatial gnosis, in drawing, in counting, in understanding sentences with spatial prepositions, and others forming the syndrome of spatial disturbances.

Luria described well the process of syndrome analysis: "In clinical work, the starting point is not a clearly defined problem but an *unknown bundle of problems* and resources: *the patient*. The clinical investigator begins by making careful observations of the patient in an effort to discover the crucial facts. In the beginning, he *can ignore nothing*. Even data that on first glance seem insignificant may turn out to be essential. At some point, the *vague contours of factors that seem important begin to emerge, and the clinician forms a tentative hypothesis about the problem*. But, it is still too early for him to say definitively whether the facts he has picked out are important to the problem or extraneous. Only when he has found *a sufficient number of compatible symptoms that together form a 'syndrome'* (does he have) a right to believe that his *hypothesis about the patient might be proved or rejected"* (Luria, 1982, p. 132).

In contrast to the psychometric approach, considering that the speed of task fulfillment determines its complexity, Luria's approach measures task complexity upon inclusion of additional factors such as spatial synthesis, increased volume of perception, etc. Besides, the speed of mental functioning derives from the education system: in America, the testing in primary school is time controlled and forms the principle "quicker is better." In Russian schools, the number of mistakes is considered and the time is not as important. This explains why a comparative study of American and Russian students revealed a predominance of American students in all neuropsychological tests with limited time of fulfillment (Agranovich, 2004).

The Lurian type of analysis not only permits an understanding of why the subject was poor at or unable to perform a given task, but it also allows us to see what other tasks, with similar cognitive demands (structure), could present difficulties for this individual as well as to predict the types of tasks accessible for the patient, given the potential of self-regulatory strategies. Such an approach is individual- and process-oriented, and aims to provide brain-injured patients and learning-disabled children (as well as their therapists or teachers) with strategies they can use to be more productive in their cognitive abilities. The examination of *how a patient achieves a given level of functioning* is equally, if not more, important to the development of a rehabilitation plan than the level of psychometric scoring this individual obtains.

Therefore, Lurian and psychometric approaches have different orientations (Fig. 1).

The process is a complex of neurodynamic, executive, motivational, and instrumental components included in the structure of the presented task. Therefore, Lurian qualitative analysis is a structural one.

Another difference between qualitative and psychometric approaches consists of their center of attention. The Lurian approach is patient-centered while psychometric assessment is disease (defect)-oriented. The patient-centered approach in neuropsychological assessment means that the primary focus is on the

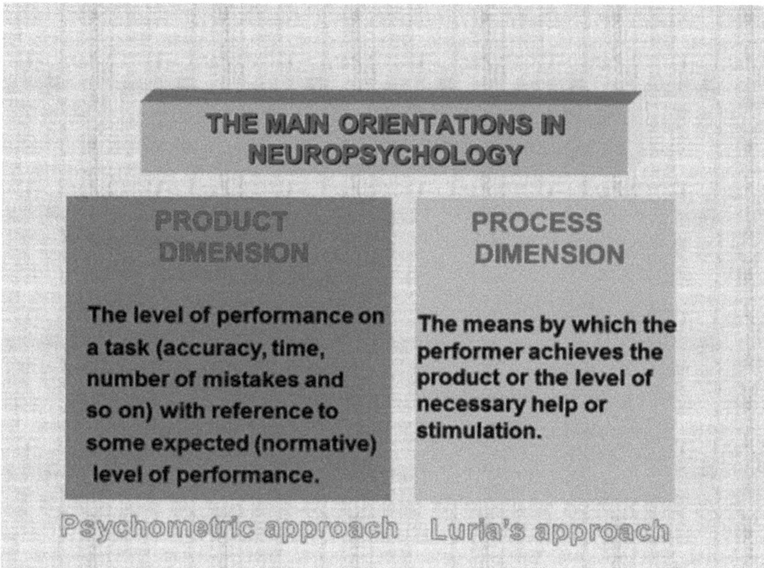

FIG. 1 Different orientations in psychometric and Lurian neuropsychological assessments.

experience of individuals, their subjective interpretation and personal knowledge of health and disease, their coping strategies, self-esteem, emotional well-being, and social interaction.

On the other hand, quantitative evaluation is of primary value for determining the dynamics of change in cognitive functioning and for measuring the outcome of rehabilitative or remedial procedures. Thus, there is a clear-cut benefit to both approaches as well as disadvantages to each.

Analysis + measurement

Therefore, *both qualitative and quantitative evaluation approaches are recognized as necessary* in Russian and American neuropsychology (Luria & Majovski, 1977). This should provide complementary information toward the goal of a comprehensive and logical evaluation of impairments of higher mental functions in patients with a brain injury or mentally delayed children.

Following the task and main orientation of the neuropsychological assessment, the methods used can be either standard (the same for all subjects) or individual for different cases; a battery or separate techniques; quantitatively (psychometric) oriented on the result of the assessment; or qualitatively oriented on the process of test fulfillment and mistake analysis.

The quantitative approach is combined with the qualitative one in modern Russian neuropsychology, but the system of scoring (or actually rating) is based on the psychological evaluation of each task's structure and the *qualitative evaluation of processes necessary for task fulfillment* (Glozman, 1999, 2012).

Likewise, numerous authors in contemporary North American and European neuropsychology currently emphasize the need for the qualitative analyses of psychometric testing results. For example, the Boston Process Approach represents a major application of qualitative analysis (Kaplan, 1983; Kaplan, Fein, Morris, & Delis, 1991). Another example is the Barcelona test that presents a modular structure, determining intra- and intermodule dissociations. The first version of the test was published in 1991 (Peña-Casanova, 1991). It is an instrument of neuropsychological research, developed by Prof. Jordi Peña-Casanova under the influence of Luria's ideas. The new version has both traditional (paper-based) and computerized forms (included in a workstation) with the capability to realize different tests or modules separately, which is more efficient in practical work (Liutsko et al., 2018). The "most qualitative" among psychometric scales is probably the NEPSY battery (Developmental Neuropsychological Assessment), created in 1980 in Finland and later standardized in America (Korkman, 1999; Korkman, Kirk, & Kemp, 2007). The authors differentiate primary and secondary defects, and the child's strengths and weaknesses. This scale is also flexible (hypothesis-oriented), permitting select tests for each child or problem. The rating system has a choice of scores from 0 to 2, which are, as in the Lurian system, penalty scores, that is, 0 is the best result. Some tests such as "Word List Interference" repeat Luria's tests. The NEPSY also permits some forms of examiner assistance, which are not allowed in most psychometric approaches but are very important for Lurian ones. Luria used to say that a good neuropsychological assessment is a part of education (Leontiev et al., 1968).

The Lurian tests are methods currently used in Russia. While qualitative syndrome analysis is the cornerstone of this approach, Luria himself proposed a four score rating system, where the score 0 means absence of defects in test fulfillment, the score 1 equals mild defects, 2 equals moderate defects, and 3 equals impossible to perform the task (Luria, 1973, 1999). It should be noted that it correlates with the Reitan and Wolfson (1993) General Neuropsychological Deficit Four Point Scale (GNDS), with 0 indicating above average performance, 1 indicating average performance, 2 indicating mild brain damage, and 3 indicating moderate to severe brain damage.

A new scoring/rating system has been developed in the last few years, with scoring being dependent upon qualitative features of the patient's performance (Glozman, 2012). We will briefly summarize the general aspects of this scoring, although the actual criteria for scoring each functional area varies slightly according to the function addressed.

A 0 (normal) to 3 (severely abnormal) six point scoring system is used, with intermediate points located between the extremes representing different aspects of the performance, primary or secondary defects, and the conditions (level of help) underlying correction of the mistakes. For example, scores of 0.5 or 1 generally indicate that the patient can perform the task adequately, but makes a few self-corrected errors. A score of 1.5 or 2 generally means that the patient makes more or less severe errors that are only corrected upon examiner recognition and prompting. A score of 3 indicates that even upon significant examiner intervention and assistance, the task is impossible for the patient.

We attempted to combine the Lurian and Halstead-Reitan batteries for a neuropsychological assessment of an adult brain-injured patient (Glozman & Tupper, 1995).[a] The test results will be described quantitatively and qualitatively using Luria's categorization of findings, with the aim of syndrome analysis.

Case study

F.R. was a 50-year-old female who was injured in an automobile accident while on vacation with her husband in another state. Her husband was killed in the accident and F.R. suffered a closed head injury and associated injuries consisting of a scalp laceration, left frontal skull fracture, and a perforated sigmoid colon. She was hospitalized for about 6 weeks prior to being admitted to rehabilitation. Her hospital stay was lengthened due to aspiration pneumonia and a pelvic abscess associated with the laparotomy she underwent to repair her colon.

The *neurological evaluation* of F.R. during her hospital stay, following her regaining of consciousness (loss of consciousness was several days), noted a right lid ptosis, left-sided weakness, equal pupils, bilaterally down going toes, returning speech, and some confusion. An early CT scan performed soon after her accident and a repeated CT scan done about 4 weeks after the injury showed a moderate subdural collection of CSF seen in the left frontoparietal region with some mass effect upon the adjacent frontoparietal regions. A questionable hemorrhagic contusion was also noted in the right parietal lobe subcortically, which presumably represents an area of countercoup injury.

Premorbidly, F.R. worked as a secretary in a printing shop with her husband. F.R. has a high school education. She was left-handed and reported a family history of left-handedness.

By the time she entered rehabilitation, F.R. had improved significantly in her responsiveness, and was generally oriented and alert. She was cooperative for all testing and treatment and tried hard to do well. She had a very involved and supportive daughter.

Combined neuropsychological evaluation

The combined neuropsychological evaluation we performed took place over the course of a week approximately 2 months after the injury. The traditional psychometric measures administered (HRNB) were given and scored in standard fashion. Where appropriate, results were converted to standardized scores and compared via T-scores or percentiles with available normative data (e.g., Heaton, Grant, & Matthews, 1991). Besides, we applied Luria's tests to study

a. A similar attempt to combine Lurian and psychometric tests for a neuropsychological assessment of children is described in Chapter 4 of this book.

six mental spheres, traditionally selected by Luria, with qualitative and quantitative analysis, using the scoring system, described above.

Patient's general characteristics

A clinical interview with the patient showed that she had a clear state of consciousness, and was oriented in time and situation. She remembered all the steps of her injury (except for a period of retrograde amnesia), she had a critical attitude to her own behavior and awareness of specific defects, and she presented adequate emotional reactions to them. The patient complained during the interview of poor memory, especially spatial memory. In particular, the patient complained of not remembering her own house and its layout. She indicated difficulty in finding her way around the inside of the institution. Other complaints centered on weaknesses in her left hand and instability while walking. So, F.R. had scores of 0 for adequacy, critical attitude, and orientation in time and situation.

The assessment of her level of attention and mental activity showed that a mild impairment of cortical activity was present, but with preserved purposefulness and control of her own activity. Traditional psychometric tests thought to tap into attentional processes, such as the Visual Search and Attention Test and the Trail Making Test, were mildly to moderately impaired. The results of a test of visual attention from Luria's battery (the Shulte tables; these tables require the patient to point to and read out loud the numbers from 1 to 25 in order) not only confirmed the mild decrease in her mental activity, but also revealed its instability; she spent 70 s on the first Shulte table,[b] 80 s on the second table, and 60 s on the third one (Score 1.5). She did show an ability to activate herself and improve her time when she was told that it was the last table. This indicated good potential for her self-regulation in the rehabilitative process.

Assessment of motor activity

The assessment of F.R.'s motor functions showed the superiority of her left hand on the Purdue Pegboard and on the Finger Tapping Test. She showed the expected dominant hand superiority on the Finger Tapping test, but showed a markedly better performance with the left hand on the Purdue Pegboard. It should be noted that all motor performances were slowed and her grip strength was approximately equal bilaterally. A similar predominance of her left-hand skill as well as mild disturbances of bimanual coordination (score 1) were revealed on the Oseretsky Test of Reciprocal Coordination (from Luria's battery). In spite of a premorbid preference of her left hand and better performance with that hand on several motor tests, special tests of praxis from Luria's battery showed that her defects in praxis were more pronounced in her left hand. For instance, her mistakes in postural praxis were twice as frequent with the left

b. The normative standard is up to 60 s for each table.

hand than with her right hand (Score 1.5 for this test). This suggested the lateralization of a lesion in the right hemisphere, right premotor zone. The qualitative analysis of F.R.'s mistakes in the motor sphere showed their relationship to disturbances in the spatial organization of movements (a "mirror" symptom). This led us to suspect a disturbance of the right parietal region. The same type of mistake was seen in spatial praxis (Head's test). Defects in her spatial organization of motor activity were most pronounced in measures of her constructional praxis and her drawing (Score 2 for each test). The Block Design subtest, for instance, was extremely difficult for the patient. She was able to perform only the first three designs on her own. On more difficult designs, she not only failed to reproduce the internal spatial relationships between the elements of the sample, but she could not reproduce the general structure of the design (Fig. 2).

These performances indicated that her impairment of spatial organization was related to disturbances of the factor of the simultaneous organization of elements, both of which implied a lesion in parietal cortical regions.

A similar mechanism was revealed in F.R.'s drawing, both in copying the Rey-Osterrieth complex figure and in drawing simpler objects on command. When drawing a table on command, F.R. could not produce the three-dimensional aspects of the representation. Additional instructions (explanations) only partially assisted her. A visual sample provided for her to copy permitted her to overcome these difficulties for a more simple image of the table, but not for the more complicated drawing of a cube—Score 2 (Fig. 3).

Thus, she was able to profit from instructional assistance and visual cues; this demonstrated her good learning potential. However, this level of assistance was not sufficient for her to complete more complicated tasks (for instance,

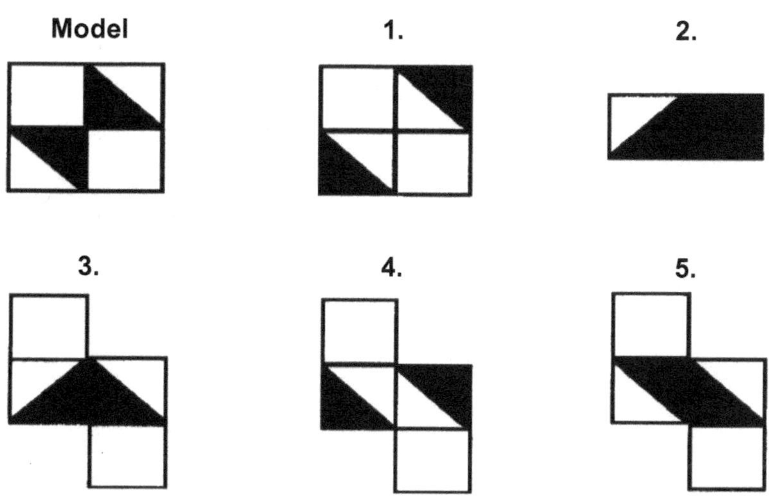

FIG. 2 F.R.'s performance on trial 4 of the WAIS-R Block Design subtest. The numbers represent the sequence of her attempts.

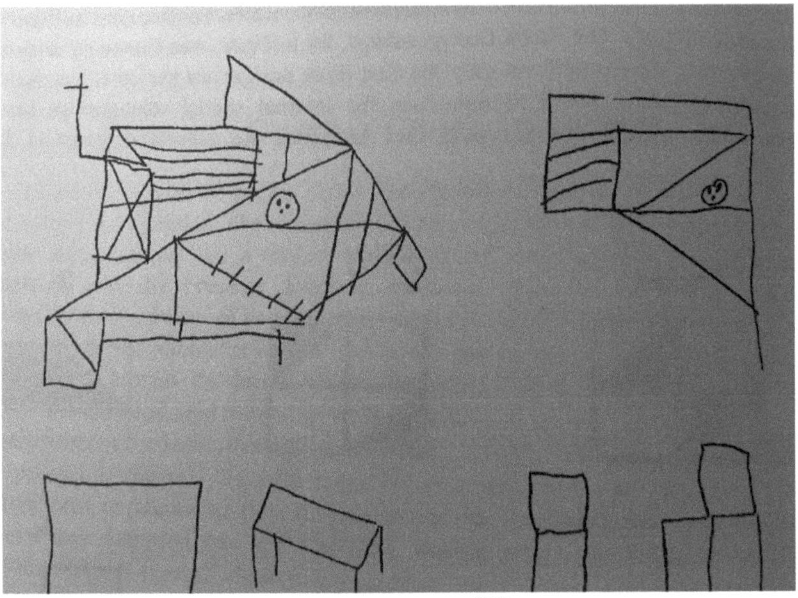

(A)

(B) (C)

FIG. 3 F.R.'s drawings. (A) The Rey-Osterrieth complex figure, copy (left) and delayed reproduction (right); (B) a table on command (left) and copy with assistance (right); and (C) a cube on command (left) and copy (right).

drawing a cube), which was impossible both on command and when copying. The psychological analysis of these tasks helped us to explain the difference between them: copying the Rey-Osterrieth figure as well as the cube necessitated not only the spatial orientation of the items but also their integration into a whole structure, effectuated by the right parietal cerebral region. More intensive assistance will be necessary to overcome both disturbed mechanisms.

It should be noted that F.R. was very aware and able to self-monitor and control herself on all these tasks. She had no problems in conventional and conflicting motor reactions (Score 0), and showed only a slight tendency toward perseveration in kinetic praxis tasks, which was very well corrected by the patient herself (Score 1). These aspects led us to suspect generally preserved frontal cortical functions, despite the evidence of a left frontal cranial fracture and hygroma at the time of injury.

The summarized score for six Lurian tests for motor activity was 7.5/6 = 1.25.

Evaluation of gnostic functions

All tests of visual matching (Benton Visual Form Discrimination, Raven's Colored Progressive Matrices, and the matrices items on the Kaufman-Brief Intelligence Test) were performed well by the patient. Luria's tests of visual perception (recognition of superimposed and masked images) revealed the symptom of fragmentary perception: The patient made a conclusion on the basis of only one perceived item, and was unable to unify all of the items represented into a single gestalt (Score 1). The same difficulties were seen on the Hooper Visual Organization test and the WAIS-R Picture Completion subtest; not only were her performances and quantitative scores low on these measures, but a qualitative analysis of her mistakes clearly showed these problems. F.R. did well when she needed to analyze a single object; for example, a missing leg of an animal. She failed, however, when several items needed to be integrated into a gestalt, as when she had to unify a pitcher with a glass through the missing stream of water. Therefore, we can see the same mechanism of disturbances in the simultaneous integration, related to the right parietal-occipital area, that was observed during the assessment of her motor activity.

F.R. also had demonstrable spatial perceptual difficulties which were not clearly reflected in her level of performance on some tests. For instance, in the same Picture Completion subtest, which of course was not specially designed to assess spatial orientation, the analysis of some of F.R.'s mistakes proved their spatial nature. The patient could understand very well a discrepancy between the number of diamonds and the digit 9 on the playing card with a central diamond missing, but she could not localize the missing item. She had mild difficulties in differentiating the Roman numerals XI and IX in Luria's battery (Score 1). It appeared that practical aspects of everyday living may help her to compensate for some of these difficulties. Also, F.R. was generally good at reading time from a schematic watch without the figures on it.

All tests of acoustic perception were performed well by the patient, in spite of a mild unilateral hearing decrease in the left ear (Reitan-Indiana Sensory-Perceptual Examination and an independent hearing screening examination). More complex testing within the normal limits included rhythm perception and reproduction tasks from the Luria battery (Score 0). Tactile and somesthetic perception, as measured by Reitan's Tactile Form Recognition test, showed a slightly better performance with the right hand, and Luria's tests of stereognosis showed minor difficulties in the left hand (Score 0.5). The summarized score for four Lurian tests for gnostic activity was $3.5/4 = 0.85$.

To qualify the gnostic findings, it can be concluded that aside from left-sided decrease in auditory and tactile perception, similar disturbances of the simultaneous integration and spatial analysis of information were revealed by the joint assessment in this functional sphere.

Evaluation of verbal functions

The spontaneous speech of F.R. was sufficiently fluent that she demonstrated only mild word-finding problems in daily interactions, and carried on extended conversations with little effort (Score 1 for spontaneous speech). However, F.R. performed noticeably poorly on a quantitative measure of word generation, the NCCEA Word Fluency subtest, and she received a typically aphasic score when compared to aphasic norms. She had no fluency or word-finding problems when completing the Reitan-Indiana Aphasia Screening test and no difficulties on the vocabulary section of the Kaufman-Brief Intelligence Test or other verbal tests such as the WAIS-R and the Luria test of naming (Score 0).

The comprehension subtest was generally completed within normal limits for her background. F.R. had a very high volume of acoustic perception and performed well on the NCCEA Sentence Repetition subtest (score at the 80th percentile), and on Benton's Serial Digit Learning Test (97th percentile). Her academic scores on measures of single word reading and spelling (the WRAT-R) were actually higher than her level of education (high school graduate). No difficulties in understanding logico-grammatical constructions were revealed by the Luria battery testing (Score 0).

These results demonstrated little clear-cut language disturbance in F.R., and the relative intactness of the middle and posterior left hemisphere structures. The only major test that F.R. performed poorly on was the test of word fluency, and we can hypothesize that her verbal expressive difficulties become more pronounced when she becomes more fatigued because this test was given toward the end of the assessment.

The summarized score for three Lurian tests for verbal activity was 1/3 = 0.33.

Memory assessment

F.R. showed mild to moderate disturbances of memory, manifested as slight decreases in the productivity (volume) of memory and an increased inhibition of stimuli by interfering activities. These defects were revealed in verbal (Score 1), visual (Score 0.5), and kinetic (Score 1.5) memory, so they were material nonspecific impairments, but her verbal memory was more unstable during delayed reproduction while her visual memory was more disturbed in terms of the productivity of her learning (number of items retained both immediately or after a delay). These differences may be related to differences in successive/simultaneous processing in each kind of mnestic activity.

It should be noted, that items semantic organization helped F.R. to ameliorate some of the memorization difficulties; the verbal stories were retained better than words, sentences, or spatial memory (Rey-Osterrieth figure). Spatial memory was disturbed to a greater degree than memory for other material; most of the memory traces of the performed drawing disappeared after interference, and F.R. could not even identify the general configuration of the Rey-Osterrieth drawing after this interference and delay (Fig. 3). Spatial recall was similarly impaired on several new visual memory tests (complex pictures) from Luria's battery (Score 2) (the summarized score for four Lurian tests for mnestic activity was 5/4 = 1.25).

Supplementary qualitative analyses of verbal memory were also possible with the California Verbal Learning Test (CVLT). While her level of performance ($T = 18$) was only mild to moderately impaired, and she clearly did not use an active learning strategy, F.R.'s score for serial learning was 4 standard deviations above the mean and her recall was primarily from the end (standard score = +4) and somewhat from the beginning of the list (standard score = +1), thus demonstrating a predominant primacy-recency effect. Cued recall did not appear to assist her significantly in short or long delays. We can see from Luria's testing that the semantic organization of the material to be learned, particularly for spatial memory, and other active mediational strategies were able to assist and increase the level of F.R.'s mnestic activity. Pure cueing, as done on the CVLT, was not always enough to help her in verbal memory. These findings were of prime importance in her rehabilitation, all of which needed to be taken into account in her rehabilitation planning and the development of remedial strategies.

Evaluation of intellectual processes

F.R.'s level of overall intellectual functioning was within the average range on the K-BIT. The patient had no difficulty understanding the meaning of stories she read or of thematic pictures. No defects in picture arrangement were seen using either the WAIS-R Picture Arrangement or the Luria sequencing of picture materials (Score 0). No verbal conceptual difficulties in similarities from the WAIS-R were seen. F.R. was able to classify objects based on a general concept and to exclude objects not belonging to this category (from Luria's battery). For example, she was able to identify three pictures (out of four) that share a similar concept of motorized vehicles, and excluded the hot air balloon as not motor-driven (Score 0). On the Wisconsin Card Sorting Test (WCST), F.R. could complete five out of the six categories requiring changes of the mental set, but demonstrated some fluctuations in her attention, scored as perseverative responses.

Nevertheless, given these relatively good intellectual performances, rather poor results were revealed on the matrices portion of the K-BIT (standard score of 90; 25th percentile). Although this test had not been widely used in neuropsychological assessment—and was even discouraged from a neuropsychological viewpoint in the manual by Kaufman & Kaufman, 1990—to understand her results from a cognitive standpoint, we performed a psychological task analysis of the K-BIT.

As was described in "From measurement to analysis" section, to find the analogical principle in the K-BIT matrices, the examinee needed to actualize different types of relationships and to perform different kinds of mental activities. We were able to differentiate seven groups of items representing different cognitive activities on this test: (1) Analogies based upon syntagmatic (situational) relationships. (2) Analogies based upon paradigmatic (categorical) relationships. (3) Analogies based upon perceptual matching. (4) Analogies necessitating perceptual matching and integration (synthesis of details). (5) Analogies based upon perceptual matching along with the analysis of spatial relationships (e.g., rotated figures). (6) Formation of abstract logical concepts. (7) Formation of abstract logical concepts including the analysis of spatial relationships.

We then rated F.R.'s mistakes using the above task analysis. This comparison revealed that 50% of all her mistakes were made on items that necessitated **perceptual matching and integration** (type 4); 33% of her mistakes were on items that included analysis of spatial relationships (types 5 and 7); and only 17% of her mistakes were made on conceptual items not related to spatial characteristics (e.g., two alike, one different).

A similar analysis of mistakes on the Raven's Colored Progressive Matrices showed four possible mechanisms of mistakes: (1) visual matching, (2) visual matching combined with the analysis of spatial relationships, (3) logical concept formation, and (4) logical concept formation and the analysis of spatial relationships. The qualitative analysis of errors made by F.R. demonstrates that 45% of the mistakes she made on items included **difficulties in the analysis of spatial relationships**.

We were able to conclude that F.R.'s difficulties on the K-BIT Matrices and Raven's Colored Matrices were not indicative of primary disturbances in cognition or intelligence (abstraction, generalization, reasoning, and so on), but were related to a **disorder of the same mechanisms of spatial analysis and simultaneous integration** that was seen in other mental activities. The same can be said of her performance on the Short Category Test.

Another problem for F.R. appeared with calculation and problem-solving. Her achievement in basic arithmetic (WRAT-R) was much worse than her achievement on the reading and spelling subtests. F.R. made a large number of mistakes in serial subtraction ($100-7=\ldots$) from Luria's battery. Her quantitative score on this task (1) was rather low. Other tests for acalculia from Luria's battery do not identify primary acalculic symptoms (Score 0), and similar difficulties were also not seen on the arithmetic items from the Aphasia Screening Test. Her concepts of quantity and the inner structure of numbers were preserved. The deficits identified in counting and problem solving were shown by a qualitative analysis to be related to **memory difficulties**; the patient would forget the intermediary results. When she was assisted in remembering the last result in the calculation, she succeeded quite well in the calculation. The summarized score for intellectual processes = 0.33.

The scoring procedure in Lurian testing allows a comparison of the level of disturbances in different mental spheres: the highest scores were in neurodynamic (Score 1.5), motor, and mnestic (Score 1.25 for each) functions; the gnostic disturbances were less pronounced (Score 0.85). The scores for verbal and intellectual spheres were relatively low (0.33 for each), and the general characteristics of the patient (personality and self-regulation features) were intact.

A qualitative analysis of both Lurian and psychometric tests proved that the **main mechanisms of disturbances were spatial organization and simultaneous synthesis in all mental functions**. This approach was close to Reitan's "intraindividual comparison procedure (a comparison of the subject's own performances on various tests) and helps identify the uniqueness of an individual's ability structure" (Reitan & Wolfson, 1986, p.139).

We used the data of this combined neuropsychological assessment for planning the rehabilitation program for this patient. The program stimulated first the indicated weak factors in all mental functions, using as a support the strengths—good executive functions, self-regulation, high motivation for rehabilitation, and good intellectual capacities. This program based on neuropsychological assessment was very effective and efficient.

Conclusions

To conclude, we have to say first that by using a combined neuropsychological evaluation with this patient, we found a large correspondence between the clinical data and the results obtained by both the Russian and the American methods of neuropsychological assessment. Thus, many of the methods proved to be mutually complementary. Although the methods were compatible and complementary, most individuals, based on their training, will use the methods with which they are most familiar. In this case, the variety of verbalized and nonverbalized methods used allowed us to comprehensively evaluate a holistic system of mental functions in voluntary conditions. Likewise, other aspects of information processing were also utilized.

Throughout this case assessment, Luria's qualitative emphasis on syndrome analysis, used as a guiding principle, not only helped us to reveal the mechanisms (factors) underlying the observed defects, but also allowed us to analyze and explain the apparent contradictions in some of the testing results. The principle of the syndrome analysis, whether applied to Lurian assessment methods or more psychometric measures in general, helped us to identify the main goals of the patient's rehabilitation program and to determine the optimal strategies for effectiveness. The latter was demonstrated by the logical consistency of the data and by the improvement F.R. made during her treatment.

We hope that the discussion we have presented of this case shows the strengths of a combined qualitative and quantitative analysis in the assessment and development of rehabilitative interventions for a person with brain injury. We believe that such cross-cultural sharing of methods and approaches strengthens not only the field of neuropsychology worldwide, but also directly benefits individual patients.

Acknowledgment

The study has been supported by the Russian Foundation of Fundamental Investigations (grant RFFI #18-013-00721).

References

Agranovich, A. (2004). Cross-cultural differences in neuropsychological performance: a comparison between Russian and American samples. In T. V. Ahutina, J. M. Glozman, L. I. Moskovich, & D. Robbins (Eds.), *A.R. Luria and contemporary psychology: Festschriftcelebrating the centennial of his birth* (pp. 181–188). NY: Nova Science.

Akhutina, T. V., & Pylayeva, N. M. (2008). *Surmounting learning disabilities. Neuropsychological approach*. Moscow: Peter [in Russian].

Ananiev, B. G. (1973). *Problems of a comprehensive study of intelligence and personality development*. In *A man and the society. Problems of intellectual and cultural development of students*. (pp. 3–7). Leningrad: Leningrad University Press. [in Russian].

Cicerone, K. D., & Tupper, D. E. (1986). Cognitive assessment in the neuropsychological rehabilitation of head-injured adults. In B. P. Uzzell & Y. Gross (Eds.), *Clinical neuropsychology of intervention* (pp. 59–83). Boston: Martinus Nijhoff.

Christensen, A. L. (1979). *Luria's neuropsychological investigation: Text, manual, and test cards* (2nd ed.). Copenhagen: Munksgaard.

Comrey, A. L. (1951). Mental testing and the logic of measurement. *Educational and Psychological Measurement, 11*, 323–334.

Glozman, J. M. (1999). Qualitative and quantitative integration of Lurian procedures. *Neuropsychology Review, 9*(1), 23–32.

Glozman, J. M. (2007). A.R. Luria and the history of Russian neuropsychology. *Journal of the History of the Neurosciences, 16*, 168–180.

Glozman, J.M. (2012). *Neuropsychological assessment: Qualitative and quantitative evaluation of data*. Moscow: Smysl Publishing House [in Russian].

Glozman, J. M. (2013). *Developmental neuropsychology*. London/New York: Psychology Press/ Taylor and Francis Group.

Glozman, J. M., & Tupper, D. E. (1995). Converging impressions in Russian and American neuropsychology: Discussion of a clinical case. *Applied Neuropsychology, 2*, 5–23.

Golden, C. J., Hammeke, T. A., Purisch, A. D., Berg, R. A., Moses, J. A., Jr., Newlin, D. B., et al. (1982). *Item interpretation of the Luria-Nebraska neuropsychological battery*. Lincoln, NE: University of Nebraska Press.

Golden, C. J., Purisch, A. D., & Hammeke, T. A. (1985). *Luria-Nebraska neuropsychological battery: Manual*. Los Angeles: Western Psychological Services.

Gould, S. (1981). *The mismeasure of man*. NY: W.W. Norton.

Groth-Marnat, G. (2009). *Handbook of psychological assessment* (5th ed.). San Francisco, CA: John Wiley and Sons.

Harlage, L. C. (1975). Neuropsychological approaches to predicting outcome of remedial education strategies for learning disabled children. *Pediatric Psychology, 3*, 23–28.

Heaton, R. K., Grant, I., & Matthews, C. G. (1991). *Comprehensive norms for an expanded Halstead-Reitan battery: Demographic corrections, research findings, and clinical application*. Odessa, FL: Psychological Assessment Resources.

Homskaya, E.D. (2005). *Neuropsychology* (4th ed.). Saint Petersburg: Peter [in Russian].

Horton, M. A., & Puente, A. (1986). Human neuropsychology: An overview. In D. Wedding, A. Horton, & J. Webster (Eds.), *The neuropsychology handbook: Behavioral and clinical perspectives* (pp. 3–22). N.Y: Springer.

Kaplan, E. (1983). Process and achievement revisited. In S. Wapner & B. Kaplan (Eds.), *Toward a holistic developmental psychology* (pp. 13–156). Hillsdale, NJ: L. Erlbaum.

Kaplan, E., Fein, D., Morris, R., & Delis, D. C. (1991). *WAIS-R as a neuropsychological instrument: Manual*. San Antonio: The Psychological Corporation.

Kaufman, A. S., & Kaufman, N. L. (1990). *Kaufman brief intelligence test: Manual*. Circle Pines, MN: American Guidance Service.

Korkman, M. (1999). Applying Luria's diagnostic principles in the neuropsychological assessment of children. *Neuropsychology Review, 9*, 89–107.

Korkman, M., Kirk, U., & Kemp, S. (2007). *NEPSY II*. San Antonio: Harcourt Assessment, Inc.

Leontiev, A. N., Luria, A. R., & Smirnov, A. A. (1968). On diagnostic techniques in psychological assessment of schoolchildren. *Sovetskaya Pedagogica, 7*, 65–77 [in Russsian].

Liutsko, L., Peña-Casanova, J., Rivera-Avila, N., Vinaixa-Campos, L., Cáceres-Guillén, I., Quiñones Úbeda, S., et al. (2018). *Neuropsychological test Barcelona-2: Theoretical and practical aspects*. In *The fifth international Luria Memorial Congress (Lurian approach in international psychological science), KnE life sciences* (pp. 1–4).

Luria, A. R. (1965). Neuropsychological analysis of focal brain lesions. In B. B. Wolman (Ed.), *Handbook of clinical psychology* (pp. 689–754). New York: McGraw-Hill.

Luria, A. R. (1969). *Higher cortical functions in man* (2nd ed.). Moscow: Moscow University Press [in Russian). (English translation, New York: Basic Books, 1980].

Luria, A. R. (1973). *The working brain*. New York: Basic Books.

Luria, A. R. (1982). *The making of mind*. Moscow: Moscow University Press [English edition: Cambridge, MA: Harvard University Press, 1979].

Luria, A. R. (1999). Outline for the neuropsychological examination of patients with local brain lesions. *Neuropsychology Review, 9*(1), 9–22.

Luria, A. R., & Majovski, L. V. (1977). Basic approaches used in American and Soviet clinical neuropsychology. *American Psychologist, 32*, 959–968.

Partington, J., & Leiter, R. (1949). Partington's pathway test. *The Psychological Service Center Bulletin, 1*, 9–20.

Peña-Casanova, J. (1991). Programa integrado de exploración neuropsicológica-test Barcelona: Bases teóricas, objetivos y contenidos. *Revista de Logopedia, Foniatría y Audiología, 11*(2), 66–79 [in Spanish].

Reitan, R. M. (1955). Investigation of the validity of Halstead's measures of biological intelligence. *Archives of Neurology and Psychiatry, 73*, 28–35.

Reitan, R. M. (1964). Psychological deficits resulting from cerebral lesions in men. In J. M. Warren & K. Akert (Eds.), *The frontal granular cortex and behavior* (pp. 295–312). New York: McGraw-Hill.

Reitan, R. M., & Wolfson, D. (1986). The Halstead-Reitan neuropsychological test battery. In D. Wedding, Horton, A. M.Jr., & J. Webster (Eds.), *The neuropsychology handbook: Behavioral and clinical perspectives* (pp. 134–160). New York: Springer.

Reitan, R. M., & Wolfson, D. (1993). *The Halstead-Reitan neuropsychological test battery; theory and clinical interpretation* (2nd ed.). Tucson, AZ: Neuropsychology Press.

Ryan, C., Vega, A., Longstreet, C., & Drash, A. (1984). Neuropsychological changes in adolescents with insulin-dependent diabetes. *Journal of Clinical Psychology, 3*, 335–342.

Semago, N. Y., & Semago, M. M. (2010). Theory and practice of evaluation of child's mental development. In *Preschoolers and schoolchildren*. Saint Petersburg: Rech [in Russian].

Smith, G., Ivnik, R., & Lucas, J. (2008). Assessment techniques: tests, test batteries, norms and methodological approaches. In J. Morgan & J. Ricker (Eds.), *Textbook of clinical neuropsychology* (pp. 38–57). NY: Taylor & Francis [2nd ed., London: Routledge, 2018].

Swiercinsky, D., & Leigh, G. (1979). Comparison of neuropsychological data in the diagnosis of brain impairment with computerized tomography and other neurological procedures. *Journal of Clinical Psychology, 35*, 242–246.

Tuokko, H., & Hadjistavropoulos, T. (1998). *An assessment guide to geriatric neuropsychology*. London: Lawrence Erlbaum Associates, Publishers.

Walsh, K. W. (1978). *Neuropsychology: A clinical approach*. NY: Churchill Livingston.

Wechsler, D. (1974). *Manual: Wechsler intelligence scale for children—Revised*. NY: The Psychological Corporation.

Wedding, D. (1980). Implication of computerized axial tomography for clinical neuropsychology. *Professional Psychology*, 31–38.

Williams, M. A., & Boll, T. J. (1997). Recent advances in neuropsychological assessment of children. In G. Goldstein & T. Incagnoli (Eds.), *Contemporary approaches to neuropsychological assessment* (pp. 231–276). NY: Plenum Press.

Further reading

Glozman, J. M., & Tupper, D. E. (2005). Converging impressions in Russian and American neuropsychology. In T. V. Ahutina, J. M. Glozman, L. I. Moskovich, & D. Robbins (Eds.), *A.R. Luria and contemporary psychology: Festschriftcelebrating the centennial of his birth* (pp. 187–195). NY: Nova Science.

Halstead, W. C. (1947). *Brain and intelligence*. Chicago: University of Chicago.

Luria, A. R. (1947). *Traumatic aphasia*. Moscow: USSR Medical Academy Press [English translation. The Hague: Mouton, 1959].

Reitan, R. M. (1955). Certain differential effects of left and right cerebral lesions in human adults. *Journal of Comparative and Physiological Psychology*, *48*, 474–477.

Chapter 4

Combining qualitative and quantitative measures in the evaluation of executive functions in ADHD

Irina Shevchenko
Neuropsychological Remediation Center "Cortex", Krasnogorsk, Moscow Region, Russian Federation

Introduction

Attention deficit/hyperactivity disorder (ADHD) is one of the most common neurobehavioral disorders in children. The urgency of the problem is difficult to overestimate. Even with sufficiently high intellectual capabilities, children with ADHD often fail in school and experience difficulties in social adaptation in children's teams (Osipova & Pankratova, 1997). Most children with ADHD continue to suffer from it throughout their life, and they continue to show signs of social maladjustment, including deviant behaviors. Numerous studies consistently report links between ADHD and higher involvement in other risky behavior, such as drug use, reckless driving, gambling, and engaging in sexually risky behavior (Spiegel & Pollak, 2019). In this regard, ADHD is a major social problem that concerns both parents and specialists in different fields—teachers, psychologists, psychotherapists, neurologists, psychiatrists, medical psychologists, and speech therapists.

In 2004, ADHD was recognized by the International Association for Child and Adolescent Psychiatry and Allied Professions (IACAPAP) as the number one problem for the health of children and adolescents (IACAPAP, 2004).

According to various studies, the frequency of childhood ADHD in Russia is from 3% to 20%. In the United States, more than 5 million children (or 9.5%) in 2007 were diagnosed with various forms of ADHD, and it is considered a relatively common childhood disease (Breggin, 2011). In several other countries, the percentage of school-age children with ADHD was < 10%, including Great Britain—1.9%–5% (Murphy, McCarthy, Baer, Zima, & Jellinek, 2014), China—5% (Shan, 2007), Germany—4.8% (Huss, Hölling, Kurth, & Schlack, 2008), and Spain—6.8% (Catalá-López et al., 2012).

Evaluation and Treatment of Neuropsychologically Compromised Children
https://doi.org/10.1016/B978-0-12-819545-1.00004-7

According to the Diagnostic Handbook DSM-5 (American Psychiatric Association, 5th ed., 2013), ADHD has three types:

- Inattentive
- Hyperactive-impulsive
- Combined inattentive and hyperactive-impulsive

Children with attention deficit disorder without hyperactivity are rare. They tend to have significant difficulty in concentrating. About these children, we can say that they "fly in the clouds," "are absent," "hang," and slowly and sluggishly respond to external stimuli. They also process information much more slowly than other children do. As a result of bad switching, any job causes difficulties for such children. It is difficult for a child to understand what he or she should do, and they make a lot of mistakes. From the outside, such a child may seem to be involved in the work, sitting quietly and calmly, but the child does not understand the essence of the task and does not perform it.

Children with hyperactive-impulsive ADHD, in addition to the problems of socialization, have learning difficulties because of their own impulsivity (unformed executive functions). Such children usually do tasks very quickly and sacrifice accuracy for the sake of speed. Hyperactive children often perform tasks inattentively because they do not have the patience to view all the conditions and observe them.

Children with inattentive-hyperactive-impulsive combined ADHD have all the symptoms listed above.

Despite the fact that this disorder is widely studied by specialists, there are still a large number of questions about the etiology, clinical pattern, diagnosis, prognosis, and treatment of this syndrome.

Luria's neuropsychological approach allows us to qualitatively characterize the structure of ADHD, to reveal its biological and social mechanisms, and to develop effective approaches to its remediation, that is, to the resolution of this urgent and significant social problem.

At the same time, knowledge of the structure of this disorder allows us to reveal an individualized program of neuropsychological remediation and to increase its efficacy.

Therefore, in the assessment of the executive functions in ADHD, we used a combination of the Lurian approach and various psychometric measures.

Rationale for the choice of measures

Studying the qualitative and quantitative features of ADHD, we conducted a neuropsychological assessment primarily using tests proposed by Luria (1969), adapted for children by Glozman, Potanina, and Soboleva (2008), Glozman (2012), and Glozman and Soboleva (2013) to reveal difficulties in learning and behavior caused by the functional immaturity (developmental delay) of certain brain structures of children.

Conners' scale (Conners, 1997) helps to reveal the presence or absence as well as the degree of severity of attention deficit and hyperactivity.

To reveal the complications in prenatal, perinatal, and early childhood development as well as problems of communication in the family and the children's team in the primary evaluation of the child, we used the parent questionnaire of early child development (Glozman et al., 2008). This makes it possible to reveal sociobiological risk factors for ADHD.

To determine the profile of the child's lateral organization, we used the questionnaire of M. Annet and tests "clock," "telescope" (Homskaya, 2005).

In addition, we used psychometric measures to clarify the structure of executive defects: the Hailing Test (Burgess & Shallice, 1997) studies the functions of control and regulation; the Numeric Stroop test (Shallice et al., 2002; Stroop, 1935) is aimed at measuring the resistance of brain activity and attention to interference; the Daily Planning Test (Funke & Krüger, 1993) is used to study the ability for stage-by-stage planning as well as to compare the plan and its implementation; and the Iowa Gambling Task (Bechara, Damasio, Damasio, & Anderson, 1994; Bechara, Damasio, Damasio, & Lee, 1999; Bechara, Damasio, Tranel, & Anderson, 1998; Bechara, Damasio, Tranel, & Damasio, 1997; Bechara, Tranel, & Damasio, 2000) sets the task to study the relationship between emotional and speech regulation through studying the regulatory functions in emotionally charged decision-making in a situation of uncertainty.

We will now focus on each method in more detail.

Luria's qualitative methods of neuropsychological assessment

Using the battery of neuropsychological assessment of seven areas of mental functioning, developed by Luria (1969) and adapted for children of different ages by Glozman et al. (2008), Glozman (2012), and Glozman and Soboleva (2013), we have conducted a complex neuropsychological assessment of children with qualitative and quantitative processing of the results of the assessment (Glozman, 2012). For quantitative evaluation, we used a penalty point system based on a qualitative analysis of defects and the possibilities of their correction in terms of Luria's dialogue interaction with the child, where:

0—Error-free test execution
0.5—Single errors with self-correction or slow entry into the task
1—Insignificant error, self-corrected or after minimal stimulation by the neuropsychologist
1.5—Numerous errors corrected through an external organization of the child's attention
2—Multiple errors with an incomplete correction even after the deployed tips
3—Implementation of the test is impossible even with different types of assistance by the examiner

This assessment allows us to determine the nature of disturbances of mental functions (neuropsychological symptoms) and, not just their presence, but to reveal preserved components for further remediation work with the child.

Before conducting Luria's neuropsychological assessment, we determined the lateral organization for hand, foot, eye, and ear functions using the questionnaire by M. Annette (Homskaya, 2005), and two additional tests–the "clock" and the "telescope." We asked the child to show some preferred actions using a pencil or a ball: "to brush the hair," "to brush the teeth," to write something on paper, to beat the ball with one hand, to cross hands, to cross fingers, to jump on one foot, to lean one knee on the seat of the chair, to look into the "telescope," to hear the ticking wristwatch, and to answer the "ringing" phone.

Let us describe the studied mental spheres.

General characteristics of the child

Evaluation begins with a talk with the child to establish rapport with him and to obtain information regarding his general knowledge (orientation in where and about), his awareness of his own problems, his adequate attitude about them, and his adequate behavior in the process of assessment (in preschoolers—name and surname, age, birthday, time of year, address, with whom the child lives, the names of parents, whether he/she attends kindergarten). In school-age children, in addition to the previous questions, we ask the relevant year, month, date, and day of the week as well as the school grade, names and places of work of parents, the specialist consulted, and problems about which the child was brought for assessment, all from the child's perspective. Thus, we estimated three areas of general characteristics of the child's mental functioning:

- Orientation in where and about
- Adequacy of behavior
- Critical attitude to oneself

Assessment of mental activity

For children up to 8 years, a proof-reading test is used where the child is invited to cross out as many figures as possible of the type indicated by the neuropsychologist during 1 min. The number of correctly found figures and the number of errors of two types are fixed: confusions with visually similar or different figures.

From the age of 8, the child performs a test for the fastest possible finding of numbers from 1 to 25 from the Schulte tables (Glozman & Soboleva, 2013). The average implementation time of three tables is fixed.

Assessment of movements and actions

In the study of motor functions in neuropsychological assessment, we used and estimated the performance of the following tests from Luria's battery:

- Test for reciprocal coordination of hand movements
- Digital praxis test

- Oral praxis test
- Dynamic praxis test
- Head's test on the spatial praxis (from age 9)
- Copying of three-dimensional image of a house with a tree
- Copying of the table for school-age children or simple geometric figures for preschoolers
- Test for conditioned motor reactions
- Test for reproduction of rhythmic structures

Assessment of gnosis

The study of gnostic functions included:

- Test for recognition of real and masked images
- Test for acoustic gnosis
- Recognition of spatially oriented simple shapes (Benton's test)
- Test for identification of emotions
- Test for facial gnosis (from age 9)
- Test for letter gnosis (from age 8)
- Test for tactile gnosis
- Test for stereo gnosis

Assessment of verbal functions

The study of verbal functions included:

- Evaluation of spontaneous speech (smoothness, expansion, grammatical, and lexical correctness)
- Studying of automatized speech
- Studying of phonematic discrimination
- Test for naming
- Test for understanding words (correlation with pictures)
- Test for understanding logical and grammatical structures
- Assessment of writing the words, phrases, and text (from age 8)
- Studying of reading words, phrases, and text (from age 8)

Assessment of memory

The study of mnestic functions included:

- Test for auditory memory (memorization of a series of semantically unrelated words and their subsequent reproduction after heterogeneous interference; the number of presented words depended on the child's age)
- Test for motor memory (memorization of a series of movements and their transfer to the other hand)
- Visual memory test: memorizing a series of real and geometric (from age 9) images in a given sequence

Assessment of reasoning

In the study of intellectual functions, the following tests and tasks were done:

- Test for understanding the meaning of the story
- Test for understanding the meaning of stories in pictures and a series of pictured stories
- Formation of analogies
- Generalization and exclusion of concepts: picture test "4th extra" for preschoolers and verbal test "5th extra" for school children
- Sequences of subtraction (from age 8)
- Solution of arithmetic tasks (from age 7), differentiated for each grade of school

Conners' scale

Conners' scale was created to assess the presence and degree of severity of ADHD. This questionnaire is widely used in Russia and other countries to describe the overall picture of the child's disorder. It helps in the evaluation process, identifies children with difficulties, determines their degree of severity, and is used to create special training programs for children with ADHD. It also helps in the development of treatment plans and the determination of their efficacy.

There are two forms of the questionnaire: long (CPRS-R:L) and short (CPRS-R:S) (Conners, 1997; Passolt, 2004; Porter & Cirino, 2016).

The Conners CRSR:S diagnostic questionnaire (Connors's revised rating scale short versions) has three forms:

- For parents
- For teachers
- Questionnaire to be filled out by the child

We only used the scale for parents. In the short form, there are 10 questions and the parent indicates the frequency of occurrence of certain types of their child's behavior for the previous 6 months.

The evaluation criteria of attention deficit and hyperactivity/impulsivity are supplemented by a psychometric scale: absent, low, quite high, and very high. The maximum score on the scale is 30 points. The diagnostic value is the result of more than a 15-point difference. A score from 16 to 19 indicates a mild degree of ADHD; from 20 to 24 is moderate; and from 25 to 30 is a high severity of ADHD (Altherr et al., ed. Passolt, 2004).

In the long version, parents are asked to answer 80 questions.

The criteria on the Conners-80 scale are as follows:

- Scores above 60—a sign that the child may have emotional, behavioral, or academic problems such as ADHD;

- At the same time: scores from 61 to 70—a sign that the child's emotional, behavioral, and academic performance problems are a little atypical or moderately pronounced;
- Scores above 70 are a sign that emotional, behavioral, or academic performance problems are very atypical or more serious.

These completed forms help to reveal emotional, behavioral, and academic difficulties. Together, they help to make an exhaustive list of characteristics of the child's behavior.

Questionnaire of early child development

Additional information about the child is provided by a questionnaire filled out by parents who seek the services of a neuropsychologist (Glozman et al., 2008). The questionnaire provides information about the particularities of pre-, peri-, and postnatal development of the child (that is, the pregnancy, delivery, and the first year of life of the child), his/her problems in family and children's team relations, any injuries and chronic diseases, etc.

The complaints of parents on the child's behavior and development are investigated in detail. We determine the age the pathological manifestations first appeared; their nature and changes in the course of the disorder in the child's growth; any particularities of development and behavior; his/her relationship with peers and adults; the propensity to certain activities; and the actual level of the child's readiness for school. A special section of the questionnaire is devoted to neurological and somatic concerns.

Because biological and social factors play an important role in the development of the child, it can be assumed that these factors become even more important in abnormal development. The primordial cause of a disturbed development is often an organic (biological) defect, but the conditions of the social environment can either compensate for these consequences, or, conversely, strengthen their negative effects.

Quantitative assessment measures

One of the founders of American clinical neuropsychology, who developed and used test batteries for the neuropsychological evaluation of children's brain-behavior functioning, was Ralph M. Reitan (Hom & Nici, 2015; Reitan, 1962, 1974). He was a mentor to many students who used his innovative ideas to make additional contributions to this field. Thus, the psychometric assessment methods that allow us to clarify the structure of ADHD include, but are not limited to, the following methods:

The Hayling Test

The Junior Hayling Sentence Completion Task (sentence ending test) is a neuropsychological test for the study of control and regulation functions (executive functions) (Burgess & Shallice, 1997). The test assesses the ability to inhibit the stereotypical response and suppress the involuntary response to the task to complete sentences. In the first part of the test, (A), consisting of 10 sentences, the child should finish the sentence with a word that fits the meaning, for example, on the sentence "The cat ran for a long time, but caught..." the child must give the answer "mouse." The second part of the test, (B), also consists of 10 sentences where the child needs to finish the sentence with a word that is not related in meaning to the sentence (for example, the sentence "In autumn there is a fall of..." the child can answer "TVs," "skates," "gloves," etc.). This requires the suppression of an involuntary response "leaves." If the child gave the wrong answer, we fixed the errors. The children were asked to respond as quickly as possible. The response time was measured using a stopwatch, from the moment when the last word of the presented unfinished sentence was read out until the child's answer. Part A is not quantified, but if the child does not do it, Part B is not given. In Part B, three penalty points means not corresponding to the instructions for the correct completion of the sentence (for example, in the sentence "With racket and ball you can play in..." the child gives the answer "tennis"), one point for a word semantically associated with a sentence or a missing word (for example, in the sentence "At the traffic light the car stops if the light is..." the child says "green"), and 0 points for words that are not appropriate in meaning. Herewith, we analyzed the used strategy that helped the child finish the sentence (for example, observing the room). The total number of penalty points (maximum number of points is 30) and the time of the test are calculated. From the total time of completing 10 sentences of Part B, we subtracted the total time of completing 10 sentences of Part A.

Numeric Stroop test (modified Stroop test)

This test aims to measure the resistance of brain activity and attention to interference. It is used to diagnose cognitive style: the flexibility/rigidity of cognitive control. This cognitive style characterizes the degree of subjective difficulty in changing the ways of information processing in a situation of cognitive conflict. Rigid control indicates difficulties in the transition from verbal to sensory-perceptive functions due to the low degree of automation while flexible is the relative ease of such a transition due to the high degree of automation.

Available data for using the Stroop test in neuropsychology showed the sensitivity of this test to understand the work of different parts of the frontal lobes of the brain in providing specific components of attention (Korsakova, 2014; Shallice et al., 2002). The classic version of the Stroop test consists of reading words when the color of the words does not coincide with the content of the written words (for example, the word "red" is written in blue) (Stroop, 1935). In the modification of the test proposed by Italian neuropsychologists (Shallice et al., 2002), children had to count the number of digits. The test material consists of two sets of tasks. In the first part, the child was asked to count the number of stars in each of the 12 squares. The number of errors, the counting time of 12 squares as a whole, and the average for one square were recorded. In the second session, the child was given the task to count the number of represented digits (but not to call the digit itself) in each of the 75 squares. The number of errors (the child named the digit, but not the number of digits), the time for 75 squares with numbers, and the average of one were measured. Then the time of interference influence was calculated (from the average time of counting the digits in one square of the second series and the average time of counting stars in one square of the first series was subtracted).

Daily Planning Test

This test is used to study the ability for stage-by-stage planning and for comparing the plan to its realization (Funke & Krüger, 1993; Holt et al., 2011). The child has to imagine that he/she returned from school and he/she needs to do 10 actions until the end of the day (the actions are presented in a random order):

- Go to the sports hall for basketball training with Mike (after all the homework is done)
- Buy bread for grandmother
- Take Mike home after training
- Do geometry homework (this requires a new ruler)
- Put on a sport suit
- Go for Mike
- Buy a new ruler
- Take break to grandmother
- Do the hometask in the native language (this requires a new notebook)
- Buy a new notebook for the native language

Also, the map of places where the child had to go was presented. This map should help the child to plan everything in the correct sequence. The child's task was to make a plan of the day in the optimal sequence (to write the actions in the order in which he/she will do them, to indicate the start and finish, and to map out the route on the map and the approximate time for the way). Herein, the map shows all the buildings—bakery, sports hall, etc.—as well as the child's current location. The effectiveness of the planning, the violation of planning logic (for example, going to grandmother before he/she bought bread, which he/she needs to bring her), the correct planning time, the test time (maximum 30 min), and the adequacy of self-control (accordance of self-evaluation and correct planning) were evaluated.

This test is an effective way to measure planning ability in children with executive function deficits. Because the ability to plan is important in a school-age child's daily life (for example, buying goods, preparing homework, or playing sports), the experimental measurement of this ability is an important link in the assessment of children with ADHD.

Iowa Gambling Task (test "Risk and benefits")

The study of decision-making has been the subject of investigation for more than 20 years, and many publications have appeared in recent years (Lin, Song, Chen, Lee, & Chiu, 2013; Overman & Pierce, 2014; Rodrigo, Padrón, de Vega, & Ferstl, 2014; Sallum, Mata, Miranda, & Malloy-Diniz, 2013; Singh, 2014; Van den Bos, Koot, & de Visser, 2014). The results of numerous studies, however, are difficult to integrate and interpret because of the large differences in the methodology and tasks of the analysis.

The Iowa Gambling Task (IGT)—the test of "Risk and benefits" was developed in 1994. The authors investigated one of the most difficult tasks—studying executive functions in uncertain and emotionally heightened decision making conditions (Bechara et al., 1994, 1997, 1998, 1999, 2000).

IGT was originally designed to test the ability to make decisions and the functioning of the frontal cortex in highly ambiguous circumstances, with the aim of imitating real-life behavior trials. The dorsolateral and lateral orbital prefrontal cortex are involved in making right and wrong decisions as well as in predicting their future consequences (Damasio, 1994; Damasio, Tranel, & Damasio, 1991; Eslinger & Damasio, 1985).

Over the past few years, various versions of IGT have been created (Bechara, 2007; Bechara et al., 1994, 2000). Most of the versions confirmed the correctness of the basic assumptions that the emotional decision-making system normally allows the person to foresee the long-term benefits of specific variants.

The test can be used from age 8, and can be used to assess the executive functions of school-age children.

Children were asked to play the card game "Risk and benefits," where they have to intuitively determine the internal rules of the game. Players were offered four decks of cards—A, B, C, and D. Children were informed that decks A and B win more, but have a higher chance to lose. In decks marked C and D, the gain is less, but so is the possible loss. Players are informed that they have 40 trials and that they must win as much as possible or lose as little as possible.

The goal of the game is to get the maximum profit. The child takes one card from any deck. Cards from decks A and B value 10 conventional points, and decks C and D value 5 conventional points. When the child selects a card, he/she looks on the back side. If the reverse side is clean, the child gets 5 or 10 conventional points (depending on which deck the card was in.) A penalty can, however, be indicated on the reverse side, and then the child pays the penalty from his/her recorded earnings. Thus, the child sees the "structure" of his/her own wins/losses. For example, winning/losing alternate through one card, or for a long time the child wins (about 7–8 trials in a row), and the next turn receives a very large penalty. Thus, the child should evaluate the risks and develop a winning strategy.

The basic idea is that there is a conflict between short-term and long-term rewards. If the child continues to select cards with a higher short-term reward (a more risky strategy), then he/she will lose money in the long term. These risky strategies correlate with various risky behaviors in real life, including rash behavior, impulsive reactions, etc.

Results of evaluation of executive functions in ADHD

Luria's approach

The application of Luria's approach to study the structure of defects in regulation and control in ADHD children was analyzed. These methods proved to be sensitive enough to differentiate children with and without ADHD in terms of regulation and control features. Our study involved 33 school-age children (28 boys and 5 girls aged 8–11 years) with ADHD diagnosis confirmed neurologically, supported by the Conners' scale (Conners' score higher than 15 points in the short version questionnaire/or higher than 60 points in the long version questionnaire), and 33 children (23 boys and 10 girls aged 8–12 years) with learning and behavior problems at school, but without an ADHD diagnosis and without data on pre- and perinatal pathology—"visually healthy children."

The initial focus was on the analysis of the most pronounced symptoms indicated by the parents of school-age children diagnosed with ADHD when filling out Conners' questionnaires:

- Excitability, impulsiveness
- Inattention, easy distraction
- A lot of speaking
- Errors due to negligence
- The tendency to interfere in or interrupt the conversations and activities of others
- Fidgeting on the spot, hanging out with hands and feet
- Uneven handwriting
- Easy distraction to extraneous stimuli

These data fully corresponded to the description of ADHD presented in DSM-5 (American Psychiatric Association, 5th ed., 2013).

The learning difficulties in children without the ADHD diagnosis were established according to complaints from parents and teachers ("scattered, quickly forgets everything, cries at school," "inattention, bad handwriting, difficult concentration," "a lot of mistakes in writing," "cannot remember the days of the week, months, seasons, miswriting of letters and numbers," "problems with reading," etc.), the study of school documentation and notebooks of the child, and the qualitative analysis of the Conners' scale. Thus, the most frequent defects of behavior in the Conners' questionnaire filled in by parents are the following:

- Difficulties in organizing own work
- Inattention, easy distraction
- Errors due to negligence

- Distracted or narrow attention
- Uneven handwriting
- General distraction, disorganization at home and school
- Easy distraction to extraneous stimuli

A comparative diagram of the most pronounced difficulties of school-age children with and without ADHD diagnosis, where 0 is the absence of a symptom and 3 is a very high degree of its manifestation, is illustrated in Fig. 1.

As can be seen in Fig. 1, children without an ADHD diagnosis have a lower degree of severity of difficulties compared with children with ADHD, but it is not enough for academic success.

At the same time, parents of school-age children without ADHD note the almost absolute absence of the following features of their children's behavior—"leaves the classroom without permission," "angry, vindictive," "quickly loses friends," "poorly controls behavior in stores," "interferes with other children"—while parents of school-age children with ADHD indicate these symptoms quite often.

In the neuropsychological study of ADHD using Luria's approach, the significant differences in higher mental function (HMF) delay in these two groups were observed in the areas of general characteristics, praxis, intelligence, neurodynamics, and in the total neuropsychological penalty score.

The penalty score in the field of general characteristics–orientation of the child in time and what about, general knowledge, control of own behavior, critical attitude in assessment, and the adequacy of the perception of mistakes made—is significantly higher in the group of school-age children with ADHD compared with school-age children without this diagnosis. Also, the number of defects in this area is higher in the former.

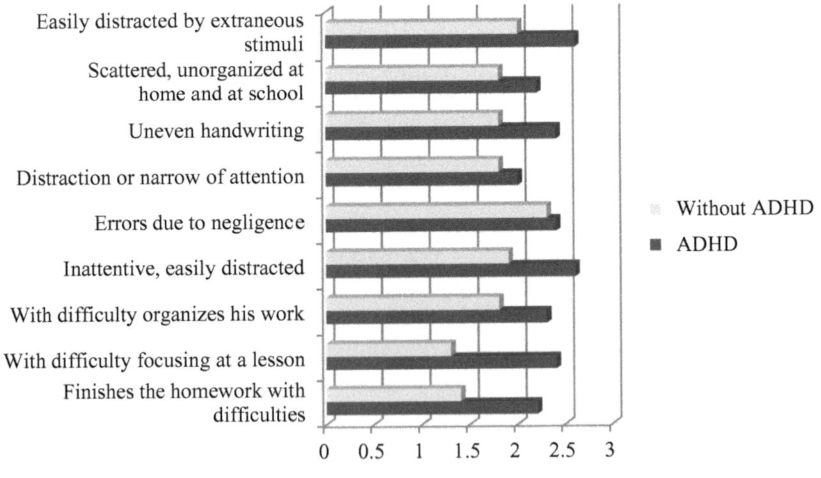

FIG. 1 Comparative data of the most pronounced difficulties of learning of school-age children with and without the ADHD diagnosis.

School-age children with learning difficulties (but without an ADHD diagnosis) also have significantly lower penalty points in praxis tests as compared with school-age children with ADHD, which indicates larger difficulties in their motor sphere. While the overall motor skills of children with hyperactivity disorder are well developed, they experience significant difficulties in performing movements that require a high degree of successive organization and coordination (for example, turning the hands inside and out or rapid alternating movements) as well as in the coordination of small movements (when writing, difficulties in tying shoelaces, and buttoning). This correlates with data from other authors. According to a number of similar studies (Carte, Nigg, & Hinshaw, 1996; Denckla & Rudel, 1978; Steger et al., 2001), coordination disorders in general motor skills were found in about half of ADHD cases.

Penalty points for neurodynamic parameters (mental activity) were also significantly lower in a group of school-age children without ADHD. In this area, the number of defects in students with ADHD is higher than in students without ADHD. For example, school-age children without ADHD very rarely encountered such neurodynamic symptoms as fluctuations in mental activity. These findings suggest that children with ADHD have more neurodynamic difficulties than school-age children with learning difficulties, but without this diagnosis.

According to the work of Ahutina, Matveeva, and Romanova (2012), the weakness in activity regulation (reduced level, fatigue, exhaustion of mental processes, attention fluctuations, etc.) is characteristic, at least to a small degree, of all children with learning problems. This data supported the above studies—among children with learning difficulties, but without the diagnosis of ADHD, there is a low level of activity. At the same time, the combination of deficiency in neurodynamic functions with the weakness of programming and control functions in ADHD children leads to significantly worse indicators in this area compared to their same age peers without this diagnosis.

Children with ADHD have disorders associated with an insufficiency of the activating effects of subcortical structures on the cerebral cortex, and hyperactivity is a kind of compensation for insufficiency of brain activity (Agris, 2015; Glozman, 2017; Goryacheva & Sultanova, 2005). That is why such children have a high level of exhaustion, an imbalance and instability of attention, and low mental activity. Moreover, with increasing school requirements, it is more difficult for these ADHD children to compensate for their difficulties.

According to the neuropsychological research of Glozman, Ravich-Scherbo, and Grishina (2007), children with severe clinical signs of deficiency in the neurodynamic components of activity cope much worse with neuropsychological tests, with the greatest difficulties noted in mnestic and intellectual functions. Among children with a pronounced neurodynamic deficit, their teachers and parents classified 60% of them as failing in school while in the group without signs of weakness of this function, that number was only 20%. Thus, in conclusion, the neurodynamic difficulties of ADHD children are obvious and cause many problems for them.

Despite the fact that the intellectual component of mental activity in ADHD children, as a rule, does not suffer primarily, and that the development of intellectual operations (generalization, logical reasoning, nonverbal intelligence) generally match to age peers, ADHD children are extremely poor in tasks that require programming, building an algorithm of activity (e.g., in maps or planning a day). At the same time, school-age children without this diagnosis rarely had such symptoms, such as an inability to understand the meaning of a told or pictured story, impulsiveness in the analysis of a picture or story, impulsive solution of a math problem, generalization, or making analogies.

The difference in the summarized neuropsychological penalty score was the most important and significant in the comparison of the two groups. In the ADHD group, it was 6.49 (diagnostic value is the result of more than 2.9 points), which characterizes the severe degree of delay in higher mental function formation. In school-age children without this diagnosis, an average score was 3.95, which corresponded to the mild delay in higher mental function formation. Consistent with this study's results, many authors consider the primary defect for most ADHD children to be a functional deficiency of subcortical brain structures, which leads to various defects in the development of higher mental functions (HMFs).

Quantitative methods

The applied quantitative methods in this study allowed for expansion of the investigation of ADHD through the inclusion of such little-studied categories as violation of step-by-step planning of self-activities, resistance to interference, and difficulties in decision-making in a situation of emotional uncertainty.

In the test "Risk and benefits," exploring the function of planning and the ability to make effective decisions, the average "gain" in the group of ADHD children was much lower (−82 conventional units) than in the second group of children (+35 conventional units), that is, the members of the ADHD group ended in debt. According to the procedure, during every 10 trials of the game, the child was asked how he/she made a choice, whether he/she saw any trends, etc. Children without ADHD, as a rule, during the first 5–10 trials tried to understand the system, opening the cards at random. After 10 trials, as a rule, there was no clear understanding of the structure, but the intended way to win was outlined. Already after 20 trials, the vast majority of children began to understand the possible variants of development, and would say such statements as: "In 'C' I realized the pattern," "In 'A' and 'C' cards with penalties alternate through one, in 'B' and 'D' a long time is a plus, and then a huge penalty falls." Respectively, further actions only strengthened their confidence in the chosen strategy; they said: "I will not change my strategy, I will not take more 'A' and 'C' cards, there are big disadvantages," "It is better to earn such a small pace, but without large penalties." These children emotionally assessed and "notice a mismatch, an inconsistency of individual elements, but the resulting goals were aimed at finding, from their point of view, an adequate explanation that turned a contradictory situation into a noncontradictory one" (Krasnoryadtseva, 2012, p. 46). As a result, with an average gain of +35 conventional units, the deviation was from −100 conventional units up to +130 conventional units.

Children with ADHD after 10 trials noted: "I have no scheme," "I try to see through the card," "I need to sort everything out," "Just take," etc. After 20 trials, at the moment when children without ADHD have already created a strategy, school-age children with a diagnosis of ADHD commented: "While at random, well, in 'C' now got a minus, probably I will not take more there," "Just take," "And what patterns can be here?". After 30 trials, the children's answers were different—some continued to act impulsively at random, without thinking about a strategy, while others looked partially for a strategy: "In 'B' risky, it seems," "In 'B' a lot of winning is given." The results after 40 trials in ADHD children were as follows: with an average result of −82 conventional units, the deviation was from −230 conventional units up to +35 conventional units. The quantitative results of the task can be seen in Fig. 2.

Brown (2005) describes many adults with ADHD as having money problems. They may be shopaholics (from small purchases to large and expensive ones). At the same time, as a rule, they do not take into account that part of the money from their income is already taken as expenses for monthly payment for the apartment or a car. An acute problem arises with plastic credit cards. People are surprised at the amounts spent because they perceive each purchase as separate, not considering their relationship with the accumulated debt on the credit card. This study fully confirms the facts described by Brown. Comparatively, children with learning difficulties, but without an ADHD diagnosis, have a positive final balance. As for ADHD school-age children, their average result was reduced to a noticeable minus (that is, at the end of the task they were in considerable debt).

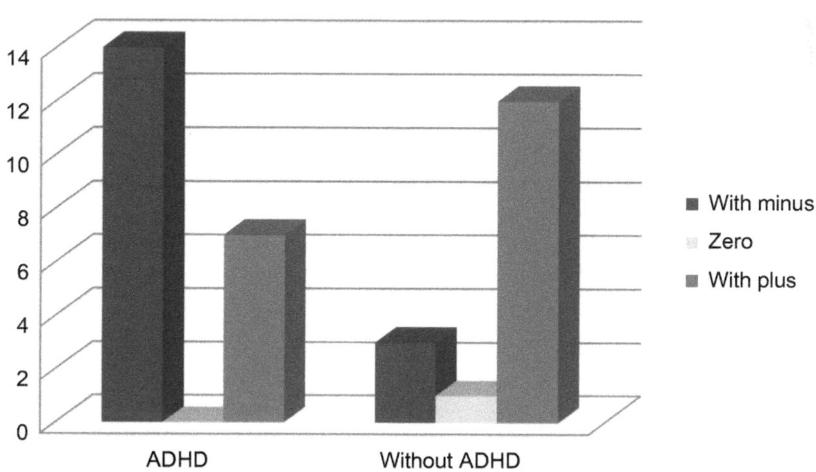

FIG. 2 Results of "Risk and benefits" test (number of children).

In summary, impairment in the planning component of executive functions and in the ability to make an effective decision, especially when the decision has to be made in emotionally charged conditions, were significant in ADHD children. The psychometric methods used in this study revealed significant differences in the number of errors on the Stroop test, which aimed to evaluate the stability of the regulation of activity in interference conditions. Among children with learning difficulties but without ADHD, a lower average number of errors (r)=1.2 was found, in contrast to the ADHD group (r=3.6). Thus, in the table consisting of 75 graphs, ADHD children often did not call the number of digits (for example, 4) in the square, but rather the digit to be counted (for example, 3, because these 4 digits represent "threes"). They often did not notice their mistakes, unlike their peers without ADHD, who usually self-corrected their rare wrong answers. The average execution time was also registered on the table. In ADHD children it was 2 min 25 s while in children without ADHD it was 1 min 55 s on average. Recent complementary data have allowed a comparison of neurodynamic parameters in the two groups of children. Thus, current research supports the notion of low resistance of brain activity and attention to interference in ADHD children. In the present study, the tests performed under interference conditions, such as the Stroop test, caused special difficulties for ADHD children. In these conditions, the number of errors increases impulsiveness, a finding that correlates with the data of other authors (Barkley, 1997; Pennington & Ozonoff, 1996).

In the Hayling Test, significant differences were revealed in the final score. For children without ADHD, the average score was 1.8 while for ADHD school-age children it was 3.7. This test evaluated the inhibition of involuntary response, and found a lower capacity for inhibition in the ADHD children compared to their school-age peers with learning difficulties alone.

This test revealed significant differences in the types of errors: instead of completing a sentence with a word that does not fit the sentence at all, the ADHD children ended it with either a semantically associated or a correct missing word. For example, the phrase "Tricycle is a Bicycle with three…" the child ends with the word "wheels," which is completely contrary to the instruction (three penalty points). Or, another example, the sentence "In autumn there is a fall of…" the child ends with the word "flowers," and this answer is associated with the meaning of the missing word (one penalty point). In the first case, the child did not inhibit his/her immediate reaction. In the second example, the child attempted to follow the instruction, but could not implement the full program. Note that in school-age children without ADHD, the average score for this type of error was 1.6 while in their ADHD peers it was 3.1.

Conclusion

The quantitative methods of ADHD assessment espoused by Reitan and his colleagues, but nontraditional for Russian neuropsychologists, made it possible to clarify the structure of defects in regulation and control in this group of children and to include these defects in the phased planning of their activities. Low resistance to interference and difficulties in decision-making in a situation of uncertainty in ADHD children were also found.

At the same time, Luria's methods allowed not only to qualitatively characterize the structure of the attention deficit/hyperactivity disorder, but also to reveal its biological and social mechanisms and to develop effective approaches for prevention and remediation.

A better understanding of the structure of this disorder also allowed the creation of effective, individualized programs of neuropsychological interventions, thus demonstrating the importance of utilizing an integrated qualitative and quantitative approach to the evaluation of ADHD.

References

Agris, A. R. (2015). *Deficiency of neurodynamic components of activity in children with learning problems* [PhD dissertation]. Moscow State University [in Russian].

Ahutina, T. V., Matveeva, E. Y., & Romanova, A. A. (2012). Application of Luria's principle of syndrome analysis in the processing of neuropsychological examination data of children with developmental disabilities. *Bulletin of Moscow University, 2*, 84–95 [in Russian].

American Psychiatric Association. (2013). *Diagnostic and statistical manual of mental disorders* (5th ed.). Arlington, VA: American Psychiatric Publishing.

Barkley, R. A. (1997). *ADHD and the nature of self-control*. NY: Guildford.

Bechara, A. (2007). *Iowa Gambling Task professional manual*. Lutz: Psychological Assessment Resources, Inc.

Bechara, A., Damasio, A. R., Damasio, H., & Anderson, S. (1994). Insensitivity to future consequences following damage to human prefrontal cortex. *Cognition, 50*(1–3), 7–12.

Bechara, A., Damasio, H., Damasio, A. R., & Lee, G. P. (1999). Different contributions of the human amygdala and ventromedial prefrontal cortex to decision-making. *Journal of Neuroscience, 19*, 5473–5481.

Bechara, A., Damasio, H., Tranel, D., & Anderson, S. W. (1998). Dissociation of working memory from decision making within the human prefrontal cortex. *Journal of Neuroscience, 18*, 428–437.

Bechara, A., Damasio, H., Tranel, D., & Damasio, A. R. (1997). Deciding advantageously before knowing the advantageous strategy. *Science, 275*, 1293–1295.

Bechara, A., Tranel, D., & Damasio, H. (2000). Characterization of the decision-making deficit of patients with ventromedial prefrontal cortex lesions. *Brain, 123*(11), 2189–2202.

Breggin, P. R. (2011). A.D.H.D. is a misdiagnosis. *The New York Times*, [Electronic resource]. http://www.nytimes.com/roomfordebate/2011/10/12. (Accessed October 12, 2014).

Brown, T. E. (2005). *Attention deficit disorder: The unfocused mind in children and adults*. Yale: Yale University Press.

Burgess, P., & Shallice, T. (1997). *The Hayling and Brixton tests*. Pearson: Thurston Suffolk.

Carte, E., Nigg, J., & Hinshaw, S. P. (1996). Neuropsychological functioning: Motor speed and language processing in boys with and without ADHD. *Journal of Abnormal Child Psychology, 24*, 481–498.

Catalá-López, F., Peiró, S., Ridao, M., Sanfélix-Gimeno, G., Gènova-Maleras, R., & Catalá, M. A. (2012). Prevalence of attention deficit/hyperactivity disorder among children and adolescents in Spain: A systematic review and meta-analysis of epidemiological studies. *BMC Psychiatry, 12*, 168.

Conners, C. K. (1997). *Conners' rating scales revised: Technical manual*. North Tonawanda, NY: Multi-Health Systems.

Damasio, A. (1994). *Descartes' error: Emotion, reason, and the human brain* (p. 1994). New York: Grosset/Putnam.

Damasio, A., Tranel, D., & Damasio, H. (1991). Somatic markers and the guidance of behavior: Theory and preliminary testing. In H. S. Levin, H. M. Eisenberg, & A. L. Benton (Eds.), *Frontal lobe function and dysfunction* (pp. 217–229). New York: Oxford University Press.

Denckla, M. B., & Rudel, R. (1978). Anomalies of motor development in hyperactive boys. *Annual Neurology*, *8*, 231–233.

Eslinger, P., & Damasio, A. (1985). Severe disturbance of higher cognition after bilateral frontal lobe ablation: Patient EVR. *Neurology*, *35*, 1731–1741.

Funke, J., & Krüger, T. (1993). *"Plan-A-Day" (PAD)*. Bonn: Psychologisches Institut der Universität Bonn [in German].

Glozman, J.M. (2012). *Neuropsychological assessment: Qualitative and quantitative evaluation of data*. Moscow: Smysl Publishing House [in Russian].

Glozman, J.M. (2017). *Neuropsychology of childhood: A textbook for undergraduate academic* (2th ed.). Moscow: Yurait [in Russian].

Glozman, J. M., Potanina, A. Y., & Soboleva, A. E. (2008). *Neuropsychological evaluation in preschool age*. Saint Petersburg: Peter [in Russian].

Glozman, J.M., Ravich-Scherbo, I. V., & Grishina, T. V. (2007). Neurodynamic factors of individual differences in school success. In V. A. Moskvin (Ed.), *Neuropsychology and psychophysiology of individual differences* (pp. 103–113). Moscow/Belgorod: POLITERRA [in Russian].

Glozman, J. M., & Soboleva, A. E. (2013). *Neuropsychological assessment of school-children*. Moscow: Smysl Publishing House [in Russian].

Goryacheva, T. G., & Sultanova, A. S. (2005). *Neuropsychological features of mental development of children with hyperactivity disorder*. In *Vol. 3(2). Proceedings of the Russian scientific-practical conference "V. M. Bekhterev and modern psychology", Kazan* (pp. 91–100) [in Russian].

Holt, D. V., Rodewald, K., Rentrop, M., Funke, J., Weisbrod, M., & Kaiser, S. (2011). The Plan-a-Day approach to measuring planning ability in patients with schizophrenia. *Journal of the International Neuropsychological Society*, *17*, 1–9.

Hom, J., & Nici, J. (2015). Ralph M. Reitan: The Pioneer of Clinical Neuropsychology. *Archives of Clinical Neuropsychology*, *30*, 724–732.

Homskaya, E.D. (2005). *Neuropsychology* (4th ed.). Saint Petersburg: Peter [in Russian].

Huss, M., Hölling, H., Kurth, B.-M., & Schlack, R. (2008). How often are German children and adolescents diagnosed with ADHD? Prevalence based on the judgment of health care professionals: Results of the German Health and Assessment Survey (KiGGS). *European Child & Adolescent Psychiatry*, *17*, 52–58.

IACAPAP. (2004). *Abstracts of the 16th world congress of the International Association for Child and Adolescent Psychiatry and Allied Professions (IACAPAP)*. Berlin, Germany: Steinkopff Darmstadt.

Korsakova, N. K. (2014). Neuropsychology of attention and the Stroop task. *Bulletin of Moscow University*, *3*, 26–33 [in Russian].

Krasnoryadtseva, O. M. (2012). Features of "sensitivity to problems" in children of primary school age as a manifestation of self-regulation of mental activity. *Theoretical and Experimental Psychology*, *5*(3), 42–47 [in Russian].

Lin, C. H., Song, T. J., Chen, Y. Y., Lee, W. K., & Chiu, Y. C. (2013). Reexamining the validity and reliability of the clinical version of the Iowa Gambling Task: Evidence from a normal subject group. *Frontiers in Psychology*, *4*, 220.

Luria, A.R. (1969). *Higher cortical functions in man and their disturbances after local brain lesions* (2nd ed.). Moscow: Moscow University Press [in Russian].

Murphy, J. M., McCarthy, A. E., Baer, L., Zima, B. T., & Jellinek, M. S. (2014). Alternative national guidelines for treating attention and depression problems in children: Comparison of treatment approaches and prescribing rates in the United Kingdom and United States. *Harvard Review of Psychiatry*, *22*(3), 179–192.

Osipova, E. A., & Pankratova, N. V. (1997). Dynamics of neuropsychological state in children with different types of attention deficit/hyperactivity disorder. *School of attention,* 4 (pp. 31–43). [in Russian].

Overman, W. H., & Pierce, A. (2014). Iowa Gambling Task with non-clinical participants: Effects of using real + virtual cards and additional trials. *Frontiers in Psychology*, *4*, 935.

Passolt, M. (Ed.), (2004). *Hyperactive children: Correction of psychomotor development: Textbook for students of higher school.* (2nd ed.). Moscow: Academy [in Russian].

Pennington, B. F., & Ozonoff, S. (1996). Executive functions and developmental psychopathology. *Journal of Child Psychology and Psychiatry*, *37*(1), 51–87.

Porter, E., & Cirino, E. (2016). Conners scale for assessing ADHD. *Healthline*, [Electronic resource]. http://www.healthline.com/health/adhd/conners-scale#1. (Accessed April 19, 2016).

Reitan, R. M. (1962). Problems in evaluating the psychological effects of brain lesions. *APA Division 22 Newsletter*, [Special supplement].

Reitan, R. M. (1974). Psychological effects of cerebral lesions in children of primary school. In R. M. Reitan & L. A. Davison (Eds.), *Clinical neuropsychology: Current status and applications* (pp. 53–90). Washington, DC: Hemisphere.

Rodrigo, M. J., Padrón, I., de Vega, M., & Ferstl, E. C. (2014). Adolescents' risky decision-making activates neural networks related to social cognition and cognitive control processes. *Frontiers in Human Neuroscience*, *8*, 60.

Sallum, I., Mata, F., Miranda, D. M., & Malloy-Diniz, L. F. (2013). Staying and shifting patterns across IGT trials distinguish children with externalizing disorders from controls. *Frontiers in Psychology*, *4*, 899.

Shallice, T., Marzocchi, G. M., Coser, S., Del Savio, M., Meuter, R. F., & Rumiati, R. I. (2002). Executive function profile of children with attention deficit hyperactivity disorder. *Developmental Neuropsychology*, *21*(1), 43–71.

Shan, H. (2007). ADHD affects over 15 million Chinese children. *Chinaorgcn*, [Electronic resource]. http://www.china.org.cn/english/China/219830.htm. (Accessed September 29, 2015).

Singh, V. (2014). A potential role of reward and punishment in the facilitation of the emotion-cognition dichotomy in the Iowa Gambling Task. *Frontiers in Psychology*, *4*, 944.

Spiegel, T., & Pollak, Y. (2019). Attention deficit/hyperactivity disorder and increased engagement in sexual risk-taking behavior: The role of benefit perception. *Frontiers in Psychology*, *10*, 1043. https://doi.org/10.3389/fpsyg.2019.01043.

Steger, J., Imhof, K., Coutts, E., Gundelfinger, R., Steinhausen, H. C., & Brandeis, D. (2001). Attentional and neuromotor deficits in ADHD. *Developmental Medicine & Child Neurology*, *43*, 172–179.

Stroop, J. R. (1935). Studies of interference in serial verbal reactions. *Journal of Experimental Psychology*, *18*, 643–662.

Van den Bos, R., Koot, S., & de Visser, L. (2014). A rodent version of the Iowa Gambling Task: 7 years of progress. *Frontiers in Psychology*, *5*, 203.

Further reading

Luria, A. R. (Ed.), (1973). *Outlines of the neuropsychological assessment*. Moscow: Moscow University Press [in Russian].

Chapter 5

Ralph M. Reitan and the clinical interpretation of neuropsychological test data

Arthur MacNeill Horton Jr.
Neuropsychology Section, Psych Associates of Maryland, Bethesda, MD, United States

Portions of this chapter were drawn from chapter 7 in Horton and Wedding's (1984) *Clinical and Behavioral Neuropsychology* and the Halstead Reitan Chapters in the first, second and third editions of the *Neuropsychology Handbook*.

Introduction

Ralph M. Reitan was credited with developing a standardized neuropsychological battery approach, in which the same set of neuropsychological tests was given to child and adult patients. This approach allows for a comprehensive assessment of a wide variety of brain-related behaviors and provides a consistent information base for research purposes from which validated data interpretations may emerge (Horton & Wedding, 1984).

The Halstead-Reitan Neuropsychological Test Batteries for children and adults were developed from research studies by Ward Halstead and his doctoral student Ralph M. Reitan (Halstead, 1947; Horton & Wedding, 1984; Reitan, 1964, 1974a, 1994; Reitan & Wolfson, 1985). The adult battery was based on experimental psychology procedures first used by Halstead to investigate the human abilities that were compromised by brain injury (Horton & Wedding, 1984). Halstead conceptualized the concept of *biological intelligence*, which was defined as the adaptive capacity of the brain dependent upon its organic integrity and related to frontal lobe functioning (Halstead, 1947). Many neurosurgical patients who had documented brain injuries were assessed and the test results were factor analyzed, suggesting a four-factor model of neuropsychological abilities. The factors were a central integrative field factor, an abstraction factor, a power factor, and a directional factor (Halstead, 1947). Ralph M. Reitan was a doctoral student with Halstead and, rather than studying the concept of biological intelligence, he modified and augmented the Halstead-Reitan

Evaluation and Treatment of Neuropsychologically Compromised Children
https://doi.org/10.1016/B978-0-12-819545-1.00005-9

Neuropsychology Test Battery (HRNB) for the purpose of better assessing children and adults with brain injuries (Horton & Wedding, 1984; Reitan, 1974b; Reitan & Wolfson, 1993). Reitan added measures of intelligence, measures of aphasia, constructional dyspraxia, sensory-perceptual functioning, and motor functioning (Horton & Wedding, 1984).

Research status

The HRNB was and is recognized as the premier neuropsychological test battery in neurological, neurosurgical, rehabilitation, and psychiatric settings (Hartlage & Telzrow, 1980; Seretny, Dean, Gray, & Hartlage, 1986). This was due to the extensive body of research conducted by Ralph M. Reitan, PhD, and a variety of investigators demonstrating the validity of this battery for assessing brain-damaged patients (Reitan, 1994; Reitan & Wolfson, 1986). As was noted by Reitan and Wolfson (1986):

> *The Halstead-Reitan Battery has probably been researched in more detail than any other set of neuropsychological tests. Through the close cooperation between neuropsychologists, neurologists, neurological surgeons, and neuropathologists it has been possible to compose groups of subjects with definite, unequivocal evidence of cerebral damage and compare these persons with subjects who have no history or present evidence of cerebral damage or disease. This approach has a tremendous advantage over research oriented toward development of constructs such as intelligence, affective disorders, emotional maturity, and so forth. In attempting to validate psychological measures against such constructs, there has been the continual criterion problem of not having an unequivocal definition of the condition being evaluated. In neuropsychology, however, it has been possible not only to identify the presence or absence of cerebral damage but also to provide more detailed information regarding localization type, duration, and acuteness or chronicity of lesion. (p. 140)*

The research approach used by Reitan and his coworkers was to compare control subjects to persons known to have different types of brain lesions in various locations and to identify the tests that were most sensitive to the general condition of the brain. The validity of the HRNB was documented in an extensive number of research studies (Boll, Heaton, & Reitan, 1974; Wheeler, Burke, & Reitan, 1963; Wheeler & Reitan, 1962, 1963).

The HRNB was primarily developed to be sensitive to neurological, as opposed to behavioral, variables such as age and education (Reitan & Wolfson, 1986). The crucial concern was the biological condition of the human brain. Reitan used empirical methods to determine if specific neuropsychological tests were "brain-related." As noted by Reitan and Wolfson (1986):

> *We have found that the best way to answer this question has been to examine carefully an individual's neuropsychological test data and, from that information, predict the neurological status. To implement this procedure data were collected on*

> *thousands of patients using a three-step process: (1) administering a comprehensive battery of neuropsychological tests to the patient without knowing any of the patient's neurological findings; (2) making a written prediction of the patient's neurological status based solely on his or her neuropsychological test results; and (3) comparing the neurological diagnosis with the neuropsychological test results.*
>
> *Using this procedure, we have learned that certain variables contribute little to neurological conclusions (even though they may serve as comparison variables in certain respects), whereas other combinations of test results are of unequivocal significance. This procedure has permitted us to gradually refine clinical interpretation of results on individual subjects to a high degree of accuracy, as will be illustrated later.*
>
> *Certain neuropsychological test data are particularly helpful in determining whether brain damage is present; other test results are especially useful for lateralizing and localizing cerebral damage; certain patterns of results relate to generalized or diffuse cerebral damage; other test results, particularly as they reflect the entire configuration of data, are used to differentiate the chronic, static lesion from the recent acutely destructive or rapidly progressive lesion; and still different findings aid the interpreter in deciding whether the cerebral damage was sustained during the developmental years or adulthood.*
>
> *One can readily see that in addition to formal, controlled research studies (the type usually published in the literature) there are challenging tasks that involve development of valid clinical interpretation of results for individual subjects. Achieving this aim required the development of a test battery that represented at least a reasonable approximation of the behavioral correlates of brain function. (p. 136)*

The HRNB research was the basis for the development of a theoretical-conceptual model of brain-behavior relationships (Reitan & Wolfson, 1986). As noted by Reitan and Wolfson (1986):

> *The battery consists of tests in five categories: (1) input measures; (2) tests of verbal abilities; (3) measures of spatial, sequential, and manipulatory abilities; (tests of abstraction, reasoning, logical analysis, and concept formation; and (5) output measures. The tests cover a broad range of difficulty: both very simple and quite complex tasks are included. Attention, concentration, and memory are distributed throughout the tests in the battery, just as they appear to occur in the tasks that people face in everyday living. Many of the tests require immediate problem-solving capabilities, others depend on stored information, and some require simple perceptual skills that focus principally upon the sensory modalities of vision, hearing, and touch. (pp. 136–137)*

Methodological contributions

Ralph M. Reitan's most important methodological contribution was the recognition of the need to use multiple methods of inference (Horton & Wedding, 1984).

Reitan proposed four methods of inference: (1) level of performance, (2) patterns of performance, (3) pathognomonic signs, and (4) right-left comparisons for evaluating neuropsychological test data. As described by Reitan and Wolfson (1986):

> *First, it is necessary to determine how well the subject performs on each of the measures included in the battery. This approach essentially refers to level of performance and, on most of the measures, is represented by a normal distribution for non-brain-damaged subjects. Since some persons perform quite well and others perform more poorly, it clearly would not be possible to accept a level-of-performance strategy alone as a basis for diagnosing cerebral damage. In other words, there are some persons who demonstrate above-average ability levels in spite of having sustained cerebral damage and some persons with below-average ability levels who do not have cerebral damage. A level-of-performance approach represents an interindividual inferential model. It is useful for comparing subjects, but offers relatively little direct information regarding the brain functions of the individual subject. (As the reader has probably noted, this is the model used in most research studies.)*
>
> *A second approach, introduced by Babcock (1930), postulated that differences in levels of performance on various tests might denote impaired brain functions, or at least a loss of efficiency in psychological performances. This approach has also been used to compute the Deterioration Quotient, based on comparison of scores from different subtests of the Wechsler Scale (Wechsler, 1955). This method represents an intraindividual comparison procedure (a comparison of the subject's own performances on various tests) and helps identify the uniqueness of an individual's ability structure. Research with the tests included in the Halstead-Reitan Battery has produced a number of intraindividual patterns that are quite useful for assessing differential functions of the brain and identifying impaired areas within the brain.*
>
> *A third approach incorporated into the Halstead-Reitan Battery is the identification of specific deficits on simple tasks of the type that occur almost exclusively among brain-damaged persons. Deficits on these simple tasks may not only identify the presence of cerebral damage but also indicate areas of maximal involvement (Wheeler & Reitan, 1962). The reader should be aware, however, that this inferential strategy fails to identify a significant proportion of brain-damaged persons who do not show the specific deficit in question (false negatives).*
>
> *The fourth measurement strategy used in the Halstead-Reitan Battery to identify cerebral damage is one which compares motor and sensory-perceptual performances of the same type on the two sides of the body, thus permitting inferences regarding the functional status of homologous areas of the two cerebral hemispheres. This method is also based on intraindividual comparisons, using the subject as his or her control. When positive findings occur they may have unequivocal significance for cerebral damage. (Reitan & Wolfson, 1986, pp. 138–139)*

Test battery components

The names of the batteries for adults (15 years and older), older children (ages 9–14), and younger children (ages 5–8) require some clarification. The adult battery was based on the Halstead battery that was originally 10 tests but reduced to seven tests and augmented by a number of other tests based on the work of Reitan. Initially, the adult battery was known as Halstead's Neuropsychological Battery for Adults (Reitan & Davidson, 1974). Over the years, however, because of Reitan's major contribution, the battery is now most often referred to as the Halstead-Reitan Neuropsychological Test Battery for Adults (HRNB) (Reitan & Wolfson, 1985).

Originally, the battery for older children (ages 9–14) was named the Halstead Neuropsychological Battery for Children (Reitan & Davidson, 1974), but now the older children battery is most often referred to as the Halstead-Reitan Neuropsychological Test Battery for Older Children (HRNB-OC) (Reitan & Davidson, 1974) because of Reitan's modifications and augmentation. For the younger children's (ages 5–8) battery, the original name was the Reitan-Indiana Neuropsychological Test Battery for Children (RINB), as Halstead had no role in developing most of the tests and the major development occurred while Reitan was at the Indiana University School of Medicine.

The major tests most commonly used in the Halstead-Reitan Neuropsychological Test Batteries for children and adults are described below.

The Category Test

The Category Test measures the patient's ability to learn general abstract principles from sets of stimulus items (Horton & Wedding, 1984). The patient responds to each stimulus by selecting a number from one to four to represent the principle that is used in a particular subtest. Feedback is given regarding the correctness of the response. A single response is permitted for each stimulus presentation. The Category Test is believed by many to be the HRNB subtest most sensitive to brain damage in adults (Reitan & Wolfson, 1993).

Tactual Performance Test

The Tactual Performance Test (TPT) uses a form board slanted at a 45-degree angle that has geometric spaces. The test requires a blindfolded patient to place geometric blocks into matching geometric spaces on the form board where the blocks fit. The test is performed first with the dominant hand, next with the nondominant hand, and last with both hands. After the last trial on the TPT, the form board is taken away and the patient is requested to draw the geometric shapes that were on the form board and to place as many blocks as can be remembered in their correct location. Memory and localization scores of this test are conceptualized to be measures of incidental spatial learning (Horton & Wedding, 1984).

The TPT assesses integration of tactile and kinesthetic feedback, psychomotor skills, and spatial memory. In addition, disparities between the performance of the left and right hands are evidence for lateralization of cerebral damage. The nondominant hand, in a normal individual, should be about one-third faster than the dominant hand, and both hands are one-third faster than the nondominant hand. If either hand or both hands are slower than expected, the integrity of the contralateral hemisphere can be questioned if peripheral damage (e.g., broken wrist, carpel tunnel syndrome) can be ruled out (Horton & Wedding, 1984).

Speech Sounds Perception Test

The Speech Sounds Perception Test requires that the patient attend to tape-recorded stimulus words that are variations of an "ee" sound and requires the ability to sustain attention, perceive speech sounds, and read words (Horton & Wedding, 1984). The task is to match the auditory stimuli item with the correct printed word made up by the sound. The patient is to select (by circling) the correct printed version from four alternatives (three alternatives for older children) (Horton & Wedding, 1984).

Rhythm Test

The Rhythm Test measures auditory memory, rhythmic discrimination, and attention ability (Reitan & Wolfson, 1993). Thirty pairs of rhythms are presented via a sound recording. The patient evaluates each pair as either the same or different by writing "S" or "D" on a test form (Horton & Wedding, 1984).

Trail Making Test

The Trail Making Test for adults and older children consists of two parts labeled "A" and "B." It requires visual tracking, simple and complex set-shifting, and sequencing ability (Horton & Wedding, 1984). Trail A consists of numbered circles that the patient connects by drawing a line to each circle of a higher number. Trail B consists of circles with series of numbers and letters printed within the circles on the same page. The patient is required to draw a line that alternately connects numbers and letters (i.e., 1-A-2-B-3-C...) (Horton & Wedding, 1984) as quickly as possible. The scores are the amounts of time required to complete each page (Horton & Wedding, 1984).

Finger Tapping Test

The Finger Tapping Test is a measure of gross motor speed (Horton & Wedding, 1984). The patient taps, with the index finger of each hand, a key counter that is mounted on a board for multiple trials for adults and older children. For younger children, there is an electronic finger tapper apparatus. The ideal result is five consecutive trials of 10 s with a range of no more than five taps. Performance with the dominant hand is expected to be better than the performance with the nondominant hand by a preset amount. Interpretations regarding lateralization of brain damage require that there are no peripheral injuries. Comparison of hand speed performances on the Finger Tapping Test is helpful for localization of brain injuries (Horton & Wedding, 1984).

Reitan-Indiana Aphasia Screening Test

The Reitan-Indiana Aphasia Screening Test assesses symbolic language-related deficits such as difficulty reading, writing, naming, spelling, performing arithmetic, and repeating words and phrases (Reitan & Wolfson, 1993). The patient also performs nonlanguage tasks such as drawing quasigeometric figures (square, Greek cross and triangle) and left-right confusion tasks (Horton & Wedding, 1984), which are sensitive to lateralized brain damage (Wheeler & Reitan, 1962).

Reitan-Klove Sensory-Perceptual Examination

The Reitan-Klove Sensory-Perceptual Examination is a standardization of a behavioral neurological examination, which assesses visual, auditory, and tactual sensory abilities as well as an examination of tactual perceptual functioning (Reitan & Wolfson, 1993). The purpose is to assess sensory-perceptual functioning for visual, auditory, and tactual stimuli on either side of the body.

Reitan-Klove Lateral Dominance Examination

The Lateral Dominance Examination assesses preferences for use of hand, foot, and eye, as determined by brief motor requests. Lateral dominance is important in interpreting tests that compare the two sides of the body.

Strength of Grip

Gross motor strength for both hands is assessed by two alternating trials with a hand dynamometer and is important in comparing motor abilities of the two sides of the body.

Additional tests for the HRNB

The Halstead-Reitan Neuropsychological Test Batteries also have included measures of intelligence, academic achievement, emotional functioning, memory, or executive functioning. A misunderstanding is that Reitan was inflexible regarding test selection. He did think that it was best to have a comprehensive neuropsychological evaluation and his battery had the most extensive research support. At the same time, Reitan had no problem with the addition of other neuropsychological tests to assess specific abilities, such as memory, or to limit the number of tests when an individual was severely impaired.

Children's versions

As noted earlier, the HRNB was first developed with research on adults. At that time in the 1940s, it was clear that intelligence tests were inadequate to fully assess adults with known brain injuries. The limitations of intelligence tests were a major reason Halstead first attempted to develop a test battery that would be sensitive to brain integrity. As earlier mentioned, Reitan saw the potential of adapting Halstead's tests to clinical purposes so that the treatment of brain-injured patients could be improved. Reitan wished also to assess brain damage in children as he saw the potential to improve the care of brain-injured children. In order to do this, Reitan modified the HRNB for testing children (Reitan & Wolfson, 1992a, 1992b). The adult version of the HRNB was found to be appropriate for assessing brain-behavior relationships in adolescents down to age 15 (Reitan & Wolfson, 1993) but below age 15, modifications of test materials were needed.

Older children (ages 9–14) needed the Category Test, the Trail Making Test, and the Tactual Performance Test to be shortened, and choices on the Speech Sounds Perception Test were reduced to three (Reitan & Wolfson, 1992b). Younger children (ages 5–8) required more extensive changes to test material and procedures. As mentioned earlier, because of small hands, an electric finger tapper was used. Also, the Trail Making Test was modified by using figures within figures to guide set-shifting and renamed the Progressive Figures Test. In addition, the Category Test and Tactual Performance Test and the Reitan-Klove Sensory-Perceptual Examination were further simplified to make them more appropriate for younger children (ages 5–8) (Reitan, 1974a, 1974b; Reitan & Wolfson, 1992a).

General Neuropsychological Deficit Scale (GNDS)

Reitan and Wolfson (1988) devised a summary index of overall brain damage, the General Neuropsychological Deficit Scale (GNDS). The GNDS utilizes 42 separate test variables from the Halstead-Reitan Neuropsychological Test Battery that are arranged according to Reitan's methodological methods of inferences (Horton & Wedding, 1984; Reitan, 1974a). As noted earlier, these are the patient's level of performance, specific deficits/pathognomonic signs, patterns of performance, and comparisons of the two sides of the patient's body on motor and sensory-perceptual measures. Each GNDS test score is put on a weighted 4-point scale with 0 indicating above-average performance, 1 indicating average performance, 2 indicating mild brain damage, and 3 indicating moderate to severe brain damage. The GNDS was validated by studies (Reitan & Wolfson, 1988; Sherer & Adams, 1993) as well as a cross-validation by Reitan and Wolfson (1995).

Horton and Sobelman (1994) also examined how the severity of brain damage is evaluated by the GNDS relative to the Halstead Impairment Index (HII), an earlier overall measure of brain impairment devised by Halstead. The Pearson correlation between the two scales was statistically significant, 0.43 ($P < .02$) confirming the significant relationship between the two summary indexes. Pearson product-moment correlations for age on the GNDS and the HII were for the GNDS 0.382 ($P < .06$) and not statistically significant for the HII, 0.177 ($P = .40$). Pearson correlations for education on both scales were nonsignificant, GNDS −0.186 ($P = .374$), and HII −0.191 ($P = .362$).

Reitan and Wolfson (1992b) later developed a Neuropsychological Deficit Scale for Older Children (GNDS-OC). The GNDS-OC measure has a similar format to the adult GNDS. The GNDS-OC includes 45 test scores from the Halstead-Reitan Neuropsychological Test Battery for Older Children (ages 9–14) (Reed, Reitan, & Klove, 1965). There is, however, not a GNDS for younger children (ages 5–8).

Alternative Impairment Index

The Alternative Impairment Index (AII; Horton, 1995a) is a measure of neuropsychological impairment that is composed of selected scores from a number of tests of the HRNB (Halstead, 1947; Reitan & Wolfson, 1992a, 1992b) including the Category Test, the Rhythm Test, the Speech Sounds Perception Test, the Finger Tapping Test for both dominant and nondominant hands, and the Trail Making Test, both parts A and B. The new index was developed to assess the severity of brain damage when time and resource constraints prevent the entire Halstead-Reitan Neuropsychological Test Battery from being given. Horton (1995a) examined how the AII compared relative to the GNDS and the HII and found that the AII hit rates were 60% with the HII and 64% with the GNDS. A later cross-validation of the initial results (Horton, 1995b) found a hit rate of the AII and the HII of 66%. Horton (1997) evaluated a modified AII, which used a set of weighted scores, the Alternative Impairment Index-Revised (AII-R). Agreement hit rates for level of severity for the HII and AII-R were 60% (i.e., 15/25), and for the GNDS and AII-R were 72% (i.e., 18/25). Horton (1995a) found similar results for the AII-R/HII (60%) versus the AII/HII comparison (60%) and better results for the AII-R/GNDS (72%) versus the AII/GNDS (64%) comparison.

Children's version of the AII

Given promising results with the AII and AII-R, a children's version of the AII was developed. An initial study of Alternative Impairment Index-Children's Version (AII-CV; Horton, 1995c) found poor prediction (56% correct prediction). Development of the Revised Children's Version of the Alternative Impairment Index (AII-CV-R; Horton, 1996) modified the AII-CV to use the sum of selected weighted scores divided by the number of test measures contributing to the sum of weighted scores, but the hit rate for severity of the AII-CV-R with the GNDS-OC (Reitan & Wolfson, 1992b) was in poor agreement (i.e., 50%, or 8/16 correct agreement).

The sensitivity of subtests from an earlier version of the Wechsler Scales to brain damage has been shown to be superior to those from subtests of the

Halstead-Reitan Neuropsychological Test Battery (Reed et al., 1965; Reitan, 1974b) for older children and children of early school age. Horton (1998) demonstrated that a short form screening index based on performance subtests from the Wechsler Intelligence Scale for Children-Revised (WISC-R) significantly predicted the severity of brain damage on the GNDS-OC (hit rate 75%, or 15/20 correct agreement). A later study using WISC-R subtests found that a subtest measuring processing speed was able to substantially predict the severity of brain damage (70%) on the GNDS-OC (Horton, 1999b).

Clinical interpretation of the HRNB

Reitan devised a multistep method for interpreting the test data from the Halstead Reitan Neuropsychological Test Battery (Reitan & Wolfson, 1986). The first step requires consideration of the patient's premorbid level of functioning. The particular measures Reitan found most useful were intelligence subtests of information, comprehension, similarities, and vocabulary (Reitan & Wolfson, 1986). As noted by Reitan and Wolfson (1986):

> *If these subtest scores are low, one cannot use them as a contrast for poor scores on neuropsychological (brain-sensitive) tests. If these scores are relatively good, one can presume that circumstances in the past have been adequate to permit development of these abilities; poorer scores on tests that are more specifically sensitive to the biological condition of the brain may be subject to interpretation as evidence of impairment. The Wechsler subtests may be used for more specific aspects of interpretation as well but only after reviewing the results obtained with the remaining tests of the Halstead-Reitan Battery. (p. 142)*

The next step in interpretation was to consider the results on the most sensitive measures of the Halstead-Reitan Neuropsychological Test Battery. With the development of the GNDS, Reitan added that measure as a general indicator of brain integrity and considered it along with other particularly sensitive single measures of brain damage. As noted by Reitan and Wolfson (1986):

> *If these tests were performed poorly and the Wechsler scores suggest that the person had developed relatively normal abilities in the past, a presumption may be made that the person has suffered some neuropsychological deficit resulting from brain damage; inferences of severity may also be drawn. However, each of these four measures is a general indicator and does not have significance for localization of cerebral damage, even though focal lesion (regardless of localization) and generalized or diffuse damage may have pronounced effects on general indicators. (p. 142)*

The next step in interpretation of the Halstead-Reitan Neuropsychological Test Battery was to consider indicators of lateralization and localization of functions and utilize measures of inference other than level of performance, such as patterns of performance, pathognomic deficits, and comparison of the two sides of the body on motor and sensory-perceptual measures. The most useful indicators were motor and sensory perceptual findings on the Finger Tapping Test, the Tactual Performance Test, the Strength of Grip Test, and the Reitan-Klove Sensory-Perceptual Examination, evidence for language and/or constructional dyspraxia on the Reitan-Indiana Aphasia Screening test, visual field losses, and intelligence test results (Reitan & Wolfson, 1986).

The fourth step in interpretation involved making a prediction of brain injury progression such as progressive, chronic, or recovery from a brain injury. Focal lesions were most commonly associated with a static or chronic course but a progressive course showed severe generalized effects. In predicting degree of recovery (Reitan & Wolfson, 1986), found the Speech-Sounds Perception Test, the Rhythm Test, and the Trail Making Test to be good measures of recovery from a brain injury (Reitan & Wolfson, 1986). Another option for prediction of the course of brain damage was to conduct repeated evaluations over time.

The fifth step was to identify the type of neurological condition present. As noted by Reitan and Wolfson (1986):

> *Skill in this area obviously requires knowledge of neurology and neuropathology, and the neuropsychologist should be familiar with the major categories of neurological disease and damage. (p. 143)*

Drawing psychological inferences from neuropsychological test data is a complex task and involves knowledge based in personality assessment, treatment of psychiatric disorders, and vocational rehabilitation, among other areas of expertise. Supplementation of the HRNB with additional tests such as memory and executive functioning as well as collateral information and school and work records is often wise when faced with this complex task. Clinical neuropsychologists must draw on their clinical experience and consider the ecological validity of neuropsychological assessment (Sbordone & Long, 1996).

Screening for brain damage

When screening a great number of patients is needed and the base rate estimate of brain damage in the sample population is known to be very low, then brief screening procedures would be indicated. For the HRNB, Reitan and Wolfson (2004a, 2004b, 2006) developed methods to screen for brain damage in child samples with predominantly normal brain function. These screening procedures are able to correctly identify brain-damaged children at impressive rates (young children, 88%; older children, 91%), but further research appears warranted.

Factor structure of the HRNB for older and younger children

As noted earlier, Halstead (1947) conducted a factor analysis of his battery. A later study of adults (Fowler, Zillmer, & Newman, 1988) found five factors (verbal comprehension, perceptual organization, sensory-attention, primary-motor, and tactual-spatial abilities). A factor analysis study with older children (Brooks, Dean, & Gray, 1989) found four factors (simple motor, tactile kinesthesis, memory/attention, and nonverbal visual-spatial memory). Another later study with children ages 9–12 (Francis, Fletcher, Rourke, & York, 1992) found a five factor model (simple motor skill, complex visual-spatial relations, simple spatial motor operations, motor steadiness, and speeded motor sequencing). A factor analysis study of the young children's version of the HRNB with children aged 5–7 years (Foxcroft, 1989) revealed six factors (analytic-synthetic visual motor ability, perceptual organization, cross-modality motoric efficiency, directed motor speed patterned critical discrimination, and strength). It is possible that different patient samples of children produced different factors but there does appear to be some consistency. Clearly, there is great need for further confirmation of the factors that underlie the HRNB at ages 9–14 and 5–8.

Conclusion

The HRNB provides the best and most complete American comprehensive assessment available in clinical neuropsychology for the clinical neuropsychological assessment of children.

References

Boll, T. J., Heaton, R. K., & Reitan, R. M. (1974). Neuropsychological and emotional correlates of Huntington's chorea. *Journal of Nervous and Mental Disease*, *158*, 61–69.

Brooks, D. A., Dean, R. S., & Gray, J. W. (1989). HRNB factors with simultaneous-successive marker variables. *International Journal of Neuroscience*, *46*(3–4), 157–160.

Fowler, P. C., Zillmer, E., & Newman, A. C. (1988). A multifactor model of the Halstead-Reitan Neuropsychological Test Battery and its relationship to cognitive status and psychiatric diagnosis. *Journal of Clinical Psychology*, *44*(6), 898–906.

Foxcroft, C. D. (1989). Factor analysis of the Reitan-Indiana Neuropsychological Test Battery. *Perceptual and Motor Skills*, *69*(3 pt. 2), 1303–1313.

Francis, D. J., Fletcher, J. M., Rourke, B. P., & York, M. J. (1992). A five-factor model for the motor, psychomotor and visual-spatial tests used in the neuropsychological assessment of children. *Journal of Clinical and Experimental Neuropsychology*, *14*(4), 625–637.

Halstead, W. C. (1947). *Brain and intelligence: A quantitative study of the frontal lobes*. Chicago: University of Chicago Press.

Hartlage, L. C., & Telzrow, C. F. (1980). The practice of clinical neuropsychology in the U.S. *International Journal of Clinical Neuropsychology*, *2*, 200–202.

Horton, A. M., Jr. (1995a). The alternative impairment index: A measure of neuropsychological deficit. *Perceptual and Motor Skills*, *80*, 336–338.

Horton, A. M., Jr. (1995b). Cross-validation of the alternative impairment index. *Perceptual and Motor Skills*, *81*, 1153–1154.

Horton, A. M., Jr. (1995c). Children's version of the alternative impairment index. *Perceptual and Motor Skills*, *81*, 217–218.

Horton, A. M., Jr. (1996). Revised Children's version of the alternative impairment index. *Applied Neuropsychology*, *3*, 178–180.

Horton, A. M., Jr. (1997). Alternative impairment index-revised: A neuropsychological pilot study. *Applied Neuropsychology*, *4*, 176–179.

Horton, A. M., Jr. (1998). Development of a short-form screening index for severity of brain damage in older children. *Applied Neuropsychology*, *5*, 48–50.

Horton, A. M., Jr. (1999b). Prediction of severity of brain damage by a processing speed variable in older children: A brief report. *International Journal of Neuroscience*, *99*, 233–238.

Horton, A. M., Jr., & Sobelman, S. A. (1994). The general neuropsychological deficit scale and the Halstead impairment index: Comparison of severity. *Perceptual and Motor Skills*, *78*, 888–890.

Horton, A. M., & Wedding, D. (1984). *Clinical and behavioral neuropsychology*. New York: Praeger.

Reed, H. B. C., Reitan, R. M., & Klove, H. (1965). The influence of cerebral lesions on psychological test performance of older children. *Journal of Consulting Psychology*, *29*, 247–251.

Reitan, R. M. (1964). Psychological deficits resulting from cerebral lesions in man. In J. M. Warren & K. A. Akart (Eds.), *The frontal granular cortex and behavior* (pp. 23–34). New York: McGraw-Hill.

Reitan, R. M. (1974a). Methodological problems in clinical neuropsychology. In R. M. Reitan & L. A. Davison (Eds.), *Clinical neuropsychology: Current status and application* (pp. 19–46). New York: Wiley.

Reitan, R. M. (1974b). Psychological effects of cerebral lesions in children of early school age. In R. M. Reitan & L. A. Davison (Eds.), *Clinical neuropsychology: Current status and application* (pp. 53–90). New York: Wiley.

Reitan, R. M. (1994). Ward Halstead's contributions to neuropsychology and the Halstead-Reitan Neuropsychological Test Battery. *Journal of Clinical Psychology*, *50*(1), 47–70.

Reitan, R. M. & Davidson, L. A. (Eds.), (1974). *Clinical neuropsychology: Current status and applications*. New York: Wiley.

Reitan, R. M., & Wolfson, D. (1985). *The Halstead-Reitan Neuropsychological Test Battery: Theory and clinical interpretation*. Tucson, AZ: Neuropsychology Press.

Reitan, R. M., & Wolfson, D. (1986). The Halstead-Reitan Neuropsychology Test Battery. In D. Wedding, Horton, A. M.Jr., & J. S. Webster (Eds.), *The neuropsychology handbook* (pp. 134–160). New York: Springer Publishing Company.

Reitan, R. M., & Wolfson, D. (1988). *Traumatic brain injury: Vol. 2. Recovery and rehabilitation*. Tucson, AZ: Neuropsychology Press.

Reitan, R. M., & Wolfson, D. (1992a). *Neuropsychological evaluation of younger children*. Tucson, AZ: Neuropsychology Press.

Reitan, R. M., & Wolfson, D. (1992b). *Neuropsychological evaluation of older children*. Tucson, AZ: Neuropsychology Press.

Reitan, R. M., & Wolfson, D. (1993). *The Halstead-Reitan Neuropsychological Test Battery: Theory and clinical interpretation* (2nd ed.). Tucson, AZ: Neuropsychology Press.

Reitan, R. M., & Wolfson, D. (1995). Cross-validation of the general neuropsychological deficit scale (GNDS). *Archives of Clinical Neuropsychology*, *10*, 125–131.

Reitan, R. M., & Wolfson, D. (2004a). The Trail Making Test as an initial screening procedure for neuropsychological impairment in older children. *Archives of Clinical Neuropsychology*, *19*, 281–288.

Reitan, R. M., & Wolfson, D. (2004b). Use of the Progressive Figures Test in evaluating brain damaged children, children with academic problems, and normal controls. *Archives of Clinical Neuropsychology*, *19*, 305–312.

Reitan, R. M., & Wolfson, D. (2006). *Screening for neuropsychological impairment using subtests from the Halstead-Reitan Battery*. In: *Workshop presented at the third annual meeting of the coalition of clinical practitioners in neuropsychology, Las Vegas, Nevada, January.*

Sbordone, R. J., & Long, C. J. (Eds.), (1996). *Ecological validity of neuropsychological testing*. Delray Beach, FL: St. Lucie Press.

Seretny, M. L., Dean, R. S., Gray, J. W., & Hartlage, L. C. (1986). The practice of clinical neuropsychology in the United States. *Archives of Clinical Neuropsychology*, *1*, 5–12.

Sherer, M., & Adams, R. L. (1993). Cross-validation of Reitan and Wolfson's neuropsychological deficit scales. *Archives of Clinical Neuropsychology*, *8*, 429–435.

Wheeler, L., Burke, C. J., & Reitan, R. M. (1963). An application of Discriminant' functions to the problem of predicting brain damage using behavioral variables. *Perceptual and Motor Skills*, *16*, 417–440.

Wheeler, L., & Reitan, R. M. (1962). The presence and laterality of brain damage predicted from responses to a short Aphasia Screening test. *Perceptual and Motor Skills*, *15*, 789–799.

Wheeler, L., & Reitan, R. M. (1963). Discriminant functions applied to the problem of predicting cerebral damage from behavior tests: A cross validation study. *Perceptual and Motor Skills*, *16*, 681–701.

Further reading

Guilmette, T. J., & Faust, D. (1991). Characteristics of neuropsychologists who prefer the Halstead-Reitan or the Luria-Nebraska Neuropsychology Battery. *Professional Psychology: Research and Practice*, *22*(1), 80–83.

Horton, A. M., Jr. (1994). *Behavioral interventions with brain-injured children*. New York: Plenum.

Horton, A. M., Jr. (1999a). Prediction of brain damage severity: Demographic corrections. *International Journal of Neuroscience*, *97*, 179–183.

Horton, A. M., Jr., Anilane, J., Slone, D. G., & Shapiro, S. (1986). Development and cross-validation of a short-form impairment index. *Archives of Clinical Neuropsychology*, *1*, 243–246.

Chapter 6

Executive functions defined

Darlyne G. Nemeth, Kayla Mckenzie Chustz
The Neuropsychology Center of Louisiana, LLC, Baton Rouge, LA, United States

Background information

In her book, *The Everything Parent's Guide to Children with Executive Functioning Disorder*, Rebecca Branstetter, Ph.D., (2014) defined executive functional skills as "all of the cognitive skills needed to regulate your thinking, feeling, and behavior often to reach a goal" (p. 14). Being a clinical and school psychologist, she further explained that "executive functioning skills are needed for all the other cognitive processes as well, such as memory, attention, motor skills, verbalizing, visualizing, and completing learning tasks. Executive functioning skills are also used to regulate emotions." Furthermore, executive functioning skills are required for effective working memory, which acts as "the mortar between the bricks" (Nemeth, Chustz, & McElroy, 2019) as children learn. Branstetter offered this analogy, "If the brain is the engine of learning and self-regulation, executive functioning is the driver of that engine" (p. 14).

Branstetter used the following phonetic example of executive functions (ĭg-zĕk'yə-tĭv fŭngk'shəns) before her concise definition, "the cognitive processes necessary to think, manage oneself, evaluate and solve problems, and achieve goals" (p. 10). Although these definitions are very straightforward, they are hardly simple. Just as with Einstein's famous equation, $E=mc^2$ ($E=mc^2$ Explained, 2005), they are the product of years of scientific investigation.

In Russia, the investigations by Lev Vygotsky, Alexander Luria, and Janna Glozman are well documented. Likewise, in the United States, the efforts of Halstead, Reitan, and Reed, just to name a few, are groundbreaking. Although many miles and cultures apart, these Russian and American pioneers were studying the same concepts—those variables that comprise the general organization of executive functions.

As early as 1932, Luria defined "a higher mental function" as "a functional system consisting of many components, each of which is based on the work of a special area of the brain and performs its special role in the system" (as cited in Glozman, 2007, p. 172). Luria was able to further his study of executive functions as a result of World War II.

Evaluation and Treatment of Neuropsychologically Compromised Children
https://doi.org/10.1016/B978-0-12-819545-1.00006-0

Likewise, in the United States, Ward Halstead and his colleague, Ralph Reitan, conducted many evaluations of World War II soldiers. These studies eventually lead to Reitan's development of the Halstead-Reitan Neuropsychological Test Battery (HRB) for adults, the HRB-OC for older children, and the Reitan-Indiana Neuropsychological Test Battery (RINB) for children—quantitative approaches to the understanding of brain-behavior functions. In Russia, however, Luria's approach relied on a rather qualitative analysis of brain-behavior functions. For Luria, "the main task of the neuropsychological assessment is not so much diagnostic but prognostic and corrective" (as cited in Glozman, 2007, p. 177).

The value of play in executive functions

Over a century ago, Vygotsky, a Russian developmental psychologist, emphasized the role of play in child development (as cited by Bodrova, Germeroth, & Leong, 2013, p. 111). As Vygotsky contended, in play a child becomes "a head taller than himself" (Bodrova et al., 2013, p. 112) because successful play requires self-regulation—a major component of executive functions. This is especially true in child-specific "make believe" play where "children create an imaginary situation, take on and act out roles, and follow a set of rules determined by these specific roles" (Zaporozhets, 1986, as cited in Bodrova et al., 2013, p. 112–113). In such play, young children learn to suppress their immediate impulses to achieve a goal. Thus, according to Vygotsky and Elkonin, play supports the development of self-regulation "because it requires that players observe and restrain themselves" (Bodrova et al., 2013, p. 113). This involves voluntarily following the rules, which the children themselves create; developing a plan of action; engaging in reflective thinking; and, perhaps, engaging in socially desirable roles (e.g., children may play a doctor or a teacher). Thus, according to Elkonin (1978, as cited in Bodrova et al., 2013, p. 114), "By imitating these figures and behaviors in play, children learn to adjust their actions to conform to the norms associated with the behaviors of these role models, thereby practicing the planning, self-monitoring, and reflection assented for intentional behavior" (Bodrova et al., 2013, p. 114). In other words, via play, young children (e.g., age 5) are developing executive functions or "mature play" via the zone of proximal development. When entering school, however, Elkonin suggests that teachers may not always support "mature play," and therefore children may experience regression to more primitive forms of play. Thus, according to Smirnova and Gudareva (2004, as cited in Bodrova et al., 2013, p. 117), "the ability to follow directions at all ages and in all conditions has generally declined." Bodrova et al., along with several other cited colleagues, conclude that, without adult involvement and without mature play, "declining self-regulation in young children … puts them at risk of later cognitive and social-emotional problems." Instead, current play methods, which isolate the child to computer games and building sets where the child merely follows directions, do not promote the development of executive functions. Perhaps this is one of many reasons for the development of executive dysfunction.

Learning emotional regulation via play

Part of developing emotional executive functions is helping the child learn to recognize, label, and share feelings. This starts with recognizing one's own and others' feeling states. As cultural differences in expression can be quite significant, drawings of bears were used to teach six base feelings: happy, sad, anxious, embarrassed, angry, and nervous (Nemeth, Ray, & Schexnayder, 2003, p. 80–81). Furthermore, this book, *Helping Your Angry Child*, is completely interactive. Parents and children learn together to express their feelings in an effective manner. The use of electronics as babysitters and/or teaching tools was and still is not a part of this approach. Children and their parents learn together, thus fostering more positive relationships. For example, both learn the advantage of polite and courteous feedback using the "X, Y, Z" approach (i.e., When you do **X**, I feel **Y**, I would prefer **Z** instead). This effective process allows children to be heard, not hurt.

As "make-believe" play is finding less and less space in the homes and learning environments of young children, is it possible that more executive function disorders are on the rise?

Defining executive functions—American style

Many American clinicians and researchers have sought to define executive functions. They include but are not limited to the following:

1. In 1987, Stuss defined executive functioning as "the ability 'to extract and use information from the posterior brain systems, and to anticipate, select, plan, experiment, modify, and act on such information in novel situations'" (as cited in Adams, Parsons, Culbertson, & Nixon, 1996, p. 40).
2. Johnstone and Stonnington (2001) defined executive functions as "the ability to plan, organize, and reason" (p. 218). They proposed that "executive functions should be conceptualized in terms of disorders of initiation, termination, and self-regulation, as a common framework for describing and treating these impairments" in order to "advance the state of the field" (p. 121).
3. Sohlberg and Mateer (2001) define executive functions as "the cognitive abilities involved in the initiation, planning, sequencing, organization, and regulation of behavior" (p. 111). In 1999, Mateer conceptualized the following domains of executive functions as having clinical relevance: (1) initiation and drive, (2) response inhibition (stopping behavior), (3) task persistence (maintaining behavior), (4) organization (organizing actions and thoughts), (5) generative thinking (creativity, fluency, cognitive flexibility), and (6) awareness (monitoring and modifying one's own behavior)" (p. 235). Furthermore, Sohlberg and Mateer indicate that the tests that are most sensitive to dysexecutive symptoms included "measures of working memory and attention, fluency, and problem-solving" (p. 236). Consistent with the

theories of Luria, Sohlberg and Mateer found that "observation of behavior in naturalistic settings, using tasks that place demands on frontal lobe abilities, is perhaps the most revealing assessment approach" (p. 238).

4. Cummings and Mega (2003) defined executive functions as "higher-order cognitive abilities mediated primarily by the dorsolateral prefrontal cortex and subcortical structures lined to this region."
5. Rizzo and Eslinger (2004) defined executive functions as the diverse psychological processes that: (1) "Control the activation and inhibition of response sequences that are guided by internal neural representations (e.g., verbal rules, biologic needs, somatic states, emotions, goals, mental models)," (2) "For the purpose of meeting a balance of immediate situational, short-term, and long-term goals and demands," and (3) "that span physical-environmental, cognitive, behavioral, emotional, and social domains of functioning" (p. 440). They also offered a more concise definition for executive functions as "a neuropsychological term meant to describe the diverse higher cognitive functions that underlie planning, organization, goal-directed behavior, and the integration of cognitive and emotional processing in decision-making and adaptation" (p. 1124).
6. Miller and Cummings (2007) reported that "Executive cognitive functions are defined as (and the term is limited to) high-level cognitive functions, believed to be primarily controlled by the LPFC [left prefrontal cortex], that are involved in the control and direction (e.g., planning, monitoring, energizing, switching, inhibiting) of lower-level, more automatic functions" (p. 293).
7. Dawson and Guare (2010) defined executive function as "a neuropsychological concept referring to high-level cognitive processes required to plan and direct activities, including task initiation and follow-through, working memory, sustained attention, performance monitoring, inhibition of impulses, and goal-directed persistence" (p. vii). They concluded that executive functions "allow us to organize our behavior over time and override immediate demands in favor of long-term goals" (p. 1). They further explained that "executive skills enable us to manage our emotions and monitor our thoughts in order to work more efficiently and effectively. Simply stated, these skills help us to regulate our behavior."
8. Raskin (2011) explained that "the term executive functions encompasses the collection of high-order cognitive abilities that allow us to behave in a flexible and goal-directed manner by inhibiting our inappropriate behaviors and thoughts, planning our future behavior, directing our attention, and monitoring our actions" (p. 233). He reported that "executive functioning can at times seem to be a catch-all term used to refer to any higher-order brain ability. Planning, concept formation, mental flexibility, insight, higher-level attentional skills, sequencing, working memory, behavioral regulation, and social cognition, among others, have all been subsumed under the heading of executive functions" (p. 257).

9. Lezak, Howieson, Bigler, and Tranel (2012) stated that "executive functions consist of those capacities that enable a person to engage successfully in independent, purposive, self-directed, and self-serving behavior" (p. 37). They further explained that executive functions "have to do with how behavior is expressed" (p. 20). Reportedly, "As the most complex of behaviors, executive functions are intrinsic to the ability to respond in an adaptive manner to novel situations and are also the basis of many cognitive, emotional, and social skills. The executive functions can be conceptualized as having four components: (1) volition; (2) planning and decision-making; (3) purposive action; and (4) effective performance" (p. 666).
10. Diamond (2013) stated that "Executive functions (EFs; also called executive control or cognitive control) refer to a family of top-down mental processes needed when you have to concentrate and pay attention, when going on automatic or relying on instinct or intuition would be ill-advised, insufficient, or impossible." Diamond explained that EFs "make it possible for us to mentally play with ideas, quickly and flexibly adapt to changed circumstances, take time to consider what to do next, resist temptations, stay focused, and meet novel, unanticipated challenges." Therefore, "using EFs is effortful." Diamond reported that "there is a general agreement that there are three core EFs": inhibition, working memory, and cognitive flexibility. "From these, higher-order EFs are built, such as reasoning, problem solving, and planning." It is important to note that Diamond concluded that "EFs can be improved."

Executive function questionnaires—An American perspective

The primary questionnaire of executive functioning used in the United States is the **Behavior Rating Inventory of Executive Function, Second Edition (BRIEF-2)** by Gioia, Isquith, Guy, and Kenworthy (2015). The first edition of this questionnaire was published in 2002. According to Isquith (personal communication, 6/6/19), the BRIEF has been cited in more than 1500 peer-reviewed articles. Isquith further stated that all the authors are practicing clinicians whose "hour-long problem interviews" lead to the choice of items and the standardization of the original BRIEF. As Isquith stated, "behavior tells the story." This concept, which is in harmony with Luria's qualitative approach to such interviews, has now been taken one step further, as is the American tradition, and has been quantified.

In the BRIEF-2, executive functions are defined as a "broad umbrella construct within which a set of interrelated subdomains could be defined via behavioral manifestations. This umbrella is responsible for guiding, directing, and managing cognitive, emotional, and behavioral functions, particularly during active, novel problem solving" (Gioia et al., 2015, p. 1). Gioia and colleagues described executive functions as the "conductor of the orchestra" (p. 2). Furthermore, Gioia and colleagues described the most unique feature of executive functions as "their prolonged developmental course" (p. 5). Thus, executive functions are dynamic, not static. Therefore, Gioia and colleagues developed the original BRIEF as a series of rating scales that are "intended as complementary measures to traditional performance measures," which they perceived as "inadequate for assessing executive function because they artificially and ambiguously fractionate an integrated system" (p. 5). Of the three rating scales—Parent, Teacher, and Child—Gioia and colleagues found that the "BRIEF Teacher ratings were the best predictor of performance on statewide academic testing relative to executive function measures or broadband rating scales" (p. 6). Furthermore, they determined that "Teacher rating scales of 4-year-old preschool children's everyday executive functions were more predictive of math achievement at age 6" (p. 6).

The BRIEF-2, which applies to children ages 5 to 18, is composed of the following:

- The **Behavioral Regulation Index (BRI)** represents an individual's ability to regulate and monitor behavior effectively. Individuals who are unable to inhibit impulses and monitor their impact on others and their surroundings are likely to exhibit difficulty with several aspects of cognitive regulation. The BRI is comprised of the following two scales:
  - **Inhibit**—assesses inhibitory control, including the ability to stop one's own behavior at the appropriate time.
  - **Self-Monitor**—assesses awareness of the impact of one's own behavior on other people and outcomes. Self-monitoring is the capacity to observe and evaluate one's own behavior as others experience it and includes an understanding of one's own strengths and weaknesses, the ability to monitor the impact one is having on others, awareness of one's own effectiveness in problem solving, and the ability to monitor other important outcomes.
- The **Emotion Regulation Index (ERI)** represents a child's ability to regulate emotional responses, including in response to changing situations. The ERI is composed of two scales:
  - **Shift**—assesses the ability to move freely from one situation, activity, or aspect of a problem to another as the circumstances demand. Key aspects of shifting include the ability to make transitions, problem solve flexibly, switch or alternate attention, and change focus from one mindset or topic to another. Caregivers often describe children who have difficulty with shifting as rigid or inflexible. Such children often require consistent, predictable routines.
  - **Emotional Control**—addresses the manifestation of executive functions within the emotional realm and an individual's ability to modulate emotional responses. Poor emotional control can be expressed as emotional lability or emotional explosiveness.

- The **Cognitive Regulation Index (CRI)** represents an individual's ability to control and manage cognitive processes and problem solve effectively. Appropriate cognitive regulation is required for higher-order problem solving, learning, recall of complex information, and strategic application of knowledge. The CRI is composed of five scales:
  - **Initiate**—includes items related to beginning a task or activity and independently generating ideas, responses, or problem-solving strategies. Individuals with initiation problems typically want to succeed at a task, but they cannot get started. Caregivers of such children frequently report difficulty with getting started on homework or chores and a need for extensive prompts or cues to begin a task or activity.
  - **Working Memory**—measures the capacity to hold information in mind for the purpose of completing a task. Working memory is essential to carrying out multistep activities, completing mental arithmetic, or following complex instructions.
  - **Plan/Organize**—measures an individual's ability to manage current and future-oriented task demands.
  - **Task-Monitor**—assesses difficulty noticing minor errors in work output, such as missing operation signs on a math worksheet, making spelling errors, and not paying attention to details. In general, the Task-Monitor scale captures ineffective monitoring of work product or producing a final work product that does not represent a child's full knowledge or problem-solving capacity.
  - **Organization of Materials**—measures orderliness of work, play, and storage spaces (e.g., desks, lockers, backpacks, bedrooms). This scale assesses the manner in which children order or organize their world and belongings.
- The **Global Executive Composite (GEC)** is a summary score of all the nine scales listed above.

As cited below, one example of the BRIEF's broad application can be summarized in the research of Chavez-Arana et al. (2019). Another popular questionnaire for executive functions, used both in the United States and Russia, is the Conner's Scales, analyzed in Chapter 3 of this book.

Executive function dysregulation profile

Chavez-Arana and her colleagues (2019) have defined the childhood dysregulation profile as frequently including "impairments in cognitive, behavioral, and emotional regulation." This profile may include clinically significant deficits in "shift, initiate, working memory, planning and social skills, and mild deficits in inhibit, emotional control, and task monitor," post acquired brain injury (ABI). Proximal environmental stressors, such as dysfunctional parenting practices, may often exacerbate this profile and put children "at risk" for future mental health problems. According to Chavez-Arana and her colleagues, the BRIEF

Parent Form (Spanish version) can be very helpful in identifying these "at-risk" situations, which can become evident as early as age 7 (p. 14). Likewise, Kak et al. (2014, as cited in Chavez-Arana et al., 2019) concluded that the "presence of warm parent-child interactions" as early as 3 years of age was associated with the more effective development of EFs. In conclusion, Chavez-Arana and her colleagues hypothesized "that parents' optimal parenting practices and mental health may enhance the development of EFs and protect children from developing mental health problems following ABI". In general, these conclusions can be applied to all families. The healthier the home, the healthier the child—regardless of the child's overall health status.

A more recent example of an approach to the measurement of executive functions has been offered by McCloskey (2016). From the **McCloskey Executive Functions Scale (MEFS)** manual, the following excerpts are now offered:

- According to McCloskey, the impetus for the development of the MEFS was "to facilitate the identification of executive function (EF) strengths, executive function deficits, and executive function skills in children" (p. 1).
- According to McCloskey, Perkins, and Van Divner (2009), executive functions can be thought of as a set of direct capacities (managers at varying levels) that are responsible for a person's ability to engage in purposeful, organized, strategic, self-regulated, self-aware, goal-directed processing of perceptions, emotions, thoughts, and actions" (p.2).
- They propose a holarchical, multidimensional functional model of executive functions (HMEF), in which "the term executive functions is viewed as an overarching neurological construct that is used to represent a set of mental capacities that can be used to direct, cue, coordinate, and integrate multiple aspects of perception, emotion, cognition, and action" (p. 3).
- "The MEFS operationalizes the HMEF into 31 self-regulation capacities that are used to varying degrees and in varying combinations to cue and direct perceiving, thinking, feeling, and acting" (p. 4). These executive functions are grouped within seven overarching clusters: "attention, memory, engagement, optimization, efficiency, inquiry, solution."
- McCloskey differentiates between the concept of an executive function and the concept of an executive skill. According to McCloskey, "the executive function is responsible for becoming aware of the need for self-regulation, and for cueing the executive skills. The executive skill is then defined as being "responsible for directing perceptions, feelings, thoughts, and actions in a manner consistent with the awareness of the need to self-regulate" (p. 7). Therefore, McCloskey perceives two important managers, "one who becomes aware of the need to direct, and one who actually does the directing" (p. 5). These functions and skills operate in four different arenas: the intrapersonal arena, the interpersonal arena, the environment arena, and the symbol system arena. Beyond these self-regulation abilities are one's self-realization and self-determination skills. Thus, a multitier framework of executive functions is offered by McCloskey.

- In agreement with the authors of the BRIEF, McCloskey cites executive function development as a "slow, gradual process" (p. 13).

Defining executive functions—Russian style

Psychologist Lev Vygotsky (1896–1934) developed the cultural-historical theory of mind. His theory of development, co-authored by Luria, evolved between the years 1926 to 1931, but was not initially published in English until 1960. This work focused on the study of higher mental functions (HMFs) from a cultural-historical perspective. Thus, Vygotsky's "new psychology" was "built upon three concepts, that of 'higher mental functions,' that of 'cultural-historical development,' and that of 'mastering one's own behavioral processes'" (p. 14, as cited by Kozulin, 1985, p. 324). Vygotsky focused on two major trends: (1) "The acquisition and mastering of such cultural means of mental development as language, writing, drawing, and counting" and, simultaneously, (2) "the development of higher functions (such as) voluntary attention, logical memory, formation of concepts, etc." (p. 24, as cited by Kozulin, 1985, p. 325). He also focused on the acquisition of the "psychological tools" needed to master each developmental stage. Vygotsky described this as the "process of internalization." For example, making choices was thought, by Vygotsky, to be an "example of mastering one's own behavior" (Kozulin, 1985, p. 325).

Luria (1973) defined executive functions as "the ability to evaluate a problem, plan a response, carry out that plan, and assess the adequacy of the response within the context of the ongoing environment" (as cited in Reynolds & Fletcher-Janzen, 1989, p. 301). Thus, executive functions are "complex, rather subtle when operating effectively, and appear to mature with age" (p. 301) (Please read Chapter 3 for a more comprehensive review of Luria's qualitative approach to examining executive functions).

Measuring executive functions–An American perspective

Though American neuropsychologists have a more quantitative approach to evaluation and treatment, there are few quantitative measures available for measuring executive functions. Some of the most popularly used measures of executive functions include the Halstead Category Test (HCT), the Delis-Kaplan Executive Function System (D-KEFS), and the Wisconsin Card Sort Test (WCST).

The purpose of the **Halstead Category Test (HCT)** is "to evaluate the subject's ability in abstraction and concept formation" (Reitan & Wolfson, 1992, p. 444). It is used to assess executive functions and higher-order logical analysis. This test is a complex measure of novel problem solving, judgment, abstraction, reasoning, concept formation, and mental flexibility. Reitan and Wolfson note that the HCT has several characteristics differentiating it from many other tests. "It is a relatively complex concept formation test (that) requires the ability to (1) note recurring similarities and differences in stimulus material, (2) postulate reasonable hypotheses about these similarities and differences, (3) test these hypotheses by receiving positive or negative reinforcement (bell or buzzer), and (4) adapt hypotheses based on the reinforcement following each response" (Reitan & Wolfson, 1992, p. 320–321). The HCT has been adapted for adults, older children, and younger children (Please see Chapter 4 for a comprehensive discussion of the HRB and the HCT).

Delis and colleagues hypothesized that an executive functioning test required "a combination of higher-level cognitive abilities as well as fundamental skills such as attention, perception, and language" (Shunk, Davis, & Dean, 2006, p. 277). The **Delis-Kaplan Executive Function System (D-KEFS)**, developed by Delis, Kaplan, and Kramer in 2001, reportedly uses "a psychometric and a behavioral neurological approach to offer both a quantitative and qualitative interpretation of executive functions" (Shunk et al., 2006, p. 278). As Kaplan concluded, "why the task was failed was more clinically and theoretically relevant than that it was failed (Weintraub, 2011, p. 953). The D-KEFS often includes a qualitative understanding of the results. The D-KEFS consists of nine tests that measure a wide spectrum of verbal and nonverbal executive functions. Eight of the nine tests can be used with both children and adults ages 8 to 89. The D-KEFS Proverb Test, however, can only be used from ages 16 to 89. Descriptions of each of the subtests follow:

- The Word Context Test is a means of evaluating executive functions in the verbal modality, and of assessing the following skills: (1) deductive reasoning, (2) integration of multiple bits of information, (3) hypothesis testing, and (4) flexibility of thinking.
- The Sorting Test measures the following components of concept formation and problem-solving skills: (1) Initiation of problem-solving behaviors, (2) verbal concept formation skills, (3) nonverbal concept formation skills, (4) transfer of concepts into action, (5) abstract expression of conceptual relationships, (6) flexibility of thinking, and (7) flexibility of behavioral response.
- The Twenty Questions Test taps on the following executive functions: (1) the ability to identify the various categories and subcategories represented in the 30 objects, and (2) the ability to formulate abstract, yes/no questions that eliminate the maximum number of objects regardless of the examiner's answer.
- The Tower Test measures the following key executive functions: (1) spatial planning, (2) rule learning, (3) inhibition of impulsive responding, (4) inhibition of preservation responding, and (5) establishing and maintaining the instructional set.
- The Color-Word Interference Test measures the inhibition of a more automatic verbal response (reading) in order to generate a conflicting response of naming dissonant ink colors. Basic naming of color patches and basic reading of words that denote colors printed in black ink are required. This test measures both inhibition and cognitive flexibility.

- The Verbal Fluency Test involved letter fluency, category fluency, and category switching. It taps the ability to (1) generate words fluently in an effortful, phonetic format, and (2) form over learned concepts while (3) simultaneously shifting between over learned concepts.
- The Trail Making Test is a measure of flexibility of thinking. It requires number sequencing, letter sequencing, and motor speed.

The authors believe that "some forms of executive functioning, such as organizing, searching, verification of hypotheses, and impulse control, are already formed by age 10" (p. 18) while others such as planning remain immature even at age 15 (p. 18)." Furthermore, they conclude that most executive cognitive changes occur between the ages of 5 and 8, and that by ages 9 and 10, are stabilized.

The Wisconsin Card Sorting Test (WCST) was developed by Berg and Grant in 1948, and is still widely used today. "The purpose of this test is to assess the ability to form abstract concepts, to shift and maintain set, and utilize feedback" (Spreen & Strauss, 1998, p. 219). For qualitative analysis of this test in Russia, see Glozman, Levin, and Tupper (2004).

Understanding executive functions from a Russian perspective

According to Voronova, Korneev, and Akhutina, HMF components include "voluntary regulation of activity, serial organization of movements and actions, processing of kinesthetic, auditory, visual, and visual-spatial information, and regulation of activation" (2015, p. 16–17). Some forms of executive functioning—organized searching, verification of hypotheses, and impulse control—"are already formed at age ten, while others (such as planning) remain immature even at age twelve" (p. 18). Therefore, their research focused on: (1) voluntary regulation of activity, (2) serial organization of movements and actions, (3) kinesthetic information, (4) auditory information, (5) visual information (6) visual-spatial information, and (7) neurodynamics. They concluded that "almost all HMFs developed with age during the course of systematic instruction" (p. 22). Vygotsky pointed out that "for successful cognitive development, education must certainly be more demanding (of the school children), relying not on matured, but on maturing functions" (Vygotsky, 405, as cited in Voronova et al., 2015, p. 31). Thus, as Vygotsky concluded, "The only good teaching is that which outpaces development" (1991, p. 386, as cited in Voronova et al., 2015, p. 32) (Please see Chapter 2 for a more comprehensive discussion of Luria's approach to evaluation).

Luria's approach

Luria divided his understanding of brain functions into three units. Unit 1 focused on the energy component of mental activity, which included neurodynamics. Unit 2 focused on perception, processing, and storage of information, primarily through visual information and visual-spatial information. Unit 3 focused on executive functions, regulation, and control, and included an understanding of the serial organization of movements and actions. Voronova et al. (2015) noted that there is a strong connection between executive functions and motivation, whereas Luria concluded "that the most complex forms of regulation of conscious activity are aimed at 'the activating influence of motives, formulated with the help of speech'" (1973, p. 197, as cited in Voronova et al., 2015, p. 31).

In conclusion

So many researchers, both American and Russian, have devoted years of clinical research to develop a better understanding of the role of executive functions in learning and behavior. Some believe that executive functions make people uniquely human. These abilities are designed to regulate thinking, feeling, and behavior, but they must be learned. In this regard, healthy parenting is essential.

As children develop, they begin to play. Through imitation, initiation, and discovery, children enter the wonderful world of make-believe. By age 3, they begin to recognize, label, and share their feelings, to understand the feelings of others, and to self-regulate. By age 5, children are capable of developing mature play.

For many, the next step is school. In a healthy school setting, the playful joy of discovery is present and allowed to flourish. In rather rigid school settings, playfulness is often discouraged, if not eradicated. Conformity, not creativity, is what is required.

Yet, the developmental abilities to foster the growth of executive functions are still in progress. When thwarted, this can result in executive function dysregulation. That is why it is so important for parents, teachers, and the children themselves to understand the proximal zone of development of executive functions. Without this understanding, learning is so much harder.

With all of the many definitions of executive functions offered in this chapter as well as the variously cited questionnaires, measures, and observations of both American and Russian researchers, one common goal remains—that of offering a clear and concise definition for all. Rebecca Branstetter (2014) has done just that: "all of the cognitive skills needed to regulate your thinking, feeling, and behavior, often to reach a goal" (p. 2).

Thus, regardless of the setting, our children need to learn to ask themselves the following questions:

1. What is the problem?
2. How can I solve it?
3. Am I using an effective plan?
4. Was my plan successful?

In **summary**, in order to move forward, we all must use our executive functions wisely.

References

Adams, R. L., Parsons, O. A., Culbertson, J. L., & Nixon, S. J. (Eds.), (1996). *Neuropsychology for clinical practice: Etiology, assessment, and treatment of common neurological disorders*. Washington, DC: American Psychological Association.

Bodrova, E., Germeroth, C., & Leong, D. L. (2013). Play and self-regulation: Lessons from Vygotsky. *American Journal of Play*, *6*(1), 111–123.

Branstetter, R. (2014). *The everything parent's guide to children with executive functioning disorder*. Avon, MA: Adams Media, a division of F + W Media, Inc.

Chavez-Arana, C., Catroppa, C., Yáñez-Téllez, G., Prieto-Corona, B., de León, M. A., García, A., et al. (2019). Parenting and the dysregulation profile predict executive functioning in children with acquired brain injury. *Child Neuropsychology*, *25*(8), 1125–1143. https://doi.org/10.1080/09297049.2019.1589442.

Cummings, J. L., & Mega, M. S. (2003). *Neuropsychiatry and behavioral neuroscience*. New York, NY: Oxford University Press, Inc.

Dawson, P., & Guare, R. (2010). *Executive skills in children and adolescents: A practical guide to assessment and intervention* (2nd ed.). New York, NY: The Guilford Press.

Diamond, A. (2013). Executive functions. *Annual Reviews Psychology*, *64*, 135–168.

E=mc2 Explained. (2005). Retrieved from: https://www.pbs.org/wgbh/nova/einstein/lrk-hand-emc2expl.html.

Gioia, G. A., Isquith, P. K., Guy, S. C., & Kenworthy, L. (2015). *Brief-2: Behavior rating inventory of executive function, second edition: Professional manual* (2nd ed.). Lutz, FL: Psychological Assessment Resources.

Glozman, J. (2007). A.R. Luria and the history of Russian neuropsychology. *Journal of the History of the Neuroscience*, *16*(1–2), 168–180. https://doi.org/10.1080/09647040600550368.

Glozman, J. M., Levin, O. S., & Tupper, D. (2004). Executive behavior after cortical and subcortical brain damage. In T. V. Ahutina, J. M. Glozman, L. I. Moskovich, & D. Robbins (Eds.), *A.R. Luria and contemporary psychology: Festschrift celebrating the centennial of his birth* (pp. 65–77). NY: Nova Science.

Johnstone, B., & Stonnington, H. H. (Eds.), (2001). *Rehabilitation of neuropsychological disorders: A practical guide for rehabilitation professionals*. Philadelphia, PA: Psychology Press.

Kozulin, A. (1985). Review of Istorija razvitija vysšych psichičeskich funkcij (History of the development of higher mental functions) by Lev Vygotsky. *Studies in Soviet Thought*, *29*(4), 324–326. https://www.jstor.org/stable/20079605.

Lezak, M. D., Howieson, D. B., Bigler, E. D., & Tranel, D. (2012). *Neuropsychological assessment* (5th ed.). New York, NY: Oxford University Press.

Luria, A. R. (1973). *The working brain*. New York: Basic Books.

McCloskey, G. (2016). *McCloskey executive functions scale (MEFS)*. Stoddard, WI: Schoolhouse Educational Services, LLC.

McCloskey, G., Perkins, L. A., & Van Divner, B. (2009). *Assessment and intervention for executive functions*. New York, NY: Taylor and Francis.

Miller, B. L., & Cummings, J. L. (Eds.), (2007). *The human frontal lobes: Functions and disorders* (2nd ed.)New York, NY: The Guilford Press.

Nemeth, D. G., Chustz, K. M., & McElroy, P. (2019). *Creating executive functions in tweens with learning disabilities*. In *Presented at the CW Austin learning disability conference, Baton Rouge, LA*.

Nemeth, D. G., Ray, K. P., & Schexnayder, M. M. (2003). *Helping your angry child*. Oakland, CA: New Harbinger Publications, Inc.

Raskin, S. A. (Ed.), (2011). *Neuroplasticity and rehabilitation*. New York, NY: The Guilford Press.
Reitan, R., & Wolfson, D. (1992). *Neuropsychological evaluation of older children*. South Tucson, AZ: Neuropsychology Press.
Reynolds, C. R., & Fletcher-Janzen, E. (Eds.), (1989). *Handbook of clinical child neuropsychology*. New York, NY: Plenum Press.
Rizzo, M., & Eslinger, P. J. (Eds.), (2004). *Principles and practice of behavioral neurology and neuropsychology*. Philadelphia, PA: W.B. Saunders Company.
Shunk, A. W., Davis, A. S., & Dean, R. S. (2006). Test review: Dean C. Delis, Edith Kaplan, & Joel H. Kraamer, Delis-Kaplan Executive Function System (DKEFS). *Applied Neuropsychology*, *13*(4), 275–279.
Sohlberg, M. M., & Mateer, C. A. (2001). *Cognitive rehabilitation: An integrative neuropsychological approach*. New York, NY: The Guilford Press.
Spreen, O., & Strauss, E. (1998). *A compendium of neuropsychological tests: Administration, norms, and commentary* (2nd ed.). New York, NY: Oxford University Press.
Voronova, M. N., Korneev, A. A., & Akhutina, T. V. (2015). Longitudinal study of the development of higher mental functions in primary school children. *Journal of Russian & East European Psychology*, *52*(3), 16–35. https://doi.org/10.1080/10610405.2015.1175833.
Weintraub, S. (2011). A tribute to Edith Kaplan (1924–2009). *Journal of the International Neuropsychological Society*, *17*(6), 953–955.

Further reading

Glozman, J. (2013). *Explorations in developmental psychology: Developmental neuropsychology*. New York, NY: Routledge.
Lezak, M. D. (1995). *Neuropsychological assessment* (3rd ed.). New York, NY: Oxford University Press.

Chapter 7

Understanding "hot and cold" executive functions in children and adolescents

Darlyne G. Nemeth, Kayla Mckenzie Chustz
The Neuropsychology Center of Louisiana, LLC, Baton Rouge, LA, United States

Introduction

In Chapter 5, we cited the following questions for effective executive function problem solving:

(1) What is the problem?
(2) How can I solve it?
(3) Am I using an effective plan?
(4) Was my plan successful?
Yet, a fifth question must be addressed,
(5) Did my feelings help or hinder success?

The first four questions address the logical aspects of problem solving. According to Chavez-Arana et al. (2018), these include, but are not limited to, cognitive flexibility, attention, inhibition, and memory. They are referred to as the "cold" aspects of executive functions (EF). But whether a logical plan is successful depends on the "hot," or affective components, of EFs. Healthy emotional and behavioral regulations promote good decision-making, social skills, insight, and most of all, empathy. These skills are just as important, if not more important, to children's adaptive functioning and well-being. They may be referred to as the "soul of the mind." At times, they are elusive, but their presence often determines the outcome of a child's cognitive efforts.

This has especially been observed in our Summer Build-A-Brain programs for tweens (ages 10–14) who struggle in math. The primary deterrent to their success has been affect, not cognition. Therefore, we spend considerable time helping them develop the affective and behavioral controls needed for academic success in mathematics (this very successful program will be cited in the chapter by Fernando Pastrana, Ph.D, clinical and neuropsychologist). Suffice it to say that over the past three summers, we have seen tweens fall under the weight of

Evaluation and Treatment of Neuropsychologically Compromised Children
https://doi.org/10.1016/B978-0-12-819545-1.00007-2

their anxieties and fail to flourish in mathematics. As a result, they have exhibited behavioral difficulties. Thus, we have concluded that controlling one's anxiety and behavior is key to academic success. These abilities are seldom taught in the school setting. Yet, what if children leave having not developed these skills? Is this really emotional dysregulation? As Glozman (2013) stated, you cannot rehabilitate what has not been learned. These skills must be created, that is, learned by children and their parents in a warm and accepting environment.

Defining "hot and cold" executive functions

According to Kerr and Zelazo (2004, as cited in Chavez-Arana et al., 2018), "cold EFs refer to purely cognitive EFs while hot EFs refer to the affecting aspects of these cognitive skills." Cold EFs include being able to manipulate "abstract concepts, numbers, or letters" (p. 929), whereas hot EFs, which have a socioemotional domain, are typically "evoked by motivating and emotionally meaningful contexts (Chavez-Arana et al., 2018, p. 929). According to De Luca and Leventer (2008, as cited in Chavez-Arana et al., 2018), behavioral regulation, emotional regulation, affective decision-making, social skills, and theory of mind (i.e., empathy) are hot EFs, whereas metacognition, cognitive flexibility, attention, inhibition, working memory, planning, and problem-solving are considered cold EFs.

As Chavez-Arana and her colleagues point out, "EFs are required in children's daily activities. Children with deficits in cold EFs tend to forget instructions, misplace school supplies, have difficulties in concentrating on daily homework, make careless mistakes, and try a solution repeatedly even if it is not useful (Castellanos, Sonuga-Barke, Milham, & Tannock, 2006; Gioia, Kenworthy, & Isquith, 2010; as cited in Chavez-Arana et al., 2018, p. 929). However, "Children with impairments in hot EFs are more likely to interrupt conversation, make risky decisions, present anger outbursts, and misinterpret others" (Castellanos et al., 2006; Gioia et al., 2010; Zelazo & Carlson, 2012; as cited in Chavez-Arana et al., 2018, p. 929).

In their review of various intervention methods to improve hot and cold EFs, improving a combination of child emotional and behavioral regulation skills and improving parenting practices were deemed the most effective (Chavez-Arana et al., 2018, p. 936). Less effective were interventions aimed at improving a child's "cold" EFs alone. Furthermore, metacognition and problem solving were found to be best enhanced in group sessions, whereas individual sessions and homework were most effective to improve working memory and attention (Chavez-Arana et al., 2018, p. 936). Chavez-Arana and colleagues cited the attention treatment model of Sohlberg and Mateer (1987), which addressed five levels of attention: "focused, sustained, selective, alternating, and divided" (2018, p. 937). Their effort was to improve cold EFs, whereby "the interventions attempted to create real-life context, by teaching metacognitive skills and providing participants with the space to use them in the company of peers" (Chavez-Arana et al., 2018, p. 937).

On the other hand, according to Chavez-Arana and colleagues, affect was targeted in 50% of the intervention studies regarding hot EFs. Chavez-Arana and colleagues concluded that "by comparing the interventions (cold versus hot), we can see that recovery of hot EFs seems to require more time in comparison to cold EFs" (2018, p. 937). Adult participation was cited by Ylvisaker and Feeney (2009), and was crucial to the success of intervention programs (as cited by Chavez-Arana et al., 2018, p. 937). Furthermore, they pointed out that EF deficits "can be exacerbated when they are surrounded by unfavorable family circumstances" (Taylor et al., 2002, as cited in Chavez-Arana et al., 2018, p. 937). Reducing parental stress by involvement in the children's treatment program was seen as crucial.

In the final analysis, Chavez-Arana and colleagues noted that "real-life contexts may be more challenging to the child because they require hot and cold EFs to work together toward adaptive function" (Zelazo & Carlson, 2012, as cited in Chavez-Arana et al., 2018, p. 938). This reinforces a "balance between cognition and emotion for self-regulation (Blair and Diamond, 2008, as cited in Chavez-Arana et al., 2018, p. 938).

The executive functioning dysregulation profile

In their 2019 study on executive function dysregulation regarding children with acquired brain injury (ABI), Chavez-Arana and colleagues concluded that "parenting and the dysregulation profile predict executive functioning in children" with ABI. This profile is "characterized by impairments in cognitive, behavioral, and emotional regulation." Although specifically targeting parenting practices as well as children's EF difficulties, we conclude that these problems can be generalized to non-ABI children (Chavez-Arana et al., 2019, p. 1).

According to Althoff and colleagues, poor self-regulation is an early prediction of a variety of mental health problems in adulthood. It involves integrated "emotional, cognitive, and behavioral regulation" (Althoff, Verhulst, Rettew, Hudziak, & Van der Ende, 2010, as cited in Chavez-Arana et al., 2019, p. 2). If dysregulated, children can develop anxiety, depression, bipolarity, drug abuse, self-harm, etc. Chavez-Arana and colleagues also noted that the development of integrated EFs is dependent on "an intact central nervous system and a healthy environment" (Ryan et al., 2016; Spencer-Smith & Anderson, 2009; as cited in Chavez-Arana et al., 2019, p. 3). Distal (socioeconomic) environment stressors and proximal (dysfunctional parenting) add to the child's developmental problems. Regarding parenting behaviors, low warmth and lax discipline are cited as especially problematic for children with ABI. Chavez-Arana and colleagues pointed out that "self-regulation is more reliable at 7 years of age" (Spencer-Smith & Anderson, 2009, as cited in Chavez-Arana et al., 2019, p. 14). Furthermore, the "growing into deficits" model was cited and defined as "when consequences of a brain insult are initially silent and become evident over time" (Anderson, Spencer, & Wood, 2011; Lipska, Jaskiw, & Weinberger,

1994; as cited in Chavez-Arana et al., 2019, p. 13). Again, this is true of non-ABI children as well. Therefore, the younger the age at intervention (which should include the children and their parents), the better the outcome. Kok and colleagues concluded that "the presence of warm parent-child interactions at 3 years of age was associated with better EFs for nonclinical pediatric populations (Kok et al., 2014, as cited in Chavez-Arana et al., 2019, p. 12).

IQ versus EQ

Before the advent of the "hot" versus "cold" EF theory, many researchers focused on the "IQ" versus "EQ (EI)" concept. For example, Checa and Fernández-Berrocal (2015) concluded that "not only is IQ crucial, but also competences related to EI [emotional intelligence] are essential to human cognitive control processes" (p. 1). These researchers stated that "Fluid intelligence refers to the capacity to solve and think logically about novel problems" (p. 1). In many respects, this definition is similar to that of "cold EFs" in that "crystallized intelligence," which "depends on experience and knowledge," is defined as the "ability to use these factors" (p. 1). In mixed models, EI is conceptualized as "a conglomeration of mental abilities and personality traits such as optimism, motivation, and stress tolerance" (Mayer et al., 2008; Webb et al., 2013; as cited in Checa & Fernández-Berrocal, 2015, p. 2). The ability model, in contrast, defined EI as "the integration of several capacities" including, but not limited to, "the ability to perceive accurately, appraise, and express emotion; the ability to access and/or generate feelings when they facilitate thought; the ability to understand emotion and emotional knowledge; and the ability to regulate emotions to promote emotional and intellectual growth" (Mayer & Salovey, 1997, as cited in Checa & Fernández-Berrocal, 2015, p. 2).

Checa and Fernández-Berrocal note that "EI enhances the ability to learn and solve problems" (p. 2), concluding that "people with a higher EI are able to generate a mood that allows them to do better on challenging cognitive tasks" (2015, p. 2). Thus, EI appears to be conceptually similar to "hot EFs." They hypothesize that controlling impulsivity (i.e., premature execution of the response) is important for emotional regulation, whereas controlling interference (i.e., the ability to inhibit processing of irrelevant information) is important for cognitive regulation.

Benedek, Jauk, Sommer, Arendasy, and Neubauer (2014) explored the relationship between intelligence, creativity, and cognitive control, and the involvement of EFs therein. They studied the EFs of **updating, shifting,** and **inhibiting**. They concluded that EFs are involved in creative thought and cited the positive relationships between intelligence and creativity (defined by novelty and usefulness) (p. 73).

Updating, which is associated with the concept of working memory, refers to "the monitoring of incoming information and the revision of working memory content by replacing obsolete information with information that is new and relevant for the current task" (Benedek et al., 2014, p. 74).

"**Shifting** refers to the process of switching between different tasks and mental sets" (Monsell, 1996, as cited in Benedek et al., 2014, p. 74).

Inhibition can be "defined as the suppression of dominant but irrelevant response tendencies" (Benedek et al., 2014, p. 75).

These researchers define EFs as "basic cognitive processes that control thought and action" (Benedek et al., 2014, p. 74). In either case, flexibility of thought, updating, and inhibiting are essential elements of creativity. As updating involves working memory, which is a "primary resource for the control of attention … creative ideas originate from the successful association of previously unrelated concepts taken from memory" (Engle, 2002; Kane, Bleckley, Conway, & Engle, 2001; Koestler, 1964; Mednick, 1962; as cited in Benedek et al., 2014, p. 79). They further purport that "people with higher working memory capacity may more easily keep all goals active throughout the task, whereas people with lower working memory capacity may fall back on less-specific goals" (Benedek et al., 2014, p. 79). Thus, consistent with Nemeth, Chustz, and McElroy (2019), working memory may be defined as "the cement between the bricks." The stronger the cement, the better the outcome.

Personality characteristics are also important. One personality characteristic, which Benedek and colleagues found to be significantly correlated with intelligence and creativity, was **openness**, wherein people are receptive to new ideas. Furthermore, the consistent relationship between intelligence and creativity suggests an executive nature of creativity.

Cabello and Fernández-Berrocal (2015) focused on the essential characteristics of intelligence and emotions. They used the Mayor-Salovey-Caruso Emotional Intelligence Test (MSCEIT) to explore people's implicit theories about the influence of EI on emotional abilities. EI was defined, in reference to mixed models, as "a conglomeration of characteristics, including empathy, motivation, persistence, optimism, and social skills" (Cabello & Fernández-Berrocal, 2015, p. 1). Again, EI seems to be correlated with "hot EFs."

The MSCEIT assessed four abilities: perceiving, facilitating, understanding, and managing emotions (Mayer et al., 2003, as cited in Cabello & Fernández-Berrocal, 2015, p. 3). Results suggested that one's EI ability may vary with age and gender. Furthermore, implicit theories are involved in the ways "people interpret themselves and others" and "profoundly affect human behavior" (Dweck, 2012; Leithetal., 2014; as cited in Cabello & Fernández-Berrocal, 2015, p. 2). They effect and influence intelligence, emotion, social skills, relationships, management skills, social judgment, and stereotyping (Dweck, 2012, as cited in Cabello & Fernández-Berrocal, 2015, p. 2). Yet, emotions are viewed as more malleable than intelligence (Tamir et al., 2017, as cited in Cabello & Fernández-Berrocal, 2015, p. 2). Furthermore, multiple researchers concluded that "**training** in social and emotional competencies should begin in (the) early years and continue throughout one's lifetime" (Ruiz-Aranda et al., 2012; Rivers et al., 2013; Kumschick et al., 2014; as cited in Cabello & Fernández-Berrocal, 2015, p. 7).

Anxiety and cognition

Perhaps one of the most debilitating effects on EFs can be observed from the presence of anxiety. Just as the presence of a reasonable amount of anxiety can be a motivating factor, too much anxiety can negatively impact EFs. There is a point on an anxiety scale wherein, when crossed, it becomes debilitating. This point, often displayed on a bell-shaped curve, is called the **Just Noticeable Difference (JND)**. This concept, referred to as the Weber-Fechner Law (1834, as cited in Cherry, 2019a), is defined as "the amount something must be changed in order for a difference to be noticeable, or detectable at least half the time (absolute threshold)" (Just-Noticeable Difference, n.d.). Another way of understanding this concept, developed over a century ago by psychologists Robert Yerkes and John Dillingham Dodson (1908), is called the "Inverted U-Model," wherein there is a level of optimal arousal and optimal performance. Up to that level, anxiety can be helpful in increasing attention and interest, but over that level, anxiety can impair performance (Cherry, 2019b). This Yerkes-Dodson Law also notes that high arousal levels are "generally associated with panic, anxiety, lower concentration, physically tensing up, inability to make decisions, overreacting," etc. (Shrestha, 2017).

The impact of anxiety on both hot and cold cognition is quite significant (Robinson, Vytal, Cornwell, & Grillon, 2013, p. 1). **Hot cognition** involves emotionally laden information, whereas **cold cognition** involves emotionally neutral information. Both may include sensory-perceptual, attentional/control, memory, and/or executive functioning information, which are strongly influenced by stress.

There are two types of anxiety—s**tate** and **trait** (Spielberger, 2010). **State anxiety**, which is a consequence of external events, results from the overfunctioning of the "alerting and orienting networks" (Pacheco-Unguetti, Acosta, Callejas, & Lupiáñez, 2010, p. 6). **Trait anxiety** is related to deficiencies within the internal executive control network (Pacheco-Unguetti et al., 2010, p. 6).

There is an important difference between anxiety and fear. Anxiety may be described "by the anticipation of (an) unspecific, future threat," whereas fear is defined as "the emotional response following real or perceived imminent threat" (Stegmann, Reicherts, Andreatta, Pauli, & Wieser, 2019, p. 1). Thus, the hallmark of an anxiety disorder may be described as a "heightened sensitivity to unpredictable threat" (Stegmann et al., 2019, p. 7).

In **summary**, according to Vytal, Cornwell, Letkiewicz, Arkin, and Grillon, "anxiety can be distracting, disruptive, and incapacitating" (Vytal, Cornwell, Letkiewicz, Arkin, & Grillon, 2013, p. 1).

Case illustration

A case illustration involves a tween boy who developed familial stomach migraines secondary to the stress he experienced in math class. This physiological reaction was so debilitating that he almost failed math for the entire year.

Via individual and group sessions, cognitive-behavioral therapy, biofeedback training, and medication management with fluoxetine, he learned to anticipate and ameliorate these devastating symptoms and has done quite well ever since. Because children who experience stomach migraines frequently develop migraine headaches as adults (Abdominal Migraine, 2016), these interventions were considered both corrective and preventative.

Depression and cognition

Current researchers Barch, Harms, Tillman, Hawkey, and Luby (2019) have found a strong correlation between mood disorders (e.g., unipolar depression, bipolar depression, major depression, and situational depression) and cognitive dysfunction. Furthermore, the younger the age and the more severe the circumstances, the greater the effect on cognition and episodic memory (Barch et al., 2019). Episodic memory, first described by Endel Tulving in 1972, is defined as "one of the main neurocognitive memory systems" (Schacter & Tulving, 1994, as cited in Tulving, 2002, p. 5) that allows individuals to consciously recall personal experiences and events that happened in the past (Williams, n.d.). It "makes possible mental time travel through subjective time, from the present to the past, thus allowing one to reexperience … one's own previous experiences" (Tulving, 2002, p. 5). In their 2013 article, *Hot and Cold Cognition in Depression*, Roiser and Sahakian highlighted the importance of understanding how these significant aspects of cognition affect depression and vice versa.

Because "depression is the leading cause of disability worldwide" (Roiser & Sahakian, 2013, p. 1), and because of its negative effects on cognition, the younger the age of intervention, the more hopeful the outcome. This is especially true in late adolescence when the final stages of cognitive development are coalescing. Peterson, Porter, and Miskowiak hypothesize that "cognitive deficits in younger patients may be especially disabling because they impede educational attainment (as well as) occupational and interpersonal functioning" (Jaeger et al., 2006, as cited in Peterson, Porter, & Miskowiak, 2019, p. 770).

Even though **hot** (emotion-dependent) and **cold** (emotion-independent) cognitions are often researched separately, they are not independent of one another (Roiser & Sahakian, 2013, p. 8). Sometimes seemingly cold cognitions, which may simply involve information processing, can become highly emotionally charged in specific circumstances. This is especially true during times of acute stress. These stressful situations can cause maladaptive decision-making (Alexander, Oliver, Burdine, Tang, & Dunlop, 2017, p. 386).

In both bipolar and major depressive patients, Mann's decisional conflict model (Janis & Mann, 1977, as cited in Alexander et al., 2017, p. 387), was cited as defining one adaptive decision-making choice (vigilance) and three maladaptive choices (hypervigilance, buck-passing, and procrastination) as being associated with problem-focused coping strategies. This "decisional conflict model" (Alexander et al., 2017, p. 387) involved three processes: (1) awareness of the risks and alternatives, (2) hope of identifying a good alternative, and (3) belief in adequate time to choose. They concluded that depressed patients engaged in more maladaptive decision-making than nondepressed individuals.

Case illustration

This case illustration is of a teenage girl who made many maladaptive decisions due to poor vigilance, a trait characteristic of bipolar disorder patients (Alexander et al., 2017, p. 390). For example, she was expelled from high school for drugs and sent to a reform school. Secondary to her drug use, she developed a serious medical condition, hepatitis C. A recent article in the Baton Rouge Advocate newspaper reported that hepatitis C was the deadliest infectious disease in America, killing more than 20,000 people a year (Crisp, 2019). As a result of this serious infection, she was ill for many years, and was unable to complete high school or seek employment.

With family support, this bipolar adolescent was able to enroll in a university drug trial for a hepatitis C drug. She was placed in the experimental group and was cured. Although her medical treatment was successful, she was basically homebound with little hope of a decent future. Instead of returning to street drugs, with the encouragement of her supportive family, she sought mental health treatment. This intervention, which included cognitively based individual therapy, educational remediation, and medication management, was conducted in coordination with her family physician and university specialist. They approved her mental health medication regimen, which this chapter's first author prescribed.

Although she had lost significant cognitive and educational skills, they were rebuilt over time. After several years of trying, she was able to achieve a graduate-equivalent high school diploma and begin a part-time job. After completing the psychological aspects of her intervention program, she was successfully regulated on the following medications: Bupropion XL 300 mg, Lamotrigine 200 mg, Clonidine HCL ER 0.1 mg BID, and Cerefolin NAC. Six years postdespair, this young woman now has a bright future.

Conclusions

For successful problem-solving, both the hot and cold aspects of executive functions must be integrated. This integration allows for emotional and behavioral regulation and promotes healthy decision-making, social skills, insight, and empathy. These skills must be developed. Without such development, emotional dysregulation dominates. Hot EFs refer to the emotional aspects of cognition. Cold EFs refer to neutral cognition. In general, hot EFs are required for living, and cold EFs are required for learning. Both must be present in healthy children and adolescents. Without this integration, behavioral regulation skills become problematic. Healthy EFs must work together to produce healthy adaptive functions; the balance is crucial. Without this balance, EF dysregulation may emerge. In order for children and adolescents to develop these integrated skills, positive parenting is essential.

Another understanding of hot versus cold EFs has been offered by theorists who have proposed the IQ versus EQ (EI) phenomenon. Basically, these theories are different approaches to similar outcomes. Regardless of which theory is utilized, working memory, or the "cement between the bricks," so to speak, is crucial for successful learning and adaptation.

References

Abdominal Migraine. (2016). Retrieved from https://americanmigrainefoundation.org/resource-library/abdominal-migraine/.

Alexander, L. F., Oliver, A., Burdine, L. K., Tang, Y., & Dunlop, B. W. (2017). Reported maladaptive decision-making in unipolar and bipolar depression and its change with treatment. *Psychiatry Research, 257*, 386–392. https://doi.org/10.1016/j.psychres.2017.08.004.

Barch, D. M., Harms, M. P., Tillman, R., Hawkey, E., & Luby, J. L. (2019). Early childhood depression, emotion regulation, episodic memory, and hippocampal development. *Journal of Abnormal Psychology, 128*(1), 81–95. https://doi.org/10.1037/abn0000392.

Benedek, M., Jauk, E., Sommer, M., Arendasy, M., & Neubauer, A. C. (2014). Intelligence, creativity, and cognitive control: The common and differential involvement of executive functions in intelligence and creativity. *Intelligence, 46*, 73–83. https://doi.org/10.1016/j.intell.2014.05.007.

Cabello, R., & Fernández-Berrocal, P. (2015). Implicit theories and ability emotional intelligence. *Frontiers in Psychology, 6*, 1–8. https://doi.org/10.3389/fpsyg.2015.00700.

Chavez-Arana, C., Catroppa, C., Carranza-Escárcega, E., Godfrey, C., Yáñez-Téllez, G., Prieto-Corona, B., et al. (2018). A systematic review of interventions for hot and cold executive functions in children and adolescents with acquired brain injury. *Journal of Pediatric Psychology, 43*(8), 928–942. https://doi.org/10.1093/jpepsy/jsy013.

Chavez-Arana, C., Catroppa, C., Yáñez-Téllez, G., Prieto-Corona, B., de Léon, M. A., García, A., et al. (2019). Parenting and the dysregulation profile predict executive functioning in children with acquired brain injury. *Child Neuropsychology*, 1–19. https://doi.org/10.1080/09297049.2019.1589442.

Checa, P., & Fernández-Berrocal, P. (2015). The role of intelligence quotient and emotional intelligence in cognitive control processes. *Frontiers in Psychology, 6*, 1–8. https://doi.org/10.3389/fpsyg.2015.01853.

Cherry, K. (2019a). *Just noticeable difference (JND) in psychology*. Retrieved from https://www.verywellmind.com/what-is-the-just-noticeable-difference-2795306.

Cherry, K. (2019b). *The Yerkes-Dodson law and performance*. Retrieved from https://www.verywellmind.com/what-is-the-yerkes-dodson-law-2796027.

Crisp, E. (2019, July 23). La.'s Hep C model draws interest. *The Advocate*, 7A.

Glozman, J. (2013). *Explorations in developmental psychology: Developmental neuropsychology*. New York, NY: Routledge.

Just-Noticeable Difference. (n.d.). Retrieved from https://courses.lumenlearning.com/wm-biology2/chapter/just-noticeable-difference/.

Nemeth, D. G., Chustz, K. M., & McElroy, P. (2019). *Creating executive functions in tweens with learning disabilities*. In: *Presented at the CW Austin learning disability conference, Baton Rouge, LA, February*.

Pacheco-Unguetti, A. P., Acosta, A., Callejas, A., & Lupiáñez, J. (2010). Attention and anxiety: Different attentional functioning under state and trait anxiety. *Psychological Science*, 1–7. https://doi.org/10.1177/0956797609359624.

Peterson, J. Z., Porter, R. J., & Miskowiak, K. W. (2019). Clinical characteristics associated with the discrepancy between subjective and objective cognitive impairment in depression. *Journal of Affective Disorders*, *246*, 763–774. https://doi.org/10.1016/j.jad.2018.12.105.

Robinson, O. J., Vytal, K., Cornwell, B. R., & Grillon, C. (2013). The impact of anxiety upon cognition: Perspectives from human threat of shock studies. *Frontiers in Human Neuroscience*, *7*, 1–21. https://doi.org/10.3389/fnhum.2013.00203.

Roiser, J. P., & Sahakian, B. J. (2013). Hot and cold cognition in depression. *CNS Spectrums*, *18*(3), 1–11. https://doi.org/10.1017/S1092852913000072.

Shrestha, P. (2017). Motivation emotion: Yerkes-Dodson law. *Psychestudy*. Retrieved from https://www.psychestudy.com/general/motivation-emotion/yerkes-dodson-law.

Sohlberg, M. M., & Mateer, C. A. (1987). Effectiveness of an attention-training program. *Journal of Clinical and Experimental Neuropsychology*, *9*, 117–130.

Spielberger, C. D. (2010). State-trait anxiety inventory. In *Corsini encyclopedia of psychology*. Hoboken: John Wiley & Sons, Inc. https://doi.org/10.1002/9780470479216.corpsy0943.

Stegmann, Y., Reicherts, P., Andreatta, M., Pauli, P., & Wieser, M. J. (2019). The effect of trait anxiety on attentional mechanisms in combined context and cue conditioning and extinction learning. *Scientific Reports*, 1–12. https://doi.org/10.1038/s41598-019-45239-3.

Tulving, E. (2002). Episodic memory: From mind to brain. *Annual Review of Psychology*, *53*, 1–25. Retrieved from https://www.annualreviews.org/doi/10.1146/annurev.psych.53.100901.135114.

Vytal, K. E., Cornwell, B. R., Letkiewicz, A. M., Arkin, N. E., & Grillon, C. (2013). The complex interaction between anxiety and cognition: Insight from spatial and verbal working memory. *Frontiers in Human Neuroscience*, *7*, 1–11. https://doi.org/10.3389/fnhum.2013.00093.

Williams, Y. (n.d.). Episodic memory: Definition and examples. Retrieved from https://study.com/academy/lesson/episodic-memory-definition-examples-quiz.html.

Ylvisaker, M., & Feeney, T. (2009). Apprenticeship in self-regulation supports and interventions for individuals with self-regulatory impairments. *Developmental Neurorehabilitation*, *12*, 370–379.

Zelazo, P. D., & Carlson, S. M. (2012). Hot and cool executive function in childhood and adolescence: Development and plasticity. *Child Development Perspectives*, *6*(4), 354–360. https://doi.org/10.1111/j.1750-8606.2012.00246.x.

Further reading

Rock, P. L., Roiser, J. P., Riedel, W. J., & Blackwell, A. D. (2013). Cognitive impairment in depression: A systematic review and meta-analysis. *Psychological Medicine*, *44*(10), 2029–2040. https://doi.org/10.1017/S0033291713002535.

Tecce, J. J. (1965). Relationship of anxiety (drive) and response competition in problem solving. *Journal of Abnormal Psychology*, *70*(6), 465–467.

Chapter 8

Preparing children to learn through early intervention

Carla Anauate[a,b,c,d], Edna Maria Severino Peters Kahhale[b]
[a]*CINAPSI—Centro Integrado de Neuropsicologia e Psicologia, Integrated Center of Neuropsychology and Psychology, São Paulo, Brazil,* [b]*PUCSP—Pontifical Catholic University of São Paulo, Department of Psychology, São Paulo, Brazil,* [c]*Department of Psychology, Emory University, Atlanta, GA, United States,* [d]*CENSUPEG—College of Science, Education, Health, Research and Management, Joinville, Brazil*

Introduction

Alexander R. Luria and Ralph M. Reitan are icons of neuropsychology recognized worldwide from, respectively, Russia and the United States. Both were concerned with the evaluation of brain lesions and/or impairments as well as developmental neuropsychology. Both were scientists who left a legacy to the world in terms of the extension of their work and their discoveries as well as the number of followers who use their evaluation batteries and concepts, then build new forms of clinical applications on them. By studying these two renowned neuropsychologists, scientists from all over the world use their concepts and studies to think beyond and adapt and actualize new forms of working with the human being. In this way, it is very important to have a solid base, a structural theoretical base, to be able to work on top, to progress, and to think beyond.

Luria and Reitan structured this base with concepts, research, and evaluation batteries that many actual neuropsychologists use to produce and renew practices actualizing studies and theory. Both lived in an era without technological supplies. I wonder how their theories and evaluations would be in the present when technology is one of our important tools of communication? Luria focused mainly on a qualitative evaluation and Reitan more on a quantitative evaluation. Both were interested in explaining how the brain works, and on forms of evaluating to help identify the compromise to rehabilitate based on more precise data. Neither worked specifically with early intervention, but both studied and developed concepts, theories, and practices that have led to scientists who followed their principles, updating their ideas and clinical applicability.

In the following paragraphs, the intention is to briefly introduce both Luria and Reitan regarding their main works as neuropsychologists who are

Evaluation and Treatment of Neuropsychologically Compromised Children
https://doi.org/10.1016/B978-0-12-819545-1.00008-4

recognized and studied all over the world. It is important to emphasize that not much was explored concerning the fetus stage and infancy. When researching children, both Luria and Reitan studied the early years of childhood, comparing and contrasting disabled, brain-damaged, and typical groups but not much more in the earlier years.

Alexander R. Luria

Luria (1902–1977) researched psychology and the brain in a very broad sense, including studies of psychoanalysis, reflexology, personality traits, linguistic aphasia, anterior lobe pathology, speech dysfunction, and child neuropsychology, among other areas related to both psychology and neuropsychology. Luria not only had a vast investigation regarding the functions of the human brain, but also focused his work on the development of psychopathology and the managing of neural injuries.

Luria, together with Vygotsky and Leontiev, worked to establish the cultural-historical approach in psychology, which enabled them to study the way in which natural processes such as physical maturation and sensory mechanisms together with culturally determined processes produce psychological functions. It concerns the cultural mediation in the constitution of human psychological processes and the role of the social environment in structuring the means by which children appropriate the cultural tools of the environment where they grew up in the process of ontogeny (Luria, 1979).

In the early 1930s, Luria went to Uzbekistan, where he investigated changes in perception, problem solving, and memory associated with changes in economic activity and schooling. During this decade, he also had an opportunity to study identical and fraternal twins raised in a large residential school, where he considered the relations between phylogenetic and cultural-historical factors in the development of language and thought (Glozman, 2013).

The author emphasizes that in sequence, Luria entered medical school where he studied the relation between language and thought, specializing in the study of aphasia. During World War II, Luria was based in a hospital in Kisegach in Ural, Russia. There he conducted a large study of several forms of traumatic brain injury, which gave him a lot of material for developing his theories of brain function and methods for the remediation of focal brain lesions. It was during this period that he developed the systematic approach of brain and cognition, which served as the foundation of neuropsychology.

After World War II, Luria did his pioneer research in child neuropsychology through a series of studies of the development of language and thought in intellectually disabled children at the Institute of Defectology in Moscow. Homskaya, Luria's former student, summarizes his approach as:

> *The application of the Method of Motor Associations (which) allowed investigators to reveal difficulties experienced by (unskilled) children in the process of forming conditioned links as well as restructuring and compensating by means of*

speech ... (Unskilled) children demonstrated acute dysfunction of the generalizing and regulating functions of speech.

Homskaya (2001, p. 46)

The author affirms that Luria explored his ideas about the differences of neurodynamic processes in different functional systems, primarily in verbal and motor systems. For Luria, the regulating function of speech is a main factor in the formation of voluntary behavior, in which first the activating function is formed, and only afterward is the inhibitory function formed.

Luria and Simernitskaya's studies concluded that damage to the left and right hemispheres provoked different types of dysfunctions in children than in adults. This started several other investigations regarding changes in the localization of higher psychological functions during the process of development.

Luria, through the functional system named by him, affirmed that human mental processes represented complex functional systems that involved groups of brain areas working in concert, each making a unique contribution to the organization of this system. Luria studied the three principal functional units of the brain necessary for human mental processes: the first unit regulates the tonus and vigilant stages, the second unit obtains, processes, and stores the information, and the third unit programs, regulates, and verifies the mental activity (Luria, 1981). These three units will be addressed later in this chapter with practical examples to be used as clinical applications of post-Luria principles.

Ralph M. Reitan

Reitan (1922–2014), on the other hand, investigated the neuropsychological effects of several neurological diseases and disorders, including cerebral tumors, traumatic brain injury, cerebrovascular disease, Huntington's disease, multiple sclerosis, Parkinson's disease, mental retardation, alcoholism, substance abuse, epilepsy, hypertension, and aging. Reitan also studied the neuropsychological correlates of psychiatric disorders, learning disabilities, aphasia, brucellosis, agenesis of the corpus callosum, elevated serum cholesterol levels, sensorimotor deficits, visual field defects, and myxedema (Hom & Nici, 2015).

The authors mention that one of Reitan's most important contributions to neuropsychology was a battery called the Halstead-Reitan Neuropsychological Test Battery (HRB), which he organized and which was based and named after his former teacher, Ward Halstead. The tests he used in the battery were a sample of important human abilities and were selected on an empirical basis that went beyond theory itself. The battery of tests included measures of sensory-perceptual tasks, motor tasks, psychomotor, attention/concentration, visual-spatial relationships, memory and learning, aspects of language, abstraction, problem-solving procedures, and concept formation. Although more quantitative, HRB has also qualitative ways of being analyzed. It is regularly used associated with the Wechsler scales, the MMPI, and the WRAT to better understand the individual's neuropsychological condition.

Reed and Reed (2015) stated that besides studying adults with brain lesions, Reitan had a definite but secondary interest in programs for children. He modified the Halstead tests to make them suitable for children from 9 or 10 years of age through the teen years. For still younger children, tests similar to those designed for older subjects were identified and developed. Even new tests were added that included concept formation and psychomotor abilities. Reitan would normally use the children's form of the Wechsler test to complement his data.

Reitan did some more modifications to the test procedures so that he could test even younger children. He organized some new tasks that would be more appropriate for children ranging from 5 to 8 years old, calling this new test the Reitan-Indiana Neuropsychological Test Battery. One of the additional modifications that Reitan made was the Category Test, in which the change was done so that the answers were based on color and not on number. With even more additional test modifications and procedures, the test was designed for even younger children, starting at 3 years old. Unfortunately, Reitan never had the opportunity to test out this battery (Hom & Nici, 2015).

Reitan also researched children regarding the area of learning disabilities. He and his colleagues examined three groups of children: a group with brain damage, a group with normal neurological exams but significant academic delay, and a group of normal controls. Selz and Reitan (1979) mentioned that the performances of the learning-disabled children fell in between the performances of the normal controls and those children with brain-damage. It was observed that the group that included learning-disabled children was similar to the control group on tasks that had a motor component. On the other hand, the group of children with learning disabilities performed similar to the brain-damage group on tasks with cognitive or attentional demands. The conclusion was that the effects of brain damage in infancy or childhood can limit the potential for normal development and may result in delays on achieving cognitive and behavioral milestones.

> *While our results suggest that early damage has relatively severe consequences, it is possible that the plasticity of the immature brain may, in some instances, permit adaptation to the damage. Probably, however, the more frequent result is that damage to the immature brain imposes a limitation on the potential for acquisition of abilities in the developmental years of childhood.*
>
> Reitan (1974, p. 70)

Early intervention—Prenatal stage

When we consider all the background in neuropsychology and previous studies of Luria, Reitan and their followers plus the clinical application of their theories about the brain and brain functions, early intervention, in our point of view, starts before the child has ever been conceived. It all starts with the desire to become parents and the preparation that this involves, leading to the healthy development of a child. People who organize themselves and their routines for raising a child are already thinking in preventive measures, which are themselves early intervention. This preparation involves a life change, organization, and planning to include this new being inside the womb of a family. Internal, including both physical and psychological preparation, plus external, including housing, economic, and time preparation, have to be done. To raise a child is a life-changing and challenging experience. Therefore, it is fundamental to use all preventive measures possible to aim at healthy and positive results regarding the new life to be conceived.

Early intervention should emphasize important issues that can prevent psychological and neuropsychological disturbances from occurring and can enhance learning abilities. Some important orientations to be given to couples who wish to become parents include: (a) avoid using alcohol, drugs, and cigarettes; (b) live an organized life; (c) do physical activity; (d) get plenty of rest, live a healthy life in a calm and safe environment, as a calm attitude and positive emotions are key; (e) drink plenty of fluids, eat healthy food, avoid eating raw meat and raw fish; (f) avoid contact with rodents, cats, and wild pigeons, which can transmit sicknesses such as toxoplasmosis; (g) have a good relationship with the partner; (h) hear nice music that encourages happy and calm feelings; (i) doctors should orientate the use of prenatal vitamins; (j) avoid X-rays, hot tubs, and saunas; and (k) make use of therapeutic practices when needed, among other specific orientations based on the individual needs of the parents (Anauate, 2017).

Public health should be the main channel to direct information to the population so that it reaches the largest amount of people. Unadvised people can make mistakes, but knowledgeable people have a choice to follow orientations and proceed with a healthy lifestyle regarding their pregnancy and their relation with the baby. Being able to make a choice involves responsibility and commitment. In this way, it is fundamental to be able to have all the information available in a broad sense, using media and other public resources so that people can make choices.

This preparation will continue throughout the whole pregnancy wherein mother and father will enjoy the pregnancy in order to start an important and affectionate bond with the baby. Early intervention during pregnancy includes group orientation activities, which can be provided by medical assistance professionals with the intention to promote and stimulate these bonds. Weekly meetings can be an opportunity for pregnant couples to meet and exchange ideas, doubts, and wishes. In these meetings, it would be good to emphasize the importance of the relation with the belly, such as talking to the baby, tenderly passing the hand on the belly (both father and mother), and other bond development activities that can aid this relation. A lively and affectionate climate should be present within motherhood.

Another nice intervention activity to suggest is to cut out a cardboard paper with a drawing that the couple likes, for example, a flower, a heart, or any other symbol. In a dark room, tenderly pass a flashlight around the picture drawn while talking or singing tenderly to the baby. This activity, besides the need to focus attention, can also have a response from the baby's pushing against the belly. Another intervention and relaxing activity to do during pregnancy is to put, close to the belly, a speaker or headphones with a style of music that the couple likes and that makes them feel calm, arousing a loving and tender feeling. The orientation would be to pass the hand on the belly and kindly talk to the baby while listening to the music.

Studies were made with this speaker activity in which a speaker was put in the womb and the baby's heart rate increased with loud noise and decreased with a female voice, proving that the fetus discriminates sounds and physically reacts to them. The repetition of the sound stimulation slows down the reaction because there is a habituation or memorization. It was proven that the fetus can be very specific, hearing and even discriminating different syllables and memorizing sounds and songs that his parents heard (Busnel, 2003).

The author points out that studies show that the simple thought of the mother directed to the fetus wakes him up because the mother, when thinking about the fetus, undergoes physiological changes. Regarding the newborn, Busnel (2003) mentions that he prefers to listen to the voice he knows than to other voices he has never heard. He responds more when his mother's voice addresses him than when an unknown voice talks to him.

An important part of early intervention is also being able to do a good prenatal follow-through. From the beginning of pregnancy, a woman should be followed closely, preferably by the same doctor that will be the one present at the delivery of the baby. Preparation should be done with orientations from the first trimester. A monthly appointment should be scheduled to check the growth of the baby and to inform the parents about what changes will occur to the mom and to the fetus during that specific month. This monthly follow up can prevent and treat emotional problems that can arise during pregnancy.

As the fetus pays attention to what happens inside and outside the womb, it is important to give psychological and physiological support to a mother who is suffering so as to improve the psycho-physiological situation of the baby at birth. This support can prevent permanent effects on the baby that can result in developmental compromises (Busnel, 2003).

The author concludes that babies who underwent stress during pregnancy have less ability to withstand stress in adult life. Fetuses of anxious or stressed mothers were found to be much more active and fearful while crying more, having more digestive disorders, and sleeping less. Busnel (2003) mentions that these babies were described by researchers as difficult-tempered, overactive, always hungry, often crying, and having frequent cramps. Research shows that women who experienced stress, especially in the third trimester of pregnancy, are at an increased risk of having small children due to the interruption of breathing and hardening of the umbilical artery, causing a reduction in placental irrigation as well as a reduction of movement and weight. They are also at higher risk of preterm birth, a weaker APGAR, and a longer hospitalization period.

Wilheim (1992) mentions that other emotional states of the mother such as sadness and depression, which result in an elevation of the cortisol level, are also passed to the fetus, causing him to close himself as self-protection. The author believes that injuries to the baby's emotional structure produce traumatic imprints.

All sociocultural, psychological, and family interventions designed to help mothers understand and solve their problems have the effect of reducing or even nullifying the effects of stress. The most urgent need, however, is to create mechanisms to help pregnant women who are experiencing difficulties to get in touch with their babies and reduce the stress effect (Busnel, 2003).

Prenatal orientations, in the third trimester of pregnancy, together with medical and psychological monitoring of the mother and the fetus are important to welcome and discuss the fantasies, fears, expectations, etc. Some important bonding activities should be addressed and taught at this time, which is a time very close to delivery, to knowing the baby. These issues include using shantala techniques, singing, dancing, and talking to the baby to promote relational bonds among parents and the baby as soon as he is born. These orientations are part of early intervention methods in applied clinical work.

Other important orientations should also be given to the parents at the last trimester of pregnancy to prepare them to be attentive parents: pay attention to the baby's initiatives and respond to them by showing that you are present in this dynamic relationship; look the baby in the eyes, talk to him, and touch him as you change diapers, breastfeed, and during all situations that you are together to create visual, auditory, and tactile contact. Use all the baby's senses; let feelings of tenderness arise and name them; establish a relationship with your baby; hold the baby tightly and securely to pass safety; be entire and complete in the relationship; when the baby makes a gesture, do the same gesture back to show that you are following him, paying attention to him; and when the baby makes a sound, repeat this sound back to the baby. Tell the baby what you understand that this sound means, name the sound, communicating in a sensitive way with your baby (Anauate, 2017).

The preparation for delivery is also very important because it works toward the feelings of safety and well-being of the mother. When the mother feels safe and cherished as well as closely followed by a trustful doctor, she will welcome the baby more secure of herself as an entire human being. The best option will be for the same doctor who was present during the prenatal process to be the same one on the delivery. This acts in favor of safety and the security feelings of the mother. Odent (2017) points out that studies show that if the baby participates in the labor process, he will be more ready to be born, therefore providing better conditions of development. So, even if the mother and/or doctor chooses a C-section, it would be important for it to be at the baby's pace, or else provide an opportunity for the baby to experience labor conditions for at least a short period of time.

The bonds between mother and baby during delivery are already constituted and will show themselves strong at the first encounter face to face. It is a magical moment that should be lived in its intensity. The participation of the father is also important. The father at this point has an important task in helping the mother to bond with the baby as well to himself. From day one, parents will just increase and deepen their bonds with the baby as well as provide developmental opportunities to their child.

Early intervention—Postnatal

To clinically apply early intervention, it is important to pay attention and promote the development of all the areas fundamental to the development of the baby in each skill as the baby grows and develops. If possible, the development of the baby should be observed following a medical scale. The scale SGSII, the *Schedule of Growing Skills II* (Bellman, Lingham, & Aukett, 1996), is recommended. It has 10 detailed spheres of development to serve as orientation: passive and active postural control, visual, manipulative, locomotor, hearing and speech, talk and speech, social interaction, personal autonomy, and cognitive. All these spheres should be analyzed month by month to see if the baby/child achieves the milestones necessary for his adequate development because each sphere has a chronological step-by-step development. All the spheres follow ontological milestones and aim at the healthy development of the child.

The brain doubles in size and quadruples in synaptogenesis during the first year of life (Tau & Peterson, 2010). In this way, it is fundamental to apply a proposal of early intervention to optimize this developmental stage of life. The early intervention can be applied by a significant other, an adult, or a caregiver, as suggested below, and should be applied if delays are noticed. Reitan (1974) mentions that a training program should be established to suit the unique and individual needs of children who have specific deficits. Therefore, preventively speaking, let us examine each sphere contemplated on the SGSII (Bellman et al., 1996) and suggest some ways to enhance child development and learning abilities as the baby grows.

Orientations to caregivers based on the spheres of SGSII

First sphere: Passive postural control

- The caregiver should use his own body to give support for the baby to help him to keep his head and back straight;
- The caregiver should help the baby to look at his feet by giving support to his legs and/or putting a rattle on his ankles so he would be curious to look at them;
- The caregiver should give hands for the infant to rise from the lying position to the sitting position;
- The caregiver should play and use a multisensorial ball to massage the body and feet of the baby;
- The caregiver should slide the baby on top of a blanket on the floor of a room.

Second sphere: Active postural control

- The caregiver should give support for the child to rise to the sitting position and stay seated;
- The caregiver should slide the child on ramps;
- The caregiver should give contour to the child while holding him;
- The caregiver should roll the baby with his belly down on a roll pillow using a toy, which the child will want to grab, as bait;
- The caregiver should roll the baby with his belly down on a Bobath ball;
- The caregiver should play with the baby, putting him on the lap and bending the knees up and down;
- The caregiver should give support for the child to stay standing and provide secure places for the child to hold while standing.

Third sphere: Locomotor

- The caregiver should put a toy out of the baby's reach and ask him to crawl or walk in his direction to get it;
- The caregiver should give support to the child for him to walk around;
- The caregiver should stimulate the baby to walk from one adult to the other, offering support;
- The caregiver should call the baby to go in his direction so both can do an activity together;
- The caregiver should open the space for the child to walk;
- The caregiver should promote walking and jumping activities such as walking on top of a line or jumping from one side of the room to the other with both feet or on one foot;
- The caregiver should support and help a child to climb the stairs on a secure space (cushion stairs) where the child can go up and down, first crawling and then walking;
- The caregiver should promote opportunity for the child to repeat motor activities associated with the words of the music, such as "The wheels of the bus go round and round…" Sing and show the baby how to turn his arms around and around in front of his chest as well as other movements related to the song.

Fourth sphere: Manipulatives

- The caregiver should put rattles on the wrist of the baby so he is motivated to look at his hands and play with them;
- The caregiver should give a toy to the baby so he can grab it as well as motivate him to pass the toy from one hand to the other or even unite two toys, such as cubes, in which a cube is in each hand;
- The caregiver should demonstrate how to play with particular toys, such as playing with the keys of a piano;
- The caregiver should present finger puppets to the baby and let the baby touch and interact with the puppets;

- The caregiver should present a book to the baby so that he can flip the pages and point to characters, stimulating joint attention;
- The caregiver should present tactile materials to the baby so that he can feel the different textures;
- The caregiver should stimulate the baby to clap his hands together with the music;
- The caregiver should give cubes to the baby so that he can put them inside a container or so that he can build a tower with them;
- The caregiver should give a pencil to the child so that he can scribble and as he matures, the caregiver should ask him to draw geometric figures or even the human figure.

Fifth sphere: Visual

- The caregiver should pass a toy in front of the baby's eyes from one side to the other so that he can look and follow the toy; the caregiver should increase the distance as the baby grows and matures;
- The caregiver should point to objects and name them, stimulating joint attention;
- The caregiver should present to the baby objects with different colors;
- The caregiver should present to the baby story books with colorful drawings;
- The caregiver should show to the baby very colorful and singing videos;
- The caregiver should present to the baby toys that light up;
- The caregiver should demonstrate the songs with motor acts that the child can visualize;
- The caregiver should hide behind a little cloth or behind his hands and play hide and seek with the baby;
- The caregiver should hide the toys that the baby likes to play with under a piece of cloth so that the baby is challenged to look for them;
- The caregiver should give to the baby a wooden board with figures that come out so that he can practice taking them out and putting them back in.

Sixth sphere: Auditory and language

- The caregiver should name objects and the world to the child;
- The caregiver should talk and sing to the child;
- The caregiver should call the child by his name;
- The caregiver should practice waving goodbye, saying "no," and balancing the finger, introducing negative phrases to the baby and sending kisses;
- The caregiver should play music and music videos and sing along, clapping hands and doing the movements that the song suggests;
- The caregiver should repeat and name the gurgling sounds the baby emits;
- The caregiver should introduce to the baby the parts of the body, objects, colors, animals, etc., so that he can practice asking the child to give him what he asks for;
- As the baby matures, the caregiver should practice giving simple orders to the baby so that he can practice to do what he is asked.

Seventh sphere: Speech and language

- The caregiver should return to the baby an answer to all the sounds that he emits being responsive to the baby's initiative, establishing a dialogue with him;
- The caregiver should name the world to the baby and give name to his guttural sounds;
- The caregiver should tell a story to the child and ask for the child to name the sounds of the animals within the story, for example, "the cow goes moooooooo";
- The caregiver should ask, "Where is __________ (name of the baby)?";
- The caregiver should encourage the child to sing along with the music and to rhyme phrases and words;
- The caregiver should play talking on the phone with the child, saying "Hello! How are you?" and wait for the child's response;
- The caregiver should talk to the baby using full words so that both can start to introduce a conversation.

Eighth sphere: Social interaction

- The caregiver should smile to the baby and caress him;
- The caregiver should show how to caress one another;
- The caregiver should talk to the baby using a low pitch tone of voice;
- The caregiver should give a pleasant bath with toys and a lot of talking and singing;
- The caregiver should clap hands and send kisses when playing with the baby;
- The caregiver should introduce a ball and play with this ball, rolling it back and forth to and from the baby;
- The caregiver should hold a toy close to the ear, as if it were a telephone and ask for the child to imitate him and simulate a conversation;
- The caregiver should wave and say goodbye;
- The caregiver should provide opportunity for the baby to share toys and play with siblings and friends;
- The caregiver should give a notion of limitation to the children (do not hit the friend, caress without force);
- The caregiver should play hide and seek;
- The caregiver should hide a toy and ask the baby to find it.

Ninth sphere: Personal autonomy

- The caregiver should, when giving the bottle to the baby, stimulate him to hold the bottle and afterward do the same with a cup;
- The caregiver should encourage the baby to play with toys of his choice;
- The caregiver should call the baby when he is far away or ask him to bring something to him to encourage him to walk around the room;
- The caregiver should give the baby a hand to stimulate him to climb the stairs;

- The caregiver should let the baby eat the food you give him by himself, such as fruits, and as he matures, should provide opportunity for the baby to hold a spoon and then a fork;
- The caregiver should start potty training, permitting the child to know when she is dirty and needs help to be cleaned;
- The caregiver should wash the baby's hands before feeding him and stimulate him to do it as he matures;
- The caregiver should let the baby help with dressing himself and when he matures, give him the clothes and let him dress alone.

Tenth sphere: Cognitive

- The caregiver should pick up an object or bring a hand to the ear and say "Hello," pretending it is a telephone;
- The caregiver should provide opportunity to do motor activities as soon as music starts playing, as in the song "The wheels of the bus go round and round," when the caregiver should start moving the arms around and around;
- The caregiver should hide toys under the leg or a piece of cloth to encourage the child to look for the hidden object;
- The caregiver should, while playing, see if the baby is able to take turns and see if he can wait for his turn;
- The caregiver should give cubes to the baby so he can put them inside a container or so that he can build a tower;
- The caregiver should give him a pencil so he can scribble and as he matures, ask him to draw geometric figures or even the human figure;
- The caregiver should point to objects and name them;
- The caregiver should present objects with different colors;
- The caregiver should present story books with colorful drawings;
- The caregiver should hide the toys that the baby likes to play with under a piece of cloth so that the baby is challenged to look for them;
- The caregiver should give the baby a wooden board with figures that come out so that he can practice taking them out and putting them back in;
- The caregiver should provide playing conditions with different children for them to explore social relations as well as different games, toys, and turn-taking.

Attachment and brain development

Neuropsychology, as a science, is present in the lives of people as soon as early childhood when counseling is given to parents of babies aiming at prevention and health promotion. It concerns early orientation regarding the importance of bond formation related to cognitive development. The bond between parents and children is fundamental in early intervention, promoting the learning abilities of a child.

Cozolino (2013) states that during the first year of attachment, relationships and emotional regulation are developed. The right hemisphere has more growth at this time, which is an important period of learning, in the areas related to bonding, emotional regulation, and self-esteem. High levels of maternal attention result in more benzodiazepine, oxytocin, and glucocorticoid receptors being formed in more regions of the brain, increasing attention, curiosity, and the exploratory behavior of the baby. Current evidence suggests that parental attachment ability is associated with how a child experiences this relationship with his parents. Children need their family's support to feel safe to manage the challenges of life.

The author states that newborns mimic the faces of adults around them due to the mirror neuron. The adult opens his mouth, puts his tongue out, makes sad or happy faces, and the baby imitates it in a reflective way. Imitation is essential for learning, interpersonal bonding, and brain development. This emotional resonance between mother and baby becomes an important step toward empathy as well as future functioning, including more time in social engagement, better emotional regulation, engagement in symbolic play, higher IQ, and greater ability to comment on feelings and inner experiences. People must be tuned in to be able to connect, bond, and learn from others. Sculpting the brain networks through early relationships allows people to think about themselves, to trust themselves, to regulate their emotions, to maintain positive expectations, and to use their intellectual and emotional intelligence in making decisions. Maternal care increases brain growth and function. Fonseca (2013) mentions that a baby is a social human being and that attachment is the first step to learning and development.

Luria (1991, 1992, 2001) agrees and considers that the experiences lived by the child from 0 to 3 years have a potential force in brain development and affirms that a child who lacked experiences and stimulus can have delays in his speech, reading, singing, and dancing. The author believes that it is essential that children have shared experiences with adults to enhance language and communication. "The formation of a functional system of speech is influenced by the interaction of the child with the surrounding adult" (Glozman, 2013, p. 44).

In this way, Busnel (2003) points out that studies show that the baby prefers the mother talk to him in a higher-frequency pitch, with stronger modulation and slower speech than when a human voice is addressed by another adult. The baby prefers the tone of voice that expresses happiness; he connects and attunes more to these adults as a whole.

Vygotsky (1994) states that man constitutes himself within social relations. Relations will constitute this person as a human being who will internalize the world as it is presented to him, transforming objectivity, the external world, into subjectivity, the internal world. The author explains this when he affirms that instruments, actions, and social relations are first presented to the child in an interpsychological and social level, and only afterward will it occur in an intrapsychological, internal, and subjective level through the process of internalization.

These concepts are very important when we talk about early intervention because, more than what is given to the child, it is important to focus on how it is given. In other words, the HOW is more important than the WHAT. The "how" involves relations that constitutes man as a unique human being, which will internalize the world his own way, the way he was brought up, within his culture and within his emotional experiences.

Solovieva and Rojas (2016) mention that Vygotsky considers that affection is the basis of all the psychological development of the child. The existence of a positive emotional life from birth is considered to be an important step in child development because affection and intellect do not exist in separate ways.

In this way, a good bond that provides and forms relations is important for the development and maturation of a child. Because of this, it is necessary to respect the initiatives of the child and then respond to them, showing that he is an authentic person with desires and needs that must be expressed, heard, and addressed throughout his development.

Social encounters take place as an emotional exchange, which occurs in a sequence of communication in a go-and-come-back way (Leal, 2003). Soboleva mentions that the formation of higher mental functions—attention, memory, psychomotricity, language, perception, and executive functions—improves school performance, as it develops not only affective but also communicative abilities that are fundamental for school readiness and preparation for learning (Glozman, 2013).

Luria's studies of brain activity show the value of communication to the mental development of children, in which language is one expression of reality (Luria, 1991). The development of language is a result of the interaction between mother and baby in which there is the negotiation of meanings. The communicative ability is formed in a social environment since birth. It is a product of the interaction of people, which also produces social learning. A group involving two or more people is the most appropriate environment for people to master their skills in a social context.

Rojas and Solovieva (2013) report that words spoken aloud lead to changes in the intellectual activity of a child and that the participation of language in problem solving facilitates and directs the search for the correct answer. Language, therefore, has the power to act on the intellectual development of a child. In the beginning, the child formulates concepts from a direct relation that he shares with the concrete reality to gradually realize increasingly complex abstractions and generalizations (Vygotsky, 1998a, 1998b).

Leal (2003) affirms that playing is an effective and relational way to do this because it favors self-awareness as well as emotional involvement and motivation, culminating in learning and internalization. Cozolino (2013) considers that the brain is constructed and regulated within interpersonal relationships that occur by facial expressions as well as physical and ocular contact. In this sense, the human brain is known to be the most dependent and adaptive in the world.

Winnicott (1975) argues that a sufficiently good mother promotes conditions of dependability, allowing security to be established so that the baby can integrate and become a part of the world. It is this confidence, generated within a facilitating environment, that promotes healthy maturation. This trust established in a facilitating environment promotes healthy development. Bowlby (1988) affirms that a child raised by a sufficiently good mother will most probably have an adequate brain structure, develop a safe system of attachment, and have trust internalized. In this way, the child will be able to have a trustful relationship with the world that surrounds him, with courage to face the challenges and dangers that will arise while he is brought up, becoming resilient. Resilience suggests flexibility and elasticity to deal with adversities and get over them, reaching good results independent of the events of life and circumstances (Cassidy, 2015).

> *In this way, it is fundamental to create a physical, ecological and cultural environment, from gestation to the puerperium, an environment that has space to experience interpersonal relationships, that promote resources and / or conditions for an effective and affective contact that enables child development. We believe that this environment must be reliable, supportive and facilitating, providing growth as well as cognitive and personal maturity to the baby.*
>
> Anauate (2017, p. 50)

Leal (2003) mentions that the baby has an innate impulse to seek the reaction of the other person and to relate to the other, who seems to be a legitimate and responsive person. The author affirms that, within dialogical relationships, the baby's brain develops and matures by increasing his brain networks.

The bases of learning are located in the structural and functional modifications of the neuron and its connections. Lashley (1929) states that alterations occur in the functioning of the neuron according to both chemical and physical changes. Chemical changes happen due to an increase in the amount of neurotransmitters produced by neurons. Physical changes occur due to the increase of the number of branches that interconnect the neurons as well as the increase of the number of synapses or points of communication of each branch.

Schore (2003) points out that the first 2 years of a baby's life are the critical years of brain growth and that these 2 years are directly related to the period of bonding established between the baby and his primary caregiver, which, most of the time, is the biological mother. This relationship will significantly influence the maturation of the right side of the baby's brain that occurs through the caregiver and baby relationship in the postnatal period. The orbitofrontal region of the brain is responsible for the regulation of affective, motivational, and cognitive adaptive functions. Other areas of the developing brain that are also impacted by relational communication that results in safe bonding experiences include the areas in the limbic system, especially the amygdala (Schore, 2003).

Leal (2003) emphasizes that back-and-forth communication is observed very early in the life of a baby. The author considers that this is the root of motor, affective, and cognitive development. The interaction, in itself, builds the brain of the interlocutors, optimizing the plasticity and the construction of new neuronal structures. It is in this critical period of neuronal growth and brain organization, more than in others, that the relationship experiences associated with feelings of security, bonding, and sense of self become essential (Cozolino, 2013).

Glozman (2013) affirms that many forms of social influence will have an implication on the formation of the higher mental functions of the child as well as stimulate the maturation of the brain structures. Anauate (2017) states that in this way, the interaction of two people in joint activity, regulated by language, is crucial for this formation, as it involves the internalization of social meanings. The environment impacts human development, which includes both the physiological and anatomical maturation of the brain. We believe that biological and social development factors are closely related and interdependent.

> *The development of language – one of the first subjects studied by the young Luria - was never seen by him as an anatomic development of 'language areas' in the brain, but as resulting from the interaction of mother and child, from the negotiation of meanings between mother and child, as being in the mode of interaction or 'betweenness' and this as a prerequisite for, and needing to be structuralized in, the developing neurolinguistics systems of the brain.*
>
> Sacks (1990, p. 188)

The social situation during the development of a child is determined by the learning activity. This activity at primary school will shape the child's personality and mental processes. The learning activity has a goal to master science and cultural objects so that the child can act and evolve with them. The learning of concepts forms the internal action plan of children, allowing anticipation of their actions and transformation of objects. The main issue is for the child to be able to learn in an independent way. This way the child will become the subject of change in the learning activity, building it while assimilating the concepts (Glozman, 2013).

The author mentions Elkonin's point of view of the learning activity as including learning objectives, educational action concerning the assimilation of the educational material; control, to see if the student does the action according to the model; and evaluation to determine if results were achieved. In this way, the learning activity is not given to the child, but is built in forms of joint activity between the adult and child within meaningful actions.

Childhood interventions

Glozman (2013) states that the readiness to go to school, according to Elkonin, involves a verbal regulation of behavior, where internal and external instructions regulate the way the child chooses his actions. The author continues saying that the child should be able to work independently to maintain control and self-control as well as the development of the function of programming, regulation, and control and coordinating the action regulation and the coordination of the action. In this way, external rules become an internal representation of how to act in situations. When a child enters school, he changes his relation with the world around him. Two types of relationships start to form: child-adult and child-child, both connected to cognitive and play activity. The learning activity recruits the child to himself, requiring reflection and analysis. The author points out that the learning activity includes learning objectives, educational actions, control, and evaluation. Nonetheless, learning has to be constructed in joint activities, with the use of communication, to compose the higher mental functions.

In the below paragraphs, joint activities will be suggested as childhood interventions aimed at enhancing learning abilities and the development of the superior mental functions—attention, memory, perception, language, psychomotricity, reasoning, and executive functions—using as a base important concepts established by the Russian troika, Luria, Vygotsky, and Leontiev.

To Vygotsky (1998a, 1998b), a playing activity is connected to the process of learning. To play is to learn. While playing, the child will learn to act in a cognitive sphere and will achieve the base for future complex and elaborate learning abilities. Therefore, playing is an educational proposal to deal with the difficulties of the process of learning abilities. For example, it is through the playing activity that the child will be able to separate thinking from an object, thus enabling the action to emerge from ideas and not from things. In this way, through the toy, the child will start to understand the meaning of concepts and objects.

The process of learning is very complex and involves all the spheres mentioned in this chapter. Mostly, however, we believe that it occurs, as Vygotsky (1994) explains, in the zone of proximal development, in which someone who knows more helps and promotes the passage from a level of potential development, when the child still needs help, to real development, when the child is already able to do the activity himself. It is important to emphasize that significant relational and interpersonal contact promotes development.

Be aware and consider that each individual person has different personality characteristics. For better learning, teach children individually because they are different people, therefore unique and particular. Respect the initiatives of each person and try to respond by always leaving a pause for the next initiative to emerge. Work in a go-and-come-back rhythm, initiative, response, pause, initiative, and so on. Look the child in the eyes and be sensible to his needs. Propose teamwork where two people work together; people working together exchange information and practice their relations. All these basic orientations are fundamental to be taken into consideration in the process of learning, enhancing individuals in their own particular moment and need.

Luria's functional system

To be able to give some examples of what could be done concerning childhood intervention, it is important to introduce Luria's functional system. Luria (1981) emphasized that brain functions are performed by a set of neurons forming a functional system. This system was studied and organized by Luria as a result of his work with injured soldiers during World War II. The system is composed of three functional units, which will be summarized below.

The **first functional unit** is located on the brain stem and on the areas around it, and is responsible for brain activation as well as the vigil state. As a clinical application, several psychomotor exercises can be done to provide brain activation. Below, there are some suggestions of exercises that can be done, such as "Simon says" in which the participants should only obey the command when Simon says. If "Simon says" is not said before a command, the activity should not be done. Another movement exercise to activate the child is "head, shoulder, knees, and toes, knees and toes..." Then, take away the words and just do the movements. Practice memory exercises like "John went to the fair and bought an orange..." The next person continues saying "John went to the fair and bought an orange and Jack went to the fair and bought an apple..." These exercises, which recruit attention, activate the brain and provide a good field of concentration.

Some attention games that can be used are fast games. These games are played by two or more players and have to be played in a correct and fast way. An example of these games is "Spot it," in which two or more players have to find a figure in common in their first card of their deck that matches the figure that is on the card on the table. Another game is "Wanted," in which the player has to pay attention to the four characters of the game and has to accordingly do movements when the character is using his correct clothes and doing the correct action. Books like "Where is Wally," in which people have to do a visual search to find Wally among many confusing figures, is also a focusing visual attention activity. "Halli Galli" is another game that trains visual attention and processing speed as well as math abilities and the control of impulses. Many other games that are directed to draw people's attention to conclude a certain task can be used to activate Luria's first functional unit.

The **second functional unit** is located on the posterior part of the brain, including the parietal, temporal, and occipital lobes, and is responsible for the reception, storage, and analysis of information. Primary areas receive auditory, visual, and somesthetic messages connecting the outside world with the secondary areas. Secondary areas process information and give meaning by integrating perceptions and gnosias. The tertiary areas are for association, which will reach the symbolic and conceptual level, such as oral and written language, the notion of body schema, space, time, and calculation. Many activities can be done that emphasize oral and written activities as well as the use of different noises as well as the use of different noises and of visual and tactile stimuli.

Regarding auditory stimuli, it is interesting to work with musical instruments that stimulate the perception of loudness, pitch, and different frequencies as well as to work with rhythms, such as clapping hands following the rhythm of a musical piece, or even work with the memory of sounds in which several small plastic boxes with different things inside would be used for the person to recognize different patterns and styles of sounds. Concerning visual stimuli, it is interesting to use picture books or flashcards and work with recognition or memory games. Regarding tactile stimuli, several different materials can be available for a blindfolded person to recognize: sand, flour, rice, beans, paint, water, body lotion, and clay. Another form of exercising tactile functions is to put several small objects into a black bag and the person will need to identify what objects are in the bag without seeing them (Dreyfuss, 2017). The use of all the senses with their particular stimuli will enhance even more learning abilities. Repetition is also important for the storage of information as well as using all the senses, providing more opportunities for learning to occur.

The **third functional unit** is located on the frontal lobe and is responsible for programming, regulating, organization, planning, anticipation of action, problem solving, correction of errors, and postponement of impulses; it is the core of the executive functions. The use of games and activities is important to stimulate the thought and planning from both a psychomotor point of view as well as from a cognitive aspect. Before one does a motor exercise or speaks, one has to plan all the details of the action. This part of the brain is responsible for doing it. Some advised games that work the executive functions and abilities such as volition, planning, purposeful action, inhibition, alternation, and operational memory include the following: chess, Mastermind, mancala, SET, and sudoku, among others, that train problem-solving abilities.

Therefore, the development of brain functions, which is the primordial base of the learning activities, passes through the following stages: development of the ascending reticular substance, which is in full action at 12 months; development of the motor and primary sensory area, which is present in the first 2 years of life; the functional maturation of secondary areas, which begins at age 2 and lasts up to 5 years, in which language development and lateralization of the cerebral hemispheres occur; the development of the tertiary areas of the second unit, allowing the production of complex mental activities related to the symbolic and conceptual level, which occurs between the ages of 5 and 12; and the development of the third functional unit of the prefrontal region, where formal operations such as abstractions occur from the age of 12 up.

Luria (1981) affirms that the brain works as in a concert, as all three units work together to form the functional system. One unit helps the other in an interdependent way. Nevertheless, these activities should be developed with a purpose, with an intention so that they become meaningful. Leontiev (1978) explains that all activities proposed should have meaning to the persons who are executing them. They should be driven to a specific objective already foreseen by them. Meaningful actions make sense to the subject and, in this way, are more easily internalized and generalized, enhancing learning abilities and development. Glozman (2013) agrees and adds that purposeful play activities contribute to the child's cognitive and personal growth.

Recent studies

Recent researchers have been studying interventions with the aim of enhancing child development. Below, we will cite some interesting studies that can serve as references for forms of working with early intervention.

Low birth weight

A study on psychomotor development in babies born with low birth weight, according to Alexander Luria's conception, has been recently published. González, Solovieva, Rojas, Meza, and Arce (2016) affirm that low birth weight has a negative impact on the baby's psychomotor development, mainly in the motor and perceptive functions. The authors suggest that cortical activation, related to the first functional unit, using psychomotor and cognitive regulation exercises, vestibular and proprioceptive exercises combined with direct emotional contact between the baby and the adult, promote a better functioning of the brain and can act towards overcoming the impact of low weight and/or prematurity.

This study was conducted in Mexico with 25 babies born with low birth weights and with their parents. The objective of this study was to emphasize that the preventive action in a zone of proximal development is fundamental because it is of empirical and theoretical knowledge that infants who are born with low weight can suffer subsequent developmental consequences if an effective intervention is not performed. The stimulation program carried out had as its main component the relation of the adult parents toward the baby. Adults were asked to speak with a highly positive emotional tone, an expressive attitude, and a smile on their face to the baby using verbalizations, songs, or melodies while performing the exercises. Stages of the program included 1st-month assessment of the baby, 5 months of intervention, evaluation after the 5th month, plus 3 months of intervention and reevaluation in the 8th month.

The results demonstrated a good involvement of the parents after the second month of execution of exercises with positive evaluation of them in relation to the improvement, both relationally and in terms of the baby's movements. It was also noticed, after the eighth month of intervention, that the child showed progress in psychomotor development. The authors emphasized that parents not only learned how to perform all the exercises that would benefit the baby, but also changed the way they related to him, focusing on positive emotional contact and greater conversation, which resulted in positive responses from the baby.

González et al. (2016) concluded that during the first months of life, infants benefit from early stimulation through joint activity with adults, and this is of great importance for the later creation of systems for regulating behavior.

They also believe that emotional communication with parents is essential if the expected levels of development are to emerge, even in babies at risk, such as those born with low birth weights.

Early stimulation

Another interesting intervention material was developed by Guimarães, Assis, Vieira, and Formiga (2015) to guide caregivers and daycare teachers regarding child development. They conducted a survey in Goiânia, Brazil, with 23 subjects: 7 parents and/or guardians of children, 7 nursery teachers, and 9 physiotherapists. They used the following instruments: personal data sheet, an instruction book with accessible language, and demonstrative figures of some exercises.

The authors defined development as the ability to perform complex functions as a result of the interaction between intrinsic factors of the individual and extrinsic factors such as the environment. They concluded that, when development is atypical or with delays, it is important to give extra attention and use preventive actions. They reported that the early years of a baby's life are critical because of brain growth and because of both cognitive and sensorimotor advances due to the intense plasticity of the human brain, which enhances the babies' potential.

> *Various biological and environmental conditions may increase the likelihood of deficits in child development. Among the main biological risk factors are: prematurity, low birth weight, cardiovascular, respiratory and neurological disorders and malnutrition. The environmental risk factors include the physical space where the child lives, parents' schooling, family dynamics, family purchasing power and family relationships.*
>
> Guimarães et al. (2015, p. 1)

The authors discuss the early stimulation that favors the development of the child, which consists of adequate human contact and exploration of objects and spaces at the right moment and with the right amount. In this sense, Guimarães et al. (2015) mentioned that the mediating agent is fundamental for the promotion of child development, and because children typically stay in the daycare center for many hours a day, it is necessary for the professionals who work there to study and collaborate for the prevention of neuropsychomotor delays, establishing intervention strategies that promote development.

The didactic material manufactured and used by the authors was positively accepted by the participants in the study and considered a facilitator of the practice because it standardized the guidelines, aiding in the memorization of the contents. The research had a favorable result because with the use of the booklet, it was possible to identify delays in the development of children as well as instruct the caregiver with simple measures of stimulation through play activities aimed at child development.

Interactive activities

A study was carried out by Soto (2018), at the Benemerit Autonomous University of Puebla, Mexico, which contemplated the precepts of the cultural-historical theory linked to Luria's theory of neuropsychology. It included the accomplishment of a series of interactive activities that promoted the development of indicators of development related to babies between 2 and 14 months of age. The parents were instructed on how to carry out the activities so that they could be inserted into the daily routine of their children. The study included 17 babies, 12 in the intervention group with interventions during 8 months, and 5 in the control group. Both groups were evaluated using T. Hellbrugge's "Evaluation of the psychomotor development of the baby," the "Kinesiological evaluation of the first year" of V. Vojta, the "Neuropsychological assessment for children from 2 to 14 months of age," and a questionnaire for parents.

A series of activities was done based on the results found in the qualitative evaluation of the quality of the infants' relationship with their primary caregivers. They were taught to interact with the baby to promote the development of regulation mechanisms. The intervention itself is based more on making a previous diagnosis of risk factors and facilitating, inhibiting, or modifying behavior that favors the child to develop in a harmonic and integral way.

The study was based on the four periods characterized by Lisina (1987): (1) animation complex, observed up to 3 months of age and based on the positive emotional response of the child to the interaction with the adult, such as social smiles, body animation, and sounds emitted; (2) interaction with objects, observed from 4 to 6 months and based on the possibility of the child to interact with the objects proposed by the adult; (3) social communication skills, observed between 8 and 11 months, and the initiative of communication by the baby in relation to the adult or toward attractive objects; and finally (4) directed guidance, observed between 12 and 14 months, related to the possibility of the child to follow a proposed play activity established by the adult. Interaction proposals were made for each of these periods using the following parameters: what is the communicative situation, what are the objectives, what are the brain circuits, what are the proposed activities, what are the proposed contexts, and what is the frequency.

The results of this study were that the intervention reached the goals because the results showed that the spontaneous actions and those during the four established periods were always superior in the infants of the intervention group compared to the control group. The intervention program also favored the development of infants facilitating the psychological neoformations, showing that the instruments used were reliable instruments and that works such as this one add much to the area of neurodevelopment in the first year of life. Nevertheless, it is essential to continue to work to improve the discussion of better forms of intervention. In this way, they conclude that the intervention program confirms that the brain can be modified by the influence of these experiences. The activities used showed that both natural and cultural development intertwined constitute a process of biological and social formation of the child's personality.

Extreme vulnerability

Murphy et al. (2015) carried out a study in a place of extreme vulnerability in New York City, where a group intervention was done with families who had babies from 0 to 3 years old. Vulnerability was defined in relation to bonds as well as family history of adverse experiences in childhood. These authors mention the attachment theory, developed by Bowlby, as the guiding principle of the study, saying that the child needs a caregiver who is older, stronger, and wiser than himself to serve as a source of safety. In this way, a programmed group intervention, aimed at bonding, has shown that it is possible, even for cases that have experienced poor childhoods, to form safe and protective bonds. The main objective of this intervention was to prevent disorganization and help parents to identify, address, and resolve traumas or losses experienced in the past, preventing the transmission of social, behavioral, and mental health problems between generations. The intervention proposed in this study was based on a group study with the following principles: reflexive functioning, which allows a person to put himself in the other's shoes; emotional attunement; affective regulation; reticence, which is associated with the time each has to discover and name their own emotions; intergenerational patterns; and soothing. Although this study was of group intervention, it also included individual psychotherapy.

The study was conducted with a group of 60 families with the use of questionnaires, checklists, and the intervention mentioned above. The results concluded that the intervention program led to a decrease in adverse experiences in the lives of the infants of the participating families. Mothers wanted to keep custody of their babies and also provide love and protection, thereby redeeming and repairing their own adverse childhood experiences. Finally, it was concluded that this intervention was promising in reversing the transmission of intergenerational trauma and could be replicated and followed up in a more systematized way to better evaluate long-term results.

The importance of early intervention

All these studies have confirmed the importance of interventions related to bond experiences, plus the motor and cognitive measures that aim at neurocognitive development. They all suggest broader and cross-cultural research to validate, in a global way, the importance of information and intervention practices to improve brain development and promote psychological maturity from early childhood.

Conclusion

The brain develops better within a stable environment of support and low levels of stress. Safe relations are the key to healthy development of the brain as well as emotional regulation that encourages learning and adaptation to reality. It is very important to produce a cozy and welcoming environment so that the child can establish significant relations to consolidate himself as an autonomous and capable human being who can build significant subjective life experiences. It is very important that teachers and caregivers permit children to be authentic, truthful, and respected in their choices and behaviors, within previously established parameters and limits. This objective allows for the formation of an original and spontaneous human being. Therefore, education can be a creative process in which a child can live in harmony within his surrounding world (Glozman, 2013).

Regarding the formal educational process at school, Solovieva and Rojas (2017) mention that independent of the subject material, the teacher will introduce the concept by means of a gradual orientation, creating within the students an internal and solid level of learning. In this way, the teacher will guide the students in an organized way through orientation, execution, verification, and control toward the process of internalization. Social roles are also important because they provide the development of the following activities: symbolic, voluntary, reflective, communicative and imaginative, which provide important tools for the child to use in his life as well as in society (Moreno, Solovieva, & Rojas, 2014).

Although neither Luria nor Reitan were able to deepen their studies about intervention in early child development, both were aware of the need for standards regarding both evaluation and developmental milestones as well as how human interaction enhances human abilities in general. "Vygotsky proved that education leads development" (Glozman, 2013, p. 149).

Neuroscientists point out that the interaction itself, materialized by communication, enables the development and reconfiguration of the brain, building new structures and neural networks optimizing cerebral plasticity. Relationships are fundamental to the formation of the so-called social brain. In this way, the anatomy and biochemistry of the brain are related to our social relations. Thus, the brain, as a social organ, supports the influence that relationships have on health, neuroplasticity, and learning. The ability to learn, in itself, connects our brain and our bodies to our physical, emotional, and social survival (Cozolino, 2013).

Bock, Gonçalves, and Furtado (2002) affirm that man transforms and is transformed in a constant process. Therefore, relationships involve exchange, in both ways, one constitutes the other, transforms the other, in a process that focuses the best path to promote holistic health and adaptation to reality. Teamwork among school, community, and family is fundamental to enhance learning abilities. Parents, teachers, and communities in general should establish good relationships with their children and students, considering them unique individuals and allowing development to occur. Parents and teachers who received a good orientation and are interested in the well-being of the child are able to promote holistic health to the child which includes a healthy environment, a healthy community, a healthy infrastructure, and a healthy family, all forming a healthy individual who is capable of learning, developing, and coping with life's many demands.

References

Anauate, C. (2017). Orientação a pais: prevenção necessária. In C. Anauate & J. Glozman (Eds.), *Neuropsicologia Aplicada ao Desenvolvimento Humano*. São Paulo: Editora Memnon.

Bellman, M. H., Lingham, S., & Aukett, A. (1996). *Schedule of Growing Skills II: References manual*. London: NFER Nelson.

Bock, A. M. B., Gonçalves, M. G. M., & Furtado, O. (2002). *Psicologia Sócio-Histórica (uma perspectiva crítica em psicologia)*. São Paulo: Cortez Editora.

Bowlby, J. (1988). *A secure base. Parent-child attachment and healthy development*. New York: Basic Books.

Busnel, M. C. (2003). Quinta Conferência. In J. Wilheim (Ed.), *Relação mãe-feto: visão atual das neurociências e humanização do nascimento*. São Paulo: Casa do Psicólogo.

Cassidy, S. (2015). Resilience building in students: The role of academic self-efficacy. *Frontiers in Psychology*, *6*, 1781.

Cozolino, L. (2013). *The social neuroscience of education: Optimizing attachment & learning in the classroom*. New York, London: W. W. Norton & Company.

Dreyfuss, J. C. (2017). Habilitação neuropsicológica. In C. Anauate & J. Glozman (Eds.), *Neuropsicologia Aplicada ao Desenvolvimento Humano*. São Paulo: Editora Memnon.

Fonseca, V. (2013). *Cognição, Neuropsicologia e Aprendizagem*. Petrópolis, RJ: Editora Vozes.

Glozman, J. A. (2013). *Developmental neuropsychology*. New York: Routledge.

González, H. J. P., Solovieva, Y., Rojas, L. Q., Meza, V. R., & Arce, R. M. J. (2016). Proposal for psychomotor development in newborns with low weight according to A.R. Luria's conception. *Psychology in Russia: State of the Art*, *9*(4), 152–162.

Guimarães, F. A. B., Assis, C. D., Vieira, M. E. B., & Formiga, C.K.M.R. (2015). Avaliação de Material Didático Elaborado para Orientação de Cuidadores e Professores de Creches sobre o Desenvolvimento Infantil. *Journal of Human Growth and Development*, *25*(1), 27–40.

Hom, J., & Nici, J. (2015). Ralph M. Reitan: The Pioneer of Clinical Neuropsychology. *Archives of Clinical Neuropsychology*, *30*(8), 724–732.

Homskaya, E. (2001). *Alexander Romanovich Luria: A scientific biography*. New York: Plenum Publishers.

Lashley, K. S. (1929). *Brain mechanisms and intelligence*. Chicago: University of Chicago.

Leal, M. R. M. (2003). *Comunicação Primária e Intercâmbio Mutuamente Contingente*. São Paulo: Terceira Margem.

Leontiev, A. N. (1978). *Activity, consciousness, and personality*. Englewood Cliffs, NJ: Prentice Hall.

Lisina, M. I. (1987). La Genesis de las formas de Comunicación en los Ninos. In M. Shuare (Ed.), *La Psicologia Evolutiva y Pedagogica en la URSS*. Moscou: Editorial Progreso.

Luria, A. R. (1979). *The making of mind: A personal account of soviet psychology*. Cambridge, MA: Harvard University Press.

Luria, A. R. (1981). *Fundamentos da Neuropsicologia*. [J. A. Ricardo, Trans.]. São Paulo: Editora da Universidade de São Paulo.

Luria, A. R. (1991). *Curso de Psicologia Geral. (Vol. I)* (2nd ed.). Rio de Janeiro: Civilização Brasileira.

Luria, A. R. (1992). *A Construção da mente*. São Paulo: Ícone.

Luria, A. R. (2001). O cérebro humano e a atividade consciente. In L. S. Vigotskii, A. R. Luria, & A. Leontiev (Eds.), *Linguagem, desenvolvimento e aprendizagem*. São Paulo: Editora Ícone [M. P. Villalobos, Trans.].

Moreno, C. X. B., Solovieva, Y., & Rojas, L. Q. (2014). El Juego temático de roles sociales: aportes al desarrollo en a edad pré-escolar. *Avances em Psicologia Latinoamericana. Bogotá*, *32*(2), 287–308.

Murphy, A., Steele, H., Bate, J., Nikitiades, A., Allman, B., Bonick, K., et al. (2015). Group attachment-based intervention trauma-informed care for families with adverse childhood experience. *Family & Community Health, 38*(3), 268–279.

Odent, M. (2017). Stress deprivation and Caesarean birth. *Nursing, Pediatrics, Women's Health*, (22nd March).

Reed, J. C., Reed, H. B., Jr. (2015). Contributions to Neuropsychology of Reitan and Associates: Neuropsychology Laboratory, Indiana University Medical Center, 1960s. *Archives of Clinical Psychology: The Official Journal of the National Academy of Neuropsychologists, 30*(8), 751–753.

Reitan, R. M. (1974). Methodological problems in clinical neuropsychology. In R. M. Reitan & L. A. Davison (Eds.), *Clinical neuropsychology: Current status and applications*. Washington, DC: V.H. Winston & Sons.

Rojas, L. Q., & Solovieva, Y. (2013). *Avaliação das neoformações psicológicas da idade pré-escolar* [C. Morais, J. Chastinet, Trans.]. Uberlândia, MG: Editora da Universidade Federal de Uberlândia.

Sacks, O. (1990). Luria and "romantic science". In E. Goldberg, A. R. Luria, & G. Elkohonon (Eds.), *Contemporary neuropsychology and the legacy of Luria* (pp. 181–194). Hillsdale, NJ: Lawrence Erlbaum Associates.

Schore, A. N. (2003). Early relational trauma, disorganized attachment, and the development of a predisposition to violence. In M. F. Solomon & D. J. Siegel (Eds.), *Healing trauma attachment, mind, body, and brain*. New York, London: W. W. Norton & Company.

Selz, M., & Reitan, R. M. (1979). Neuropsychological test performance of normal, learning-disabled, and brain-damaged older children. *The Journal of Nervous & Mental Disease, 167*(5), 298–302.

Solovieva, Y., & Rojas, L. Q. (2016). *La Actividad de Juego en la Edad Preescolar*. Mexico, DF: Editorial Trilhas.

Solovieva, Y., & Rojas, L. Q. (2017). *Métodos de la ensenanza y el desarrollo de nino: juntos o aparte? Psicopedagogia histórico-cultural. Vol. 24(2)* (pp. 553–566). Uberlandia, MG: Ensino em Re-vista [jul./dez.].

Soto, S. I. O. (2018). *Programa de Intervención Neuropsicológica para ninos de 2 a 14 meses de edad* [Masters dissertation]. Mexico: Benemérita Universidad Autonoma de Puebla.

Tau, G. Z., & Peterson, B. S. (2010). Normal development of brain circuits. *Neuropsychopharmacology, 35*(1), 147–168.

Vygotsky, L. S. (1994). *A Formação Social da Mente*. São Paulo: Martins Fontes.

Vygotsky, L. S. (1998a). Aprendizagem e desenvolvimento intelectual na idade escolar. In L. S. Vigotsky, A. R. Luria, & A. N. Leontiev (Eds.), *Linguagem, desenvolvimento e aprendizagem* (2nd ed., pp. 103–117). São Paulo: Ícone [M. P. Villalobos, Trans.].

Vygotsky, L. S. (1998b). *Pensamento e Linguagem*. Rio de Janeiro: Martins Fontes.

Wilheim, S. (1992). *O Que é Psicologia Pré-Natal. 3ª Edição*. São Paulo: Casa do Psicólogo.

Winnicott, D. W. (1975). O Papel do Espelho da Mãe e da Família no Desenvolvimento Infantil. In *O Brincar e a Realidade*. Rio de Janeiro: Imago Editora.

Chapter 9

The role of family in speech rehabilitation of children with learning disabilities: Clinical observations by Luria and Reitan

Natalyia Karpova[a], Elena Nikolaeva[b]
[a]*Psychological Institute of Russian Academy of Education, Moscow, Russia,* [b]*Herzen State Pedagogical University, Saint-Petersburg, Russia*

Introduction

Stuttering, or logoneurosis, is one of the quite frequent speech pathologies that has a complex psychological structure (a complex of disturbances of the speech fluency and personality of the patient), and it can serve as a tool for the analysis of a number of speech practices.

Because speech is a lateralized function, the analysis of the causes of speech problems in children is impossible without evaluation of both lateral preferences and the relationship of the cerebral hemispheres in the process of speech activity. These problems are presented in the works from Luria (1973) and Reitan, Wolfson, and Hom (1992). However, tomography results were not available yet to Luria while Reitan even analyzed the causes of discrepancies in the results obtained by functional tomography and clinical methods. Both authors were extremely careful in describing the functions of the left and right hemispheres, unlike most of their contemporaries and those who begin to cope with this problem nowadays. That is why their understanding of the hemispheric interactions corresponds considerably to what we have at the present time. Those ideas have formed the basis of the theoretical substantiation of the system of family logopsychotherapy when working with stuttering children and adolescents today. Logopsychotherapy (from the Greek word "logos" that is word, psyche—soul, therapia—treatment, care) is a kind of psychotherapy aimed at restoring impaired speech communication (logoneurosis). This is a term introduced by Nekrasova (1992), who created a comprehensive methodology of social rehabilitation of stuttering adolescents and adults that combined speech therapy and psychological and psychotherapeutic approaches.

Evaluation and Treatment of Neuropsychologically Compromised Children
https://doi.org/10.1016/B978-0-12-819545-1.00009-6

Genetic and psychophysiological courses of stuttering

Investigations confirm the link of stuttering with gender: male relatives have a substantially higher risk than female relatives (Drayna & Kang, 2011) and its communicative nature (Bishop, 2013; Nekrasova, 1992; Shklovsky, 1994). It is also possible to speak about the neuropsychological bases of speech disorders: the mechanism of readiness for speech is identified within the functional system of speech, and the disturbances of that mechanism contribute to the generation of stuttering. Stutterers demonstrate an increased activity of the right hemisphere and an abnormal coordination between the brain areas that plan and perform speech function, which causes learning disabilities (Glozman, 2013; Glozman, Vartanov, Kiselnikov, & Karpova, 2005).

Anatomical structures providing the processing of verbal information are already revealed in the human brain during the 29th week of gestation, that is, even a bit earlier than the final formation of the auditory system (Dehaene-Lambertz, Dehaene, & Hertz-Pannier, 2002). At birth, there are ventral projections from the temporal to the prefrontal regions, although dorsal connections from the auditory cortex end up in the premotor cortex (Brauer, Anwander, Perani, & Friederici, 2013). Tomographic assessments of newborns (Peña, Maki, Kovaĉić, Dehaene-Lambertz, & Koizumi, 2003) detect a greater activation in classical temporal and frontal language areas in response to the speech stimulus in contrast to the nonverbal stimulus. There is some contradiction in the studies; some reveal that the left hemisphere is dominant in speech from birth as in adults (Peña et al., 2003). Others show that the bilateral activation to the speech stimulus with a gradual increase in the left-hemisphere dominance during the following few months is initially fixed (Perani, Saccuman, Scifo, Anwander, & Spada, 2011).

At present, the neurobiology research of speech disorders often tests the idea that they are associated with a decrease in the language lateralization in the left hemisphere. Orton (1925) is the first who wrote about the decrease of lateralization as the cause of the change in the normal development of verbal functions. He suggests that problems with reading may be the result of a decrease in brain lateralization. This assumption was intensively studied in the 1980s. However, there are still difficulties in assessing the features of the location of speech areas. Prior to the development of tomography, the Wada test was the only reliable way to assess the location of the speech areas of the brain. This is an invasive procedure where an anesthetic is introduced into the carotid artery to cause temporary inactivation of the injected hemisphere (Abou-Khalil, 2007). This procedure may not be applied to children, which is why some additional methods have been used for years, such as dichotic testing (Nikolaeva & Borisenkova, 2008) or verbal-manual interference (Nikolaeva & Yavorovich, 2014; Yanson & Kenga, 1983).

The invention of tomography did not facilitate the task of researchers. Most of them assessed the structural brain asymmetry and seldom studied the functional activity of the hemispheres. First, the authors revealed a reduced asymmetry of the planum temporale in dyslexia—the area necessary for the perception of language. But it soon turned out that much depends on the method of assessing asymmetry (Eckert & Leonard, 2000) and on the type of speech disorder (Leonard, 2002). That led to extremely contradictory results. It was not further confirmed that the asymmetry of the planum temporale correlated with the lateralization of the brain activity in the verbal tasks.

Functional transcranial dopplerography turned out to be more adequate for those purposes. It allowed obtaining the image of blood flow in the left and right middle cerebral arteries during the solution of linguistic tasks. Blood flow in the left hemisphere increased for several seconds after the beginning of solving verbal tasks. The data were consistent with the results obtained by the Wada test (Knecht, 1998). A further decrease in lateralization was indicated by different tomographic techniques for different speech disorders (de Guibert et al., 2011).

At the same time, there is no definite data about the peculiarities of lateralization in stuttering people (2.5%–3.5% of the population suffers from that speech pathology) while there is a hypothesis that the stuttering itself is possible only in the presence of two speech areas in two hemispheres (Badcock, Bishop, Hardiman, Barry, & Watkins, 2011). This is a consequence of some impairment to the left-hemisphere speech areas and the formation of speech representation in the right hemisphere during the first year of life at the peak of brain flexibility. At any rate, when accepting any above-mentioned idea about the causes of stuttering, a question must be asked: what reason can there be for such atypical development?

Stuttering occurs at the preschool age when the main environment for the child's development is the family, and significant adults are parents. It is natural to imagine that changes in the interaction of the brain hemispheres of the child can be caused by the influence of highly emotional impact from the family that can be accepted as superstrong by the child at this age.

The most common conception about the communicative nature of stuttering falls well on the psychophysiological one about two speech representations. The activation of the right hemisphere in case of emotional problems leads to competition between two speech areas for one speech apparatus. Then, the psychotherapeutic work should ultimately be aimed at reducing the activity of the right hemisphere in the generation of speech.

Communication problems and stuttering

Nonverbal communication is a necessary condition for interaction in the family between parents and children, facilitating attachment manifestations, regulating emotion demonstrations, and determining behavior in a particular situation (Schachner, Shaver, & Mikulincer, 2005). Communication skills extracted by a child in the processing of social information (for instance, the ability to accurately send and receive nonverbal information) are essential to control any interactions (Nowicki & Duke, 2013). The research of infants in their daily lives demonstrates their striking abilities to communicate. Adamson (1996) detected biological and behavioral changes during the first months of life (eye direction, visual concentration, vocal behavior, and the ability to initiate interaction). These allow the child to gradually become a communicator. During the second half of the first year of life, children develop the ability to coordinate attention to both the social partner and external objects. That ability to engage in collaborative interaction provides the groundwork of the common experience that underlies acquiring language (Butterworth, 1991).

The sensitivity of the mother to the child's behavior is of great importance in the development of communication (Elias & Broerse, 1996). The social context, in which mothers pick up on the child's signals and respond to his or her nonverbal behavior, provides prelinguistic communication signals (Acredolo & Goodwyn, 1988). If the nonverbal signals of parents directly contradict their verbal messages, children have difficulties in recognizing emotions that affect their self-perception negatively (Grebelsky-Lichtman, 2014). Parents can show nonverbally to their children from birth that they understand their state developing the ability to reflect their own state in the future (Fonagy & Target, 1997). If parents cannot do this, there is no integration of internal experiences and their external manifestations in the child.

Studies based on fMRI scanning (functional nuclear magnetic resonance imaging) detect regions associated with the combination of speech and gestures. The bilateral activation of the posterior superior temporal gyrus, the precentral gyrus, and the lower frontal lobe that support the integration of speech and gesture has been revealed. The regions of an enhanced response are found in the left upper temporal and premotor regions. The authors (Weisberg, Hubbard, & Emmorey, 2017) suppose that those are regions within the large neuronal networks that play a dual role in the sensory and semantic information integration, whereas surrounding regions maintain the activity only for sensory or semantic information.

The peculiarity of speech pathology in the form of stuttering is that the affective component prevails over the speech defect in many individuals. It leads to a complex "set" of communication problems: fear of speaking in public, diffidence, suspiciousness, and increased anxiety about the attitude of others. Psychological factors that generate and keep stuttering are fairly well studied, and their contribution to the prediction of the effectiveness of rehabilitation is identified (Glozman, 2017; Karpova, 2011a, 2011b; Nekrasova, 1992; Shklovsky, 1994). Fixation on the defect increases over time and correlates with other speech defects and associated motor disorders while also correlating inversely with the positive results of speech therapy. Investigations also indicate the mediating role of parents in the formation of the self-esteem of a child with stuttering as well as in the effectiveness of the remediation of the disturbed speech communication (Glozman, Karpova, & Cheburashkin-Antipov, 2018).

Methods and techniques of speech remediation in children and adolescents with learning disabilities based on theories by Luria and Reitan

The essence of the work of both Reitan and Luria based on clinical observations is that the brain basis of voluntary control in a child forms quite late. The frontal lobes only begin to mature at the age of 7, and their final maturation occurs in most people after age 18 (Thompson-Schill, Bedny, & Goldberg, 2005). At the present time, the problem of control is studied within the framework of the concepts of executive functions, voluntary regulation, volitional regulation, etc. (Kelley, Wagner, & Heatherton, 2015). Because all these models have almost the same tools, the movement is toward the creation of a single model of regulatory processes (Zhou, Chen, & Main, 2012). The impact of the family may be linked not so much to the change in the lateralization itself as to the slowdown in the development of controlling functions because of stress. Therefore, a therapeutic approach covering all the aspects of the family interaction, including functions of control, is going to be effective.

System of family relations and speech disturbances

Numerous studies have shown the influence of parental behavior on the physical (Oteva, Nikolaeva, Sartakova, Nikolaeva, & Parm, 1994) and psychological state of the child as well as his cognitive abilities and emotional state (Nikolaeva & Merenkova, 2013a, 2013b). An efficient parent-child relationship is characterized by a high level of involvement of the parent in the life of the child, providing the age-appropriate autonomy and responsibility as well as using efficient monitoring strategies and child support in solving cognitive and emotional tasks corresponding to his age (Collins, Madsen, & Susman-Stillman, 2002). In Russian science, the consideration of the practical issues of the application of psychological-pedagogical techniques and methods of work with the parents of children with speech disorders is presented in the works by Bachina and Samorodova (2009), Vakulenko (2012), Perchatkina (2008), and others. At the same time, specialists note the features of parenting styles in families with children with disabilities, including speech disorders. The system of family relations—their manifestations, stability, and changes—also has influence on the formation, consolidation, and aggravation of speech disorders in the child; there is a strong relationship between the attitude of parents to the remediation process and the result of this process.

A modern integrated psychological-pedagogical approach is scientifically and practically substantiated in overcoming speech disorders: the integration of medical, psychological, and pedagogical diagnoses of children with speech disorders; the provision of medical treatment based on the assessment results; the organization of the psychological-pedagogical process of the remediation of the disturbed speech function; and the creation of conditions for the active participation of the family in the process of remediation and development of speech and communication skills. Simultaneously, specialists (speech therapists, neuropsychologists, and psychologists) point out that many parents begin realizing the speech problems of their son or daughter after explanatory work only. And it is not always possible to attain their interest and activity in the remediation of the speech development of the child.

Family group logopsychotherapy by Nekrasova and Karpova

An example of the integrated approach involving relatives to overcome stuttering is the system of family group logopsychotherapy by Nekrasova and Karpova (Karpova, 2003, 2011a, 2011b; Nekrasova, 1992, 2006; Nekrasova, Bodalev, Karpova, Suvorov, & Chudnovsky, 1996). The studies carried out within this system revealed the following:

1. Because stuttering has a strong maintaining system that seizes both the person and his or her proximal environment, a perennial practice of psychotherapy of logoneurosis shows: (a) an overlooked disharmony of family relations (between parents and children, between spouses, etc.) significantly aggravates the speech defect and its subjective experiencing by participants; (b) remaining unchanged, the pathological family relations inhibit the process of speech remediation in a stutterer in the treatment group; and (c) at the end of treatment, family conflicts can quickly cause the recurrence of stuttering.
2. An analysis of relatives' attitudes to the defect in the families of participants with stuttering reveals different types of disharmony: (a) the attitude to the stutterer as "deficient" (more often in fathers and elder brothers); (b) the exaggeration of the significance of the defect, an excessive fixation on it, and an overprotective attitude to the child, which actually creates the cult of the disease and induces the role of the "sick" child; (c) on the contrary, the downward bias of the importance of the defect: parents believe that the defect can be quickly eliminated if one increases the requirements and makes the child "work on himself/herself" more effectively. In practice, such a style of relationship creates a "pressure," controlling-regulating style in the family. It increases the child's anxiety and his or her self-doubt while blocking the speech function development even more; and (d) a "demanding" style of relations in the family when an excessive emphasis is put on the achievement of the child's success (in different activities). It leads to a constantly increased tension and, as a possible consequence, to stuttering as an excuse and self-justification of one's own failure (Karpova, 2003, pp. 49–51).

We would like to note that our studies prove the findings of psychologists (Spivakovskaya, 2000; Zakharov, 2000) regarding families with children suffering from different emotional dysfunctions.

3. More recent studies have revealed some trends in parent-child relationships that generate, consolidate, and maintain speech defects: (a) the mother's overprotection up to the desire to assume the speech functions of the child induces fixation on the defect and the cult of the disease; (b) the authoritarian style of parental relations blocks the speech function of the child and provokes its protective reactions up to the avoidance of communication; (c) the undervaluation of one's own child and pushing him/her out of the sphere of personal problems leads to a decrease in the communication value in general. And stuttering can be a way to draw the attention of parents to oneself; and (d) the overall depressive situation, an increased sense of guilt, and the emotional tension of children and parents lead to increased sensitivity and a sense of inferiority.

Neuropsychological, psychological, and psychophysiological study of participants in family logopsychotherapy

It was found out that an inter- and multidisciplinary study of the brain mechanisms of stuttering in the context of logopsychotherapeutic rehabilitation (Karpova, Pastushkova, Volkova, & Kiselnikov, 2006; Kiselnikov, 2006) over the past few years was conditioned with many psychological variable. The study of the logopsychotherapeutic group participants in comparison with people without any speech disorders at the age of 15–25 years old (17 participants) was carried out by the author's method, "the potential registration associated with the readiness to speech" (Kiselnikov, 2006). This included psychophysiological techniques and neuropsychological diagnosis according to the scheme by Luria with the quantitative assessment of the obtained data by the method of Glozman before and after treatment (Glozman et al., 2005).

The results of a system inter- and multidisciplinary study of the brain mechanisms of stuttering in the context of logopsychotherapeutic rehabilitation

The results obtained by the authors proved: (a) the data of neuropsychological assessment on the involvement of subcortical structures in the genesis of stuttering; (b) the fact of some right-hemisphere asymmetry of the found symptoms; and (c) the results of the studies of the brain mechanisms of stuttering with the help of functional nuclear magnetic resonance imaging, which showed the primary deficiency of the left hemisphere posterior regions and the compensatory activity of the homologous right hemisphere regions. That confirmed the difference in the activation of stuttering in the sample and the norms of certain subcortical structures (in particular, the right subcortical nuclei). The study also indicated that in the process of complex sociorehabilitation, the state of the mnestic ($0.73 \rightarrow 0.68$) and neurodynamic ($0.26 \rightarrow 0.24$) spheres in stutterers somewhat improved. The speech (0.16) and intellectual spheres (0.12) remained unchanged, but the differences in the event-related potentials for the process of speech readiness between the groups of stutterers and the norm during logopsychotherapy was also reduced. And the configuration of the former approached the configuration of the latter, that is, normalized (Kiselnikov, 2006).

Why during family logopsychotherapy do we need a deep study of the neuropsychological parameters for stuttering children? This type of psychotherapy is based on the "logos"—a deep awareness by parents of the causes of child's stuttering, which are largely due to the emotional relationship between children and parents. Evidently describing the high readiness of the right hemisphere to compete with the left one for speech apparatus in a stuttering child, a psychotherapist teaches parents the methods of self-control during interaction with him (her). This allows not only ensuring the long-term effect of interaction changes, but also teaching the parents to resolve independently unforeseen conflicts outside the framework of psychotherapy.

Lateral features in stutterers

Lateral features in stutterers were studied and the associations of those features with the peculiarities of cognitive processes were identified in the 2018 research. Eleven team members of the family logopsychotherapy (two girls and nine boys; mean age 21.1) were individuals under testing (Dobrin, Karpova, & Nikolaeva, 2018). The results of the study of the lateral preferences of the individuals in the sensory and motor spheres are presented in Table 1.

Table 1 shows that the number of right-handed individuals (27.2%) among stutterers sharply decreased at the expense of the increase in the number of mixed-handed (54.5%) and left-handed (18.3%) individuals. The conducted research (before the beginning of the work of the group, at the end of the work, and 6 months after its completion) confirmed the results obtained by us earlier about the increase in the number of nonright-handed individuals with regard to data in the literature (Leutin & Nikolaeva, 1985; Leutin, Nikolaeva, & Fomina, 2009).

TABLE 1 Distribution of motor and sensory asymmetries in stutterers (%).

Parameter	Left	Combined/symmetrical	Right
The leading hand	18.3	54.5	27.2
The leading leg	27.2	27.2	45.6
The leading ear	54.4	0	45.6
The leading eye	36.4	9.1	54.5
Lateral profile	36.4	27.2	36.4

However, our results did not indicate a decrease in lateralization but an increase in the number of left and symmetric features. These data matched considerably the ideas of Reitan and Luria about the change in the activity of the right hemisphere, but not any disturbances of the hemisphere's functioning.

The analysis of the results of the verbal-manual interference test in the group of stutterers revealed that only 36.3% of the participants (four persons out of 11) had the speech representation in the left hemisphere, five individuals had two speech areas, and two people had one area in the right hemisphere. At the same time, two individuals with a typical arrangement of speech areas in the left hemisphere had less pronounced speech disorders in comparison with the total sample (Table 2).

Let us emphasize that our data accord to the hypothesis of a greater probability of stuttering in individuals with speech representation in both hemispheres of the brain. It is reckoned that in this case, the second area of speech appears during the first year of life as a result of intrauterine or perinatal damage to the speech area in the left hemisphere. During the first year of life, the brain is flexible, and the right hemisphere can compensate for problems in the left hemisphere. At the same time, there are conditions for competition between the two hemispheres in utterance that lead to stuttering.

To assess verbal-manual interference (Yanson & Kenga, 1983), the participants under testing were asked to sequentially carry out tapping as quickly as possible by each hand for 10 s in the corresponding square of the sheet divided into six equal squares. When each hand performed the movements three times, everything was repeated but with a verbal task. The change in the number of taps without any verbal task and with it for each hand was evaluated. Using nouns was proposed as a verbal task. If the active hand and speech areas were in the same hemisphere, the number of taps during tapping fell significantly.

The executive functions by inhibitory control in the paradigm of go/go and go/no goes (Nikolaeva & Vergunov, 2013) were evaluated as well as the volume of working memory (Razumnikova & Savinich, 2016). Executive functions are known to be associated with the prefrontal regions of the brain (Kelley et al., 2015; Luria, 1973; Reitan et al., 1992).

TABLE 2 Distribution of the individuals under test by the parameter "arrangement of speech areas" (%).

Arrangement of speech areas		
One in the left hemisphere	Two in two hemispheres	One in the right hemisphere
36.3	45.6	18.1

Finally, the variability of the cardiac rhythm of the individuals in the calm state and when remembering emotional states (remembering the methods of punishment and encouragement in the family in childhood) was recorded. The study consisted of two parts, each of which was equal to the duration of 300 R-R intervals. That was sufficient to calculate the high and low frequency waves in the spectral analysis. In the first (background) part, 300 R-R intervals were recorded for the participants in quiet wakefulness. In the second part, they were suggested to recall unpleasant situations associated with punishment by their parents and pleasant situations associated with their encouragement. The analysis of the results showed an excessive activation of the sympathetic nervous system of the participants when remembering emotional events.

Retention of the results in the 6th month

It was also revealed that upon completion of logopsychotherapy, the volume of working memory increased significantly in the individuals. However, after 6 months, the data distribution increased and memory volume decreased in many of them. This indicated that some of the participants under testing maintained changes obtained in the process of therapy due to self-training. The others lost skills, claiming that they had not had enough time for the individual work. It reduced the effect of logopsychotherapy.

Similar changes were identified during the evaluation of inhibitory processes in the paradigm of go/no-go. Before therapy, the individuals made 10.2 ± 3.1 incorrect responses on average. Immediately after therapy, there were 7.3 ± 4.2 errors on average, that is, there was a tendency toward the enhancement of inhibitory processes. Six months later, the participants made 8.9 ± 5.6 errors on average. The data distribution increased; those who performed the necessary exercises of logopsychotherapy at the end of the course retained the effect and those who did not train on their own had decreased results.

At the same time, the absence of changes in the reaction of the sympathetic nervous system to emotional events was important. It had been preserved. This meant that stutterers needed more time to reduce the excessive activation of the nervous system, and it was necessary to follow all the instructions received in the process of logopsychotherapy (Dobrin et al., 2018).

The present investigations enable us to make the following conclusions:

1. Stuttering is not a separate speech disorder; it occurs in the syndrome of specific correctable mnestic, neurodynamic, and motor neuropsychological defects reflecting the dysfunction of posterior-frontal and deep brain structures.
2. The most defective process in stutterers is the preparation for pronouncing the word. The psychophysiological indicator of that is the change in the brain localization of the speech readiness potential. The hemispheric interaction is disturbed in stutterers during preparation for the utterance of the word, but this defect can be corrected.

3. Executive functions suffer and the average volume of working memory decreases in stutterers. This is probably because of the decrease in the controlling attention on the part of the cortical frontal lobes. The anterior parts of the brain are hyperexcited in stutterers, and the posterior parts are inhibited in comparison with the norm.
4. The comparison of the data of neuropsychological, psychophysiological, and biomechanical investigations allows assuming the unity of the brain mechanisms of motor and cognitive readiness in the mental functioning of the person.
5. Stuttering is a specific psychological syndrome connected with increased anxiety, logophobia, and maladaptive reactions in frustrating situations. The remediation of stuttering has a positive impact both on those defects and on psychophysiological and neuropsychological disturbances (Glozman et al., 2005).

Using the Luria battery in assessment of communication in stuttering

An expert evaluation of speech and personal problems associated with speech communication and a neuropsychological assessment based on the Luria battery of methods were carried out during the study of two different age groups of stutterers (in 2017 and 2018) before and after the course of family logopsychotherapy (Glozman et al., 2018). The degree of speech and personality disorders was calculated in points according to the method by Karpova and Yakovistenko (Yakovistenko, 2008).

Group 1: 12 individuals from 7 to 35 years old (three females and nine males. This corresponded to the gender distribution of stuttering in the population on the whole). Prior to treatment, according to the stuttering severity, four persons (33%) had a high degree of speech disorders (2.5–3.0 points), five individuals (42%) had an average degree (1.5–2.0 points), and three persons (25%) had mild speech disorders (1 point). *According to the degree of personal problems* associated with speech communication, eight of 12 group members (67%) had severe personal disturbances (3 points), three had an average degree of personal defects (1.5–2.0 points), and only one 7-year-old child had mild disorders (1 point).

Group 2: Eight persons from 14 to 43 years old (two females and six males). Prior to treatment, according to the stuttering severity, two persons (25%) had a high degree of speech disorders (2.5–3 points) and the remaining six persons (75%) had an average degree of speech defects (1.5–2 scores). There were no stutterers with mild speech disorders (1 point) in this group. According to the degree of personal problems related to speech communication, three of the eight participants of the group (37.5%) had severe personal problems (2.5–3 points) and the remaining five had an average degree of personal problems (1.5–2 points). There were no stutterers with a mild impairment in speech communication (1 point) in this group.

A comprehensive neuropsychological assessment of the participants in both groups before and after the course of social rehabilitation showed that deviations from norm were revealed in all the stutterers before treatment as well as positive dynamics by the end of logopsychotherapy. At the same time, the most evident dynamics were in the younger individuals under testing. That allowed us to talk about "the effect of the group"—the influence of the entire intensive process of social rehabilitation. The results of logopsychotherapy were the recovering fully fledged speech communication of most stutterers and the expending their social activity. Thus, it was confirmed experimentally that the complex system of family group logopsychotherapy had a significant impact on both the fluency of speech and cognitive functions in the participants and on their personal characteristics (Glozman et al., 2018).

Involvement of family members of individuals in active participation during the remediation of verbal communication in family group logopsychotherapy

In the system of family group logopsychotherapy for stuttering children, adolescents and adults from 7 to 45 years old (the different age groups included 8–12 stutterers and their parents and relatives), all participants took the course consisting of four main stages:

I Diagnostic, which lasts for 6 months at least. It is based on the dynamic psychotherapeutic diagnosis developed by Nekrasova, namely the method of bibliotherapy (treatment through directed reading activity) (Nekrasova, 1991).

II A session of emotional-stress psychotherapy by Dubrovsky. "Stuttering withdrawal" in the presence of parents or relatives lasts for 1–1.5 h.

III Active group family logopsychotherapy. Daily sessions of 7–8 h are held with the participants for 3–5 weeks in which their parents and/or relatives participate actively. In addition to special verbal-motor exercises and psychotherapeutic discussions, unusual methods of treatment in the group form are used such as bibliotherapy, kinesitherapy (influence on the mental functions and the personality of the participant through work with the body), and symbol therapy (therapy with therapeutic symbols). Cinema therapy was introduced in 2005 (the use of the therapeutic potential of specially selected films). A series of neurocorrection sessions was introduced in 2015.

IV Maintaining logopsychotherapy—6 months after the main treatment course—lasts for 2 weeks. On a new and higher level, this stage repeats the basic elements, techniques, and methods of the active group family logopsychotherapy (Karpova, 2003, 2011a, 2011b).

Based on the dynamic psychotherapeutic diagnostics worked out by Nekrasova for stuttering adolescents and adults (Nekrasova, 1991), a diagnostic unit for their parents and relatives was developed. It confirmed the basic principle of our approach: diagnostics may become therapy simultaneously (Karpova, 1994).

An assessment of 64 families of candidates in the group of family logopsychotherapy during 1993–97 showed that 35 families of the participants manifested a high involvement in the process of completing all the tasks (they performed 4–5 sets of tasks out of 5). All the relatives in 23 families worked until the end during the initial (diagnostic) stage. The relatives in 18 families completed tasks partially (2–3 out of 5), with both parents in nine families. The relatives of six participants took part in testing only. So, more than 80% of the relatives participated actively in the diagnostic work (Table 3).

Considering the motive as a systematic and holistic way of organizing human activity (in this case, it was about the formation of the motivation of relatives to actively engage them in the process of remediation), we supposed that there would be two groups performing tasks: those involved in the process of work actively, and those involved formally. The motivational involvement in the process of logopsychotherapy was arranged at all stages by means of specific methods and techniques (Karpova, 2003).

One of the main objectives of **the first (diagnostic) stage** held for several months "at a distance" was *motivating-stimulating*. Diagnosis was carried out in the form of correspondence. The participant and then the relatives were invited to give feedback on a certain work of art and to perform a specially selected psychological test or questionnaire at a time (Nekrasova, 1991, 1992). Such unusual diagnosis aroused interest in the upcoming work in the parents and

TABLE 3 Data on the involvement of participants and their relatives at the initial stage.

Participants ($N=66$) involvement	Parents and relatives—64 families	
	Involvement	Quantity of families (%)
High 45 individuals (68.2%)	- High - Medium - Low - No participation	30 (45.5%) 10 (15.2%) 2 (3.0%) 3 (4.5%)/2 single individuals of them
Medium 18 individuals (27.3%)	- High - Medium - Low - No participation	5 (7.6%) 7 (10.7%) 3 (4.5%) 3 (4.5%)
Low 3 individuals (4.5%)	- High - Medium - Low - No participation	0 (0%) 1 (1.5%) 1 (1.5%) 1 (1.5%)

participants while also changing their needs, motivations, and ideas about their role in the process of remediating.

Bibliotherapeutic tasks began with tales by H.Ch. Andersen, then stories by A. Chekhov, I. Turgenev, and R. Bradbury, novels by A. Marshall and E. Porter, B. Shaw's play "Pygmalion," a number of other works, and the parables by R. Bach at the end (Nekrasova, 2006).

At the initial (diagnostic) stage, most participants are relieved of possible resistances, a desire to understand personal and family problems appeared through empathy and emotional identification with the characters of specially selected highly artistic works, their literary metaphors and senses. This makes it possible to deepen and complement "the portrait of uniqueness," not only of the participants (Nekrasova, 1991) but also their family members as well as to create "the portrait of the uniqueness" of each separate family that gives the necessary diagnostic and informative material for the logopsychotherapist. At the beginning of therapy we often hear such sentences from parents and relatives of participants: "We only hope for You," "I think I have too little energy to achieve the goal alone" and "Only You can help my son ...." Later during the therapy, they started talking: "I am ready to help my son," "Together we are adjusted for the victory!" (Karpova, 2003).

At **the second stage** of the work—during the session called "the withdrawal of stuttering"—the participant experiences personal-motivational explosion leading to emotional and behavioral changes. The picture of the change in motivation is observed in the parents and relatives: from the initial involvement ("observer")—to the further involvement—active empathy to all the participants of the session. It also supports a pronounced motivation to remediate the relative.

This state of activity aimed at participation in the treatment process is fixed at **the third stage** during the course of active family group logopsychotherapy. The task at this stage for both participants and their relatives is the active performance of all the elements of the technique, including the orientation to success during intensive speech communication. Symbol therapy contributes to the introduction of the group members into a particular symbolic structure of the language of training by means of getting acquainted with medical symbols of the technique: "the iceberg of stuttering," "scales for good speeches," "Narcissus," "Pygmalion," etc. The symbolism forms an attitude for creative work in interpersonal communication, improving and enhancing the motivation for recovery through the extension and change of the usual forms of communication (Nekrasova, 2006). In the course of psychotherapeutic discussions, important topics for family relations are "anxiety," "offense," "conflict," "education," etc.

The fourth stage of the work is a 2-week course of the supportive family group logopsychotherapy contributes to the maintenance of the active and creative participation in the treatment process both participants and their relatives. Nontraditional methods are employed: bibliotherapy and symbol therapy in the group to prepare and hold logopsychotherapeutic discussions and to develop and fix spontaneous speech.

Parents talk about the results of the great common creative work: "One cannot write everything. There is one important thing: 'ugly duckling' (and not the single!) soared in the sky as a Swan!" wishing that such groups should be created not only for stutterers (Karpova, 1994, 2003). The analysis of the results of the speech and personal changes of the stutterers in family group logopsychotherapy also identifies the direct dependence of the degree of involvement of both the participants and their relatives in the social rehabilitation process.

Psychological mechanisms of the remediation process and general principles of social rehabilitation

During many years of our work, the psychological mechanisms of the motivational involvement in the logopsychotherapeutic process have been identified and described:

(a) The mechanism of *coparticipation* is realized in the participation of the parents and relatives of participants at all stages of social rehabilitation, taking into account their specific features; the ways and methods of creating "the coparticipating environment" by a supervisor are indicated. They cause a high level of motivational involvement in the logopsychotherapeutic process of all the participants.

(b) *The mechanism of adequacy* is the development of an adequate attitude to the defect (disadvantages) as a significant condition for the establishment of motivational involvement in the education and reeducation. The awareness of the mechanism of occurrence, fixation, and development of logoneurosis is as a translation of pathological behavioral structures from parents to children.

(c) *The mechanism of the aspiration toward "ideal self"* is based on the difference of potentials between "everyday" and "ideal self." It is indicated that bringing up the need for "ideal self" creates an additional "power base" for motivational involvement.

(d) *The mechanism of the realization of the goal in the ideal image* is considered on the content of bibliotherapy. The functions of the ideal image in the process of social rehabilitation and education are shown: the image as a state regulator, the image as an "initiator" of development, and the image as a factor of creating the common "semantic field" in participants and their relatives.

(e) *The mechanism of "the Pygmalion effect"* is an appropriation of a new positive image created by the participant as a successful speech communicant with the support of a group—"a collective psychotherapist."

The precondition for the effectiveness of social rehabilitation is the use of an integrated system of those mechanisms interacting with one another (Karpova, 2003).

The analysis of the work of the groups for family logopsychotherapy in 2009 in Moscow (11 participants and their 27 relatives), Vladivostok (nine stutterers and their 22 relatives), Taganrog (eight stutterers and their 15 relatives), and Samara (nine stutterers and 16 relatives), with the participation of 60 graduates of the previous groups and their relatives, revealed the following:

1. The evidence of the development of motivational involvement, dialogical communication, and the dynamics of personal growth in social rehabilitation obtained in previous experimental studies is confirmed in the new groups of family logopsychotherapy, taking into account the age-related features of their participants.
2. The revealed new psychological mechanisms of forming the dialogue ability and dialogical communication as well as the mechanisms of facilitation of the personal growth of younger adolescents in different age groups do not contradict the previously revealed psychological mechanisms of the development of motivational involvement in the social rehabilitation activities, but complement and clarify them in new aspects.
3. The efficiency of the logopsychotherapeutic work in different age groups rises with the active inclusion of the entire family of stutterers at any age in the educational and therapeutic-rehabilitation process.

Based on the system of family group logopsychotherapy, the following **general principles of social rehabilitation** have been worked out:

The principle of "the universal importance of the process of social rehabilitation." The process of social rehabilitation has not only private and "therapeutic" value, but also general psychological and pedagogical value. It reveals the essence of the general problems of personality development. Therefore, it is rational to use the experience accumulated in the process of social rehabilitation in solving the common problems of education and the development of personality.

The principle of the moral-psychological approach to the problem of norm pathology. In social rehabilitation, it is necessary to solve the problem of restoration of an individual's physical and mental health with the obligatory consideration of the moral space of his vital activity.

The principle of the unity of psychological-pedagogical and psychotherapeutic effects. Humanistic pedagogy and pedagogical psychology should be penetrated with the psychotherapeutic approach. Psychotherapeutic effects should not be limited to narrow therapeutic functions but contribute to the task of personality development. It is this "trinity" of influences that can give the optimal effect in social rehabilitation.

The principle of social rehabilitation as an integral process: in any complex system of social rehabilitation, not only the individual stages and methods should be developed in detail but their relationship, interpenetration, and interdependence should be organized, particular mechanisms that work at each stage should be identified, and the place, function, and significance of this stage in the whole process of "medical reeducation" should be determined (Myasishchev, 2004).

The principle of the preparation of "the psychological ground" (Chudnovsky, 2006). This principle is realized by means of the purposeful generation of "sanogenic" (Orlov, 2006, "healing") mental states in participants at each stage of work. These positive states contain a powerful communicative potential and are characterized by the mobilized readiness of the participant to perceive new treatment information as well as by internal playback of the optimistic model of the future.

The principle of the dynamic psychotherapeutic diagnosis and the internal representation of health. The basis of this principle is positive sources in a person and positive emotional states. In addition to the well-known "portrait of the disease" ("the internal representation of the disease" according to Luria, 1977), the purpose of diagnostic techniques is to create "a portrait of the uniqueness" of each participant (Yu. B. Nekrasova), that is, to identify his peculiar unique personality traits as well as "the portrait of the uniqueness" of his or her family (Karpova, 2011a, 2011b).

The principle of a different-age psychotherapeutic group: one of the leading factors in the treatment of participants in the system of logopsychotherapy is a psychotherapeutic team. It is born at the diagnostic stage and passes through all stages of social rehabilitation, reaching the optimal level at the stage of active logopsychotherapy. As the analysis shows, it continues to persist and act after the treatment course. The unity of goals and common difficulties and experiences as well as a high level of interpersonal and intrapersonal communication all contribute to the creation of a group with high vitality and efficiency (Nekrasova et al., 1996).

Conclusion

Many years of the successful work of more than 90 groups in family logopsychotherapy in several centers—Moscow, Taganrog, Samara and the Samara region, Vladivostok, Saratov, and Yekaterinburg—show that the active participation of the parents and relatives of stutterers in the remediation of verbal communication skills contributes to the development of a healthy and able-for-communication personality and the improvement of parent-child relationships. The practical employment of the principles, techniques, and methods of family group logopsychotherapy in the remediation of disturbances in written speech in primary school children is also convincing regarding the opportunity of applying this system to other speech disorders. We emphasize the effectiveness of the identified psychological mechanisms developing the motivational involvement and regulation of communication in social rehabilitation. At the same time, all the mechanisms ("coparticipation," "adequacy," "the aspiration" toward the "ideal self," and "the Pygmalion effect") as the principles of preparation of "the psychological ground" and the moral-psychological approach to the problem of "norm pathology" reveal themselves in the intrafamily interactions that effect the remediation process.

It is also noteworthy that regulatory mechanisms are currently considered under different models, and the scholars distinguish several brain networks that control different states. The default mode network (the network that works during the rest state but influences all active states), which includes the medial prefrontal cortex, the cortex of the posterior cingulate gyrus, and the lateral, medial, and lower parietal cortex, reflects the fact that any problems arising within this system lead to a variety of diseases from depression to autism (Singh et al., 2019). The disturbances of regulatory functions in infants lead to severe avoidance behavior in adult life (Bäuml et al., 2019). This network is active at rest, that is, it is the network of the passive mode that controls the internal activity of rest.

Some researchers single out the executive network or executive control network, which includes the regions of the dorsolateral prefrontal cortex and the back of the parietal cortex (Seeley et al., 2007). It is possible to suppose that the complex training aimed at increasing the efficiency of the regulation of the mental state of parents and children will promote a greater activation of both the default network and the executive control network in all participants, and will cause positive changes in the parent-child relationship. This would help solve many psychophysiological, neuropsychological, and psychological problems. One may consider the present modern studies as an extension of the work by Luria and Reitan.

Acknowledgments

The study has been supported by the Russian Foundation of Fundamental Investigations (grant RFFI #18-013-00721).

References

Abou-Khalil, B. (2007). Methods for determination of language dominance: The Wada test and proposed noninvasive alternatives. *Current Neurology and Neuroscience Reports*, *7*, 483.

Acredolo, L., & Goodwyn, S. (1988). Symbolic gesturing in normal infants. *Child Development*, *59*, 450–466.

Adamson, L. B. (1996). *Communication development during infancy*. Madison, Wis: Westview.

Bachina, O. V., & Samorodova, L. N. (2009). *Interaction of a speech therapist and a child's family with speech disabilities*. Moscow: Sphere (in Russian).

Badcock, N., Bishop, D., Hardiman, M., Barry, J. G., & Watkins, K. (2011). Co-localization of abnormal brain structure and function in Specific Language Impairment. *Brain and Language*, *120*, 310–318.

Bäuml, J. G., Baumann, N., Avram, M., Mulej, B. S., Breeman, L., Berndt, M., et al. (2019). The default mode network mediates the impact of infant regulatory problems on adult avoidant personality traits. *Biological Psychiatry: Cognitive Neuroscience and Neuroimaging*, *4*(4), 333–342.

Bishop, D. V. M. (2013). Cerebral asymmetry and language development: Cause, correlate or consequence? *Science*, *340*(6138), 123–131.

Brauer, J., Anwander, A., Perani, D., & Friederici, A. D. (2013). Dorsal and ventral pathways in language development. *Brain and Language*, *27*, 289–295.

Butterworth, G. (1991). The ontogeny and phylogeny of joint visual attention. In A. Whiten (Ed.), *Natural theories of mind: Evolution, development, and simulation of everyday mind-reading* (pp. 223–232). Oxford: Blackwell.

Chudnovsky, V. E. (2006). *Formation of personality and the problem of the meaning of life*. Moscow: Modek Nekrasova (in Russian).

Collins, W. A., Madsen, S. D., & Susman-Stillman, A. (2002). Parenting during middle childhood. In M. H. Bornstein (Ed.), *Children and parenting*: Vol. 1. Handbook of parenting (pp. 73–101). Mahwah, NJ: Erlbaum.

Dehaene-Lambertz, G., Dehaene, S., & Hertz-Pannier, L. (2002). Functional neuroimaging of speech perception in infants. *Science, 298*, 2013.

Dobrin, A. V., Karpova, N. L., & Nikolaeva, E. I. (2018). The relationship of the lateral features with cognitive processes in individuals with stuttering. *Psychology of Education in the Multicultural Environment, 3*(43), 8–16. https://doi.org/10.24888/2073-8439-2018-43-3-8-16 (in Russian).

Drayna, D., & Kang, C. (2011). Genetic approaches to understanding the causes of stuttering. *Journal of Neurodevelopmental Disorder, 3*(4), 374–380.

Eckert, M. A., & Leonard, C. M. (2000). Structural imaging in dyslexia: The planum temporale. *Mental Retardation and Developmental Disabilities Research Reviews, 6*, 198.

Elias, G., & Broerse, J. (1996). Developmental changes in the incidence and likelihood of simultaneous talk during the first two years: A question of function. *Journal of Child Language, 23*, 201–217.

Fonagy, P., & Target, M. (1997). Attachment and reflective function: Their role in self-organization. *Development and Psychopathology, 9*(4), 679.

Glozman, J. M. (2013). *Developmental neuropsychology*. L–NY: Psychology Press; Taylor and Francis Group.

Glozman, J. M. (2017). *Psychology. Communication and personal health* (2nd ed.). Moscow: Yurait. Rev. and add. textbook for undergraduate and graduate programs (in Russian).

Glozman, J. M., Karpova, N. L., & Cheburashkin-Antipov, D. N. (2018). The dynamics of personality disorders and fluency of speech in the course of logopsychotherapy of stuttering. *Defectology, 5*, 51–57 (in Russian).

Glozman, J. M., Vartanov, A. V., Kiselnikov, A. A., & Karpova, N. L. (2005). Neurophysiological mechanisms of readiness for speech in norm and stuttering. *Human Physiology, 31*(2), 13–17 (in Russian).

Grebelsky-Lichtman, T. (2014). Parental patterns of cooperation in parent-child interactions: The relationship between nonverbal and verbal communication. *Human Communication Research, 40*, 1–29.

Karpova, N. L. (1994). The improvement of the motivational inclusion of stutterers and their relatives in the process of social rehabilitation. *Issues of Psychology, 6*, 43–45 (in Russian).

Karpova, N. L. (2003). *The essence of the personality-oriented logopsychotherapy*. Moscow: MGU (in Russian).

Karpova, N. L. (Ed.), (2011a). *Family group logopsychotherapy: The study of stuttering*. Moscow, St. Petersburg: Resh (in Russian).

Karpova, N. L. (2011b). The system of family group logopsychotherapy: Traditions and new approaches. In N. L. Karpova (Ed.), *Family group logopsychotherapy: The study of stuttering* (pp. 27–34). Saint-Petersburg: Rech (in Russian).

Karpova, N. L., Pastushkova, L. M., Volkova, N. V., & Kiselnikov, A. A. (2006). Psychological, psychophysiological and neuropsychological studies of stuttering. *Defectology, 4*, 18–28 (in Russian).

Kelley, W. M., Wagner, D. D., & Heatherton, T. F. (2015). In search of a human self-regulation system. *Annu. Rev. Neurosci, 38*, 389–411.

Kiselnikov, A. A. (2006). *Psychophysiological and neuropsychological approaches in the study of neural mechanisms of stuttering*. Thesis, PhD Moscow: MGU (in Russian).
Knecht, S. (1998). Reproducibility of functional transcranial Doppler sonography in determining hemispheric language lateralization. *Stroke*, *29*, 1155–1162.
Leonard, C. M. (2002). Anatomical risk factors that distinguish dyslexia from SLI predict reading skill in normal children. *Journal of Communication Disorders*, *35*, 501.
Leutin, V. P., & Nikolaeva, E. I. (1985). The risk of arterial hypertension and features of the functional asymmetry of the brain in the shift workers. *Human Physiology*, *11*(6), 923–926 (in Russian).
Leutin, V. P., Nikolaeva, E. I., & Fomina, E. V. (2009). The functional brain asymmetry and incomplete adaptation. In V. F. Fokin (Ed.), *Manual on functional hemispheric asymmetry* (pp. 429–457). Moscow: Russian Academy of Medical Sciences, Scientific Center of Neurology (in Russian).
Luria, A. R. (1973). *Foundations of neuropsychology*. Moscow: Nauka (in Russian).
Luria, R. A. (1977). *The internal picture of the disease and iatrogenic diseases*. Moscow: Nauka (in Russian).
Myasishchev, V. N. (2004). Psychology of relations. In A. A. Bodalev (Ed.), *Selected psychological works*. Modek MPSI: Moscow (in Russian).
Nekrasova, Y. B. (1991). Diagnostic features in the rehabilitation of people with speech communication disorders. *Issue of Psychology*, *5*, 123–129 (in Russian).
Nekrasova, Y. B. (1992). *The psychological basis of the process of social rehabilitation of stutterers*. Thesis, DscMoscow: MGU (in Russian).
Nekrasova, Y. B. (2006). In N. L. Karpova (Ed.), *Treatment by the creative work*. Moscow: MGU (in Russian).
Nekrasova, Y. B., Bodalev, A. A., Karpova, N. L., Suvorov, A. A., & Chudnovsky, V. I. (1996). The development of new ways of social rehabilitation of people with the different disturbed communication. *The RGNF Bulletin*, *3*, 199–206 (in Russian).
Nikolaeva, E. I., & Borisenkova, E. Y. (2008). The relationship of dichotic testing with the indicators of laterality in preschool children. *Issues of Psychology*, *2*(1), 64–72 (in Russian).
Nikolaeva, E. I., & Merenkova, V. S. (2013a). Mother's caregiving and child's health. *Psychology & Health*, *28*, 279–280.
Nikolaeva, E. I., & Merenkova, V. S. (2013b). The effect of a mother's level of attachment and her emotional intelligence on a child's health during its first year of life. *Psychology*, *4*(5), 483–487.
Nikolaeva, E. I., & Vergunov, E. G. (2013). The forecast of the psychophysiological "cost" of the effectiveness of the learning process in high schoolchildren. *Psychology of Education in the Multicultural Space*, *1*(21), 47–52 (in Russian).
Nikolaeva, E. I., & Yavorovich, K. N. (2014). The specifics of the verbal-manual interference in young boys and girls with varying degrees of the manifestation of lateral symptoms. *Psychology of Education in the Multicultural Environment*, *1*(25), 30–38.
Nowicki, S., & Duke, M. (2013). Accuracy in interpreting nonverbal cues. In J. A. Hall & M. L. Knapp (Eds.), *Nonverbal communication* (pp. 441–470). New York: De Gruyter.
Orlov, Y. M. (2006) *Healthier thinking*.
Orton, S. T. (1925). Word-blindness in school children. *Archives of Neurology and Psychiatry*, *4*, 581.
Oteva, E. A., Nikolaeva, A. A., Sartakova, N. V., Nikolaeva, E. I., & Parm, Y. N. (1994). Assessment of the health state of pregnant women in the Novosibirsk scientific centre: Somatic and psychological aspects. *Obstetrics and Gynaecology*, *3*, 25–27.

Peña, M., Maki, A., Kovačić, D., Dehaene-Lambertz, G., & Koizumi, H. (2003). Sounds and silence: An optical topography study of language recognition at birth. *Proceedings of the National Academy of Sciences of the United States of America*, *100*(20), 11702–11705.

Perani, D., Saccuman, M. C., Scifo, P., Anwander, A., & Spada, D. (2011). Neural language networks at birth. *Proceedings of the National Academy of Sciences of the United States of America*, *108*(38), 16056–16061.

Perchatkina, E. (2008). Cooperation of a speech therapist and parents. *Preschool Education*, *10*, 102–108 (in Russian).

Razumnikova, O. M., & Savinich, M. A. (2016). *Author's certificate No. 2016617675. The software package to identify the characteristics of the visual-spatial memory system*. Moscow (in Russian).

Reitan, R. M., Wolfson, D., & Hom, J. (1992). Left cerebral dominance for bilateral simultaneous sensory stimulation. *Journal of Clinical Psychology*, *48*, 760–766.

Schachner, D. A., Shaver, P., & Mikulincer, M. (2005). Patterns of nonverbal behavior and sensitivity in the context of attachment relationships. *Journal of Nonverbal Behavior*, *29*(3), 141–169.

Seeley, W. W., Menon, V., Schatzberg, A. F., Keller, J., Glover, G. H., Kenna, H., et al. (2007). Dissociable intrinsic connectivity networks for salience processing and executive control. *Journal of Neuroscience*, *27*, 2349–2356.

Shklovsky, V. M. (1994). *Stuttering*. Moscow: Moscow University Press (in Russian).

Singh, A., Erwin-Grabner, T., Sutcliffe, G., Antal, A., Paulus, W., & Goya-Maldonado, R. (2019). Personalized repetitive transcranial magnetic stimulation temporarily alters default mode network in healthy subjects. *Scientific Reports*, *9*(1), 563.

Spivakovskaya, A. S. (2000). *Psychotherapy: game, childhood, family*. Moscow: April Press LLC, EKSMO-Press Publishing House (in Russian).

Thompson-Schill, S. L., Bedny, M., & Goldberg, R. F. (2005). The frontal lobes and the regulation of mental activity. *Current Opinion in Neurobiology*, *15*(2), 219–224.

Vakulenko, L. S. (2012). *Correction of violations of sound pronunciation in children*. St. Petersburg: Speech (in Russian).

Weisberg, J., Hubbard, A. L., & Emmorey, K. (2017). Multimodal integration of spontaneously produced representational co-speech gestures: An fMRI study. *Language, Cognition and Neuroscience*, *32*(2), 158–174.

Yakovistenko, A. D. (2008). *Dynamics of personal and speech characteristics in the process of social rehabilitation (by the example of family group logopsychotherapy)*. PhD Thesis, Moscow.

Yanson, V. N., & Kenga, Z. F. (1983). The relationship of the lateralization the mechanisms of speech activity with individual differences in psychophysiological reactions. *News of the Academy of Sciences of the Latvian SSR*, *17*, 112–120.

Zakharov, A. I. (2000). *Day and night fears in children*. St. Petersburg: Publishing House of the UNION (in Russian).

Zhou, Q., Chen, S. H., & Main, A. (2012). Commonalities and differences in the research on children's effortful control and executive function: A call for an integrated model of self-regulation. *Child Development Perspectives*, *6*, 112–121.

Further reading

Ardelt, M., & Eccles, J. S. (2001). Effects of mothers' parental efficacy beliefs and promote parenting strategies on inner-city youth. *Journal of Family Issues*, *22*, 944–972.

Bennett, E. M. (2006). *Working with people who stutter: A lifespan approach*. Upper Saddle River, NJ: Pearson Merrill/Prentice Hall.

Blomgren, M. (2010). Stuttering treatment for adults: An update on contemporary approaches. *Seminars in Speech and Language*, *31*(4), 272–282.

Blomgren, M., Roy, N., Callister, T., & Merrill, R. M. (2005). Intensive stuttering modification therapy: A multi-dimensional assessment of treatment outcomes. *Journal of Speech, Language, and Hearing Research*, *48*(3), 509–523.

Bothe, A. K., Davidow, J. H., Bramlett, R. E., & Ingham, R. J. (2006). Stuttering treatment research 1970–2005: I. Systematic review incorporating trial quality assessment of behavioral, cognitive, and related approaches. *American Journal of Speech-Language Pathology*, *15*(4), 321–341.

Craig, A. R. (2002). Fluency outcomes following treatment for those who stutter. *Perceptual and Motor Skills*, *94*(3 Pt 1), 772–774.

de Guibert, C., Maumet, C., Jannin, P., Ferré, J. C., Tréguier, C., Barillot, C., et al. (2011). Abnormal functional lateralization and activity of language brain areas in typical specific language impairment developmental dysphasia. *Brain*, *34*, 3044–3056.

Gregory, H. (1972). An assessment of the results of stuttering therapy. *Journal of Communication Disorders*, *5*, 320–334.

Karpova, N. L. (2006). Bibliotherapy in family logopsychotherapy. *Issues of Psychology*, *4*, 70–82 (in Russian).

Keller, S. S. (2011). Can the language-dominant hemisphere be predicted by brain anatomy? *Journal of Cognitive Neuroscience*, *23*, 2013–2018.

Kroll, R., & Scott-Sulsky, L. (2010). The Fluency Plus Program: An integration of fluency shaping and cognitive restructuring procedures for adolescents and adults who stutter. In B. Guitar & R. McCauley (Eds.), *Treatment of stuttering: Established and emerging interventions* (pp. 277–311). Philadelphia, PA: Wolters Kluwer/Lippincott Williams & Wilkins.

Luria, A. R. (1975). *Basic problems of neurolinguistics*. Moscow: Nauka (in Russian).

Nikolaeva, E. I. (2017). *Psychology of family: Textbook for universities*. St. Petersburg: Piter (in Russian).

Vygotsky, L. S. (1934). *Thinking and speech*. Moscow: Misl' (in Russian).

Vygotsky, L. S. (1984). *Collected works: In 6 vol. Vol. 5*. Moscow: Pedagogika (in Russian).

Chapter 10

Formation of higher mental functions in children with special educational needs via social interaction

Vitaly Rubtsov, Andrey Konokotin
Moscow State University of Psychology and Education, Moscow, Russian Federation

Introduction

The education of children with special educational needs (SEN) is a challenge, both to the educational practice and to scientific research. In L.S. Vygotsky's cultural-historical scientific school, this issue is framed and addressed in the context of changing the child's abilities and capacities to join a social situation and participate in various interrelations that emerge with age-mates and adults.

Vygotsky argued that neither the teacher nor the child deals with a "physical defect" directly (Vygotsky, 1983a, p. 52). The issue has to be regarded more broadly as a matter of social consequences that are triggered by the "defect," that is, as a matter of social deprivation and therefore of *underdevelopment* of higher mental functions (HMF). In its turn, the *underdevelopment* of HMF aggravates the child's social deprivation. Vygotsky regarded the issue of educating children with SEN as well as normally developing children first of all as a social challenge. His idea that the process of development is due to the social environment finds its fullest expression in the general genetic law of development of HMF, where he claims that social interactions between the child and surrounding people underlie the inner structures of the psyche. Vygotsky argued: "Every function in the child's cultural development appears on the stage twice, that is, on two planes—first, on the social plane, and then on the psychological plane; first, among people as an interpsychological category, and then within the child as an intrapsychological category"[a] (Vygotsky, 1983b, p. 145).

Developing the key principles of cultural-historical psychology, Luria followed Vygotsky in arguing that the child "from the very beginning of their life

---

a. Translated by authors.

Evaluation and Treatment of Neuropsychologically Compromised Children.
https://doi.org/10.1016/B978-0-12-819545-1.00010-2

establishes necessary relations with other people, learns the objectively existing language system, and assimilates with its help the experience of other generations. All this is the determining factor in the child's further mental development, a determining condition for the formation of those higher mental functions that distinguish the human from animals"[b] (Luria, 1962, p. 30). Studying the specificities of the development of HMF, Luria managed to unify into a comprehensive system the knowledge about the biological fabric of the brain, its physiological functioning, and the psychological concept, explaining the process of its development. Analyzing Luria's approach to studying speech, Oliver Sacks emphasizes that "the development of language … was never seen by him as an anatomic development of 'language areas' in the brain, but as resulting from the interaction of mother and child, from the negotiation of meanings between mother and child, (the) mode of interaction or "betweenness," and *this* as a prerequisite for, and needing to be structuralized in, the developing neurolinguistic systems of the brain" (Sacks, 2015, p. 32). B.D. Perry, building on research, demonstrates that the earlier the child's normal social functioning is restored, the more likely positive dynamics in their development are to be expected (Perry, 2002, p. 92–94). He argues that social deprivation has a particularly negative influence on brain development in early childhood (2–4 years), resulting in physiological underdevelopment and leading to disruptions in such mental functions as speech, attention, self-control, etc.

Thus, the above-mentioned premises imply that specially organized social interactions between child and adult represent an important factor that contributes to the child's overcoming any social and educational difficulties. Therefore, by including the child in joint activities, we create conditions for eliminating "the main cause of the underdevelopment of HMF." By developing HMF via social interactions, we give the child a chance to overcome social deprivation. This allows us to address educational inclusion as an issue of social interactions of children with SEN and normally developing children (ND), as the emerging interactions and interrelations trigger changes in the social situation of development, boosting the development of higher mental functions.

Following Vygotsky and Luria, we hypothesized that the development of HMF in children with SEN is possible in a situation of specially organized interactions with age-mates and adults, where particular processes are launched, determining emergence and development of the so-called child-adult "communities."[c] Primarily, these processes include communication and mutual understanding, which to a large extent influence joint problem solving and, eventually, the development of a child's thinking.

---

b. Translated by authors.

c. In Cultural-Historical Theory and Activity Approach by L.S. Vygotsky, A.R. Luria, and A.N. Leontiev a special notion is used—"obstchnost," which designates a particular kind of socioemotional unity of the participants of the social situation. The closest equivalent of this concept in English is "community," which we will use in this chapter.

This standpoint is confirmed by experimental data. According to F. Erdogan, cooperative learning, supported by reflective thinking activities such as writing, journal writing, reflective dialogue, and thinking aloud, contributes to the development of critical thinking skills. Erdogan illustrates this in her research on learning, where students were given the possibility to discuss with their group members and evaluate their own activities with the "group discussion strategy," which transforms reflective activity into a social activity. Erdogan found out that students who analyzed peers' activities, thoughts, and interactions, then gave feedback to each other, developed critical perspectives during the study. Thus, Erdogan argues that the very process of the analysis of children's interactions with each other paves the way for the development of thinking (Erdogan, 2019, p. 101).

N. Gagne and S. Parks, who studied interaction and mutual support in joint problem solving (Gagne & Parks, 2013, p. 205–207), argue that the success in collaborating may be due, at least in part, to the type of problem given to the child. In this study, students were given tasks designed to foster positive interdependence and individual accountability (for example, a crossword jigsaw task where the clues were distributed among the team members). Thus, the tasks themselves acted as a scaffold to facilitate interaction.

Following Vygotsky's ideas about the interrelation of development and means of learning, J.K. Hall, who investigated the development of language skills in the process of second language acquisition depending on students' participation in different classroom interactional practices, argues that: "what students take away from their classrooms in terms of target language knowledge and skills, is intimately tied to the kinds of interactional practices that teachers create in their talk with students" and that "teaching practices are simultaneously prerequisite and product, the tools and the results of language learning" (Hall, 2010, p. 12). Therefore, "the question about how language is acquired and represented in the mind of an individual learner can only be answered by looking first not at WHAT is being talked about in the classroom interaction, but at HOW the talk is being accomplished in the interactional practices used to teach" (Hall, 2010, p. 12).

E.F. Fitch and K.M. Hulgin conducted research on the process of teaching children to read in inclusive classes in a situation of joint work via dialogic learning. They managed to show that in the process of dialogue and in the course of emerging communication, children exchange standpoints and positions concerning the learning task. They also discuss, explain, and convince each other as well as evaluate each other. Thus, they develop an understanding of each other's positions–that is, mutual understanding that, according to E.F. Fitch and K.M. Hulgin, leads to the construction of a "shared meaning." They argue that, apart from developing reading skills as the result of learning, the participants of the specially organized joint activity also developed cooperation skills, which resulted in the development of their thinking abilities. Referring to Vygotsky, the authors argue that children acquired (internalized) the means of thinking (Fitch & Hulgin, 2013, p. 12).

As V.V. Rubtsov's research demonstrated in an example of joint problem solving by children aged 7–12 (i.e., tasks on including subclasses into a class by J. Piaget), there was a profound internal connection between the ways children interacted (i.e., means of cooperation) and the level of development of the operational structures of the child's thinking (J. Piaget's concept). Particularly, Rubtsov found out that a correct understanding by children of the content of multiplicative relations, which corresponds to a high level of development of operational structures, develops in a situation where an exchange of actions takes place when the very means of interaction between participants and the ways it can lead them to the right solution becomes the subject of their analysis. As was demonstrated in the research, the processes of communication and mutual understanding had a strong impact on the efficiency of exchanges in joint action. According to Rubtsov, this influence revealed itself in the fact that participants perceived the subjective content of the problem (multiplication of attributes) as an indicator of the possible means of interaction, answering the terms of the problem (the relation of attributes as a "sign of action"). This initiated the participants' new attempts to find a solution and new tests in organizing efficient interactions (Rubtsov, 1994, p. 35–47).

Aim of research and methods

Our research was aimed at revealing and experimentally investigating the processes that influenced the inclusion of children with SEN into joint problem solving. We particularly focused on the processes of communication and mutual understanding and tried to demonstrate how, in the course of these processes, new ways of interaction appear in the emerging child-adult "communities," which mediate the development of speech, attention, memory, and thinking.

In this research, the method of the "scale" was used, which was elaborated by Rubtsov and L. Martin, for studying the impact of social interactions on the efficiency of solving a set of tasks on balancing the moments of force (Rubtsov, 1994, pp. 93–106). In contrast with the earlier research, we applied this method with the aim of revealing and experimentally investigating the processes that contribute to children's inclusion into joint problem solving and their extending the boundaries of communication and interaction with each other and with the adult. In this method, a special installation was used, a "scale" (Martine, 1983, p. 76–78). This "scale" was a metal circle fastened at the center on a tripod (the center of the circle is also the center of the equilibrium). Along the diameter of the circle, an indicator line was drawn with divisions equidistant from each other. The experimenter placed on this indicator line weights (magnets) equal in weight. The participants could change the number of magnets as well as the distance to the center of the indicator line. Children were sequentially offered 12 tasks on balancing the "scale" (Fig. 1). For solving the task, children had to jointly figure out the equilibrium of the moments of force in relation to the center of gravity. Observing the interaction of children in the process of problem

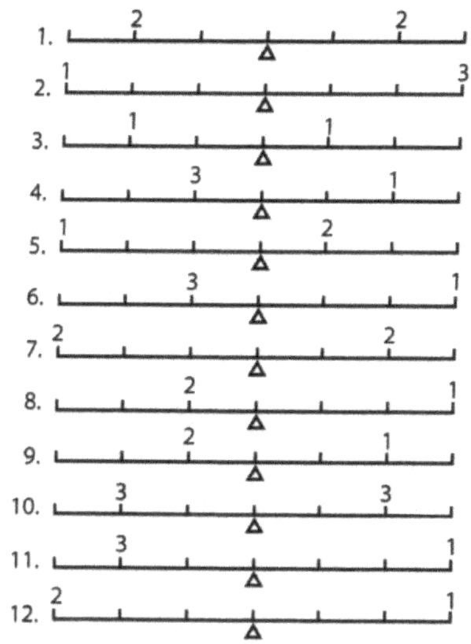

FIG. 1 Examples of experimental tasks (the numbers on the picture indicate the number of weights, and the markings on the line indicator represent the distance from the weights to the center of gravity).

solving made it possible to investigate the emerging communication and mutual understanding, and to evaluate how these processes influence the development of speech, thinking, and attention.

The experiment was conducted in two phases. In the first phase (individual series), each participant had to answer the question of whether the "scale" would be in equilibrium with a given distribution of weights. The weights were placed by the experimenter and the children did not replace or remove them. Depending on the orientation of children on the interrelation of factors, important for balancing the "scale" (weight and distance to the center of gravity), the differences in children's understanding the rules of the balance of the moments of force were identified and the level of development of each child's thinking abilities was indicated. In the second phase (cooperative series), children jointly solved the tasks on balancing the moments of force, which allowed us to study the peculiarities of children's interactions with age-mates and adults as well as to analyze the processes that reflected the characteristic features of the emerging "community" and, eventually, influenced the development of HMF.

The participants in the study were eight primary school children, ages 7–9, attending a public school in Moscow (Russia). There were ND children and children with SEN among the participants:

1. *Misha, age 8.1*—First-year primary school student with delayed psychological development. Had problems with contacting age-mates and adults (teachers), emotionally stunted, very passive at lessons. Did not contact his group-mates.

2. *Nikita, age 9.3*—First-year primary school student with cerebral palsy. Easily contacted age-mates and adults, shy, rarely initiated dialogue. Only active at lessons when directly addressed by the teacher.
3. *Lena, age 9.11*—Third-year primary school student with hearing impairment. Easily contacted age-mates and adults, open, communicative. Active at lessons.
4. *Grisha, age 8.10*—Second-year primary school student with severe speech deficiencies. Selective in contacting age-mates, emotionally stunted, conflicted. Had difficulty in contacting adults. Passive at lessons, completed the tasks with difficulty.
5. *Masha, age 8.2*—First-year primary school student, ND. Easily contacted age-mates and adults, communicative and open. Active at lessons.
6. *Oleg, age 8.8*—First-year primary school student, ND. Easily contacted age-mates and adults, communicative and open. Active at lessons.
7. *Samirghon, age 9.7*—Third-year primary school student, ND. Easily contacted age-mates and adults, communicative and open. Active at lessons.
8. *Arina, age 9.3*—Second-year primary school student, ND. Easily contacted age-mates and adults, communicative and open. Active at lessons.

Based on the results of the first phase of research (individual series), we identified four types of orientation[d]:

Type 1—Children with this type of orientation took into consideration exclusively the factor of weight while solving the task. This type of orientation was demonstrated, for example, by Nikita. He gave the following arguments: "It's heavier on the right because there's a small weight here and a big one here" (Task 1), "The scale will be in equilibrium because there is one weight on each side" (Task 5).

Type 2—Children with this type of orientation took into consideration mostly the weight of magnets; however, they correctly grasped the factor of distance while solving the tasks on equal weights. This type of orientation was demonstrated, for example, by Masha, Samirghon, and Oleg, who gave the following arguments: Masha: "It's in equilibrium because there's an equal number of magnets (Task 1)," "It's heavier on the side with two magnets because there are more weights and they're heavier," (Task 5), or "In equilibrium because these magnets (on the left) are closer to the edge" (Task 7); Samirghon: "In equilibrium because they are identical" (Task 1), "It's heavier on the side with two magnets," (Task 5) or "In equilibrium because the weight is located at the edge of the indicator line (on the right), but these magnets weigh more (on the left)" (Task 7); Oleg: "In equilibrium because they weigh the same" (Task 1), "To the left because they're located near the edge, and there're two magnets here and two magnets there" (Task 7).

d. Types of orientation, identified in the first phase of experiment, correspond to the types described in the works by V.V. Rubtsov and L.M. Martin (Martin, 1983; Rubtsov, 1994).

Type 3—Children with this type of orientation took into consideration mostly the distance to the center of gravity. This type of orientation was demonstrated, for example, by Misha and Grisha, who gave the following arguments: Misha: "Toward side 1 because it's at the edge" (Task 1), "Toward side 1 because it's at the edge" (Task 6), Grisha: "To the left because it's closer to the edge" (Task 3), "To the left because it's closer to the edge, and these aren't" (Task 7).

Type 4—Children with this type of orientation took into consideration both factors and correctly grasped the significance of each factor for getting the "scale" in equilibrium. They correctly identified the connection between weight and distance; however, they failed to formulate this connection in a form of equality between the moments of force, which resulted in mistakes. This type of orientation was demonstrated, for example, by Lena and Arina, who gave the following arguments: Lena: "There are three magnets here and they're closer, and there's one magnet here and it's farther" (Task 4), "To the side with two magnets because there are two magnets and they're closer, and here there's one magnet and it's farther" (Task 5); Arina: "In equilibrium because three magnets are more, but they're on a small level, and here there are fewer magnets, but they're on a bigger level" (Task 4).

In the second phase (cooperative series), the group was divided into pairs, where participants demonstrated different types of orientation. While organizing the pairs, we assumed that, apart from an intellectual gap between children with SEN and ND, there is also a social-personal gap between them, which is determined by their individual characteristics. This circumstance was particularly taken into account while organizing group work. There were four pairs who took part in the experiment:

- Misha (SEN, type 3)—Masha (ND, type 2)
- Nikita (SEN, type 1)—Oleg (ND, type2)
- Grisha (SEN, type 3)—Arina (ND, type 4)
- Lena (SEN, type 4)—Samirghon (ND, type 2)

Children were asked to bring the "scale" to equilibrium while working together, on the condition that the operations were distributed between the participants in such a way that one of them could move the weights along the indicator line on their part of the installation, and the other one could increase or decrease the number of weights on their part of the installation exclusively on the indicator line, where the experimenter had placed them. These conditions allowed us to create situations where the problem could not be solved by one participant without the other.

After the cooperative series in the second phase of the experiment, the individual series was repeated where children were once again given the tasks from the first phase. This allowed us to indicate changes that occurred (or did not occur) in the participants' understanding of the multiplicative relations. It also allowed us to link these changes with the processes of communication and mutual understanding, emerging in the situation of joint activity and interactions in the process of problem solving.

Analysis of the results

This study has shown that the interconnection between *communication, mutual understanding, and means of interaction* may be perceived as an integral indicator of children's inclusion into the joint means of problem solving and, therefore, as a substantive feature of the emerging "communities," which determines the new framework of the possibilities of development of HMF in children. The analysis of the collected data allowed us to identify four types of "communities" ("obstchnost"). The main features of each type of "community," based on the results of the empirical data, are presented in Table 1.

Let us focus on the **four types of** "communities" in more detail.

1. ***Precooperative type of*** "community" ("obstchnost")

This type of "community" is characterized primarily by a lack of productive interactions between participants. The processes of communication and exchange of actions, aimed at the search for a joint means of problem solving, did not emerge between children. In a number of cases, "speech for oneself" emerged, which accompanied individual operations (for example, "I made it heavier," "And what if I take it away?") and nondirected appeals to the experimenter (for example, "I know, I know how I can do it… like this"), identifying possible variants of the child's actions. The task to understand the partner's aims and possibilities did not acquire significance for these children. Understanding the rules of their own actions was the priority for these children. They did not get involved in the joint search for solving the problem and performed exclusively individual attempts to cope with the task.

Example 1. Misha and Masha (Misha was responsible for the weight and Masha was responsible for the distance).
Task 1.
Masha: I can move (moves the magnets).
Misha (At the same time tries to move the magnet, but turns it on the wrong end and the magnets repel). Oops. Wrong end. (turns the magnet and chooses the right side).
Masha: (Observing Misha's actions and moving her magnets to the center of gravity).
E: You can only put the magnets on the indicated places on the indicator line.
Masha: (Moves the magnet one marking on the line).
Misha: (Wants to remove one magnet).
E: Take your time. Misha put three magnets. Let's have a look at how it works.

TABLE 1 Types of children's "communities" emerging in the situation of joint problem solving (on the example of solving a class of tasks on balancing the moments of force).

Type of "community" ("obstchnost") (means of interaction)	Processes of communication and mutual understanding, characterizing the joint search for a means of solving the problem
1. *Precooperative*: There is no interaction between participants. Children are not involved in the joint search for a means of solving the problem.	Processes of communication and exchange of actions, aimed at the search for a means of solving the problem, do not emerge. There is no mutual understanding.
2. *Pseudocooperative*: Interaction between participants is substituted by actions of one of the participants. In some cases, the task is solved by one participant (individually).	Communication that emerges between participants does not affect the content of the task. There is no understanding of the possibilities of actions of the other participant and no exchange of actions, which determine the search for a joint means of solving the problem.
3. *Cooperative (organizational)*: The emerging joint action relies on the interaction of participants, based on simple cooperation of the operations performed. Children search for the solution of the problem, relying on the possibilities of individual actions without analyzing the means of interaction itself. The problem is solved.	Mutual understanding of the possibilities of individual actions and exchange of actions is determined by the search for a joint means of solving the problem. Communication is not focused on the search for a joint means of solving the problem. Participants are concentrated on solving the problem, rather than on figuring out how to organize interaction to find the right solution.
4. *Metacooperative (reflective-analytical)*: The subject of the participants' analysis is the means of interaction itself, which makes it possible to transform the means and solve the problem. The problem is solved due to the inclusion of individual actions into the joint action and exchange of actions.	Communication is aimed at discussing the possibilities of including individual actions into the joint action. The search for the correct solution is transformed for the participants into the task of interaction and revealing a joint means of solution. Mutual understanding is mediated by the search for means of interaction. Organization of individual actions in joint action becomes the goal of interaction. The way is paved for new relationships and, as a result, for the emergence of a new social situation, determining new aims and goals.

Misha: (Pointing at the installation and laughing). Wrong. (Then removes one magnet and tries to put it on the wrong end). And this is the wrong side. Flies away all the time (removes the magnet).

Apparently, the children did not grasp the content of the task, represented as an interrelation of factors. For them the task itself (to bring the "scale" in equilibrium) and the impossibility of solving it became only an indicator of the limitations of their individual actions. The necessity to overcome the emerging limitations, preceded by the requirement of the adult, led the children to the need for communicating with each other, and thus to discussing and understanding the actions envisaged for each of them.

2. ***Pseudocooperative type of*** "community" ("obstchnost")

The analysis revealed that communication that emerges in this type of "community" does not address the content of the task and does not contribute to the search for a joint means of solving the problem. Understanding the aims and possibilities of the other participant also did not emerge, and thus there was a lack of mutual understanding. However, while understanding the limitations of their own (individual) actions that were established by the experimenter via distribution, the participants empowered themselves to act "for the other," performing the action instead of the other participant ("for him") without agreeing on that.

Example 2. Misha and Masha (the same participants)
Task 4.
Masha: There should be more here (**pointing** at Misha's magnets).
Misha: (Adds one magnet)
Masha: (Moves the magnets to line 3)
...
Misha: (Removes one magnet)
Masha: (Moves her magnets to line 1). We should put more there.
Misha: (Not reacting. Playing with magnets).
E.: Misha, this won't help you to tackle the task.
Misha: (Adds one magnet)
Masha: (Moves to line 2). One should be removed from here (**pointing** at Misha's magnets).
Misha: (Removes one magnet)
Masha's attempt to include her group-mate into joint work remain unsuccessful.

Example 3. Nikita And Oleg (Nikita is responsible for weight, and Oleg for distance).
Task 3.
Nikita: (Moves his magnets closer to the edge of the "scale").
Oleg: Stop, stop, Nikita, put them here (**pointing** at line 2. Then starts gradually removing his magnets from the installation). Wait, don't do anything now.

Nikita: (Stands up, though used to sit and observe. Oleg stands up all the time).
Oleg: O, it's in equilibrium!
E: Great! Is there any other means?
Nikita: (Moving the magnets to line 3).
Oleg: Stop! Like thiiiiiiis (adds one magnet)
Nikita: Just a bit… Like thiiiis (prolongs the sounds, makes an intonation, puts the magnets between lines 2 and 3).
Oleg: No, a bit more. Put them here (**points** to line 2).

Cooperation between children in this situation was replaced by actions of one of the participants. At this point, a distinctive "manipulation" of the actions of the other could be observed as well as orientation exclusively on finding a concrete solution to the task. It is also important to highlight the emergence of the *pointing gesture*, which testifies that there was a change in how children address each other—appealing to the other became directed, and attracted the attention of the group-mate to the search for the means of solving the task. This fact is particularly meaningful for understanding the peculiarities of the indicated forms of "communities."

Vygotsky particularly emphasized the pointing gesture as "the basis for all higher forms of behavior" (Vygotsky, 1983b, p. 168), as a gesture directed toward the other person and being a means of connecting with them. It is possible to assume that the emerging form of appealing, based on the pointing gesture, may be regarded as the first stage of the change of the means of interaction between participants and the development of the joint action per se because in this case, the means of interaction became the focus of the children's attention.

In this type of "community," however, the emergence of the pointing gesture in one of the participants did not change the position of the other participant—only one participant took an active position and the task was solved only partly. That is why some of the participants could not overcome the given means of distribution of actions and make a step forward in the development of a joint means of problem solving.

The analysis of the results of joint work of Nikita and Oleg showed that this kind of "community" may not be considered fully efficient because a positive effect on development could only be noticed in one of the participants. In the second individual series, Nikita did not indicate the interrelation between the factors of weight and distance and was consistently oriented on the weight of the magnets. He also made typical mistakes in the interpretation of this factor ("Will go to the side of magnet 1 because three are more, because three are heavier," "Will go to the side with two magnets because it is lighter than one magnet"). In Oleg's case, a different picture could be observed. In the first phase, while taking into account both factors, he still did not understand the interrelation between them, and thus made mistakes. However, in the next phase, the child started to interrelate the two factors and solved the majority of the tasks ("It's in equilibrium because here it's heavy, but they're placed far, and here there's one, but it's close, very close," "To the side 3. Because they used to be here, and now they're closer here"). This testified that the child developed an understanding of the rule of balance and, therefore, indicated a step in the development of his thinking.

3. ***Cooperative type of*** "community" ("obstchnost")

Children who built this type of "community" engaged in an interaction, based on the cooperation of the actions that they performed. They searched for the solution, considering the possibilities of individual actions; however, they did not analyze the means of interaction per se. The constructed joint action remained unstable, emerging in the situation of the distribution of actions and their exchange; it was often again replaced by the participants' individual activity.

Example 4. Misha and Masha -
Task 8.
Misha: (Removing one magnet)
Masha: (Simultaneously with Misha's action) one should be removed (**pointing** at Misha's magnets with her finger)
Misha: (Moving his magnet to line 1)
(The task is solved by establishing a simple identity)
E: Is there any other solution?
Misha: (Adds one magnet)
Masha: (Moves her magnet to line 2)
(The task is solved by applying the rule on balancing the moments of force)
Masha: (Leans to reach for her magnet, but does not take it first, looking at Misha)
Misha: (Adds one magnet. Observes what Masha is doing)
Masha: (Only after Misha's actions starts moving her magnet to line 3)
(The task is solved by applying the rule on balancing the moments of force)

Task 9.
Misha: (Removes one weight and observes Masha's actions)
Masha: (Moves to line 1. The "scale" leans to Misha's side. Moves to line 3. The "scale" leans to Masha's side. Puts on the center of gravity. The "scale" leans to Misha's side again).
Misha: It's even heavier like this.
Masha: (Moves to line 3 and pointing at Misha's weights). One should be removed.

It is significant that in the process of solving Task 8, directed speech and gesture communication did not emerge. However, despite the lack of communication, the participants demonstrated orientation not on the individual, but on the joint action. They related the emerging result with the means of cooperating their own actions and by this indicated the relation of factors, determining the balance. Mutual understanding, which emerged in the process of the interaction, allowed these children not only to find the right solutions to the problem, but also to do it in a shorter period of time in comparison with the beginning of the cooperative actions (the number of testing actions decreased).

Later on, however, as the example of solving Task 9 shows, the children's joint action broke up, and orientation on the individual action and its result became the dominant means of solving the task. At the same time, the results of the second series showed that in the process of interaction, Misha demonstrated signs of the development of attention—he was not distracted by other activities (which used to happen at the very beginning of work in the second phase), and he concentrated on solving the task and controlling the actions that his groupmate was performing. In the course of interaction, a transition to the fourth type of orientation could be detected—in Misha's case that could be seen in the following remarks: "… There're three magnets here, but they moved only one circle, and here there's one magnet, but it's in the big circle," "There're two magnets in the middle circle, and here there're also two, but in the big circle."

Masha also demonstrated a transition to a new level of understanding the relation of balance. This was reflected in her answers: "In equilibrium. Because there're three here, but they're closer to the center, and here there's one, but it's closer to the edge," "To the left because there's the same number of them, but these magnets are closer to the edge."

In general, the fact that the children solved the tasks together indicated that the participants understood the possibilities of individual actions and their role in cooperation, which mediated the search for solving the task. At the same time, the analysis of the means of cooperation did not become the focus of the joint action being constructed. Thus, the main goal for these children remained solving the task, based on the relation of the factors of balance.

4. ***Metacooperative type of*** "community" ("obstchnost")

A characteristic trait of this type of "community," distinguishing it from the forms of joint work mentioned earlier, is the change of the subject of the task. In our case, the very means of interaction between participants became the subject of the task. While engaging in the search for this means, the children went beyond the substantive framework (the "barrier" of substantive content), and perceived the interrelation of the basic factors as guidance for the joint action that was being constructed. Thus, these children's search for the solution was based on the analysis of a possible means of interaction, which resulted in its transformation and in the emergence of the possibility of solving the task. This point of research might be illustrated by the following example.

Example 5. Lena and Samirghon.
Task 1.
Lena: (Moves the magnets to line 1)
Samirghon: (Adds one magnet)
Lena: It will be heavier, you have to remove a few.

Samirghon: (Removes one magnet, the "scale" is still tipped to his side).
Lena: Shall you remove one more?
Samirghon: If I remove it, it will fall down… ahhh… yes, I can remove it. (The problem is solved by applying the rule on balancing the moments of force).

Task 4.
Samirghon: (Looking at Lena and modeling her movement with his hand) I have to remove two magnets.
Lena: (Simultaneously moving one magnet forward and coordinating her actions with her group-mate's actions) OK, remove them (The task is solved by establishing a simple identity)
Experimenter: Are there any other solutions?
Samirghon: Move backwards, and I will add one weight.
Lena: (Simultaneously with Samirghon) Yes, yes (moves her magnet to line 2)

It is significant that, in this case, mutual understanding that emerged and developed between the participants was mediated by communication, and was aimed at the discussion of the interrelation of actions for each participant, and the possibilities of including these actions in a joint action. The actions for each participant were indeed no longer perceived as independent. An exchange of actions acquired a stable character and, consequently, the participants became included in a joint metasubstantive space of searching for a solution, in the framework of which the partner turned into a coparticipant of the joint activity. Such verbal traits, such as appealing to the other and putting spins on the words, prevailed in the speech of the participants. Exclamations, discussion of the possible outcomes of joint actions, and pointing gestures also emerged. These characteristics of communication indicated the emergence of a "mutual field of meaning," a new form of joint action ("collective form" in Vygotsky's terms) where the participants elaborated shared meanings and possible "scenarios" of the joint search for the solution.

In general, we observed that with the emergence of this form of "community," children made steps in the development of understanding the interrelation between factors, determining the balance of the moments of force. For example, in the second phase in the second individual series, Lena correctly interpreted the interrelation between weight and distance and, though in her answers she only mentioned one of the factors, she correctly solved the tasks: "To the left because it's further and heavier," "The same, because there are three here and three there," and they're at the same distance from the point (meaning the center of the circle). Samirghon, mentioning only one of the factors, was, however, also considering the interrelation of factors. This indicated a new level of understanding of the moments of force ("To side 1 because it's closer to the edge, and when we were solving with three magnets, it was in equilibrium").

Some concluding remarks

While studying the development of higher mental functions (HMFs) in children with SEN in social interactions, we concluded that the premises of such development should be found in the very forms of interaction and in the real relationships that emerge between participants. The results obtained in the course of this study allowed us to formulate at least four types of child-adult "communities" ("obstchnost"), differing in the processes of communication, mutual understanding, and means of interaction that emerged between participants in the situation of problem solving. The characteristic traits of the "community" where children are included in the process of joint problem solving, which distinguishes it from other possible types of bringing participants together, consist of the fact that participants are focused on the very means of interaction. Peculiarities of this "community" are reflected in a targeted search for a joint means of solution: in assessment of the limitations of "their own" actions and the actions of "the other," in mutually saying aloud and the use of symbols (short hands) of the "scenarios" of possible interactions, which might be efficient for solving the problem, and further modeling (symbolic gaming) of such interactions.

In analyzing the received data, we came to the conclusion that the transition from the focus on substantive content of the task to the analysis of the means of interaction in the process of problem solving has a particular significance for understanding the source and the mechanisms of the child's mental development. Let us once again turn to the ideas of Vygotsky and Luria. Both these scholars agreed that all higher mental functions and processes are social in origin.[e] That means that they emerge in the system of social relationships, where each function is originally divided between participants. "Behind all higher mental functions and their relationships stand genetically social relationships, real relationships, homo duplex (a dual person, Latin). From here comes the principle and method of personification in the study of cultural development, that is, (the) division of function between people, (the) personification of functions. For example, voluntary attention—one possesses, the other one acquires. Dividing again in two what had been fused into one, experimental unfolding of a higher mental process (voluntary attention) into a small drama"[f] (Vygotsky, 2005, p. 1023). Social interactions determine the mechanism of the division of functions on the one hand, and the means of their acquisition on the other. This means that the social interactions and the social relations of the participants, which originally serve as a necessary condition for the social realization of the processes of thinking and communication, start later to perform the function of self-regulation and mental representation of various kinds of information. These interactions boost the development of cognitive functions, which are not yet developed, allowing children to act on a higher cognitive level.

---

e. L.S. Vygotsky used the term "genetically social" (from Lat. "genesis").

f. Translated by authors.

There is yet one significant circumstance that has to be taken into consideration while discussing the processes that influence inclusion into the situation of social interactions, particularly in children with SEN. It is important to highlight that the change of the subject of the task, which emerges in social interactions, does not indicate exclusively the change in the subject of action. For children, this change is connected with the emergence of a new problem. The necessity of solving this new problem, therefore, triggers a new motivation, which prompts the children to organize joint actions and search jointly for a solution. Following this motivation, the participants discuss emerging limitations and model necessary exchanges, developing communication and modeling the directions of possible interactions.

In these conditions, a shared emotional-meaningful field emerges, based on the participants' mutual understanding and their emotional experience ("pereghivanije") of the new possibilities and their understanding of the sense of the actions that they perform. The importance of the emerging "pereghivanije" in the development of activity was particularly emphasized by A.N. Leontiev, who argued: "These forms of pereghivanije are the forms of the subject's relation to the motive…" and "This conscious relation of the subject of action to its motive is the sense of action; the form of pereghivanije (experience) of the sense of action is the awareness of its aim… The change of the sense of action always means a change of its motivation" (Leontiev, 1994, p. 48–49).

Summary

The results presented in this chapter highlight the significance of social interactions in the development of higher mental functions and shed light on the issue of including children (particularly with SEN) into the process of joint problem solving. There are strong grounds to believe that it is the emerging motivation, determined by the necessity to perform new interactions, that gives the impulse for the change of the social situation. The activity in this situation is based on the new meanings and relations to the performance of one's own actions and the actions of the other participants as well as on emotional experience (pereghivanije) and mutual understanding of these new meanings. With the emergence of a new motivation for a child who has limitations in performing certain actions, new possibilities emerge, and therefore new boundaries for individual actions. As a result, children try to plan new scenarios and come to new agreements concerning the real interactions as well as to model new means of joint work.

Lastly, including children with special educational needs (SEN) and normally developing children (ND) into joint learning activities is a necessary condition for the development of their higher mental functions as well as a necessary condition for organizing inclusive education.

References

Erdogan, F. (2019). Effect of cooperative learning supported by reflective thinking activities on students' critical thinking skills. *Eurasian Journal of Educational Research*, *80*, 89–112.

Fitch, E. F., & Hulgin, K. M. (2013). Achieving inclusion through CLAD: Collaborative learning assessment through dialogue. *International Journal of Inclusive Education*, *12*(4), 423–439. https://doi.org/10.1080/13603110601121453.

Gagne, N., & Parks, S. (2013). Cooperative learning tasks in a grade 6 intensive ESL class: Role of scaffolding. *Language Teaching Research*, *17*(2), 188–209.

Hall, J. K. (2010). Interaction as method and result of language learning. *Language Teaching*, *43*(2), 202–215.

Leontiev, A.N. (1994). In A.A. Leontiev & D. A. Leontiev (Eds.), *Philosophy of psychology. From scientific tribute*. Moscow: Moscow Univ. Press. 228 p. (in Russian).

Luria, A.R. (1962). *Higher cortical functions in man and their disturbances after local brain damages*. Moscow: Moscow Univ. Press. 431 p. (in Russian).

Martin, L. (1983). *Children's problem solving as inter-individual outcome*. Ph.D, Diss. San Diego: University of California. 164 p.

Perry, B. D. (2002). Brain and mind childhood experience and the expression of genetic potential: What childhood neglect tells us about nature and nurture. *Brain and Mind*, *79*(3), 79–99.

Rubtsov, V. V. (1994). *Organization and development of joint actions among children in the learning process*. New York: Nova Science Publishers.

Sacks, O. (2015). Luria and "romantic science". In A. Y. In, R. Van der Veer, & M. Ferrari (Eds.), *The Cambridge handbook of cultural-historical psychology* (pp. 517–528). Cambridge: Cambridge University Press. https://doi.org/10.1017/CBO9781139028097.028.

Vygotsky, L. S. (1983a). Foundations of defectology. In T.A. Vlasova (Ed.), Vol. 5. *Collected papers*. Moscow: Pedagogika. 368 p. (in Russian).

Vygotsky, L. S. (1983b). History of higher mental functions development. In A.M. Matiushkin (Ed.), Vol. 3. *Collected papers*. Pedagogika: Moscow. 368 p. (in Russian).

Vygotsky, L. S. (2005). *Psychology of human development*. Moscow: Smysl. 1136 p. (in Russian).

Chapter 11

Laying the framework for developing executive functions in tweens with learning disabilities

Fernando Pastrana[a,b], Patricia A. McElroy[b], Scott Johnson[c], Kayla Mckenzie Chustz[b], Darlyne G. Nemeth[b]
[a]*Neuropsychology Center of Louisiana at Gretna, LLC, Gretna, LA, United States,* [b]*The Neuropsychology Center of Louisiana, LLC, Baton Rouge, LA, United States,* [c]*Pediatric Development & Therapy Center, Our Lady of the Lake Children's Health, Baton Rouge, LA, United States*

Introduction

Tween boys ages 10–14 tend to be behaviorally impulsive and emotionally reactive (Schroeder & Kuriansky, 2009). At this age, their executive/frontal functions (Schroeder & Kuriansky, 2009) and multitasking abilities (Harasty et al., 2000) are less developed than girls' executive/frontal functions. Like some of their college counterparts, these boys tend to act without thinking rationally (Birnbaum, 2013; see Table 1) and make significant mistakes. This is especially the case in mathematics, where rational thinking is required (Young, Wu, & Menon, 2012) and emotional thinking leads to mistakes. The more errors these tweens make, the more anxious they become (Young et al., 2012). As boys develop language skills more slowly than girls (Macintyre, 2009), they are often driven by emotions that they cannot label and do not understand as well as social pressures with which they are ill prepared to cope.

Therefore, the Neuropsychology Center of Louisiana (NCLA) created a program for tweens (ages 10–14) to improve their executive/frontal functions, emotional and social skills, and mathematics abilities. After 3 years and two summer trials, the program gelled. The purpose of this chapter is to outline and analyze the efficiency and efficacy of the program for the four tween boys and the group. During this 8-week/14-session program, these students were taught to create, communicate, and compete effectively. This Build-A-Brain program was designed to teach logical thinking and assuage emotional reactivity, thus

Evaluation and Treatment of Neuropsychologically Compromised Children
https://doi.org/10.1016/B978-0-12-819545-1.00011-4

TABLE 1 Birnbaum identified two potential action sequences—The first using logic and the second using emotions to make decisions.

Rational (cold)	Emotional (hot)
Ready	Ready
Aim	Fire
Fire	Aim

allowing participants to perform better in the academic environment. One study of executive function in kindergarteners by Morgan et al. (2019) suggests that deficits in working memory, cognitive flexibility, and inhibitory control increase the risk for repeated academic difficulties.

In an explanation of this intervention to the students and their parents/parental figures/loved ones, NCLA's "Build-A-Brain" program was compared to building a house. The information on the program was given to all (see Fig. 1). "No confidentiality" agreements were explained and signed (see Fig. 2). Hold harmless and technology agreements were also explained and signed (see Figs. 3 and 4). All students received a white three-ringed binder with weekly lessons and assignments, which served as the bases of the experiential learning techniques used in this program.

A historical perspective

Five years ago, several tweens were presented to NCLA by their parents for math-related learning difficulties. Their psychoeducational evaluations revealed strengths in reading and written language, but significant weaknesses in mathematics. Several were also found to have attentional and/or anxiety disorders. Medication management helped but did not solve their apparent dyscalculia. Individual interventions including parent counseling were attempted with minimal success. These interventions were too similar to "homework." Basically, they were not fun.

Then, the idea of small group interventions emerged. At first, a mixed gender—boys and girls—group was attempted. This, however, proved to be too distracting. Second, small gender-specific groups (just boys) were attempted. These appeared to be more fruitful. After returning to school for the fall, these tween boys began to show improved grades in math (Nemeth, personal communication, November 2019). With the addition of MobyMax, a comprehensive online math curriculum designed to target and improve weaknesses (discussed in detail later in this chapter) and staff oversight, the third summer group program, described in this chapter, seemed to help prepare the

NCLA's

2019 Build-a-Brain Program

Create-Communicate-Compete

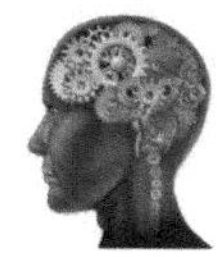

(A 14-session program to improve higher mental functions)

Your brain is just like your house. It stores everything that is important to you. It is a source of play and joy and wonder. It is filled with love and mystery. It is your special place.

All special places need love, attention, and care. That is why we are going to build new connections for more effective learning this summer.

Building can be fun. When we have fun, we learn and grow. Summertime is playtime, so let's have fun building our brain house to be more wonderful than it already is.

Through play, we will become more aware of our actions, we will better understand our freedoms and limits, we will learn to compete and cooperate with one another, and we will be able to communicate more effectively with our friends and family. First, we will think; second, we will recognize, label, and share our feelings; and third, we will choose wise actions. This is how we will do it:

Step 1: Lay the Foundation

Step 2: Build four walls and a roof.

Step 3: Add windows and doors.

Step 4: Create the interior connections.

Step 5: Add the essentials.

Step 6: Enjoy the outcome.

FIG. 1 Information sheet provided for participating tweens and their parents/guardians for the Build-A-Brain program.

boys on all levels—behaviorally, emotionally, socially, and mathematically. At the beginning, these tween boys did not appear to have the developmentally appropriate skills to benefit from such rigorous academic demands. As Vygotsky stated, the required math skills were outside their zone of proximal development (Doolittle, 1995).

NCLA

The Neuropsychology Center of Louisiana, L.L.C.

A Professional Corporation

Darlyne G. Nemeth, Ph.D., M.P., M.P.A.P.

Clinical, Medical, and Neuropsychologist

Evaluation Intervention Rehabilitation

4611 Bluebonnet Blvd., Ste. B • Baton Rouge, Louisiana 70809 • Phone 225-926-7500 • Fax 225-924-0188 • www.louisiananeuropsych.com

NCLA No Confidentiality Agreement for Adolescents, as of June 11, 2019

1. Self-harm threats or actions
2. Harm to others via threats or actions, including social media
3. Alcohol, tobacco, marijuana, and/or street drugs
4. Inappropriate decisions/actions

Should any of the above occur, discussion will ensue, either in individual, family, or group settings, and/or a call will be made to the appropriate parent figures.

Signature of Psychologist ______________________________ Date __________

Signature of Adolescent ______________________________ Date __________

Signature of Parent Figure ______________________________ Date __________

FIG. 2 Parents and tweens were provided with "No Confidentiality" agreements at the start of the program, so all participants were aware of NCLA's confidentiality practices.

Integrating the Luria and Reitan models of intervention

NCLA's Build-A-Brain program for tweens focuses on the integration of executive/frontal functions. As Glozman (2013) points out, Luria's concept of the Third Unit of Brain Functions, which provides the voluntary regulation of mental activities, usually continues to develop up to 12–15 years of age (Glozman, 2013, p. 41). This voluntary regulation, which appears to be underdeveloped in some tween boys, typically includes

Executive functions program
hold harmless release for teens

(A) Experiential learning

I understand and acknowledge that this is an experiential learning program, and not a form of counseling or therapy. I further understand that this experiential learning program is based on a model of group intervention. This model is designed to teach teens how to build more effective executive functions. Thus, I understand that this is a teaching model for teens who are dealing with difficult learning experiences and I give permission for my teen to attend.

(B) Confidentiality

I understand and agree that, during the course of this group experience, teens may share very personal information. In order for this experience to be a safe and comforting one, I agree to ask my teen not to share what others talk about; however, teen will be told that it is ok to talk about what he/she shared or learned.

(C) Voluntary participation

I understand that my teen's participation in this program is completely voluntary. I agree to hold harmless all individuals who are offering/leading this program. I also agree to hold harmless the facility in which this program is held.

(D) Research

I understand that any data gathered from this program may be used as part of a clinical and/or scientific presentations and publications. When this is done, no information that could specifically identify my teen will be shared.

(E) Missed sessions

I understand that I am financially responsible for all sessions, even those my teen does not attend. I understand that missed sessions can be made up at an individual session with Dr. Pastrana for a fee of $150/h.

By signing this release, I acknowledge the aforecited stipulations for my teen.

Name of Participant: ______________________________

Participant's Signature: ______________________________

Name of parent/grandparent: ______________________________

Parent's/Grandparent's Signature: ______________________________

Dates of Program: June 11, 2019–August 1, 2019

FIG. 3 Hold harmless releases were provided and reviewed with participating tweens and their parents/guardians.

1. "an objective setting, in accordance with motivation and purpose of actual or planned activity"
2. "planning of a program and best ways to achieve the goal"
3. "monitoring of the implementation of the program and the timely correction of inadequate action and associations"
4. "comparison of objective with intermediate and final results" (Glozman, 2013, p. 41)

NCLA

The Neuropsychology Center of Louisiana, L.L.C.
A Professional Corporation
Darlyne G. Nemeth, Ph.D., M.P., M.P.A.P.
Clinical, Medical, and Neuropsychologist
Evaluation Intervention Rehabilitation

4611 Bluebonnet Blvd., Ste. B • Baton Rouge, Louisiana 70809 • Phone 225-926-7500 • Fax 225-924-0188 • www.louisiananeuropsych.com

NCLA Technology Agreement for Adolescents, as of June 11, 2019

I understand that my teen's participation in this program requires the at-home use of a computer. I hereby acknowledge that I have a computer, and I will let my teen use it at home as needed for the purposes of this program.

By signing this agreement, I acknowledge and agree to the above stipulation for my teen.

Name of Participant: ______________________________

Name of Parent/Grandparent: ______________________________

Parent's/Grandparent's Signature: ______________________________

Dates of Program: June 11, 2019–August 1, 2019

FIG. 4 Participants and guardians were provided with a technology agreement dictating that participating tweens would have access to a computer to utilize an online program called MobyMax to improve their math skills.

As cited in Chapter 2 of this volume, Luria's Unit III, which involves programming, regulation, and control, focuses on frontal/prefrontal activities that form stable plans and interventions capable of controlling behavior and inhibition. Because Luria's Unit III (Glozman, 2013) was the focus of intervention, Reitan's Tracks B, D, and C of the REHABIT System provided the specifics for intervention. Track B focused on the verbal integration of reasoning skills; Track D focused on the nonverbal integration of reasoning skills; and Track C combined both (Reitan & Wolfson, 1992, p. 151).

Program description

The summer Build-A-Brain program took place on Tuesdays and Thursdays of each week. Tuesday's session focused on providing explanation and psychoeducation for that week's activities (setting the stage). Thursday's session focused on discussion, modeling, practice, and review. During times of review, the facilitators would often compare approaching a task/activity/discussion/interaction using the strategies being discussed versus without. This was used to concretely demonstrate their advantages and highlight their benefits. For example, "Was the task easier/more successful with a predetermined plan or without?" (benefits of planning ahead). "Would the conversation with your loved one have gone better using this tone of voice or that one?" (monitoring one's own nonverbal communication). "If a loved one is displaying the nonverbal cues of being angry or irritated, would it be a good time to ask them to take you somewhere or should you wait a little while?" (being observant of nonverbal cues of others). Cooperative and competitive play was embedded throughout the program.

It should be noted that loved ones did not directly participate in Tuesday sessions, but were encouraged to "participate" in Thursday sessions. Participation involved being able to hear (via intercom) and see (via one-way mirror) the entirety of the interactions between the participants and the facilitators (the participants were fully aware of this). With this approach, loved ones were able to hear and see the discussions being had and the activities being utilized in such a way that would facilitate out-of-session practice (modeling was being done for the children and loved ones simultaneously). A review of interventions by Chavez-Arana et al. (2018) for executive functions in children and adolescents with acquired brain injury suggests that "education for parents may be an important component of intervention" and caregiver involvement may improve effectiveness. Additionally, Weisberg, Hirsh-Pasek, Golinkoff, Kittredge, and Klahr (2016) suggest that getting a group of children together with some adult guidance setting examples of how to act socially will, in time, imprint on all participants the proper way to interact with each other in any situation. As such, loved ones were encouraged to review, discuss, and practice the topics introduced and materials covered after each session. A program facilitator was also present with the loved ones to answer any questions that may have come up.

As Glozman stated earlier, making behavioral observations can reveal essential data and can help to inform treatment/intervention. To that end, behavioral observations were collected by two observers throughout the intervention portion of the program.

Vygotsky defined the zone of proximal development as "the distance between the actual developmental level as determined by independent problem solving and the level of potential development as determined through problem solving under adult guidance or in collaboration with more capable peers" (Vygotsky, 1978, p. 86). This "Build-A-Brain" program aimed to capitalize on closing this distance.

As was indicated in the program's information sheet (see Fig. 1):

> *Your brain is just like your house. It stores everything that is important to you. It is a source of play and joy and wonder. It is filled with love and mystery. It is your special place.*

All special places need love, attention, and care. That is why we are going to build new connections for more effective learning this summer.

Building can be fun. When we have fun, we learn and grow. Summertime is playtime, so let's have fun building our brain house to be more wonderful than it already is.

Through play, we will become more aware of our actions, we will better understand our freedoms and limits, we will learn to compete and cooperate with one another, and we will be able to communicate more effectively with our friends and family. First, we will think; second, we will recognize, label, and share our feelings; and third, we will choose wise actions.

Measures/materials utilized

As cited in Chapter 2 of this volume, "quantitative evaluation is of primary value for determining the dynamics of change in cognitive functioning and for measuring the outcome of rehabilitative or remedial procedures." To that end, the program began and ended with data collection. The tools utilized included the following:

- Brown Attention-Deficit Disorder Scales: "instruments designed to elicit parent and teacher observations of symptoms in 3–12 year olds and to elicit self-report from children ages 8 years and older that may indicate impairment in executive functions related to attention deficit/hyperactivity disorders" (Brown, 2001).
- Behavior Rating Inventory of Executive Function, Second Edition (BRIEF-2) assesses executive function and self-regulation in children and teens (5–18 years) and provides information regarding behavioral regulation, emotional regulation, and cognitive regulation, which combine to form a global executive composite (Gioia, Isquith, Guy, & Kenworthy, 2015).
- The Behavior Assessment System for Children (3rd Edition) (BASC-3) measures maladaptive clinical behaviors such as aggression, anxiety, attention problems, atypicality, conduct problems, depression, hyperactivity, learning problems, somatization, and withdrawal; adaptive behaviors such as activities of daily living, adaptability, functional communication, leadership, social skills, and study skills; content scales such as anger, bullying, developmental social disorders, emotional self-control, executive functioning, negative emotionality, and resiliency; and the composite scores of externalizing problems, internalizing problems, school problems, adaptive skills, and behavioral symptoms index (Reynolds & Kamphaus, 2015).
- The math portion of the Wide Range Achievement Test (4th Edition) (WRAT-4) "measures an individual's ability to perform basic mathematics computations through counting, identifying numbers, solving simple oral problems, and calculating written mathematics problems." It consists of 40 items and 15 min are allowed for completion (Wilkinson & Robertson, 2006).

- The Repeatable Battery for the Assessment of Neuropsychological Status (RBANS-Update) is a "brief, individually administered test measuring attention, language, visuospatial/constructional abilities, and immediate and delayed memory. The test comprises 12 subtests that can be administered by trained examiners in about 20 to 30 minutes" (Randolph, 2012). The 12 subtests include list learning, story memory, figure copy, line orientation, picture naming, semantic fluency, digit span, coding, list recall, list recognition, story memory, and figure recall.
- A computerized version of the Halstead Category Test (HCT) of the Halstead-Reitan Neuropsychological Battery for Older Children (HRNB-OC; 9–14 year olds) was administered. As mentioned in a previous chapter, it measures one's ability to learn abstract principles and respond to feedback. The Trail Making Test for older children of this same battery was also administered and consists of two parts (A and B) and requires visual tracking, simple and complex set-shifting, and sequencing ability (Reitan & Wolfson, 1992).
- The Tests of Variables of Attention (TOVAs) can be administered via two versions (auditory and visual). The visual version of this test was utilized in the Build-A-Brain program. The TOVAs are "individually administered computerized tests developed to assess attention and impulse control in normal and clinical populations." "The TOVA was developed to measure attention and impulse control processes in four areas: response time variability, response time, impulse control (commission errors), and inattention (omission errors)." "The visual TOVA's stimuli are two easily discriminated geometric figures centered on the computer screen … the stimuli are squares" (Leark, Greenburg, Kindschi, Dupuy, & Hughes, 2007).
- Also completed were child personal data forms, teacher interview questionnaires, parent/teacher questionnaires, and child background questionnaires.
- Behavioral observations were being recorded throughout the intervention phase of the program and included off task, restless, verbal interrupting, easily distracted, impulsive responding, uncooperative play, and nonverbal aggression.

Program outline

A session-by-session breakdown of the summer "Build-A-Brain" program is as follows:

- Introduction: (Tuesday)
  - Welcome to the program.
  - NCLA staff introduced themselves to the participating tweens and their parents/guardians. The program details were explained. Handouts were provided and signatures were obtained for the following: no confidentiality agreement, hold harmless release, and technology agreement. Other materials were offered including Nemeth's *Helping Your Angry Child* workbook (Nemeth,

Ray, & Schexnayder, 2003) and Branstetter's *The Everything Parent's Guide to Children with Executive Functioning Disorder* (Branstetter, 2014). Directions were provided regarding the use of MobyMax (*MobyMax: Fix learning gaps*, n.d.), which was to be used at home.

- Session 1: (Thursday)
  - Pretests were completed by the participating tweens and their parents/guardians in a group setting (Behavior Rating Inventory of Executive Function—2nd ed. (BRIEF-2 SR & PR), Behavior Assessment System for Child—3rd ed., (BASC-3 SR & PR), Wide Range Achievement Test—4th ed., Math Computation (WRAT-4)).
- Session 2: (Tuesday)
  - Audio compact discs were issued to participants—Indigo Dreams (Lite, 2004) and Overcoming Anxiety series (Emery, 1989).
  - Nemeth explained what executive functions are and the role they play in learning. She explained how, when individuals struggle to regulate their emotions, they cannot efficiently utilize their executive functions.
  - Nemeth identified six basic feelings—embarrassed, anxious, scared, angry, sad, and happy—and asked each tween to describe the feelings associated with each. She emphasized the importance of being able to recognize and label emotions. Tweens completed "Matching Feelings and Faces" and "Guess the Feeling" exercises. Nemeth reviewed "Four Big Anger Sources" with the participants.
  - Nemeth explained how somatic symptoms can indicate how you are feeling (e.g., rapid breathing, stomach pain, flushed face).
  - Nemeth explained the importance of effective communication and offered strategies to use: ECOW (Eye contact, Call by name, One command, Wait for response) and XYZ (when you do X, I feel Y, I would prefer Z). Tweens practiced using these techniques and voiced anticipated concerns on practicing with family.
- Session 3: (Thursday)
  - Pastrana reviewed the three Es (emotional functioning, executive functioning, and executional functioning) and explained how all three influence one another (feeling → thinking → doing) and the six basic emotions.
  - Pastrana explained how we can read a person's body language to determine how they feel and explained what our body language communicates to other people. He explained acting out versus acting in.
    - We should recognize if we tend to act out or act in when upset and use that information as a cue to use healthy coping skills.
  - Pastrana reviewed the communication techniques previously learned and emphasized (to the tweens and loved ones) the importance of giving appropriate feedback to enhance communication/understanding:
    - "It's not what you say, it's how you say it."
    - Communication NOT manipulation.
    - Importance of being respectful.

  - The tweens played a game in which they demonstrated what each of the six basic emotions looked like on their own faces. They also drew emotion faces on the board.
  - Parents voiced their questions about the learned communication techniques and were provided guidance on how to encourage their children to participate in successful communication.
  - Importance of attention was reviewed (foundation of memory).
  - Talked about healthy versus unhealthy coping mechanisms:
    - Relaxation breathing exercise, "Breathe in the happy, breathe out the sad."
- Session 4: (Tuesday)
  - Tweens explained how they have been using communication techniques and shared any difficulties they had run into. Discussed how loved ones may consider it "talking back" (recall, loved ones were listening in on this discussion, which facilitated their understanding).
  - Tinker Toy activity:
    - Individual: "Make something that represents you, use your imagination."
    - Group: "Put individual pieces together to make a group piece."
    - Kids worked together, took turns, and shared Tinker Toys.
  - TOVA individually administered.
- Session 5: (Thursday)
  - Tweens gave feedback on using previously taught communication techniques, and gave examples of times they had used them. Loved ones did the same. Challenges were addressed.
  - TOVA scores reviewed with tweens and loved ones.
  - Tweens were individually administered Trails A and B.
  - Pastrana introduced the Four Bear Steps to Planning:
    - (Identify the problem, make a plan, evaluate the plan's efficacy, review the outcome).
  - Tween fingers sized for mood rings.
- Session 6: (Tuesday)
  - Define and prioritize creation versus education (creation must come first).
  - Play = Most effective form of development.
    - Tweens played Pyramid Game (Brain-Ade Games, 2007).
  - Discussed behavioral control and the three ways to behave: wild, weak, and wise; defined each type and explained how we can control our behavior through the choices we make. Gave examples of behaviors that will get good results (i.e., listen, understand, consider) and bad results (i.e., slam doors, yell, say mean things).
  - Nemeth brought each tween a stuffed animal to squeeze when they feel like choosing a behavior that gives bad results.
  - Nemeth explained spatial and speech control. The tweens participated in arm length exercises to learn how to position themselves properly to be heard.
  - BRIEF self scores reviewed with tweens.

- Session 7: (Thursday)
  - Pastrana led the tweens in the "RILEE Relaxation Exercise."
  - Explained that play makes learning easier. You can play games to practice competitive learning.
  - Emphasized that positive emotional involvement leads to increased social interaction, which leads to improved cognitive development.
  - Pastrana explained how emotional training will help influence math performance. Our behavior is in our control. Tasks tend to be easier when we remain calm.
  - Group Activity—Make a tower of blocks as tall as you can:
    - Tweens worked together to "establish a plan"; use four bear steps to planning.
- Session 8: (Tuesday)
  - Focus topic—improving working memory.
  - Five components of BAB program: (1) neurocognitive skills, (2) problem solving, (3) emotional control, 4) social skills, and (5) critical reasoning.
  - "Working memory is like the mortar between the bricks. It allows learning to cement/take place" ~ Nemeth.
  - Defined working memory (Auditory info = Phonological loop; Visual info = Visuospatial loop):
    - Normally takes three seconds for both loops to come together.
  - Practice—Short read about baseball; tweens instructed to read a small part, take six seconds, then tell about it. Did interference task, then asked if tweens remembered what they read.
  - Other ways to boost working memory—learn important phone numbers forward and backward (chunking).
  - Group activity—Widgets
    - Use widgets and work in pairs to build a structure, use teamwork.
    - Task completed three times, each time switching partners.
  - "Spot the Difference" exercise as group.
- Session 9: (Thursday)
  - Pastrana explained how it is naturally easier to remember something you're interested in. The Build-A-Brain program is teaching tweens to use strategies to help them learn and remember things they may not be so interested in (i.e., school instructions).
  - Changed focus from auditory memory to visual memory.
  - Individually and as a group drew Rey-Ostereith Complex Figure:
    - Copy as exactly as possible; recreate without looking.
    - How did they approach this? Did they make a plan? Did they work from the middle out, general to detailed, etc.? (Help tweens continue to use four bear steps to plan and identify their organizational techniques/inefficiencies).
  - Pastrana explained that some people are more visual learners and some are more auditory learners, but that the more parts of the brain that are

engaged in learning, the more likely learning and retention will occur (e.g., seeing and hearing info, reading aloud).
- Reviewed strategies to boost working memory (i.e., chunking).

- Session 10: (Tuesday)
  - Mood rings given out to help tweens identify/monitor how they feel (light color indicates anxiety, dark color indicates sadness, blue/blue-green indicates calm/happiness).
  - Explained the zone of proximal development:
    - Distance between what they know and is easy for them and what they do not know and is hard for them. Playing games can challenge us and help us to learn/grow.
  - Reviewed different reasons to play (social involvement, to win, motivated to do best).
  - Practiced visual discrimination (Wechsler Intelligence Scale for Children, 3rd ed. (WISC-III), Coding) and auditory discrimination (Seashore Rhythm Test).
  - Played Chinese Checkers (Western Publishing Company, Inc., 1981) (started out as cooperative, transitioned to competitive).
  - Defined three types of motivation—cooperative, altruistic, and competitive.
  - Reemphasized that remediation is not correction, it is *creation* (Glozman, 2013).
- Session 11: (Thursday)
  - Reviewed what was discussed during previous session.
  - Seashore Rhythm Test (continued to practice auditory discrimination).
  - More competitive play.
  - Task practice checked (phone numbers learned forward and backward and coding exercise).
- Session 12: (Tuesday)
  - Posttesting (group and individual).
  - Discussed self-esteem ➔ Feeling good about yourself decreases anxiety:
    - What it's composed of and what good habits promote it.
  - Drawings—self and group.
  - Discussed when to share thoughts and when to keep them to self.
  - Played game—Mighty Mind (Leisure Learning Products, Inc., 2008).
- Wrap-Up: (Thursday)
  - Reviewed post test scores.
  - Explained to loved ones how to continue MobyMax.
  - Explained importance of automatization in learning math (makes problem solving easier).
  - Encouraged tweens to continue to use mood rings to monitor their feelings and adjust behaviors accordingly.
  - Reviewed communication techniques (ECOW & XYZ) with tweens and loved ones.

- Reminded loved ones that kids and teens (up to age 15) have trouble recognizing negative words (i.e., don't and no) because their right hemisphere is not as strong in recognition as it is in adults. Therefore, the child not listening is not necessarily defiance.

Online math training software

As was previously mentioned, participants and loved ones were oriented to and encouraged to use an online learning program, MobyMax, throughout the program. According to the program's website, Moby Math helps "struggling learners quickly catch up to grade level and close learning gaps." It "finds and fixes missing math skills that are essential for math comprehension. Students increase an average of one grade level with just 20 hours of practice. Moby Math is a comprehensive math curriculum for kindergarten to 8th grade." They indicate the "primary reason that Moby Math is so effective is because students do not waste time practicing material they have already mastered. Instead, Moby Math targets areas where students are struggling and allows students to progress immediately once mastery is achieved." Moby Math reportedly "finds missing math skills with a quick, efficient placement test" and "continually updates each student's progress during practice and review to give… a current view of… progress." The program then states that the "Learn Cycle has been made more efficient by breaking math concepts into small, achievable skills and creating lesson topics that consist of a short animated Teach Me with targeted practice problems. All problems have instant feedback and all parts of the problem have a read-aloud icon for students to listen as well as read" (*MobyMax: Fix learning gaps*, n.d.). The suggested frequency for engagement with this software began at 3 days/week (30–45 min/day), with 4 or 5 days of engagement being an option. If there was difficulty maintaining this schedule, duration could be decreased to 10 min/day such that stamina could be built and lead to long enough engagement to allow for learning (*MobyMax: Fix learning gaps*, n.d.).

Methods and results

Participant demographics

As was previously mentioned, there were four cisgender males who participated in the summer program. The participants all identified as Caucasian and ranged in age from 9 to 14 (the 9 year old celebrated his 10th birthday during the program). At the time of the summer program, three of the children attended traditional schools and one was homeschooled. Their most recently completed school grade ranged from 4th to 8th. The diagnoses represented (previously identified) included dysgraphia, attention deficit/hyperactivity disorder, visual processing disorder, oppositional defiant disorder, dysgraphia, developmental delay, learning disability, and autism spectrum disorder.

Methods

Trend analysis was deployed for most conditions of the study. A t-test for one-tailed significance was utilized on the psychological tests. For behavioral observations, time sampling was deployed as an agent of change, or criteria of positive or negative outcomes. Statistics were analyzed using an Excel data analysis package.

Results—Questionnaires

A variety of questionnaires and measures were completed throughout the summer program (see Materials/Measures Utilized and Program Outline Sections above). Some were completed only in the beginning, were subjective, and will be discussed descriptively; others were completed at the beginning and end of the program and will be compared.

The descriptive results of a subjective/qualitative questionnaire (completed by a loved one) revealed general concerns regarding reading fluency, reading comprehension, spelling, written expression, listening comprehension, oral expression, communication, gross motor abilities, social/emotional/behavioral functioning, and health. It should be noted that **all** loved ones endorsed concerns regarding math calculation, math problem solving, fine motor skills, and handwriting.

Regarding behavioral performance concerns, loved ones endorsed withdrawn, anxious/nervous, demanding excessive attention, and lack of age-appropriate concern for behavior and its effects on others.

Regarding peer interactions, a mix of attributes was identified, including works well in a small group, is polite/friendly to peers, has friends, works well with peers, and has positive peer relationships. Lacks social skills, bothers other students, and is bullied were, however, also identified. It should be noted that no loved one endorsed their participant as arguing with other students, blaming others, or bullying. **None** were identified as being accepted by a majority of their peers. This representative mix of peer interaction abilities/challenges lent itself to a group dynamic in which the strengths of one could be utilized to improve the deficits of another, especially via the use of encouragement/positive reinforcement by facilitators.

The next subjective questionnaire was also completed by loved ones. This questionnaire is broken down into separate categories representing attention, mood, memory, movement, social, and perception. The first question, however, asks loved ones to categorize the participant in terms of their class rank. All answered that they ranked in the bottom third of their class.

Regarding the first content category (attention), loved ones reported the presence of appearing hypoactive, may act before thinking, distractibility, difficulty falling asleep, sleep-talking, nightmares, restlessness, and heightened sensitivity to touch. Of note, **all** loved ones reported the presence of varied attention with and/or without hyperactivity, difficulty organizing work, poor concentration/daydreams, easily forgets assignments, incomplete assignments, difficulty following directions, much repetition needed, and heightened sensitivity to sound. Many, if not all, of these descriptors are directly influenced by deficits in executive functioning and as being improved by strengthening said deficits.

The next content category (mood) is notable in that all difficulties were endorsed by at least one of the loved ones. Those included emotional volatility, heightened sensitivity, discipline problems due to poor attention span or acting out, and frequent mood changes. Additionally, the following were identified as mood difficulties for all participants: decreased self-esteem, easily frustrated, crying or temper outbursts, and impulsivity. These emotionally motivated/influenced behaviors have the capacity for improvement with the acquisition of skills utilized in this program.

Regarding memory, every loved one endorsed decreased spontaneity when writing, varied reaction times, decreased comprehension, difficulty following directions, incomplete assignments, needs much repetition of information, and needs a much longer time for answers as deficits.

Identified movement challenges for all participants included incoordination, poor handwriting, and poor balance.

Social deficits included varied peer relationships, difficulty staying on task with play activities, seems to need much supervision (endorsed by all), better on a one-on-one basis, difficulty awaiting turn when talking or playing, and difficulty reading facial expressions (endorsed by at least one).

Lastly, regarding perception, 23 of the 28 variables were endorsed by at least one loved one. The following two variables were endorsed by all: difficulty with written expression and poor copying skills.

Results—Objective measures

The Brown

Preprogram results of the Brown Attention-Deficit Disorder Scales, an instrument designed to indicate impairment in executive functions related to attention deficit/hyperactivity disorders (data available for three out of four of the participants) suggest the presence of varied observations that may indicate impairment in executive functions related to attention deficit/hyperactivity disorders. The first of the three indicated notable deficits ($T \geq 70$) in the areas of activation, focus, effort, emotion, and ADD combined total score. The second had notable deficits in focus, effort, memory, and ADD combined total score. The third had notable deficits in activation, focus, effort, memory, and ADD combined total score. These results highlight the impact attentional deficits can have on behavioral self-regulation and the need for guidance related to developing executive functions.

The BRIEF-2

The Behavior Rating Inventory of Executive Function, Second Edition (BRIEF-2) was completed by loved ones and the participants themselves at the beginning and end of the program. This measure assesses executive function and self-regulation and provides information regarding behavioral regulation, emotional regulation, and cognitive regulation, which combine to form a global executive composite (Gioia et al., 2015).

Results of this measure were interesting in that the participants rated themselves as endorsing a greater average level of deficit at the end of the program versus before on three of the four indices (emotional regulation, cognitive regulation, and global executive composite), with behavioral regulation being the only one that indicated decreased deficit (see Table 2).

However, the results of the parent report form indicated decreased deficits (improvement) in all four indices measured at the end of the program versus before (behavioral regulation, emotional regulation, cognitive regulation, and global executive composite) (see Table 3).

One potential explanation for this pattern could be that the participants became more aware, knowledgeable, and understanding of their difficulties and therefore rated themselves more accurately on the postprogram measure, whereas the loved ones saw positive change on average, which resulted in scores reflecting decreased deficit.

The BASC-3

Results of the Behavior Assessment System for Children (3rd Edition) (BASC-3) self-report form, which measures adaptive and maladaptive clinical behaviors, revealed average scores essentially unchanged from pre- to postprogram (see Table 4). Results of the parent report form could not be provided as two of the four loved ones did not complete the measure.

TABLE 2 Average BRIEF-2 self-report results.

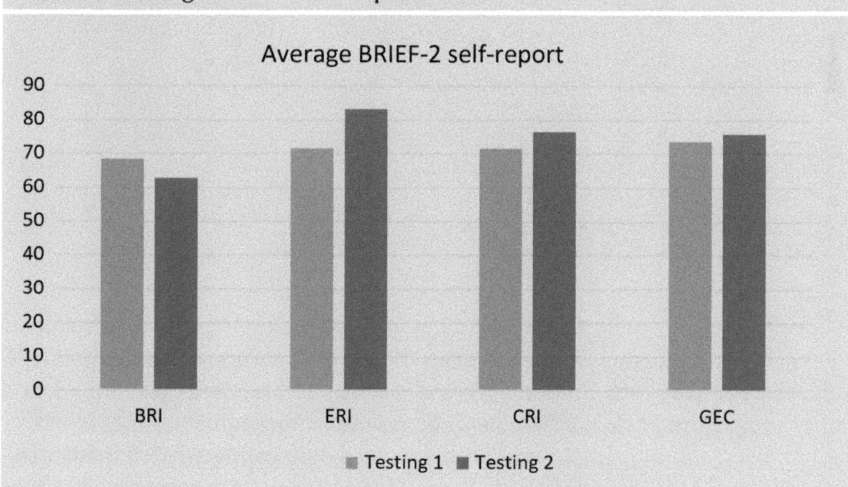

TABLE 3 Average BRIEF-2 parent report results.

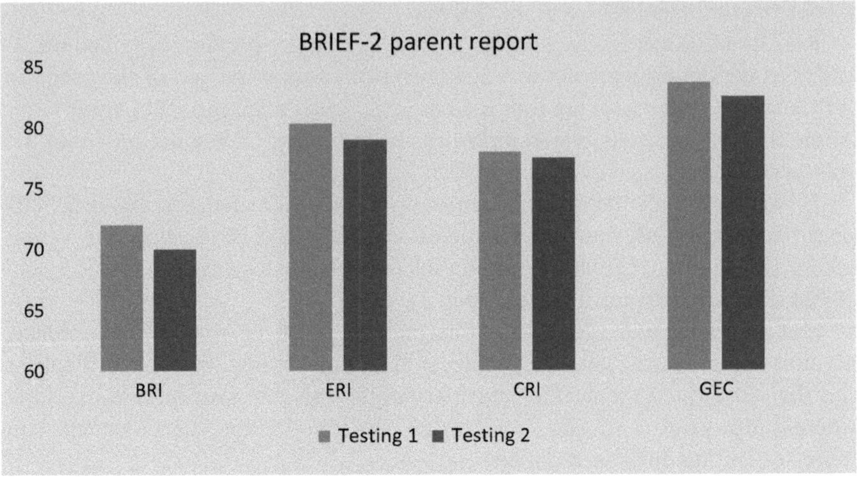

TABLE 4 Average BASC-3 self-report results.

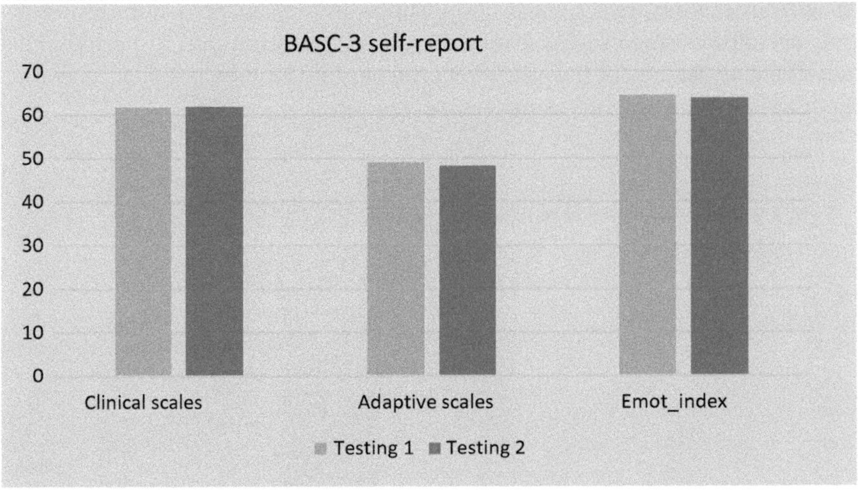

WRAT-4

Pre- versus postprogram averaged results of the math portion of the Wide Range Achievement Test (4th Edition) (WRAT-4), which "measures an individual's ability to perform basic mathematics computations through counting, identifying numbers, solving simple oral problems, and calculating written mathematics problems" (Wilkinson & Robertson, 2006) suggest the group as a whole improved by a very close to statistically significant amount at the .05 level

TABLE 5 Pre- and postscore "Build-A-Brain" program WRAT-4 math results for each participant.

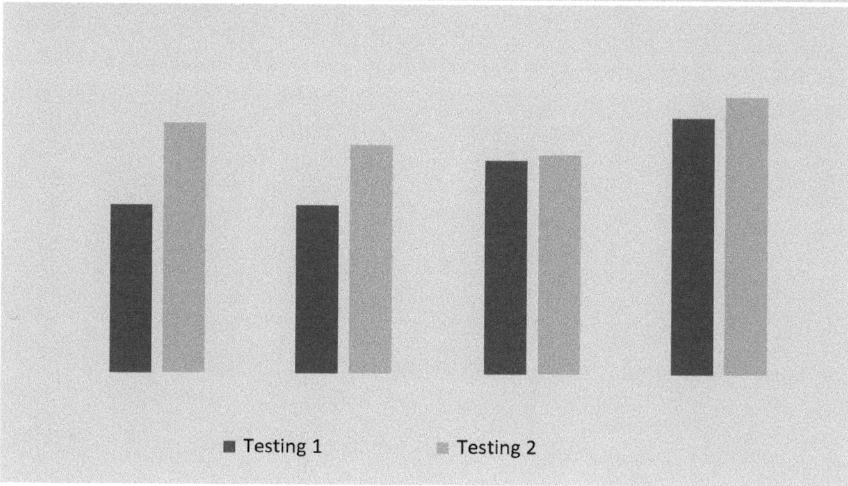

($P = .068$). Table 5 provides an individual illustration of pre- and postscore differences. These results represent the most robust documented improvement regarding pre- and postprogram change.

RBANS-update

Results of the Repeatable Battery for the Assessment of Neuropsychological Status (RBANS) a brief, individually administered test measuring attention, language, visuospatial/constructional abilities, and immediate and delayed memory, indicate that there was a .704 correlation between the total score on RBANs pre- and postadministration, suggesting a strong or very strong relationship. Also of interest is the .73 correlation that was found between delayed memory preadministration and the total score postadministration. This reveals that either high or low scores on delayed memory have a strong relationship with one another. Language scores correlated negatively with total overall scores.

HCT

The Halstead Category Test (HCT) of the Halstead-Reitan Neuropsychological Battery for Older Children (HRNB-OC; 9–14 year olds) measures one's ability to learn abstract principles and respond to feedback, an executive function. Results indicate that all three participants who completed this measure both pre- and postprogram committed fewer errors (representing improved performance) (see Table 6).

TABLE 6 Pre- and postscore "Build-A-Brain" program Halstead Category Test results for each participant.

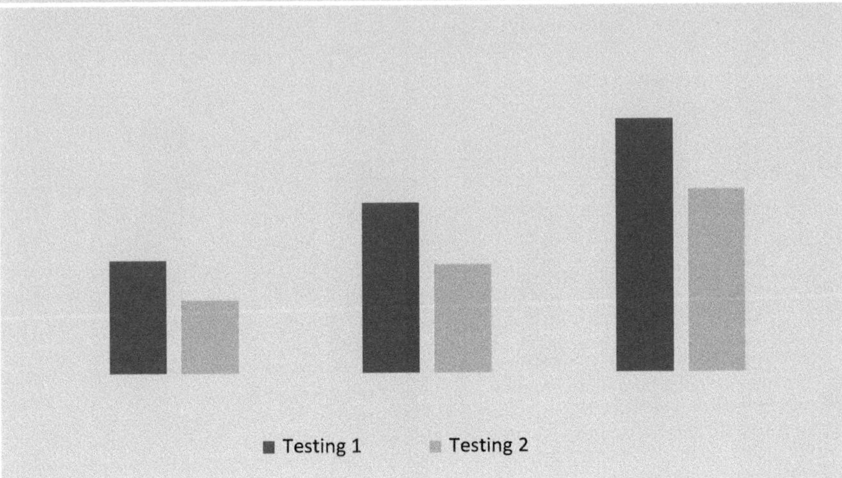

Trails A and B

The Trail Making Test, Parts A and B, which requires visual tracking, simple and complex set-shifting, and sequencing ability, could not be interpreted in its entirety due to two of the participants not completing the measure postprogram. However, the time to complete Part B decreased from 27 to 23 s for one participant and from 218 to 121 s for the other.

TOVA

The TOVA (visual version) assess attention and impulse control in normal and clinical populations and was administered to three of the four participants, both pre- and postprogram. The fourth participant attempted, but experienced sensitivity to flashing lights/screens and was unable to complete the test. Results of the three participants indicate only nominal (nonsignificant) attentional improvements as measured by this test. As they all were receiving medication for attentional issues, these findings were expected.

Behavioral observations

Results of the seven observed behaviors suggest a shift toward improvements in off task, restless, verbal interrupting, easily distracted, impulsive responding, uncooperative play, and nonverbal aggressive behaviors. More in-depth analysis is to follow.

Summary

As was mentioned in Chapter 6, one cannot rehabilitate what has not been learned. Executive functioning skills must be learned/created and are best facilitated via play, parental involvement, warmth, and a welcoming environment. The spirit behind the summer "Build-A-Brain" program was to combine the quantitative (brain-behavior) approach suggested by Reitan with the qualitative (prognostic and corrective) approach suggested by Luria while utilizing the strengths of play and the construct of the zone of proximal development.

After 14 sessions over the span of 8 weeks, using playful, interactive experiential learning techniques, changes were noticeable. The executive/frontal functions that seemed to be lacking at first began to emerge. After 2 months of cooperative play, competitive interactions were elicited. The boys began thinking before acting, and impulsivity and anxiety were reduced. The boys completed the summer program knowing how to relate, to think logically, and to cope effectively; the interventions provided necessary scaffolding to expand their zone of proximal development. As a result, they were ready to return to school with the tools needed for success at the next level. Lastly, individualized feedback was provided to the loved ones of each participant to help them maximize the potential for continued growth.

For behavioral observations, time sampling was deployed as an agent of change, or criteria of positive or negative outcomes. Results of the seven data points regarding behavioral observations suggest a shift toward improvements in off task, restless, verbal interrupting, easily distracted, impulsive responding, uncooperative play, and nonverbal aggressive behaviors.

The program goal was to reduce off-task behaviors and increase the functional qualities needed for improved academic outcomes. Using the WRAT-4, along with the prevalence of trend data, there is evidence of both positive outcomes having occurred. Further data analysis will, however, be conducted.

Limitations

The strength of this Build-A-Brain Program was its small group format (four participants to four staff with two observers). Yet, this was also its primary weakness. By offering individual and group interventions within a small group setting, these tweens were given the attention they needed to learn. Learning experiences were cooperative and competitive, playful and challenging. In previous summer programs, more participants were involved. This proved less than ideal. In the future, fewer objective measures can be utilized. Perhaps the BRIEF-2, WRAT-4 (Math), and HCT would suffice. Additional limitations include a homogeneous group regarding gender identification and ethnicity, lack of a control group, imperfect attendance and/or tardy arrival/early departure by participants, inconsistent loved one availability for Thursday participation (would often rotate weeks with other loved ones due to not being able to miss work every week), inconsistency regarding loved ones reviewing materials after each session, and inconsistent engagement with the MobyMax program.

Lastly, this intervention program was conducted in a clinical, not research, setting for the purpose of improving tweens' executive functions.

Acknowledgments

A special thank you is in order to Sarah Grimmer, M.A., and Alyssa Salcedo for their help in facilitating this summer "Build-A-Brain" program. Their biographies and contributions are as follows:

Sarah Grimmer, M.A., a doctoral candidate in clinical psychology at Fielding Graduate University, has concentrations in health psychology and neuropsychology. She is a doctoral extern at NCLA. Her contributions to the "Build-A-Brain" project included guided group discussions with the loved ones, data collection and entry, administration and scoring of objective measures, and collection of behavioral observations.

Alyssa Salcedo is an undergraduate student at California Baptist University majoring in psychology. Her summer externship duties at NCLA included reviewing and consolidating research and observing and recording child behavioral observations.

References

Birnbaum, R. (2013). Ready, fire, aim: The college campus gun fight. *Change: The Magazine of Learning*, 6–14. https://doi.org/10.1080/00091383.2013.812462.

Brain-Ade Games. (2007). *Pyramid power* [Board game]. Danvers, MA: Winning Moves.

Branstetter, R. (2014). *The everything parents guide to children with executive functioning disorder: Strategies to help your child achieve the time management skills, focus, and organization needed to succeed in school and life*. Avon, MA: Adams Media.

Brown, T. E. (2001). *Brown attention-deficit disorder scales for children and adolescents*. New York, NY: The Psychological Association, A Harcourt Assessment Company.

Chavez-Arana, C., Catroppa, C., Carranza-Escárcega, E., Godfrey, C., Yáñez-Téllez, G., Prieto-Corona, B., et al. (2018). A systematic review of interventions for hot and cold executive functions in children and adolescents with acquired brain injury. *Journal of Pediatric Psychology, 43*(8), 928–942. https://doi.org/10.1093/jpepsy/jsy013.

Doolittle, P. E. (1995). In *Understanding cooperative learning through Vygotsky's zone of proximal development. Paper presented at the Lilly National Conference on excellence in college teaching, Columbia, SC, June 2–4.*

Emery, G. (1989). *Overcoming anxiety program for self-management* [Audio Cassette]. Guilford Pr Cassettes.

Gioia, G. A., Isquith, P. K., Guy, S. C., & Kenworthy, L. (2015). *Brief-2: Behavior rating inventory of executive function, second edition: Professional manual* (2nd ed.). Lutz, FL: Psychological Assessment Resources.

Glozman, J. (2013). *Developmental neuropsychology*. New York: Routledge.

Harasty, J., Binder, J. R., Frost, J. A., Hammeke, T. A., Bellgowan, P. S. F., Rao, S. M., et al. (2000). Language processing in both sexes: Evidence from brain studies. *Brain, 123*(2), 404–406.

Leark, R. A., Greenburg, L. M., Kindschi, C. L., Dupuy, T. R., & Hughes, S. J. (2007). *T.O.V.A. professional manual*. Los Alamitos, CA: The TOVA Company.

Leisure Learning Products, Inc. (2008). *Mighty mind makes kids smarter (ages 3–8)* [Board game]. Stamford, CT: Leisure Learning Products.

Lite, L. (2004). *Indigo dreams* [CD]. Lite Books.

Macintyre, C. (2009). *Dyspraxia 5-14. Identifying and supporting young people with movement difficulties* (2nd ed.). London, New York: Routledge/Nasen.

MobyMax: Fix learning gaps. (n.d.). Retrieved from: https://www.mobymax.com/curriculum/math.

Morgan, P. L., Farkas, G., Wang, Y., Hillemeier, M. M., Oh, Y., & Maczuga, S. (2019). Executive function deficits in kindergarten predict repeated academic difficulties across elementary school. *Early Childhood Research Quarterly*, *46*, 20–32. https://doi.org/10.1016/j.ecresq.2018.06.009.

Nemeth, D. G., Ray, K. P., & Schexnayder, M. M. (2003). *Helping your angry child*. Oakland, CA: New Harbinger Publications.

Randolph, C. (2012). *Repeatable battery for the assessment of neuropsychological status: Manual*. Bloomington, MN: PsychCorp.

Reitan, R., & Wolfson, D. (1992). *Neuropsychological evaluation of older children*. South Tucson, AZ: Neuropsychology Press.

Reynolds, C. R., & Kamphaus, R. W. (2015). *Behavior assessment system for children: Manual* (3rd ed.). Bloomington, MN: NCS Pearson.

Schroeder, E., & Kuriansky, J. (2009). *Sexuality education: Past, present, and future*. Westport, CT: Praeger.

Vygotsky, L. S. (1978). *Mind in society: The development of higher psychological processes*. Massachusetts: Harvard University Press.

Weisberg, D. S., Hirsh-Pasek, K., Golinkoff, R. M., Kittredge, A. K., & Klahr, D. (2016). Guided play: Principles and practices. *Current Directions in Psychological Science*, *25*(3), 177–182.

Western Publishing Company, Inc. (1981). *Checkers & Chinese checkers* [Board game]. Racine, WI: Western Publishing Company.

Wilkinson, G. S., & Robertson, G. J. (2006). *Wide range achievement test: Professional manual* (4th ed.). Lutz, FL: Psychological Assessment Resources.

Young, C. B., Wu, S. S., & Menon, V. (2012). The neurodevelopmental basis of math anxiety. *Psychological Science*, *23*(5), 492–501.

Chapter 12

Rebuilding executive functions in environmentally traumatized children and adolescents

Judy Kuriansky[a,b], Darlyne G. Nemeth[c]
[a]*International Association of Applied Psychology, Indianapolis, IN, United States,* [b]*Teachers College, Columbia University, New York, NY, United States,* [c]*The Neuropsychology Center of Louisiana, LLC, Baton Rouge, LA, United States*

Introduction

The range of natural disasters worldwide has been considerable, including hurricanes, typhoons, tsunamis, droughts, wildfires, floods, and extreme heat occurring in all regions of the world, with the frequency having increased over the last 40 years (American Public Health Association, 2019; Guha-Sapir, Below, & Hoyois, n.d.). The World Health Organization (WHO) estimates that between 20% and 40% of populations affected by natural disasters will experience mild psychological distress, and 30%–50% will experience moderate to severe psychological distress (WHO, 2019). Children and other groups such as the elderly and disabled are especially at risk. Children vary in the nature of their responses to traumatic experiences, according to multiple factors such as culture, previous trauma exposure, available resources, and preexisting child and family problems as well as age and developmental stage (APA, 2008). When exposed to a traumatic event, children can experience symptoms on various levels. These include emotional reactions (e.g., fears, anxieties, sadness, and feelings of hopelessness and helplessness); behavioral reactions (e.g., a decline in schoolwork, anger, somatic complaints, irritability, eating and sleep disturbances, nightmares, adjustment disorders such as aggression or withdrawal, and separation anxiety leading to behavior such as school refusals); and social reactions, (e.g., alienation from peers, family, teachers, community, and other support structures).

Impacts on neurocognitive functioning include a loss of interest in normal activities, confusion, disorganization, lack of concentration and attention, disorientation, feeling in a daze or unreality (e.g., not knowing one's own name, where one is from, or what happened), loss of memory and control, and inability

Evaluation and Treatment of Neuropsychologically Compromised Children
https://doi.org/10.1016/B978-0-12-819545-1.00012-6

to problem solve or process information (Eren-Koçak, Kılıç, Aydın, & Hızlı, 2009; Helton & Head, 2012; Helton, Head, & Kemp, 2011; Silverman & La Greca, 2002). Impaired functioning can also occur on the various levels of a child's entire ecosystem, ranging from the individual and interpersonal to the social level, as defined by the Bioecological Model of Urie Bronfenbrenner (Noffsinger, Pfefferbaum, Pfefferbaum, Sherrib, & Norris, 2012).

Given that critical periods exist in infant, child, and adolescent brain development and the ability to perform cognitive tasks, children exposed to trauma are especially vulnerable because their brains are still developing (Enlow, Egeland, Blood, Wright, & Wright, 2012). Adolescence is a particularly important period as the area of the brain responsible for executive functioning—the frontal lobe—is the last area of the brain to complete the process of myelination that allows neurons to communicate. The impact of disaster on children's mental processes is scientifically underinvestigated while the importance of such assessment is being increasingly recognized (Gay, Nemeth, Kuriansky, Olivier, & Songy, 2015). As research increasingly shows the negative consequences of trauma on thinking and the ability to process information, increased importance is being placed not only on recognition of the impacts, but also on identifying interventions to ameliorate these negative effects (Roncone et al., 2013).

This chapter presents interventions applied by the first author in diverse settings worldwide. Techniques and specific activities are described that aid in regaining executive functions and related conditions underlying neurological capacity (e.g., through rebuilding a sense of safety and mastery). These facilitate logical thinking, planning for the future, and engagement with others, in contrast to symptoms of confusion, isolation, and withdrawal. Further, these activities are described in terms of brain-behavior functioning, which is consistent with models by both American and Russian neuropsychologists, neurologists, and other experts.

The importance of neurocognitive functioning was evident, as an example, in the case of a train derailment in Livingston, Louisiana, United States (Burke, 2018). Toxic chemicals were spilled, exploded, and burned for several days, then dried powder permeated the public elementary school located near the railroad tracks. Children were told to return to school, and given rags to clean off their desks (Nemeth, Personal Communication, 1984). Professionals were called in to assess the emotional state of residents and to address their fears (Lemoine, Rostow, Nemeth, & Ellis, 1984), but it became clear that the children were suffering concomitant cognitive disturbances, evidenced by the fact that they could not pay attention in class or concentrate on lessons.

The relationship of impaired cognition (as in states of dissociation) to conditions of extreme emotional distress and grief (as in posttraumatic stress disorder) is evident in studies that note that these symptoms overlap (Sachinvala et al., 2000). Further, childhood trauma has been found to be associated with cognitive function in adulthood (Majer, Nater, Lin, Capuron, & Reeves, 2010).

Conceptual and contextual framework

The approaches described in this chapter are consistent with the model of the Resilience and Empowerment Training and Workshop (RETAW) Child Ebola Version, as part of the Global Kids Connect Project, designed by the first author with activities that have been adapted and implemented in settings of postdisaster and crises around the world, including Haiti, China, Japan, Sint Maarten, Sri Lanka, Iran, Tanzania, and the United States as well as with children enduring epidemics, and Syrian refugee children in Jordan (Kuriansky, 2008, 2010a, 2010b, 2010c, 2011a, 2011b, 2012a, 2012b, 2013a, 2013b, 2013c, 2013d, 2013e, 2013f, 2015, 2016a, 2016c, 2017, 2018, in press, 2019a, 2019b, 2019c, 2019d, 2019e; Kuriansky & Jean-Charles, 2012; Kuriansky, Margevich, Jean-Charles, & Daisey, 2017; Kuriansky, Polizer, & Zinsou, 2016; Kuriansky, Wu, et al., 2015; Kuriansky, Zinsou, et al., 2015). These applications show that support is helpful on many levels, even though children can be resilient in the face of trauma (The United Nations Children's Fund (UNICEF) and The United Nations International Strategy for Disaster Risk Reduction (UNISDR), 2011). The model is designed to be implemented in a group setting with trainees of community individuals identified as potential leaders who are motivated and capable of implementing the workshop for children, even if they have minimal training in psychological techniques.

Three solid psychological concepts are highlighted in the model for recovery. The first is **resilience**, defined as the ability to "bounce back" or "the process of adapting well in the face of adversity, trauma, tragedy, threats, or even significant sources of stress" (APA, 2008) and as "being firmly grounded in the present while learning from the past, so that we can see ourselves in the future" (Nemeth & Olivier, 2017, p. xxi). The second concept is **empowerment**, the process and consequences of efforts to exert control, mastery, and influence over decisions and actions that affect one's life as an individual and as part of a community (Berry et al., 2013; Zimmerman, 2000). The third concept is **social reengagement**, namely, reestablishing relations with others that integrate the child into a supportive system. The importance of support systems in facilitating well-being and healing has been established (Dougall, Hyman, Hayward, McFeeley, & Baum, 2001; Kuriansky, 2012a, 2015; Landau & Saul, 2004; Webb, 2004). Through strong community identification, people can adapt a narrative where they no longer see themselves as passive victims, but rather as strong and active agents of change. Communities that come together after a trauma can even be stronger than before, as their collective identity becomes more tightly woven. Thus, workshops that promote group activities are excellent vehicles for rebuilding individuals and communities (Nemeth et al., 2011).

These concepts and associated techniques are consistent with research evidence on risk and resilience following trauma; applicable and practical in field settings; appropriate for developmental levels across the lifespan; and culturally informed. These techniques further help restore the "E" in the concept of "emotional resilience" in the conceptualization of the "3 E's of Recovery" from disaster, as described in a chapter included in Cherry and Gibson's forthcoming book, *The Intersection of Trauma and Disaster Behavioral Health* (Nemeth, Kuriansky, & Onishi, in press).

Executive functions

Historically, executive functions have been seen as regulated by the prefrontal regions of the frontal lobes. Moreover, while a sector of the brain such as the frontal lobe may be dominant in an activity or skill, various structures and zones of the brain are likely involved. These structures often overlap with synapses being engaged across brain regions, working in concert in a complex system. Further, the cerebellum appears to be involved in mediating certain executive functions.

The context of a model of Russian neuropsychology

Russian psychologists have pioneered an understanding of the brain's role in overall functioning. Given his studies on speech and aphasia, Russian psychologist Alexander Romanovich Luria is considered to be the father of Russian neuropsychology. Together with Lev Vygotsky, a developmental and cognitive psychologist credited with developing a sociocultural approach to cognitive development, and Alexei Nikolaevich Leontiev, a developmental psychologist who founded activity theory and contributed to the understanding of memory in children and adults, this "troika" of researchers initiated major developments in psychology, sociology, and biological theory, and originated experiments of brain impairment.

The context of a model of American neuropsychology

Advances in this field were also happening across the world in America. One of the fathers of American clinical neuropsychology, Ralph M. Reitan, is considered to have built on the work of Ward Halstead by further exploring brain-behavior relationships. His strong belief in empiricism and evidence-based practice led to the development of a neuropsychological assessment procedure, the Halstead-Reitan Neuropsychological Battery. To clinically apply his theory of brain-behavior rehabilitation to brain-compromised individuals, Reitan, with his spouse Deborah Wolfson, created the REHABIT system (Reitan & Wolfson, 1988). This challenging system of games and puzzles was intended for learning and rebuilding executive functions in a fun-filled, playful, and appealing way. It can easily be adapted to group process, allowing children and adolescents to connect, cooperate, and compete with one another in a developmentally appropriate way. This chapter's second author was one of the first to use the REHABIT system with her patients (see Appendix).

FIG. 1 An example of Reitan's REHABIT system: Track A_1, Letter Association with Pictures.

The REHABIT system addressed several areas, called "tracks." **Track A** contains equipment and procedures designed for developing expressive and receptive language and verbal skills and related academic abilities; **Track B** has language and verbal materials to integrate abstraction, reasoning, logical analysis, and organization skills; **Track C** includes tasks that focus on reasoning, organization, planning, and abstraction skills; **Track D** emphasizes abstraction abilities with materials requiring the person to use visual-spatial, sequential, and manipulatory skills; and **Track E** tasks requires the person to exercise fundamental aspects of visual-spatial and manipulatory abilities (Reitan, 1992) (Fig. 1).

Most important, these areas identified by Reitan are closely aligned with his view of brain functions (i.e., left, central, and right hemisphere processing skills). Thus, these various track activities are associated with brain-behavior functioning, an approach also used by the first author of this chapter.

The anniversary wellness workshops in the wake of natural disaster: Association to the REHABIT system

Similar to Reitan's notations of left and right brain functions and of the importance of play, the trainings and workshops developed by the first author of this chapter are also founded in brain-behavior functioning and the advantages of play. Play builds and rebuilds crucial developmental skills for children in an engaging, energizing, and entertaining way while also being healing in the context of traumas such as natural disasters. The Anniversary Wellness Workshops implemented by both authors in the aftermath of Hurricane Katrina were built on these principles. Versions were conducted in the community for adults as well as for children and their parents at the invitation of community leaders. These activities have been shown to work well in situations of an epidemic and other crises as well as natural disasters (Kuriansky, 2019a; Kuriansky, Margevich et al., 2017; Kuriansky et al., 2016).

The activities stimulate various individual or paired brain functions that are associated to the REHABIT system, as detailed below in this chapter. At the workshop, a welcome is offered by a trusted community leader. This is followed by a song. This is consistent with extensive research about musical links to neurocognitive brain functioning (Schellenberg, 2005). This process stimulates both hemispheres of the brain, namely, the right hemisphere in synthesizing and nonlinear processing with visual imagery, and the left hemisphere by engaging in linear and sequential data processing (Williams, 1986). In this case, a song called "You Are Still Loved" was recorded by well-known gospel singer and clinical psychologist Tommy Davis (2005), Ph.D., with the following original lyrics (used by permission of Davis, 2019). It is noted that the lyrics themselves evoke the right brain's efforts for emotional connections and intimacy as well as the left brain's focus on words and experiences.

You are still loved (4X)
Middle of the night and you're still awake
Seems you can't stop the heartache
You feel that you can't make it
And you're just too tired to fake it
(you are still loved)
Oh no don't you despair
(you are still loved)
There's no love that can compare
He takes away your deepest fear
Wash away all your tears
You are still loved (4X)

Workshops were also held by the authors in 2016 in response to what was referred to as the "Great Flood of Louisiana," given the prolonged and catastrophic rainfall (Peveto, 2016). In the workshops, youth and their parents completed pre- and postworkshop assessments to address assessments of Reitan's Tracks A and B, namely, basic and advanced executive functions, so that the trainers could gear the workshops to not only address the chronological age of the participants but also to coincide with their developmental levels (Nemeth, Kuriansky, et al., 2012).

The activities in the workshop as a whole addressed Track C of the REHABIT program, emphasizing integration of the left and right hemisphere functions. The components of the workshop, by this chapter's first author in her Global Kids Connect Project, include group psychosocial activities for strength building, energy regulation, and social connection; culturally appropriate creative arts activities (e.g., song, dance, and arts); creation and exchange of an art object constructed and designed by the children (e.g., a pillow) to serve as contact comfort; and a geography lesson about similarly impacted cohorts of children, where children would point out on a map where peers would be similarly suffering, thereby giving them an emotional sense of a more global connection and a feeling of not being alone. Thus, the children were able to cognitively process and generalize the experience of disastrous events (Kuriansky, 2010a, 2019b, 2019d; Kuriansky et al., 2016; Kuriansky & Nemeth, 2013; Kuriansky, Zinsou, et al., 2015). This activity aligns with Reitan's tracks D and E, as it requires visual-spatial and manipulatory skills. At the 2016 Great Flood Workshops, the pillows were exchanged among children in Haiti, Louisiana, and Japan (by the trainer bringing them from one country to another) to further facilitate the experience of connectedness, and also to stimulate a sense of compassion and empathy for others suffering similarly, thereby again engaging the left and right brain.

After a lunch of local cuisine (e.g., jambalaya and/or fried chicken fingers), the children engaged in relaxation exercises by listening to steps outlined on a CD (to the voice of a "friendly" animal called RILEE Bear to appeal to children, recorded by Davis). They were also given a copy of the CD to take home to use for relaxation at bedtime.

In other activities, Reitan's Tracks A, B, C, and D were evoked, whereby the children were asked to draw their feelings and experiences in the Great Flood and then to participate in a collective group drawing, which was posted on the wall to symbolize their shared experience. They were then invited to share the experience, which led to processing the emotions and then experiencing, once again, that they were not alone.

Other activities involved verbal and nonverbal processing with accompanying movements that relate to Reitan's left, central, and right hemisphere skills. In his system, the left cerebral hemisphere is linked to verbal and language skills and the right hemisphere is linked to spatial and manipulatory abilities (Reitan, 1992). These activities in the workshop are consistent with Reitan's goals of achieving reduced anxieties and increased joy. This process is facilitated by the group approach, which facilitated shifting from isolation to interactive play.

The multisensory approach

The activities of the workshop further facilitated healthy brain functioning and neurocognitive processing by the nature of their being multisensory. Individual activities can specifically stimulate and engage multiple dimensions, metaphorically including the brain (intellectual), the heart (emotional), and the body (physical), collectively engaging all three dimensions. This is evident in the descriptions of the activities in the below sections.

Neurocognitive aspects of the workshop activities

While most activities in the workshop for the children purposefully do not rely on extensive verbal skills or deep processing, interpretations are still encouraged in certain situations. This can happen in the safety exercise, when children are asked to find a safe place in the room and then to describe what about that place makes them feel secure and who in their life makes them feel safe.

Also, verbal processing is encouraged in the web activity, where balls of different colored yarn are tossed by the children to each other to form a web of colors. When the children are asked to describe what they have created in the web form, they often came up with creative and sophisticated observations such as, "We are all different (as in the colored yarn) but we are all together" and "We need to help each other." Similarly, processing is a valuable part of the "Pen Connection" activity, where the children balance pens between their fingers while moving in a circle in certain directions. If a pencil drops, they have to pick it up and continue following instructions to move collectively. In responding to a question about the lessons learned, they explained, for example, "When one person makes a mistake, everyone has to help them get back in the group." This activity is a metaphor for how any two people, and also a community, have to watch out for one another, notice when there is a problem for one, and work together to restore a healthy state. This processing can delve deeper into thoughts and feelings about the experience, requiring more strategic planning, analytic cognitive skills, and executive functioning.

Some children may ask for detailed instructions in the activities, reflecting verbalization activity in the brain, compared to others who copy a peer, to be sure they are performing correctly. Executive function can also be triggered in the "grounding" activity, when children are given instructions to feel their feet firmly rooted to the ground, by making cognitive associations to feeling safe.

Many children actively engage in the activities that involve pairing with a peer and verbal sharing. Indeed, many of the workshop activities encourage reconnection to others, especially after disaster when social ties are broken and people become isolated and might withdraw, yet at a time when the importance of social ties and reestablishing trust for healing is crucial (Dougall et al., 2001; Kuriansky, 2012b, 2018; La Greca, Silverman, Vernberg, & Roberts, 2002; Landau & Saul, 2004; Rodin, 2014; Walsh, 2002, 2007). Such an engaged response to workshop activities that are meant to encourage reintegration of the individual into the community is consistent with an ecological approach to disaster recovery (Harvey, 1996; Kuriansky, 2012b, 2019b, 2019d, in press).

Most children are capable of cognitive flexibility, including creatively thinking "outside the box" from different perspectives. This trait can be considered consistent with the improvisation in "cognitive control" (Mackie, Van Dam, & Fan, 2013). It is also consistent with defining resilience as not only bouncing back from a crisis, but looking forward to a better future. It is also not only a biopsychosocial phenomenon, but also a spiritual one, whereby participants thrive on spiritual development as related to understanding connections within themselves, others, the community, and the divine (Coholic, Lougheed, & Lebreton, 2009).

This adaptation, with its embrace of hope for the future, is reflected in the "Dream Ball" workshop activity, where the children toss a ball and announce their dream for the future. This encourages the transformation of helplessness and loss from the present trauma. Another activity, singing a song called

"Hope is Alive" (in a rendition adapted from many cultures by the first author and her music collaborator Russell Daisey) affirms this transformation.

Engagement in expressive arts activities of the workshop (including music, performance, yoga, drumming, drawing, and dance) stimulates adaptation and healing. These techniques are useful in disaster recovery, especially with youth (Kuriansky, 2019d). Considerable evidence shows that arts activities are an effective language-independent medium to heal children after natural disaster trauma by nurturing children's creativity and by connecting them to others. This approach is used in trauma recovery by many organizations such as the Red Cross and Red Crescent Societies (2003), and Save the Children, and is supported by research and many associations (American Art Therapy Association, n.d.; International Child Art Foundation, n.d.; Lusebrink, 2004; Malchiodi, 2005; Smilan, 2009; Story, 2011). Activity, paired with patterned and repetitive neural input, both lowers stress-response networks of the brain and releases chemicals in the brain associated with emotional integration and learning as well as pleasure (Perry, 2009).

Drawing activities further trigger creativity and concentration that lead to new connections in the brain and occupy the mind, minimizing dysfunctional cognitive symptoms. The projective nature of the drawing activities further activates brain functions. For example, in the Bridge Drawing used by the first author, the children are asked to draw a sad experience on one side of a page, a happy experience on the opposite side, and a bridge in the middle on the page fold that represents a means of getting from the sad to the happy experience. This reflects the child's perception of moving beyond barriers to resolve negativity and conflict and to experience some sense of peace and joy (Hays & Lyons, 1981; Yedida & Itzhaky, 2004). The children are then invited to share a narrative about how the bridge relates to ways they already do, or can, cope with difficulties. One 12-year-old girl in a workshop drew faint figures (of family members who died) on the left side of her page, but used a very black marker to draw a very defined bridge with different size cars that connected to her drawing on the right side of the page, which showed her playing with friends under bright sunshine. This was discussed with her as an excellent sign of her ability to transform her moods and situations from negative to positive.

Orphan children in workshops after an Asian tsunami drew their family and responded to questions like, "What quality about you was your parent most proud of?" as well as "What might your parent say to make you feel better?" A girl who originally cried, saying that, "I couldn't help my mother and sister, I lost them in the water," brightened up when answering these questions. She then added that her mother and sister would appreciate that she is clever and pretty and would tell her, "I want you to have a happy life." When the group repeated these qualities to her and affirmed her thought of her family's responses, she smiled and enthusiastically hugged the others. The shift in the cognitive framing of the experience led to an equivalent emotional shift, showing the interactivity of these two functions and how triggering one can stimulate the other.

A principle in this workshop was to encourage shifting from activities. Research has found that alternating these brain function-related activities adds to the healing response, not only by creating relaxation but also by altering neurotransmitter pathways in the brain (Salimpoor, Benovoy, Larcher, Dagher, & Zatorre, 2011). Being able to engage in multiple alternating activities is reflected in the pillow construction exercise in the workshop that encourages expressive art object creations combined with a geography lesson, which required the definition of a natural disaster (e.g., "What is a tsunami?") as well as the act of locating on a map where children are similarly coping. This act further forms helpful connections among the children. One child eagerly pointed out where Japan was located, explained what a tsunami was, and exclaimed (reflecting analytic thinking) that those children "had more water than me." Other children in the group were then inspired to go up to the map and to speak up. These combined activities trigger both analytic and creative neurocognitive recovery.

Other activities in the workshop engage multiple brain systems. In all cases, simple problem-solving skills, at the heart of executive functions, are utilized. As outlined in a previous chapter in this book, children must be guided to assess situations logically, being aware of how mental and emotional processes each play a part, in order to ask themselves the following questions: "What is the problem?," "How can I solve it?," "Am I using an effective plan?," "Was my plan successful?," and "Did my feelings help or hinder my success?"

The next sections in this chapter describe various activities in the workshop and their connection to executive function and neuropsychological brain activity.

Restoring trust

Trust is crucial to restore in trauma recovery, and involves both the left and right hemispheres. In the "Blindfold Follow the Leader" activity, pairs of children take turns to be either a leader or a follower while the follower holds his/her own hands over his/her own eyes, and the leader guides the follower in an interesting experience, being careful to keep the partner safe. To encourage a full experience of trust, no talking is allowed. The leader must exercise decision-making and alert planning while also creating right brain bonds with the follower. The children then share which role felt more comfortable and also how they felt about each role, expressing whether they were fearful or confident in their role.

Insuring safety

Safety is absolutely fundamental in disaster recovery (Herman, 1992; Miller & Cohen, 2001) and reflects multidimensional neurocognitive processes. The loss of loved ones and home in a natural disaster leads to a profound insecurity.

In the workshop, children are guided in several activities invoking safety that trigger left and right brain function in both the experience and its analysis. In **Part 1**, they become familiar with the external environment by looking around them, looking up, down, and straight ahead and noticing what they see; then, they walk around the room looking at each of the others in the room, without talking; and third, they greet others briefly. In **Part 2**, they are guided through a ritual of gathering energy from the Earth and from the Sky, bringing it into their heart and progressively announcing that they feel safe individually. They then use energy charged from the Earth and Sky to send safety to a partner. They repeat the steps to send energy to the group. In **Part 3**, they are invited to find a safe place in the room. They then describe it, share how it makes them feel and what they think about it, and expand to talk about whom and what makes them feel safe and who they help to feel safe. They can also be asked to draw a safe place, and post these drawings on the wall for a collective sense of safety. Descriptions of how they create a safe home or community are then encouraged (Kuriansky, 2011a, 2019b, 2019c; Kuriansky et al., 2016).

Assuring attention

Attention is a fundamental factor in executive functioning (Posner & Petersen, 1990). A study of the effects of trauma on attention concluded that natural disasters negatively impacted cognitive performance (Helton & Head, 2012). Furthermore, attention span was found to be affected as much as one year later, showing long-lasting negative neurocognitive effects (Cassels, 2009). Given that many children have a short attention span, and that the highest level of engagement results from switching types of activities, the activities of the workshop were selected to shift from behavioral to verbal tasks. Additionally, the workshop outline was specifically designed to balance and alternate various activities in order to capture children's attention. Additionally, activities were based on behaviors familiar to children such as jumping, play-acting as animals, and throwing balls.

Moving energy

Closely related to engaging attention is moving energy. Children are especially responsive to varying and shifting levels of energetic activity, as compared to adults who are more readily able to sustain both attention and focus on an activity that is consistently either intellectual or behavioral. Thus, a four-step process was designed to move energy from action to meditation and back to action in a controlled manner (Kuriansky, 2019a; Kuriansky et al., 2016). The exercise ends in the fourth step, in an activity whereby the children (1) choose to role play being an animal as a representation of self, (2) enact the movements and vocalizations of that animal (totem), then (3) interact with other children who have made their own choice, noticing their own and the other child's animal noises and movements; and (4) are invited to stop in front of other children and reverse roles, to mimic the sounds and movements of the other child's chosen animal. Such role-play is not only typically enjoyable for children, but has other benefits. The activity metaphorically facilitates communication skills, specifically the "active listening" technique in counseling, whereby one person empathizes with another, essentially "walking a mile in their shoes." The activity also facilitates flexible thinking, which is an important component of executive functioning.

Boosting self-esteem

Self-esteem and the related concepts of self-confidence, self-efficacy, empowerment, and mastery reflect an overall emotional as well as cognitive evaluation of self-worth that is critical in healing from disaster as well as in life in general (Bandura, 1997; Berry et al., 2013; Hand & Kuriansky, 2010; Kuriansky, 2019b, 2019d; Mruk, 2013; Pajares & Urdan, 2006; Rosenberg, 1989). Such states require balanced emotional as well as cognitive functions. In the workshop activity "Who Am I?" children first perform a little diddy song and dance and then choose someone to come into the middle of the circle, who then announces his/her name and a quality they like about themselves, with a matching movement. The group then repeats the name, quality, and movement, revealing a collective affirmation. Positive self-evaluations of emotional and cognitive qualities (e.g., "I am a good person," "I am smart") reveal the child's preference, and also become acknowledged as an important step in building self-esteem and trust as well as bonding with others.

Storytelling

Studies suggest that using the technique of narratives in a group wellness workshop format, where children tell a story, can be effective in ameliorating both the psychological and neurocognitive effects of environmental trauma (Nemeth et al., 2011; Nemeth, Kuriansky, et al., 2012; Nemeth, Songy, & Olivier, 2015). The technique of storytelling is common in many counseling programs, with the caveat that in order to avoid retraumatization, stories need to include concluding themes of overcoming the trauma.

Different learning styles

Another model of how the workshop activities relate to brain functions is evident in the following three learning styles. **Kinesthetic learners** prefer, enjoy, or require direct experience; gestures to make a point; role-play exercises over discussion groups; shaking hands with others; movements; trying new things without lengthy explanations; and "just doing it" rather than talking about it. This is evident in the workshop in the "This is the Way" dance movements and in the "Who Am I?" activity that requires doing a movement associated with the announcement of a quality one appreciates in oneself. **Visual learners** prefer, enjoy, or require graphic illustrations; maps, color coding to highlight salient information; written material and handouts to study new concepts; wall charts that display points to be remembered; written outlines; and taking notes during a lecture. **Auditory learners** prefer, enjoy, or require verbal presentation of information; group discussions to hear other points of view or practices; fast-paced verbal exchanges of ideas; a good story they can repeat for others; and music.

Discussion

This chapter makes several important observations about neurocognitive functioning in children in the context of an intervention to help them cope with the aftermath of natural disaster. The issues presented (1) highlight the importance of examining the neurocognitive impacts of natural disaster on children's functioning, given that the literature on this topic needs to be increased; (2) place neurocognitive functioning postdisaster in the context of brain-behavior functioning, from both the Russian and American perspectives; (3) examine activities in a postdisaster model of an intervention for children in light of their neurocognitive functioning (noting that observations that derive from this examination deserve further clinical application and research); and (4) show the healing impact of the combination of activities, in a group context, with expressive arts and moving energy from action to relaxation, which has been applied with children worldwide in various settings and under varied conditions.

The activities developed by the first author presented in this chapter are supported by extensive research on the value of children engaging in expressive arts. Advantages include that children can express themselves without judgment or criticism in a safe and accepting environment, process difficult experiences in a constructive and positive way, and connect with their inner selves as well as with a group, community, and larger world (Kuriansky, 2019c; Malchiodi, 2005; Smilan, 2009).

The workshops are consistent with the IASC guidelines (IASC Working Group, 2007), suggesting the need to provide basic psychosocial support and well-being to a broad group at the first and second tiers of the pyramid. The workshop is not meant to address more complicated trauma symptoms that require more intensive support and specialized services at the top tier of the pyramid.

Techniques for children must take into account their developmental stage (e.g., Vygotsky's zone of proximal development), particularly the stage of their neurocognitive abilities required to analyze situations and to verbalize feelings. Young children who have not yet learned words to express feelings and fears require interventions that focus on behavioral activities, such as those described in this chapter. These activities need to be developed to address and allow the processing of underlying neurocognitive and psychological processes required for healing.

The value of acknowledgment

A component of several activities in the workshop involves acknowledgment of the participant's behaviors and verbalizations. In the "Who I Am" activity, the group repeats back to the child the quality they appreciate in themselves. Similarly in the "Dream Ball" exercise, the group repeats back to the child their dream, deliberately as if it is true in the present tense. The child then expresses how such acknowledgment feels. Such positive reinforcement is a basic principle of operant and classical conditioning to elicit desired behaviors, especially important in child development whereby adults reward adaptive behavior. The validation offered is emotionally reassuring for the children. The trainer (group leader/facilitator) requests that the children take time to hear this validation (repeating their quality), essentially to fix it in their memory.

The value of processing anniversary reactions

Trauma is often reexperienced on or around the date of a past traumatic event that holds tremendous significance for an individual or group (Borstein & Clayton, 1972; Pollack, 2017). In such "anniversary reactions," symptoms may reemerge that characterize the original response; these can be emotional, behavioral, social, and/or neurocognitive (Kuriansky, 2013e; Kuriansky & Nemeth, 2013; Nemeth et al., 2011; Nemeth, Hamilton, & Kuriansky, 2012; Nemeth, Kuriansky, et al., 2012) Neurocognitive symptoms include, but may not be limited to, intrusive memories, reminders of the event, lack of concentration, and confusion. Even the most resilient children and adolescents may regress to earlier stages of development (e.g., crying like younger children, school phobia, overdependence). At such times, the above-described intervention of the RETAW and the Emotional Resilience Anniversary Wellness Workshops can be helpful in addressing underlying needs, without requiring deep processing (Kuriansky, 2013c, 2013d; Kuriansky & Nemeth, 2013; Nemeth, Hamilton, et al., 2012; Nemeth, Kuriansky, et al., 2012).

The value of the group format

Considerable research has shown the value of group settings for therapeutic growth, through sharing and mutual support (Alonso & Swiller, 1993; Nemeth & Songy, 2013). Creating an environment of a supportive group experience, focused on hope, provides neurocognitively challenged individuals with the opportunity to reframe their sense of self and their future (Gremillion & Nemeth, 2013; Nemeth et al., 2015). The groups for children described in this chapter follow this tripartite group format—where participants gather in a group as a whole, in a "fishbowl," and in small groups—allowing them opportunities to interact and relate in various combinations and at various comfort levels. Further, the group activities can be seen in the context of the "container-contained" model of intersubjective thinking (Billow, 2003), allowing both a cognitive container (i.e., structure) and an affective freedom of expression in a contained (i.e., safe) environment. While these conceptualizations underlie the processes, the children do not have to be aware of their dynamics, but simply gain the benefits through the activities themselves.

Long-lasting trauma

While some children, just as adults, demonstrate resilience in the face of natural disasters and are able to cope, lingering symptoms are not uncommon, regardless of the type of disaster. Ongoing reactions have been observed posttrauma after natural disasters such as the fires in California in the United States, the earthquake and flood in Haiti, hurricanes in the Caribbean, the Ebola epidemic in West Africa, and the nuclear power plant explosions in Japan and Chernobyl in the Ukraine. The pressure to "get over it" can only exacerbate lingering suffering, which must be normalized, acknowledged, and addressed.

Posttraumatic growth

The workshop has value in facilitating posttraumatic growth as defined by the ability to find benefits from the adversity in order to rise to a higher level of functioning (Tedeschi & Calhoun, 2004). As described above, the affirmations from the group as well as a positive view of the individual, the group, and the experience in totality, can inherently communicate an atmosphere of trust, caring, support, and even love that triggers positive brain functions and becomes a growth experience (Carlson & Shield, 1989).

Neurocognition in a holistic view of disaster recovery interventions

A holistic view of any intervention for disaster recovery for children must take neurocognition into account as well as other dimensions. The other dimensions may include addressing emotional well-being with interventions that encourage expression, communication, and interactions that help with positive adjustments (e.g., support groups, child-friendly spaces, family reunification, group recreation and activities); biological well-being (e.g., provision of nutrition and health services); social well-being (e.g., safety conditions, comfortable shelter, community centers and transportation access); and cultural and spiritual well-being (e.g., access to religious and cultural practices). Neurocognitive well-being may also be facilitated via access to education and information acquisition, including the use of technology.

Stages of recovery

Children experiencing environmental trauma go through similar stages in recovery as do adults. In determining disaster recovery strategies for children, neurocognition needs to be considered in all stages. These stages are used routinely in the second author's work on trauma. In Stage 1, **Shock**, it is important to maintain routines for children that are as "normal" and predictable as possible in order to restore their sense of security and safety (Nemeth & Whittington, 2012). This is particularly important in cases like in Chernobyl, or in Japan, where losses were multiplied by the dangers from the nuclear power plant explosions, merely adding to stress, fear, and disorientation (Liakhovich, 2006; Tabuchi & Wald, 2011). Similar to adults, children suffering from any disastrous event or victimization from violence include those facing immediate losses or direct experiences, as well as others not as directly affected, who can feel "survivor guilt," meaning that they believe that they somehow have caused the situation, made it worse, could have saved someone, or prevented the event from happening (Garrido, 2007). In this Shock phase, youth can either turn inward and become dysfunctional or depressed, or have the completely opposite reaction, turning outward, exhibiting affective and/or behavioral disturbance. At this stage, teddy bears are helpful for children to provide "contact comfort" and to serve as a "transitional object" to compensate for losses. Stage 2 in Nemeth's conceptualization involves **Survival Mode**, doing whatever it takes to live, whether seeking rescue or shelter. Stage 3 involves the **Assessment of Basic Needs**, including food, clean water, sleep, safety, and medical attention. Local leaders and/or authority figures play a major role to reassure safety as they are more perceived as trustworthy than outside humanitarians. For example, after Hurricane Katrina in New Orleans, Louisiana, a Louisiana native, Lt. General Russel Honoré, took over command of the chaos and restored order (Honoré, 2012). Stage 4 involves **Awareness of Loss**, when grieving and reconnecting with others is important. Noticeably, adolescents will increasingly rely on their cell phones for connection. Reconnection to community and cultural roots is critical (Nemeth & Whittington, 2012). In Stage 5, survivors are **Susceptible to Spin and Fraud**, being at the mercy of untrustworthy people who take advantage of the most vulnerable through looting and stealing. In this stage, survivors can also suffer stigmatization. For example, children and adolescents forced to move to different schools after Hurricane Katrina were often unwelcome by peers in the new school and labeled as "Katrina Kids." In Stage 6, **Resolution** of the trauma, survivors accept circumstances and adjust to the "new normal." This can take a variable amount of time, from months to years. For example, children and adolescents in Sendai, Japan, who experienced the tsunami and those in Fukushima, Japan, both of who experienced the nuclear power plant explosion, still suffered years later (Nemeth & Kuriansky, 2017, 2018).

Assessment

The authors intended to conduct psychological assessments of the children in the Wellness workshops on the anniversaries of Hurricane Katrina. Neurological assessments of cohorts of survivors of natural disasters were also planned at the time of Superstorm Sandy that hit New York and New Jersey in the United States. However as many researchers find, the logistics of such situations prioritize the need for intervention over assessment. Such measurement in the future would be extremely valuable for planning purposes. These results could form a more holistic assessment of survivors' status, including comparing and integrating neuropsychological results (e.g., measures of executive functioning) with psychological functioning (e.g., measures of anxiety and depression).

Because anxiety is a primary factor interfering with problem-solving skills, assessment is critical. A resiliency questionnaire was developed by Pastrana and Nemeth (Nemeth & Olivier, 2017, p. 68) to evaluate resilience and coping in the aftermath of the Louisiana Great Flood of 2016. This was orally administered to very young children, whereas adolescents and adults completed the questionnaire on their own.

Assessments need to be conducted over time as the long-lasting neurocognitive effects of such environmental traumas deserve more longitudinal examination and study (Brandes et al., 2002; Helton & Head, 2012; Liu et al., 2012; Nemeth, Hamilton, et al., 2012).

Applications of wellness workshops in various cultures and settings

The model of the Resilience and Empowerment Training and Workshop (RETAW) within the Global Kids Connect Project has been applied to natural disasters as well as during epidemics, on the anniversary of a terrorism event, and in conditions of poverty with orphans and other vulnerable children in diverse settings worldwide. In all cases, a team of representatives of the International Association of Applied Psychology (IAAP), a United-Nations ECOSOC-accredited NGO of which the first author is a main representative, with allied colleagues as well as students from Columbia University Teachers College, where the first author is on faculty, formed partnerships with local organizations that serve their respective communities. Whenever possible, the expressive art object creations described earlier in this chapter were exchanged with children in different countries (i.e., brought by the trainers). This added to the children's understanding that children around the world have shared similar experiences, thus enhancing the neurocognitive lesson of connectedness and being "not alone." These exercises also embellish geography lessons, wherein children point out the country from which the art objects (designed as pillows and identified by children as "gifts") came, or countries where they are going.

Similar workshops, with appropriate cultural modifications, were conducted by this chapter's first author in Haiti, Japan, Sint Maarten, Tanzania, Iran, Jordan, China, New York, Sierra Leone, and Sri Lanka.

Context of major policy agreements

Major international agreements support programs and research assessments of neurocognitive functioning of traumatized children surviving environmental disaster by promoting initiatives for mental health and well-being. Through advocacy during intergovernmental negotiations, the first author was instrumental in securing the inclusion of mental health and well-being in these agreements (Forman, 2014; Kuriansky, 2016b, 2019a, 2019c, 2019d, 2019e, in press; Masangkay, 2015). These have included the United Nations Agenda 2030 for Sustainable Development that adopted target 3.4 to "promote mental health and well-being" as a significant goal (United Nations, 2015); the Sendai Framework for Disaster Risk Reduction (UNISDR, 2015) that calls for psychosocial support postdisaster; the Global Compact for Safe, Regular, and Orderly Migration (United Nations, 2018) that makes several references to psychosocial help for children; and the Universal Health Coverage Political Declaration (United Nations General Assembly, 2019) that affirms health and mental health for all as a human right. Additionally, the first-ever national U.S. policy on "Addressing the Impacts of Climate Change on Mental Health and Well-Being," coauthored by the first author of this chapter, was adopted in November 2019 by the American Public Health Association (2019).

Recommendations

Based on the neurocognitive impacts of natural disasters on children, it is recommended that many sectors worldwide contribute to ameliorating these effects in the following manner:

1. Child neurocognitive assessments should be conducted in the immediate aftermath of natural disasters. Follow-up assessments over time are recommended as well. Such assessments should be an integral part of pre- and postevaluations of any disaster intervention.
2. When working in disaster prevention and recovery, mental health professionals should be trained in neuropsychological screenings.
3. Educational institutions should institute screening processes in order to identify neurocognitive impairments in children postdisaster. Those children needing assistance could then be identified.
4. Programs, sessions, and workshops for all children both for prevention and coping can include bereavement counseling, tutoring, and resilience-building skills.
5. Training in children's neuropsychological functioning should also be provided to teachers, nurses, staff, and available counselors.

6. Community centers and faith-based organizations can develop prevention and recovery programs, including addressing neuropsychological functioning.
7. Media should be engaged to provide public health information about symptoms and resources related to children's neuropsychological functioning.
8. Groups, especially in the health and mental health sectors, working across disciplines need to advocate for local, national, and international policies regarding disaster preparedness and recovery that include reference to children's neuropsychological functioning.
9. Research should be conducted on the impact on children's neuropsychological functions postdisaster.
10. Programs to teach children to be resilient and build or enhance their resilience, including from a neuropsychological perspective, should be developed, applied, scaled and evidence-based.
11. All policies addressing recovery of traumatized children should include references to their neuropsychological functioning.

Conclusions

Children's neurocognitive functioning can become considerably impaired both immediately and long after a natural disaster. This can result in impaired executive functioning, with symptoms that may include, but not be limited to, confusion, lack of concentration, and impaired decision-making. This neurocognitive state interacts with other levels of functioning (e.g., emotional, behavioral, and social), escalating problems in each area. Interventions for children in a group context that include activities of expressive arts as well as analytical skills, which do not require extensive verbalizations, can be useful in helping children cope. These activities help children and adolescents to move from fears to affirmation, from isolation to connection, and from victimization to empowerment. Once fears and anxieties are allayed and children are engaged within a group setting, neurocognitive functioning can be restored. In this context, the workshops described in this chapter are more than wellness and/or posttrauma interventions, but rather they are consistent with a system of neurocognitive restoration and emotional and behavioral readjustment. These activities can be further seen in the context of brain-behavior functions as defined by neuropsychologists and researchers. They are especially consistent with the Reitan REHABIT system of neurocognitive rehabilitation, and the research of noted neuropsychologists Vygotsky and Luria. More research in the areas of assessment and evidence-based intervention for children with impaired neurocognitive functioning postdisaster is needed. Multiple stakeholders, including professionals, teachers, and governments, can all play a role in supporting such efforts. This neuropsychologoical perspective must be included in policies and programs for children in diverse crises.

Appendix

THE UNIVERSITY OF ARIZONA
TUCSON, ARIZONA 85721

COLLEGE OF LIBERAL ARTS
DEPARTMENT OF PSYCHOLOGY

August 21, 1980

Dr. Darlyne G. Nemeth
The Psychology Group
707 South Acadian Thruway
Baton Rouge, Louisiana 70806

Dear Darlyne:

It certainly seems that you have an exciting prospect coming in forming your own Clinic. I certainly wish you the best of success.

You are the first person to plan to proceed with use of the REHABIT program. I have been talking with some of my students here about a possible research project, but we do not yet have a solution to many of the practical problems. I feel sure that the program will be very helpful, and in the long run, could well be an extremely exciting addition, adding a significant treatment element to the area of Clinical Neuropsychology. I do believe that documented research results will be necessary in order to develop and sustain interest in clinical application. I don't have any final ideas with respect to a research design, but I have been doing a fair amount of thinking about how such a research program may be organized. If I make more progress in developing the design I should be pleased to send you a copy of it. In any case, I certainly wish you the best of success in any work that you undertake with respect to REHABIT.

I really enjoyed seeing you and your family in Santa Fe.

Sincerely,

Ralph

Ralph M. Reitan, Ph.D.
Professor

RMR:jya We have entered your order for the tests and should be able to ship it by Sept 15-30. I presume you want it sent to the above address. Ralph

Acknowledgment letter from neuropsychologist Dr. Ralph Reitan to Dr. Darlyne Nemeth.

Acknowledgments

Much heartfelt and profound appreciation is extended to all the participants of the various trainings and workshops described in this chapter. Additionally, the valuable contributions of colleagues and students are acknowledged, with special appreciation to Russell Daisey, Father Wismick Jean-Charles, Alexandra Margevich, and Michelin Aboukasm.

References

Alonso, A., & Swiller, H. I. (1993). *Group therapy in clinical practice*. Washington, DC: American Psychiatric Press.

American Art Therapy Association (n.d.). Accessed August 2, 2018 at: https://arttherapy.org/.

American Public Health Association. (2019). *Addressing the impacts of climate change on mental health and well-being*. Policy Number: 20196. Retrieved from https://www.apha.org/policies-and-advocacy/public-health-policy-statements/policy-database/2020/01/13/addressing-the-impacts-of-climate-change-on-mental-health-and-well-being.

APA. (2008). *Children and trauma: Update for mental health professionals*. American Psychological Association Presidential Task Force on Posttraumatic Stress Disorder and Trauma in Children and Adolescents. Retrieved from: https://www.apa.org/pi/families/resources/children-trauma-update.

Bandura, A. (1997). *Self-efficacy the exercise of control*. New York, NY: W. H. Freeman and Company.

Berry, M.O'N., Kuriansky, J., Lytle, M. C., Vistman, B., Mosisili, M. S., Hlothoane, L., et al. (2013). Entrepreneurial training for girls empowerment in Lesotho: A process evaluation of a model programme. *South Africa Journal of Psychology*, *43*(4), 445–458.

Billow, R. M. (2003). Relational variations of the "container-contained". *Contemporary Psychoanalysis*, *39*(1), 27–50.

Borstein, P. E., & Clayton, P. (1972). The anniversary reaction. *Diseases of the Nervous System*, *33*, 470–472.

Brandes, D., Ben-Shachar, G., Gilboa, A., Bonne, O., Freedman, S., & Shalev, A. Y. (2002). PTSD symptoms and cognitive performance in recent trauma survivors. *Psychiatry Research*, *110*(3), 231–238.

Burke, R. (2018). *Hazmat studies: Livingston, LA, train derailment—36 years later*. Firehouse. Retrieved from: https://www.firehouse.com/rescue/hazardous-materials/article/12398893/livingston-la-train-derailment36-years-later-hazmat-studies-robert-burke.

Carlson, R., & Shield, B. (1989). *Healers on healing*. New York, NY: J. B. Tarcher.

Cassels, C. (2009). *Brains of veterans with and without PTSD differ, imaging study shows*. Medscape. Retrieved from: http://www.medscape.com/viewarticle/701855.

Coholic, D., Lougheed, S., & Lebreton, J. (2009). The helpfulness of holistic arts-based group work with children living in foster care. *Social Work With Groups: A Journal of Community and Clinical Practice*, *32*(1–2), 29–46.

Davis, T. (2005). You are still loved. *On You Are Still Loved*. [CD].

Dougall, A. L., Hyman, K. B., Hayward, M. C., McFeeley, S., & Baum, A. (2001). Optimism and traumatic stress: The importance of social support and coping. *Journal of Applied Social Psychology*, *31*(2), 223–245. https://doi.org/10.1111/j.1559-1816.2001.tb00195.x.

Enlow, M. B., Egeland, B., Blood, E. A., Wright, R. O., & Wright, R. J. (2012). Interpersonal trauma exposure and cognitive development in children to age 8 years: A longitudinal study. *Journal of Epidemiology and Community Health*, *66*(11), 1005–1010. https://doi.org/10.1136/jech-2011-200727.

Eren-Koçak, E., Kılıç, C., Aydın, I., & Hızlı, F. G. (2009). Memory and prefrontal functions in earthquake survivors: Differences between current and past post-traumatic stress disorder patients. *Acta Psychiatrica Scandinavica*, *119*(1), 35–44. https://doi.org/10.1111/j.1600-0447.2008.01281.x.

Forman, A. (2014). Five words that can change the world. *Jewish Journal*, *39*(4), 1, 9. Retrieved from: http://goodnewsplanet.com/five-words-can-change-world/.

Garrido, G. (2007). *Trauma resolution and lifestyle change*. In *Paper presented at the 60th annual United Nations DPI/NGO conference midday workshops, New York, September*.

Gay, R., Nemeth, D. G., Kuriansky, J., Olivier, T., & Songy, C. (2015). The effects of environmental trauma on our thinking. In D. G. Nemeth, J. Kuriansky, & R. Hamilton (Eds.), *Vol. 2. Ecopsychology: Advances from the intersection of psychology and environmental protection*. Santa Barbara, CA: Praeger.

Gremillion, A. L., & Nemeth, D. G. (2013). An eight-session hope group therapy program for neurocognitively impaired patients. In *Presented at the 2013 annual meeting of the American Group Psychotherapy Association in New Orleans, LA, March*.

Guha-Sapir, D., Below, R., Hoyois, P. (n.d.). Natural disasters reported. *EM-DAT: International Disaster Database*. Brussels, Belgium: Université Catholique de Louvain. Retrieved from: www.emdat.be/sites/default/files/Trends/natural/world_1900_2011/eveyr3.pdf.

Hand, E., & Kuriansky, J. (2010). *31 Things to raise a child's self esteem*. Nashville, TN: Turner Publishing Company.

Harvey, M. R. (1996). An ecological view of psychological trauma and trauma recovery. *Journal of Traumatic Stress*, *9*(1), 3–23. https://doi.org/10.1002/jts.2490090103.

Hays, R. E., & Lyons, S. J. (1981). The bridge drawing: A projective technique for assessment in art therapy. *The Arts in Psychotherapy*, *8*(3–4), 207–217. https://psycnet.apa.org/doi/10.1016/0197-4556(81)90033-2.

Helton, W. S., & Head, J. (2012). Earthquakes on the mind: Implications of disasters for human performance. *Journal of Human Factors*, *54*(2), 189–194. https://doi.org/10.1177/0018720811430503.

Helton, W. S., Head, J., & Kemp, S. (2011). Natural disaster induced cognitive disruption: Impacts on action slips. *Journal of Consciousness and Cognition*, *20*(4), 1732–1737. https://doi.org/10.1016/j.concog.2011.02.011.

Herman, J. L. (1992). *Trauma and recovery*. New York: Basic Books.

Honoré, R. L. (2012). *Leadership in the new normal: A short course*. Lafayette, LA: Acadian House Publishing.

IASC (Inter-Agency Standing Committee) Working Group. (2007). *IASC guidelines on mental health and psychosocial support in emergency settings*. Geneva: IASC.

International Child Art Foundation (n.d.). Retrieved from: www.icaf.org.

International Federation of Red Cross and Red Crescent Societies. (2003). *Community-based psychological support: A training manual*. Retrieved from: http://resourcecentre.savethechildren.se/sites/default/files/documents/2705.pdf.

Kuriansky, J. (2008). A clinical toolbox for cross-cultural counseling and training. In U. P. Gielen, J. G. Draguns, & J. M. Fish (Eds.), *Principles of multicultural counseling and therapy* (pp. 295–330). New York: Taylor and Francis/Routledge.

Kuriansky, J. (2010a). *Bringing emotional first aid and hope to Haiti*. Retrieved from: http://www.beliefnet.com/Inspiration/2010/02/Bringing-Emotional-First-Aid-and-Hope-to-Haiti.aspx?p=5.

Kuriansky, J. (2010b). Haiti pre- and post earthquake: Tracing professional and personal commitment past, present and future. *International Psychology Bulletin*, *14*(2, Spring), 29–37. Retrieved from: http://internationalpsychology.files.wordpress.com/2013/01/ipb_spring_2010_4_27_10.pdf.

Kuriansky, J. (2010c). *Stories of Haiti*. Retrieved from: http://www.humnews.com/humnews/2010/4/13/stories-of-haitiapril-13-2010.html.

Kuriansky, J. (2011a). Aftermath of the Japanese earthquake and tsunami: Immediate response and impacts of events as healing efforts. *International Psychology Bulletin*, *15*(2), 67–70. Retrieved from: https://internationalpsychology.files.wordpress.com/2013/01/ipb_spring_2011-04-16-1-forrv-9-28-2011.pdf.

Kuriansky, J. (2011b). Guidelines for mental health and psychosocial support in response to emergencies: Experience and encouragement for advocacy. *The IAAP Bulletin. The International Association of Applied Psychology Covering the World of Applied Psychology*, *23*, 30–32. http://www.iaapsy.org/Portals/1/Bulletin/apnl_v23_i1-2.pdf.

Kuriansky, J. (2012a). Christmas curse or celebration: From Superstorm Sandy to Sandy Hook to the Financial Cliff, seven questions in crisis. *Huffington Post*. Retrieved from http://www.huffingtonpost.com/judy-kuriansky-phd/sandy-hook-elementary-shooting_b_2357207.html.

Kuriansky, J. (2012b). Our communities: Healing after environmental disasters. In D. G. Nemeth, R. B. Hamilton, & J. Kuriansky (Eds.), *Living in an environmentally traumatized world: Healing ourselves and our planet* (pp. 141–167). Santa Barbara, CA: Praeger Press.

Kuriansky, J. (2013a). Helping kids cope with the Oklahoma tornado and other traumas: 7 techniques. *Huffington Post*. Retrieved from: http://www.huffingtonpost.com/judy-kuriansky-phd/helping-kids-cope-with-the-oklahoma-tornado_b_3322238.html.

Kuriansky, J. (2013b). Katrina vs. Sandy: Essays on nature-induced, human-induced, and nature + human-induced environmental trauma. *Ecopsychology*, *5*(S1), S2–S3. https://doi.org/10.1089/eco.2013.5502.

Kuriansky, J. (2013c). Superstorm Sandy 2012: A psychologist first responder's personal account and lessons learned about the impact on emotions and ecology. *Ecospsychology*, *5*(S1), S-30–S-37. https://doi.org/10.1089/eco.2013.0010. Retrieved from: http://online.liebertpub.com/doi/abs/10.1089/eco.2013.0010?src=recsys.

Kuriansky, J. (2013d). Superstorm Sandy: Coping with the one-year anniversary. *CITIZENS Magazine*, (Special (October 26)). Retrieved from: http://statenislandpolitics.wordpress.com/2013/10/26/drjudy/.

Kuriansky, J. (2013e). Talking to kids about the anniversary of Superstorm Sandy. *Huffington Post*. Retrieved from: http://www.huffingtonpost.com/judy-kuriansky-phd/talking-to-kids-about-the-anniversary-of-superstorm-sandy_b_4167294.html.

Kuriansky, J. (2013f). Thoughts on Katrina vs. Sandy: Essays on nature-induced, human-induced, and nature + human-induced environmental trauma. *Ecopsychology*, *5*(S1), S-20–S-26. https://doi.org/10.1089/eco.2013.0039.

Kuriansky, J. (2015). The role of community in the intersection of psychology and environmental protection. In D. G. Nemeth & J. Kuriansky (Eds.), *Vol. 2. Ecopsychology: Advances in the intersection of psychology and environmental protection*. Santa Barbara, CA: Praeger.

Kuriansky, J. (2016a). Psychosocial support for a burial team: Gender issues and help for young men helping their country. In J. Kuriansky (Ed.), *The psychosocial aspects of a deadly epidemic: What Ebola has taught us about holistic healing*. ABC-CLIO/Praeger: Santa Barbara, CA.

Kuriansky, J. (2016b). Report of the IAAP United Nations team: Success in the New Global Agenda Advocacy. *Bulletin of the International Association of Applied Psychology*, *28*, 80–88.

Kuriansky, J. (Ed.), (2016c). *The psychosocial aspects of a deadly epidemic: What Ebola has taught us about holistic healing*. Santa Barbara, CA: ABC-CLIO/Praeger.

Kuriansky, J. (2017). Reconstruire La Rasion et L'esprit en Haïti: Contributions du Centre de Spiritualité et de Santé Mentale. In W. Jean-Charles (Ed.), *Santé mentale & Psychothérapie en Haiti, Approaches Intégratives & Traitements Multimodeaux*. Coconut Creek, FL: EducaVision Inc. English translation: Rebuilding Mind and Spirit in Haiti: Accomplishment and Gratifications of Partnership with Father Wismick and CESSA. Retrieved from: https://www.dropbox.com/personal?preview=Haiti+chapter+for+CESSA+book+Dr+Judy+Kuriansky+2017+May+20+FINAL+THIS+ONE+English.pdf.

Kuriansky, J. (2018). Psychotherapy, psychology, psychiatry and international policy: Professional contributions and personal experiences about mental health and wellbeing, psychosocial resilience and peace. *The International Journal of Psychotherapy, Counseling & Psychiatry: Theory, Research & Clinical Practice*. Special Volume of the World Council for Psychotherapy Conference 2017, April. Retrieved from: http://ijpcp.com/journal03/j03a06.pdf.

Kuriansky, J. (2019a). A model psychosocial support training during a medical mission for Syrian refugee children in Jordan: Techniques, lessons learned, and recommendations. *Journal of Infant, Child, and Adolescent Psychology*, *18*(4), 352–366. https://doi.org/10.1080/15289168.2019.1690925.

Kuriansky, J. (2019b). Building capacity in low resource settings post-disaster: Empowerment, empathy and esteem in training comforters in the case of Haiti. In W. Jean-Charles (Ed.), *Empathie en Haïti de la Recherche à la Practique à la Croieée de Différents Regards* (pp. 207–230). Coconut Creek, FL: EducaVision.

Kuriansky, J. (2019c). Climate change and disaster recovery: Activities, achievements and contributions of the IAAP New York team. *Applied Psychology Around the World*, *1*(3), 50–56.

Kuriansky, J. (2019d). Expressive ARTS for helping children heal in crisis and disaster. In I. A. Serlin, S. Krippner, & K. Rockefeller (Eds.), *Integrated health care for the traumatized: A whole person approach* (pp. 39–58). Lathan, NY: Rowman & Littlefield.

Kuriansky, J. (2019e). Migration, refugees and mental health at the United Nations: Activities, achievements and contributions of the IAAP team at the UN. *Applied Psychology Around the World*, *1*(3), 79–87.

Kuriansky, J. (in press). Psychosocial recovery after natural disaster: International advocacy, policy and recommendations. In K. E. Cherry & A. Gibson (Eds.), *The intersection of trauma and disaster behavioral health*. New York, NY: Springer.

Kuriansky, J., & Jean-Charles, W. (2012). Haiti rebati: Update on activities rebuilding Haiti through the Global Kids Connect project. *Bulletin of the International Association of Applied Psychology*, *24*(Part 21), 116–124.

Kuriansky, J., Margevich, A., Jean-Charles, W., & Daisey, R. (2017). Resilience and recovery in natural disasters and epidemics: Comparisons, challenges, and lessons learned from Train-the-Trainer projects. In G. Rich & S. Sirikantraporn (Eds.), *Human strengths and resilience: Developmental, cross-cultural, and international perspectives*. Lanham, MD: Lexington Books. https://www.amazon.com/Human-Strengths-Resilience-Developmental-Cross-Cultural/dp/1498554830/ref=mt_hardcover?_encoding=UTF8&me.

Kuriansky, J., & Nemeth, D. G. (2013). A model for post-environmental disaster wellness workshops: Preparing individuals and communities for hurricane anniversary reactions. *Ecopsychology*, *5*(S1), S-38–S-45. https://doi.org/10.1089/eco.2013.0006.

Kuriansky, J., Polizer, Y., & Zinsou, J. (2016). Children and Ebola: A model resilience and empowerment training and workshop. In J. Kuriansky (Ed.), *The psychosocial aspects of a deadly epidemic: What Ebola has taught us about holistic healing*. ABC-CLIO/Praeger: Santa Barbara, CA.

Kuriansky, J., Wu, L.-Y., Bao, C., Chand, D., Kong, S., Spooner, N., et al. (2015). Interventions by international and national organizations for psychosocial support after the Sichuan earthquake in China: A review and implications for sustainable development. In D. G. Nemeth, J. Kuriansky, & R. Hamilton (Eds.), *Vol. 2. Ecopsychology: Advances in the intersection of psychology and environmental protection* (pp. 171–231). Santa Barbara, CA: Praeger.

Kuriansky, J., Zinsou, J., Arunagiri, V., Douyon, C., Chiu, A., Jean-Charles, W., et al. (2015). Effects of helping in a train-the-trainers program for youth in the Global Kids Connect Project after the 2010 Haiti earthquake: A paradigm shift to sustainable development. In D. G. Nemeth, J. Kuriansky, & R. Hamilton (Eds.), *Vol. 2. Ecopsychology: Advances in the intersection of psychology and environmental protection* (pp. 135–169). Santa Barbara, CA: Praeger.

La Greca, A., Silverman, W., Vernberg, E. M., & Roberts, M. C. (Eds.), (2002). *Helping children cope with disasters and terrorism*. Washington, DC: American Psychological Association.

Landau, J., & Saul, J. (2004). Family and community resilience in response to disaster. In F. Walsh & M. McGoldrick (Eds.), *Living beyond loss: Death in the family* (pp. 285–302): W. W. Norton & Company.

Lemoine, R. L., Rostow, C. D., Nemeth, D. G., & Ellis, J. S. (1984). *The Livingston train derailment accident: An evaluation of the psychological impact on community residents*. Prepared for the Plaintiff's Steering Committee.

Liakhovich, O. (2006). *After the blaze: Chernobyl 20 years on*. Retrieved from: http://sites.google.com/site/liakhovick/Index/chernobyl.

Liu, X., Betzenhauser, M. J., Reiken, S., Meli, A. C., Xie, W., Chen, B., et al. (2012). Role of leaky neuronal ryanodine receptors in stress-induced cognitive dysfunction. *Cell*, *150*(5), 1055–1067. https://doi.org/10.1016/j.cell.2012.06.052.

Lusebrink, V. (2004). Art therapy and the brain: An attempt to understand the underlying processes of art expression in therapy. *Art Therapy: Journal of the American Art Therapy Association*, *21*(3), 125–135.

Mackie, M. A., Van Dam, N. T., & Fan, J. (2013). Cognitive control and attentional functions. *Brain and Cognition*, *82*(3), 301–312. https://doi.org/10.1016/j.bandc.2013.05.004.

Majer, M., Nater, U. M., Lin, J. S., Capuron, L., & Reeves, W. C. (2010). Association of childhood trauma with cognitive function in healthy adults: A pilot study. *BMC Neurology*, *10*, 61 https://doi.org/10.1186/1471-2377-10-61.

Malchiodi, C. (2005). Using art activities to support trauma recovery in children. *Trauma & Loss: Research & Interventions*, *5*(1), 8–11.

Masangkay, M. (2015). Psychologist connects disaster-affected children around the world. *The Japan Times*. Retrieved from: http://www.japantimes.co.jp/news/2015/03/23/national/psychologist-connects-disaster-affected-children-around-the-world/.

Miller, E. K., & Cohen, J. D. (2001). An integrative theory of prefrontal cortex function. *Annual Review of Neuroscience*, *24*(1), 167–202. https://doi.org/10.1146/annurev.neuro.24.1.167.

Mruk, C. J. (2013). *Self-esteem and positive psychology: Research, theory, and practice*. New York, NY: Springer Publishing Co.

Nemeth, D. G. (1984). Personal communication.

Nemeth, D. G., Hamilton, R. B., & Kuriansky, J. (Eds.), (2012). *Living in an environmentally traumatized world: Healing ourselves and our planet*. Santa Barbara, CA: Praeger.

Nemeth, D. G., & Kuriansky, J. (2017). *Observations, teaching internet course*. Sendai, Japan: Higashi Nippon International University [Personal communication].

Nemeth, D. G., & Kuriansky, J. (2018). *Observations, teaching internet course*. Sendai, Japan: Higashi Nippon International University [Personal communication].

Nemeth, D. G., Kuriansky, J., Olivier, T. W., Whittington, L. T., May, N., Hamilton, J., et al. (2011). Group interventions for disaster/trauma anniversary reactions. *Global Horizons: The Center for Policy and Resilience*, *4*(1), 51–64.

Nemeth D.G., Kuriansky J. and Onishi Y. (in press). The 3 E's of psychosocial recovery after disaster: Practice and policy, In Cherry K. & Gibson A., (Eds.), *The intersection of trauma and disaster behavioral health.* Springer, New York, NY.

Nemeth, D. G., Kuriansky, J., Reeder, K. P., Lewis, A., Marceaux, K., Whittington, T., et al. (2012). Addressing anniversary reactions of trauma through group process: The Hurricane Katrina Anniversary Wellness Workshops. *International Journal of Group Psychotherapy*, *62*(1), 129–141.

Nemeth, D. G., & Olivier, T. W. (2017). *Innovative approaches to individual and community resilience: From theory to practice*. Cambridge, MA: Academic Press.

Nemeth, D. G., & Songy, C. M. (2013). *Using group process to address anniversary reactions: The Katrina story*. In *Presented at the 2013 annual meeting of the American Group Psychotherapy Association in New Orleans, LA, March*.

Nemeth, D. G., Songy, C. S., & Olivier, T. W. (2015). Increasing success in neurocognitively impaired patients via group therapy. *International Journal of Group Psychotherapy*, *65*(1), 125–133.

Nemeth, D. G., & Whittington, T. (2012). Our robust people: Resilience in the face of environmental trauma. In D. G. Nemeth, R. B. Hamilton, & J. Kuriansky (Eds.), *Living in an environmentally traumatized world* (pp. 113–140). Santa Barbara, CA: Praeger.

Noffsinger, M. A., Pfefferbaum, B., Pfefferbaum, R. L., Sherrib, K., & Norris, F. H. (2012). The burden of disaster: Part I. Challenges and opportunities within a child's social ecology. *International Journal of Emergency Mental Health*, *14*(1), 3–13.

Pajares, F., & Urdan, T. (2006). *Self-efficacy beliefs of adolescents: A volume adolescence and education*. Greenwich, CT: Information Age Publishing, Inc.

Perry, B. (2009). Examining child maltreatment through a neurodevelopmental lens: Clinical applications of the neurosequential model of therapeutics. *Journal of Loss & Trauma*, *14*(4), 240–255.

Peveto, K. (2016). Workshops planned to help flood survivors become more resilient. *The Advocate*, (October 30). Retrieved from: http://www.theadvocate.com/baton_rouge/entertainment_life/health_fitness/article_9973c6b8-9ba4-11e6-8a9e-e33e3bf8e108.html?sr_source=lift_amplify.

Pollack, G. H. (2017). Anniversary reactions, trauma, and mourning. *The Psychoanalytic Quarterly*, *39*(3), 347–371. https://doi.org/10.1080/21674086.1970.11926533.

Posner, M. I., & Petersen, S. E. (1990). The attention system of the human brain. *Annual Review of Neuroscience*, *13*(1), 2542. https://doi.org/10.1146/annurev.ne.13.030190.000325.

Reitan, R. (1992). *A structured program for training neuropsycological abilities*. Retrieved from: https://www.marksteinberg.com/pdf/Rehabit.pdf.

Reitan, R. M., & Wolfson, D. (1988). *Traumatic brain injury: Recovery and rehabilitation. Vol. 2.* Tucson, AZ: Neuropsychology Press.

Rodin, J. (2014). *Being strong in a world where things go wrong: The resilience dividend.* New York, NY: Public Affairs Publishing.

Roncone, R., Giusti, L., Mazza, M., Bianchini, V., Ussorio, D., Pollice, R., et al. (2013). Persistent fear of aftershocks, impairment of working memory, and acute stress disorder predict post-traumatic stress disorder: 6-month follow-up of help seekers following the L'Aquila earthquake. *SpringerPlus*, *2*(1), 636. https://doi.org/10.1186/2193-1801-2-636.

Rosenberg, M. (1989). *Society and the adolescent self-image* (Rev. Ed.). Middletown, CT, England: Wesleyan University Press.

Sachinvala, N., von Scotti, H., McGuire, M., Fairbanks, L., Bakst, K., McGuire, M., et al. (2000). Memory, attention, function and mood among patients with chronic posttraumatic stress disorder. *Journal of Nervous and Mental Disease*, *188*(12), 818–823.

Salimpoor, V., Benovoy, M., Larcher, K., Dagher, A., & Zatorre, R. J. (2011). Anatomically distinct dopamine release during anticipation and experience of peak emotion to music. *Natural Neuroscience*, *14*(2), 257–262.

Schellenberg, E. (2005). *Music and cognitive abilities. Current directions in psychological science.* Hoboken, NJ: Wiley-Blackwell.

Silverman, W. K., & La Greca, A. M. (2002). Children experiencing disasters: Definitions, reactions, and predictors of outcomes. In A. M. La Greca, W. K. Silverman, E. M. Vernberg, & M. C. Roberts (Eds.), *Helping children cope with disasters and terrorism* (pp. 11–33). Washington, DC: American Psychological Association. xvii, 446 https://doi.org/10.1037/10454-001.

Smilan, C. (2009). Building resiliency to childhood trauma through arts-based learning. *Childhood Education*, *85*(6), 380.

Story, A. (2011). The use of expressive arts with children. *Social Work Today*. Retrieved from: www.socialworktoday.com/archive/exc_020712.shtm.

Tabuchi, H., & Wald, M. L. (2011). Japanese reactor damage is worse than expected. *New York Times*, (May 12). Retrieved from: http://www.nytimes.come/2011/05/13/world/asia/13japan.html.

Tedeschi, R. G., & Calhoun, L. G. (2004). Post traumatic growth: Conceptual foundations and empirical evidence. *Psychological Inquiry*, *15*(1), 1–8.

The United Nations Children's Fund (UNICEF) and The United Nations International Strategy for Disaster Risk Reduction (UNISDR). (2011). *Children and disaster: Building resilience through education*.

UNISDR. (2015). *The Sendai framework for disaster risk reduction 2015-2030*. Retrieved June 22, 2018 from: https://www.preventionweb.net/files/43291_sendaiframeworkfordrren.pdf.

United Nations. (2015). *The United Nations 2030 agenda for sustainable development*. Retrieved from: https://sustainabledevelopment.un.org/content/documents/21252030%20Agenda%20for%20Sustainable%20Development%20web.pdf.

United Nations. (2018). *Global compact for safe, regular and orderly migration*. Retrieved November 1, 2019 from: https://www.stjornarradid.is/lisalib/getfile.aspx?itemid=7092fe59-fa1b-11e8-942f-005056bc530c.

United Nations General Assembly. (2019). *A/RES/74/2. Political declaration of the high-level meeting on universal health coverage*. Retrieved November 1, 2019 from: https://undocs.org/en/A/RES/74/2.

Walsh, F. (2002). A family resilience framework: Innovative practice applications. *Family Relations*, *51*(2), 130–137. https://doi.org/10.1111/j.1741-3729.2002.00130.x.

Walsh, F. (2007). Traumatic loss and major disasters: Strengthening family and community resilience. *Family Process*, *46*(2), 207–227. https://doi.org/10.1111/j.1545-5300.2007.00205.x.

Webb, N. (Ed.), (2004). *Mass trauma and violence: Helping families and children cope*. New York, NY: The Guilford Press.

Williams, L. (1986). *Teaching for the two-sided mind: A guide to right brain/left brain education*. New York, NY: Simon & Schuster.

World Health Organization. (2019). *Disasters and mental health*. Retrieved from: http://www.searo.who.int/bangladesh/disastersandmentalhealth/en/.

Yedida, T., & Itzhaky, H. (2004). A drawing technique for diagnosis and therapy of adolescents suffering traumatic stress and loss related to terrorism. In N. Boyd Webb (Ed.), *Mass trauma and violence: Helping families and children cope* (pp. 283–303). New York: The Guilford Press.

Zimmerman, M. A. (2000). Empowerment theory. In J. Rappaport & E. Seidman (Eds.), *Handbook of community psychology* (pp. 43–63). Boston, MA: Springer.

Chapter 13

Neuropsychological evaluation of children with complex medical concerns

Traci W. Olivier
Pediatric Development & Therapy Center, Our Lady of the Lake Children's Health, Baton Rouge, LA, United States; Neuropsychology Center of Louisiana, Baton Rouge, LA, United States

Pediatric neuropsychological evaluations

Comprehensive neuropsychological evaluations can provide invaluable information regarding children with complex medical conditions. Their utility extends beyond simply explaining a pattern of cognitive strengths and weaknesses. Accurate diagnosis, a thorough yet comprehensible discussion of difficulties as they relate to the child's medical history and targeted, individualized recommendations provide a roadmap for treatment and academic planning purposes. This section addresses some of the fundamental aspects of pediatric neuropsychological evaluations as they relate to clinical practice.

Referral source and reason for referral

Accurate identification of the referral source is a crucial component of the pediatric neuropsychological evaluation. Given high demand for services and limited numbers of qualified pediatric neuropsychologists, neuropsychological evaluations are often reduced to generic templates and fixed batteries. While these certainly have their place, and can be useful when utilized properly, pediatric neuropsychologists must work to individualize their clinical processes, test batteries, and evaluation reports. Failing to do so inevitably results in one of two issues:

1. Evaluation procedures and test batteries become unnecessarily very lengthy.
   a. *Pro*—evaluations may be thorough and comprehensive, resulting in a number of recommendations.
   b. *Con*—lengthy evaluations often result in very long wait times for patients (e.g., to be seen initially, complete testing, receive feedback, or receive the written report).

Evaluation and Treatment of Neuropsychologically Compromised Children
https://doi.org/10.1016/B978-0-12-819545-1.00013-8

2. Screening procedures or shortened batteries are utilized.
   a. *Pro*—patients who do not need comprehensive evaluations can receive services faster, and evaluation time is significantly reduced, which benefits the patient and the neuropsychologist.
   b. *Con*—overreliance on screening procedures or "cookie cutter" batteries can result in inaccurate or incomplete diagnoses, reports that are not useful, or an inadvertently longer wait time (e.g., if patients have to return to complete additional evaluation components, such as testing, parent-rating forms, record requests, etc.).

Nevertheless, pediatric neuropsychological evaluations are known to take a considerable amount of time in comparison to adult evaluations. This is due to several factors, including the request and receipt of additional records (e.g., school records) and rating forms (e.g., parent- and teacher-rating forms), which are often not returned in a timely manner; and the length of pediatric neuropsychological evaluation reports. While efforts must be made to increase efficiency (especially when managed care is involved), the evaluation should be tailored to the specific nature of the referral question. Identification of the referral source and the reason for referral, prior to seeing the patient, result in evaluations that are both useful and valued by patients and referring practitioners.

Consider the setting

Clinical neuropsychologists are primarily housed within one of three settings, which will determine the type of evaluations that are conducted. This, in combination with the reason for referral, should also be taken into consideration.

1. Outpatient settings—These include, but are not limited to, hospital ambulatory care clinics, private practices, and schools. Evaluations conducted on an outpatient basis are more "consumer focused" and may result in more direct patient care (e.g., working with families to implement recommendations). They are also generally open to more flexibility in evaluation procedures.
2. Inpatient settings—These include emergency departments and hospital units. Inpatient evaluations are often utilized to answer very specific questions (e.g., pre- and postsurgical neurocognitive functioning, presence of a neurocognitive disorder or delirium, etc.), have a very fast turnaround time, and may be limited by extraneous variables (e.g., patient availability and condition, limited motor and/or sensory functioning).
3. Rehabilitation settings—These can include step-down programs (following inpatient discharge), intensive outpatient programs/day programs, or other outpatient rehabilitation centers. Evaluations may be brief and serial during active treatment and serve to inform cognitive rehabilitation and other rehabilitation efforts (e.g., targeted recommendations for speech-language, occupational, physical, and child life therapists). Discharge evaluations may be more involved to prepare the family for transition out of rehabilitation and back into the home, school, and/or work setting.

Essential components of a neuropsychological evaluation

The initial interview

The importance of a thorough diagnostic interview cannot be overstated, particularly in pediatric neuropsychology. While standardized forms are useful supplements, they should not be utilized as substitutes for face-to-face interviews. Additional information is often spontaneously "recalled" when asked in person versus on a form. Nuances regarding birth and developmental history, which are particularly important, are often gathered throughout the course of the initial interview with the family. The initial interview also allows for clarification regarding missing or unclear information reported on forms. Though the initial interview is generally conducted with the child's parent/guardian, child interviews are also important and can be conducted at any age level. For example, preschool to school-age children can be asked about their preferred interests and activities (e.g., favorite television show, Disney characters, video/tablet games, or toys), favorite and challenging academic subjects, siblings and peer relationships, what they would like to be when they grow up, or what they would wish for if they had three wishes (with a caveat that one of the wishes cannot be for a million more wishes!). In addition to general interview questions, adolescents and young adults can be asked more targeted questions aimed at information gathering (that may not have been available in the parent/guardian interview), such as substance use/abuse history, relationship status, and sexual history. Gathering information from collateral informants is also essential, and can include other family members/caregivers, school personnel, coaches, church/community workers, counselors, and therapists.

Records review

It stands to reason that adult neuropsychological evaluations would result in a greater proportion of time spent reviewing records, given the fact that adults have simply lived longer than children. Nevertheless, pediatric neuropsychological evaluations often require extensive record reviews that include both medical and school records. Whenever possible and when applicable, the following should be requested or elicited from the parents/guardians, or directly from the source with a written authorization for release of protected health information:

- Birth records (discussed in greater detail in the relevant section below),
- School records (including report cards, previous school-based evaluations, and formalized academic supports as provided in a Section 504 Plan [i.e., student accommodations], Individualized Education Program [IEP], Individualized Health Plan [IHP], or other documents),
- Previous medical treatment (with emphasis on neurological, neurosurgical, and neuroimaging notes),
- Previous psychiatric/psychological treatment, and
- Previous neuropsychological/psychological and/or other evaluations.

With regard to previous evaluations, it is important to understand what has already been diagnosed and/or presented to the family about the child's functioning. When test scores are made available, patterns of performance and change over time can be better understood. This is particularly important for children as they progress through critical points of development and education. Reviewing previous evaluations can also provide additional historical information that may have not been otherwise available.

The neuropsychological report

Psychologists, especially neuropsychologists, are known for being quite lengthy in their writings. Postal et al. (2018) explain that this tradition arose during a time when most feedback was delivered by the patient's referring physician. "Therefore, the report was used not only to educate the referring provider so they could provide sufficient feedback to the patient, but also to provide cogent evidence of the psychologist's formulation. A clinician would be hard pressed to carry out such a mandate in one or two pages" (Postal et al., 2018, pp. 327–328). Despite the fact that most neuropsychologists now provide feedback directly to their patients, lengthy report writing traditions have persisted. This is likely due, at least in part, to a heavy emphasis on extremely detailed report writing in graduate training programs, internships, and fellowships.

As Jacobus Donders stated, "There are no shortcuts to preparing neuropsychological reports" (2016, p. xvi). Nevertheless, pediatric neuropsychologists spend more time in report writing (5–20 h as compared to ≤2 h for adult or geriatric reports) and write longer reports (11.6 pages versus 7.8 for adult and 6.3 for geriatric) than their adult colleagues (Postal et al., 2018). It typically takes at least 3 weeks to produce a pediatric neuropsychological report (Postal et al., 2018), though anecdotal observations suggest that 4–6 weeks may be more typical for many others.

Pediatric (and adult) neuropsychologists continue to grapple with report writing styles and formats with no standard consensus in sight. Though neuropsychologists in America now have access to reimbursement codes that allow report writing time to be billed to insurance companies, aggregate data regarding the consistency of reimbursement rates are not yet available. Regardless, the tradition of extensive report writing time and lengthy written reports is unsustainable and will need to continue to be addressed.

Feedback and follow-up/reevaluation

Neuropsychologists tend to view the report as the primary "product" of neuropsychological evaluations, yet feedback, to both patients and referral sources, is arguably the primary outcome. As Postal and Armstrong (2013) state, effective feedback "allows the patient and family to develop a better understanding of diagnoses, cognitive scores, and prognosis. Through the feedback session(s), neuropsychologists have the opportunity to meet patients and their families where they are, within their unique set of cognitive, emotional, and culture contexts, and help them to understand what it all means" (p. 7).

Who else on the patient's treatment team is entrusted with such a daunting yet important task? Neuropsychologists are in the unique position of explaining how a child's *brain* and *behavior* fit together. While advanced neuroimaging techniques provide information concerning *structural* changes or damages, neuropsychological evaluations provide an explanation as to *functional* changes. This entails providing clarity to otherwise elusive concepts and terms. As Vasserman and Baron state, families often have

> *...an initial lack of clarity regarding symptom presentation and appropriate treatment course. Symptoms may result from multiple alternative etiologies and the treatment course may differ depending on which clinician is conducting the evaluation and recommending treatment strategies. Thus, it often becomes the responsibility of the neuropsychologist to obtain comprehensive records and integrate this diverse information from multiple sources, with the intent that this thorough review will disambiguate the commonly contradictory information that is perplexing to the child and family. The neuropsychologist's ability to formulate a cohesive and meaningful summation based on disparate sources of information is a critical role in these complex circumstances (2016, p. 64).*

In addition to providing feedback, neuropsychologists are often called upon to follow-up with patients and their families over a period of months or even years. This is particularly important in terms of pediatric neuropsychological care, as critical points of development and educational instruction require tailored, updated recommendations. Some of these critical points are summarized below:

- Birth to 3 years: Early development. Evaluations detect subtle changes in development that may warrant early intervention, such as speech-language, physical, and/or occupational therapy.
- Age 4–5 years: School entry (e.g., kindergarten). Evaluations identify "red flags" with regard to cognitive or behavioral patterns (e.g., attention, executive functioning, visuomotor, memory) that can interfere with learning. Early intervention continues to be a focus.
- Age 8–9 years: First grade (i.e., when instruction typically shifts from *learning to read* to *reading to learn*). Evaluations identify disorders and provide tailored treatment recommendations, with a focus on maximizing educational achievement, when applicable.
- Age 14–16 years: Transition to secondary education. Evaluations provide tailored recommendations regarding maximizing educational achievement while also focusing on compensatory strategies for disorders/concerns that either were not addressed or did not respond well to previous intervention.
- Age 17–18 years: Transition to young adulthood (e.g., postsecondary school/training, occupations, independent/semiindependent living).

Complex pediatric medical conditions

Children and adolescents with complex medical conditions are at risk of being "overlooked" by parents and professionals in terms of neurocognitive functioning. These patients often present with concerns that, on the surface, look like more "typical" disorders (e.g., attention deficit hyperactivity disorder [ADHD], intellectual disability, disruptive behavior disorders, etc.). Oftentimes, however, these surface-level concerns are due to an underlying neurocognitive disorder.

The immense challenges that are faced by families must also be understood. Vasserman and Baron summarize these challenges to include four aspects:

> *First and foremost, family members must begin the process of understanding myriad facts about a disease and its treatment regimen with which they have little familiarity...Second, an added family burden is how to understand the information provided by multiple specialists encountered in the course of disease diagnosis and treatment...Third, families with medically complex children often experience a significant financial burden...Finally, for certain conditions, the impact of the illness on quality of life and cognitive functioning is so great that parents must rethink their personal expectations for their child's future functioning" (2016, pp. 64–65).*

Though a review of all complex pediatric medical conditions is beyond the scope of this chapter, particular emphasis is given to three areas: complications associated with prematurity and/or low birth weight, pediatric cancer, and acquired and traumatic brain injuries. Prematurity and birth weight are selected due to early history often being compromised in medically fragile children. Pediatric cancer, which may be initially treated at specialty hospitals, has lifelong implications and is therefore also included. Lastly, acquired and traumatic brain injuries provide important information regarding recovery and treatment trajectories, which are important across the spectrum of pediatric injuries. It should be noted, however, that a number of other pediatric conditions warrant neuropsychological evaluation and monitoring, including, but not limited to, anoxia/hypoxia, spina bifida, hydrocephalus, cerebral palsy, seizure disorders, genetic syndromes, and deafness/hearing loss.

Complications associated with prematurity and/or low birth weight

Similar to pediatric cancer survival rates, rates of survival for neonates who are born early or of low birth weight have increased rapidly since the 1960s, due to medical advances and the implementation of neonatal intensive care units (NICU; Taylor, 2010). Previous literature has demonstrated that these children are often at higher risk for neurocognitive/neurodevelopmental, behavioral, and educational difficulties (Baron & Rey-Casserly, 2010; Taylor, 2010). As the number of infants who survive increases, so does the need for comprehensive neuropsychological care across critical points of development.

An accurate early history is an essential component of a pediatric neuropsychological evaluation. Unfortunately, however, parents/caregivers are often poor historians when relaying specific details about pregnancy and delivery. Inaccuracies in reporting can occur for several reasons, including memory "lapses" due to anesthesia, pain during delivery, and/or heightened emotional responses; trouble keeping track of multiple birth histories for those who have more than one child; fear of disclosing details that may suggest harmful prenatal behaviors or events, such as substance use/abuse, use of prescribed medications during pregnancy, maternal trauma/abuse sustained during pregnancy, etc.; or lack of available information. The latter is often the case with children who have been adopted or who are living with alternate guardians (e.g., grandparents, aunts/uncles, etc.). If the child was delivered in a hospital, it is often helpful to directly request birth records, if possible, with written consent from the guardian. Directly requesting birth records ensures accuracy of details and provides more information than the parent may be able to provide.

When available, specific information of interest to neuropsychologists regarding early history includes the following:

- Pregnancy details (e.g., how soon after conception pregnancy was detected, nature and frequency of prenatal care, use of substances and/or prescribed medications, environmental risk factors [high stress, domestic violence or other abuse], maternal and/or fetal complications during pregnancy),
- Gestational age,
- Method of delivery,
- Complications during delivery,
- Need for supplemental oxygen,
- Apgar scores at 1 and 5 min postbirth,
- Newborn hearing screening results,
- Time from birth to discharge for mother and infant,
- Length of NICU admission (if applicable),
- Age of achievement for major developmental milestones (e.g., language, motor),
- Necessity of early intervention services (e.g., speech-language therapy, physical therapy, occupational therapy).

Accurate details gathered within the context of a parent/family interview aid significantly when conceptualizing data gathered from neuropsychological evaluations. While some children with compromised birth histories present with significant difficulties that can be clearly identified diagnostically (e.g., major neurocognitive disorder, intellectual disability, etc.), others present with unclear neurocognitive profiles that are often indicative of a mild neurocognitive disorder or unspecified/secondary neurodevelopmental disorder. Without a comprehensive neuropsychological evaluation, these children are at risk for improper and/or inaccurate diagnoses.

Gestational age and birth weight are arguably two of the most significant risk factors for neurocognitive/neurodevelopmental concerns. Risk increases as gestational age at delivery and birth weight decrease. Generally, full-term gestational age is 37–40 weeks postconception, and average birth weight is around 3.5 kg (or 7.5 pounds), though anything between about 2.5 kg (5.5 pounds) and 4.5 kg (10 pounds) is considered within normal limits, according to the University of Michigan (n.d.). As summarized by Cole et al. (2002, p. 1), previous studies are "consistent in demonstrating that risk of [cerebral palsy], major neurosensory, and/or neurological disability is inversely proportional to the degree of immaturity measured by gestational age or birth weight." It is important to note that risk is not eliminated by the absence of complications associated with prematurity (Cole et al., 2002). Nevertheless, some of the most common complications due to young gestational age and/or low birth weight include (Cole et al., 2002; Taylor, 2010):

- Intraventricular hemorrhage (IVH) and periventricular leukomalacia (PVL), resulting in increased risk of neurocognitive deficits secondary to brain damage.
- Retinopathy of prematurity (ROP), resulting in increased risk of vision impairments.
- Bronchopulmonary dysplasia (BPD), resulting in increased risk of long-term pulmonary issues.

The following classifications regarding gestational age and birth weight have been summarized by Taylor (2010):

- Gestational age classifications
    - Full term = 37–40 weeks.
    - Preterm birth ≤ 37 weeks gestational age.
    - Very preterm birth (VPTB) ≤ 32 weeks gestational age.
    - Extremely preterm birth (EPTB) ≤ 29 weeks gestational age.
- Birth weight classifications
    - Low birth weight ≤ 2500 g or approximately 5.5 pounds.
    - Very low birth weight (VLBW) ≤ 1500 g or approximately 3.3 pounds.
    - Extremely low birth weight (ELBW) ≤ 1000 g or approximately 2.2 pounds.

Apgar scores were developed in 1952 by Virginia Apgar in an attempt to rapidly quantify newborns' health, both 1 and 5 min following birth (Razaz et al., 2016; Ropper, Samuels, Klein, & Prasad, 2019). Though rarely recalled by parents, especially for older children, Apgar scores are typically documented in birth records. These scores have been described as "a universally used but somewhat imprecise index of the well-being of the newly born infant" (Ropper et al., 2019, p. 603), yet they have also been described as serving as a "marker for developmental vulnerability" (Razaz et al., 2016, p. F114).

Apgar scores range from 1 to 10 and measure heart rate, respiration, muscle tone, reflex response, and color. Few past studies examine the continuum of

Apgar scores as related to neurocognitive and/or developmental risk, but literature generally purports that "low" 5 min scores are associated with greater risk. More recent research, however, suggests that "the risk of developmental vulnerability at 5 years of age [is] inversely associated with the [5-minute] Apgar score and… [extends] across the entire range of scores" (Razaz et al., 2016, p. F119). The authors further explain that even scores of 9 represent "an increased risk of vulnerability on the physical and emotional domains" (p. F117), as compared to children with Apgar scores of 10. Ropper et al. (2019, p. 604) summarize the Apgar scoring system, which is provided below for reference:

- Heart rate
  - 0 = No heart rate.
  - 1 = Fewer than 100 beats per minute (low responsiveness).
  - 2 = More than 100 beat per minute (adequate vigor).
- Respiration
  - 0 = Not breathing.
  - 1 = Weak cry (e.g., whimpering, grunting).
  - 2 = Good, strong cry.
- Muscle tone
  - 0 = Limp.
  - 1 = Some flexing of arms/legs.
  - 2 = Active motion.
- Reflex response
  - 0 = No response to airway suctioning.
  - 1 = Grimace during suctioning.
  - 2 = Grimace and cough/sneeze during suctioning.
- Color
  - 0 = Whole body is completely blue/pale.
  - 1 = Good body color; blue hands/feet.
  - 2 = Completely pink/good color.

The literature debates the usefulness of developmental milestones in predicting functional outcomes. As Ropper and colleagues summarize, the "developmental scale in early life is a useful source of information, but it must be combined with a full clinical assessment" (Ropper et al., 2019, p. 604). Though a review of age-typical developmental milestones is beyond the scope of this chapter, the reader is referred to Tables 27-4 and 27-5 in Ropper et al. (2019, pp. 606–607).

Pediatric cancer

Cures for pediatric catastrophic diseases, such as pediatric cancer, have advanced tremendously within the past decades (Mulhern, Merchant, Gajjar, Reddick, & Kun, 2004; Rodgers, Withycombe, & Hockenberry, 2016), primarily due to vast amounts of new and evolving research within the fields of hematology and oncology. As such, pediatric survival rates have increased dramatically. While many researchers and clinicians have continued to work to find more cures, others' efforts have turned toward precision medicine and increasing functional outcomes at home, at school, and within the community (Conklin et al., 2012; Mulhern et al., 2004; Rodgers et al., 2016).

Pediatric neuropsychological evaluations are unique in that they help to bridge the gap between medical treatment and functional outcomes. Treatment should include medical care, neurocognitive care, and psychosocial care, and therefore does not end following surgical resection, chemotherapy, and/or radiation. While medical stabilization may have been achieved, parents are often left grappling with the reality that their child may never be the same.

Cancer and cancer-directed treatment often result in a host of physical impacts, including, but not limited to, bone marrow suppression (i.e., resulting in increased risk of infection, anemia, and bleeding); gastrointestinal concerns (e.g., mucositis/esophagitis, anorexia and cachexia, nausea, vomiting, diarrhea, constipation, weight loss/gain); sensory issues (e.g., neuropathy, decreased vision and/or hearing, changes in taste); musculoskeletal problems (e.g., bone and/or muscle tumors that can result in limb-sparing surgeries and/or amputations); skin changes (e.g., alopecia, irritation due to radiation [radiation recall], palmar-plantar erythrodysesthesia [hand-foot syndrome], extravasation, skin variations, nail dystrophies); physical pain (e.g., pain secondary to the cancer process or associated with treatment); fatigue; and sleep disorders (Rodgers et al., 2016).

Cancer and cancer-directed treatment can also result in significant psychosocial concerns. Children undergoing treatment are often removed from their typical routines for weeks, months, or sometimes even years at a time. Children who can be treated locally may miss days and weeks of school due to frequent doctor's appointments, procedures, and sickness associated with both disease and treatment. Other children must travel with their families to different cities or even countries for treatment, which typically results in long separations from family members and loved ones. Families often find themselves having to choose which parent accompanies the child for treatment and which parent stays locally to continue to work, manage the household, and/or care for the child's siblings. Financial strain is common for families of pediatric cancer patients, even when treatment is covered by insurance or mission-driven hospitals, due to parents' extended absences from work. It is not uncommon for parents to lose their jobs, and sometimes even their medical insurance, following their child's cancer diagnosis, or to be inadvertently forced to resign from their jobs to participate in treatment.

Neurocognitive late effects are common in pediatric cancer patients, particularly those who have been diagnosed with cancer that effects the central nervous system (CNS; Mulhern et al., 2004; Ullrich, 2009). Not unexpectedly, childhood brain tumor survivors are at a significantly higher risk for neurocognitive declines. Though immediate neurocognitive changes can present following diagnosis and/or treatment, those who have undergone CNS-directed treatment (e.g., chemotherapy, radiation therapy) may experience neurocognitive changes that can emerge between 2 and 5 years posttreatment and sometimes persist into adulthood (Ellenberg et al., 2009). Declines in primary neurocognitive processes, such as reasoning skills, attention, executive functioning, and processing speed, are among the most common neurocognitive late effects, which contribute to declines in both academic and functional skills (Conklin et al., 2012; Mabbott, Penkman, Witol, Strother, & Bouffet, 2008; Moxon-Emre et al., 2016; Mulhern et al., 2004; Palmer et al., 2013; Reeves et al., 2005). Further, physical impairments postdisease and treatment may exacerbate late effects (e.g., sensorimotor impairments such as decreased vision and hearing and impaired fine and gross motor skills). For example, recent research (Olivier et al., 2019) suggests that declines in reading skills posttreatment may be associated, at least to some degree, with hearing loss, which is common following certain types of cancer-directed treatment (e.g., platinum-based chemotherapy agents [cisplatin] and radiation therapy disrupting the cochlea and vestibulocochlear [eighth] cranial nerve). The authors purport that hearing loss in survivors of medulloblastoma contributes to decreased phonological awareness and processing speed, which adversely affects higher-level language skills such as reading comprehension. The risk for neurocognitive late effects is greater for children diagnosed at a younger age and for those who are identified as having high-risk disease, which therefore necessitates greater intensity of treatment (Fouladi et al., 2005; Mulhern & Butler, 2004).

Medulloblastoma, a type of embryonal brain tumor, is one of the most common types of pediatric brain tumors, arising primarily from the cerebellum/fourth ventricle (Louis, Ohgaki, Wiestler, & Cavenee, 2016). Surgical resection to remove as much of the tumor as possible is often the first line of treatment and is typically followed by craniospinal irradiation and chemotherapy (e.g., https://www.clinicaltrials.gov/, NCT01878617). Posterior fossa syndrome, often referred to as cerebellar mutism, is a complication of surgical resection that can affect up to approximately 30% of patients (De Smet et al., 2007; Gudrunardottir, Sehested, Juhler, & Schmiegelow, 2011; Schreiber et al., 2017). Damage is thought to be due to disturbances along the dentorubrothalamocortical pathway (Schreiber et al., 2017), though research efforts are actively endeavoring to clarify the nature and course of posterior fossa syndrome.

While some consider mutism a characteristic symptom of posterior fossa syndrome, research identifies a constellation of symptoms affecting speech, motor skills, and emotional presentation. Mutism is often the first observable symptom of posterior fossa syndrome, typically emerging 1–2 days postresection (though emergence up to 6 days postresection has been described) and is preceded by a period of normal speech. Speech generally returns spontaneously in an average of 7–8 weeks, though mutism can persist for up to 6 months. Residual speech difficulties, however, are often apparent (e.g., severe dysarthria). Motor difficulties include ataxia and hypotonia, and are often seen ipsilateral to the side of the cerebellar lesion and/or damage from surgical resection.

Emotional lability that presents similarly to pseudobulbar affect is also common (De Smet et al., 2007; Gudrunardottir et al., 2011; Schreiber et al., 2017).

The following points of interest are recommended for inclusion in neuropsychological evaluations of pediatric cancer survivors:

- Diagnosis (e.g., circumstances/symptoms prompting care, diagnostic course),
- Cancer-directed treatment (e.g., type of treatment—resection, chemotherapy, radiation, immunotherapy; dates initiated and completed; dose and/or treatment agents; radiation targets/dosimetry [if available]; complications during treatment course),
- Ancillary treatment (e.g., speech-language, physical, and/or occupational therapy; cognitive rehabilitation),
- Symptoms emerging during or after treatment (e.g., mutism onset and recovery),
- Neuroimaging results (e.g., magnetic resonance imaging, computerized tomography, etc.),
- Results of most recent vision and hearing examinations, and
- Amount of direct education that was missed due to disease and treatment.

Acquired and traumatic brain injuries

When adults acquire or sustain traumatic brain injuries, neuropsychological evaluations aid in quantifying existing functioning as compared to premorbid levels of function. When a child sustains a brain injury, however, special attention must be given to established skills versus skills that have yet to be developed. It is hypothesized that, for established skills, a trajectory similar to that seen with adults is expected. That is, brain-injured children will show the greatest deviations from age-typical performance immediately following injury. Though complete recovery is not always possible, as time progresses, the "gap" between their skills and those of same-age peers is expected to narrow. The opposite is hypothesized, however, for skills that the child has not yet developed. For undeveloped or emerging skills, functioning often appears age-typical immediately following injury; yet, over time, the gap between these children's performance and those of same-age peers becomes more discrepant (Taylor & Alden, 1997).

Careful consideration of the extent of injury and the timeline of symptom emergence is crucial when evaluating children who have sustained brain injuries. Parents typically seem to fall in one of three categories when attempting to make sense of neuropsychological sequelae: (a) they attribute a high number of symptoms to the injury; (b) they dismiss the possibility that the brain injury has resulted in adverse effects; or (c) they fall somewhere in the middle. Pediatric neuropsychological evaluations help to clarify these elusive neurocognitive etiologies and trajectories.

Special considerations for pediatric neuropsychologists

Intellectual assessment batteries

Advances in technology and neuropsychological assessment provide clinicians with a plethora of tools. Many tests are now computerized and can be administered with the use of computers or tablets (e.g., Apple® iPads). Updated test versions offer hopes of reduced administration and scoring time as well as greater engagement on the part of the child.

While these advances are certainly exciting and useful with many populations, pediatric neuropsychologists must be careful to utilize the most appropriate tool for individual care. For example, some children will respond better to traditional paper/pencil methods of administration while others may benefit from computer-assisted testing.

Perhaps one of the most widely assessed domains involves intellectual functioning, as intellectual measures are a standard component of nearly all neuropsychological evaluations. As such, pediatric neuropsychologists are encouraged to carefully consider patients' unique needs before assessing. Overreliance on one particular measure or battery is unwise with this population. While most patients may benefit from one particular measure, others may have needs that necessitate the use of alternative instruments. A summary of anecdotal clinical evidence surrounding some of the most commonly available measures of intellectual functioning follows:

- Wechsler Intelligence Scale for Children, Fifth Edition (WISC-V)—A widely used measure, the WISC-V is appropriate for children age 6–16 with a wide variety of cognitive concerns.
- Wechsler Intelligence Scale for Children, Fifth Edition, Integrated (WISC-V-Integrated)—This measures provides multiple-choice options for many of the subtests as well as inclusion of visual working memory tests (e.g., Spatial Span).
- Wechsler Abbreviated Scale of Intelligence, Second Edition (WASI-II)—The WASI-II is recommended for use when a full intelligence assessment is not warranted but may be needed in the near future (e.g., assessing cognitive recovery following brain injury), which aids in reducing practice effects.
- Differential Ability Scales, Second Edition (DAS-II)—The DAS-II is useful with children of lower functioning, as many of the subtests provide a lower floor than the Wechsler series subtests. Batteries for early years or school-age children can be selected.
- Stanford Binet Intelligence Scales, Fifth Edition (SB-5)—The SB-5 is useful for children with a range of cognitive skills, including higher cognitive functioning (e.g., assessing for giftedness).
- Comprehensive Test of Nonverbal Intelligence, Second Edition (CTONI-2)—In addition to reduced verbal demands, the CTONI-2 subtests also reduce motor demands.

- Leiter International Performance Scale, Third Edition (Leiter-3)—The Leiter-3 is recommended for use with children who are nonverbal, significantly impaired, or deaf/hard-of-hearing.

Performance validity tests

Though widely used in adult neuropsychology, performance validity tests (PVTs) have traditionally not been used with pediatric populations. More recently, however, the use of PVTs with children and adolescents has gained increasing popularity and utility.

Research has examined the use of the Test of Memory Malingering (TOMM) with children and adolescents and support it as a potential measure for assessing effort within these populations (Brooks, Sherman, & Krol, 2012). The use of the Rey-15 item, on the other hand, has been discouraged from pediatric use (Brooks et al., 2012; Constantinou & McCaffrey, 2003).

Additional research is needed before adult PVTs can be reliably and validly utilized with children and adolescents, as published normative data are not yet available. The Memory Validity Profile (MVP), which was recently released, is marketed as the first PVT standardized for use with individuals from ages 5 to 21 years and is supported in peer-reviewed literature (Brooks, Fay-McClymont, MacAllister, Vasserman, & Sherman, 2019). The Pediatric Performance Validity Test Suite (PdPVTS), also recently released, is another option for children ages 5–18 years.

Concluding comments

The role of the pediatric neuropsychologist in interdisciplinary care

Interdisciplinary care is becoming the standard in most healthcare settings. Now, perhaps more than ever, practitioners are encouraged to consult and collaborate rather than operate in silos. Though important across the lifetime spectrum of care, interdisciplinary care is particularly important in pediatric settings.

As discussed above, pediatric neuropsychologists are tasked with the role of integrating all aspects of a child's functioning into a coherent whole, including developmental, medical, emotional, and behavioral functioning. As such, it is important that neuropsychologists refrain from inadvertently referring to themselves as "therapists" or "technicians" or allowing themselves to be represented as such. Neuropsychologists should utilize their unique skill set as experts in brain-behavior relationships to establish themselves as a viable part of patients' interdisciplinary treatment teams. Neuropsychologists provide much more than test scores and should avoid being represented as simply "testing psychologists." As described above, giving feedback directly to patients and referring practitioners, and following up with families as necessary, are key. Lastly, more and more neuropsychologists (especially in America) are obtaining prescriptive privileges, which inevitably expands the scope of practice. As this trend continues, it is important that the nonpharmacological expertise of neuropsychologists (e.g., evaluations, cognitive rehabilitation, and psychotherapy) continues to be valued and utilized.

Promoting resilience in children and families

Resilience is defined as the "ability to be firmly grounded in today, to benefit from yesterday, and to imagine [oneself] in tomorrow" (Nemeth & Olivier, 2017, p. 20). The ultimate goal of pediatric neuropsychologists is to build resilience in children and families. Neuropsychological evaluations should provide a clear, accurate understanding of the realities of today. Pediatric neuropsychologists endeavor to help families benefit from yesterday by building upon skills that have already been developed, and they help children reach their potential so that they can imagine themselves thriving in tomorrow.

Recommendations should always balance habilitation and rehabilitation with accommodation. Continued growth and skill acquisition must be encouraged, when possible, while compensatory strategies to find "workarounds" for areas that may not be amendable to improvement, must also be addressed.

Of course, this often requires a reconceptualization of that which was previously considered "normal" or "typical." By helping families grieve and process the losses of yesterday and build strength to deal with the challenges of today, they can look forward with new hope to the future. In essence, pediatric neuropsychologists facilitate the development of *a new normal*. This should be the end goal of all work that is done. Development is ongoing, and each new day brings an opportunity for change. Though expectations must be balanced with reality, new growth is always possible.

References

Baron, I. S., & Rey-Casserly, C. (2010). Extremely preterm birth outcome: A review of four decades of cognitive research. *Neuropsychology Review*, *20*, 430–452. https://doi.org/10.1007/s11065-010-O.

Brooks, B. L., Fay-McClymont, T. B., MacAllister, W. S., Vasserman, M., & Sherman, E. M. S. (2019). A new kid on the block: The Memory Validity Profile (MVP) in children with neurological conditions. *Child Neuropsychology*, *25*(4), 561–572. https://doi.org/10.1080/09297049.2018.1477929.

Brooks, B. L., Sherman, E. M., & Krol, A. L. (2012). Utility of TOMM Trial 1 as an indicator of effort in children and adolescents. *Archives of Clinical Neuropsychology*, *27*(1), 23–29.

Cole, C., Binney, G., Casey, P., Fiascone, J., Hagadorn, J., Kim, C., … Miller, K. (2002). Criteria for determining disability in infants and children: Low birth weight. In *Evidence report/technology assessment (Summary), (70)* (p. 1). Rockville, MD: Agency for Healthcare Research and Quality (US). Retrieved 8 September 2019 from: https://www.ncbi.nlm.nih.gov/books/NBK36797/.

Conklin, H. M., Ashford, J. M., Howarth, R. A., Merchant, T. E., Ogg, R. J., Santana, V. M., … Xiong, X. (2012). Working memory performance among childhood brain tumor survivors. *Journal of the International Neuropsychological Society*, *18*(6), 996–1005.

Constantinou, M., & McCaffrey, R. J. (2003). Using the TOMM for evaluating children's effort to perform optimally on neuropsychological measures. *Child Neuropsychology*, *9*, 81–90. https://doi.org/10.1076/chin.9.2.81.14505.

De Smet, H. J., Baillieux, H., Catsman-Berrevoets, C., De Deyn, P. P., Mariën, P., & Paquier, P. F. (2007). Postoperative motor speech production in children with the syndrome of 'cerebellar' mutism and subsequent dysarthria: A critical review of the literature. *European Journal of Paediatric Neurology*, *11*, 193–207. https://doi.org/10.1016/j.ejpn.2007.01.007.

Donders, J. (Ed.), (2016). *Neuropsychological report writing*. Guilford Publications.

Ellenberg, L., Liu, Q., Gioia, G., Yasui, Y., Packer, R. J., Mertens, A., … Robison, L. L. (2009). Neurocognitive status in long-term survivors of childhood CNS malignancies: A report from the Childhood Cancer Survivor Study. *Neuropsychology*, *23*, 705. https://doi.org/10.1037/a0016674.

Fouladi, M., Gilger, E., Kocak, M., Wallace, D., Buchanan, G., Reeves, C., … Gajjar, A. (2005). Intellectual and functional outcome of children 3 years old or younger who have CNS malignancies. *Journal of Clinical Oncology*, *23*, 7152–7160. https://doi.org/10.1200/JCO.2005.01.214.

Gudrunardottir, T., Sehested, A., Juhler, M., & Schmiegelow, K. (2011). Cerebellar mutism. *Child's Nervous System*, *27*, 355–363. https://doi.org/10.1007/s00381-010-1328-2.

Louis, D. N., Ohgaki, H., Wiestler, O. D., & Cavenee, W. K. (2016). *World Health Organization histological classification of tumours of the central nervous system*. France: International Agency for Research on Cancer.

Mabbott, D. J., Penkman, L., Witol, A., Strother, D., & Bouffet, E. (2008). Core neurocognitive functions in children treated for posterior fossa tumors. *Neuropsychology*, *22*, 159. https://doi.org/10.1037/0894-4105.22.2.159.

Moxon-Emre, I., Taylor, M. D., Bouffet, E., Hardy, K., Campen, C. J., Malkin, D., … Scantlebury, N. (2016). Intellectual outcome in molecular subgroups of medulloblastoma. *Journal of Clinical Oncology*, *34*, 4161–4170.

Mulhern, R. K., & Butler, R. W. (2004). Neurocognitive sequelae of childhood cancers and their treatment. *Pediatric Rehabilitation*, *7*, 1–14. https://doi.org/10.1080/13638490310001655528.

Mulhern, R. K., Merchant, T. E., Gajjar, A., Reddick, W. E., & Kun, L. E. (2004). Late neurocognitive sequelae in survivors of brain tumours in childhood. *The Lancet Oncology*, *5*, 399–408. https://doi.org/10.1016/S1470-2045(04)01507-4.

Nemeth, D. G., & Olivier, T. W. (2017). *Innovative approaches to individual and community resilience: From theory to practice*. Cambridge, MA: Academic Press.

Olivier, T. W., Bass, J. K., Ashford, J. M., Beaulieu, R., Scott, S. M., Schreiber, J. E., … Boyle, R. Cognitive implications of ototoxicity in pediatric patients with embryonal brain tumors. *Journal of Clinical Oncology*, *37*(18), (2019). 1566–1575.

Palmer, S. L., Armstrong, C., Onar-Thomas, A., Wu, S., Wallace, D., Bonner, M. J., … Knight, S. (2013). Processing speed, attention, and working memory after treatment for medulloblastoma: An international, prospective, and longitudinal study. *Journal of Clinical Oncology*, *31*, 3494. https://doi.org/10.1200/JCO.2012.47.4775.

Postal, K., & Armstrong, K. (2013). *Feedback that sticks: The art of effectively communicating neuropsychological assessment results*. Oxford University Press.

Postal, K., Chow, C., Jung, S., Erickson-Moreo, K., Geier, F., & Lanca, M. (2018). The stakeholders' project in neuropsychological report writing: A survey of neuropsychologists' and referral sources' views of neuropsychological reports. *The Clinical Neuropsychologist*, *32*, 326–344. https://doi.org/10.1080/13854046.2017.1373859.

Razaz, N., Boyce, W. T., Brownell, M., Jutte, D., Tremlett, H., Marrie, R. A., & Joseph, K. S. (2016). Five-minute Apgar score as a marker for developmental vulnerability at 5 years of age. *Archives of Disease in Childhood-Fetal and Neonatal Edition, 101*, 114–120. https://doi.org/10.1136/archdischild-2015-308458.

Reeves, C. B., Palmer, S. L., Reddick, W. E., Merchant, T. E., Buchanan, G. M., Gajjar, A., & Mulhern, R. K. (2005). Attention and memory functioning among pediatric patients with medulloblastoma. *Journal of Pediatric Psychology, 31*, 272–280. https://doi.org/10.1093/jpepsy/jsj019.

Rodgers, C., Withycombe, J., & Hockenberry, M. (2016). Physical impact of pediatric cancer and its treatment. In A. Abrams, A. Muriel, & L. Wiener (Eds.), *Pediatric pPsychosocial oncology: Textbook for multidisciplinary care* (pp. 25–50): Springer International Publishing.

Ropper, A. H., Samuels, M. A., Klein, J. P., & Prasad, S. (2019). *Adams and Victor's principles of neurology* (11th ed.). New York, NY: McGraw-Hill Education.

Schreiber, J. E., Palmer, S. L., Conklin, H. M., Mabbott, D. J., Swain, M. A., Bonner, M. J., … Gajjar, A. (2017). Posterior fossa syndrome and long-term neuropsychological outcomes among children treated for medulloblastoma on a multi-institutional, prospective study. *Neurooncology, 19*(12), 1673–1682. https://doi.org/10.1093/neu-onc/nox135.

Taylor, H. G. (2010). Children with very low birthweight or very preterm birth. In K. O. Yeates, M. D. Ris, H. G. Taylor, & B. F. Pennington (Eds.), *Pediatric neuropsychology: Research, theory, and practice* (2nd ed., pp. 26–70). New York, NY: The Guilford Press.

Taylor, H. G., & Alden, J. (1997). Age-related differences in outcomes following childhood brain insults: An introduction and overview. *Journal of the International Neuropsychological Society, 3*, 555–567.

Ullrich, N. J. (2009). Neurologic sequelae of brain tumors in children. *Journal of Child Neurology, 24*, 1446–1454. https://doi.org/10.1177/0883073809342491.

University of Michigan (n.d.). Physical growth in newborns. Retrieved 24 August 2019 from https://www.uofmhealth.org/health-library/te6295.

Vasserman, M., & Baron, I. S. (2016). Neuropsychological evaluation of the medically complex child. In J. Donders (Ed.), *Neuropsychological report writing* (pp. 62–91). New York, NY: The Guilford Press.

Chapter 14

When medication may be helpful

John A. Flatt[a], Darlyne G. Nemeth[b]

[a]*The Jason Foundation, Inc., Hendersonville, TN, United States,* [b]*The Neuropsychology Center of Louisiana, LLC, Baton Rouge, LA, United States*

Introduction

A close working relationship between a pediatric neurologist and a pediatric neuropsychologist is of great benefit to children and their families. This synergistic experience, based on mutual respect and cooperation, produces the best possible outcomes for all involved.

Families usually consult a pediatric neurologist because of their children's symptom presentation. These symptoms can appear suddenly, for example, secondary to a seizure episode, or gradually, for example, stomach migraines or worsening tic-like behaviors.

Symptoms typically presenting to a pediatric neurologist may include, but are not limited to, alterations of consciousness or responsiveness, changes in behavior, impaired memory functions, abnormal movements, pain/abnormal sensation, impaired sleep, or a global change in functioning.

The initial neurological evaluation begins with a full and thorough history, given the potential for heritable disorders and given that many presenting symptoms may be episodic and not available for the practitioner to assess in the clinical setting. After completing the history, a pediatric neurologist may complete a full general physical examination to screen for any noted system abnormalities outside the neurological and psychological systems.

The neurological examination will tend to have two phases, a general neurological evaluation for functions not thought to be related to the reported symptoms followed by a targeted and more in-depth examination of the potentially involved functions. Neurological evaluations can vary greatly between neurologists based on their independent expertise and the resources available to them. Most commonly, screening materials for basic cognitive functioning are used in addition to the mental status examination tailored to the specific child. Oftentimes, developmental evaluations based on models such as the Denver

Evaluation and Treatment of Neuropsychologically Compromised Children
https://doi.org/10.1016/B978-0-12-819545-1.00014-X

Developmental Screening Test (Denver II) may be completed by support staff or may be done by the pediatric neurologist in a formal or fluid approach based on preference and experience.

Neuroimaging studies and neurodiagnostic testing

When appropriate, neuroimaging studies may be ordered. For children, the most common studies include magnetic resonance imaging (MRI) or computed tomography (CT) with a common focus on the head/brain. In pediatric neurology, MRI is the more preferred diagnostic modality, as the ability to distinguish between different tissues in the brain and also potential brain lesions is greater when compared to CT. Looking for malformations of the brain resulting from genetic or acquired causes is commonly used in children with epilepsy and developmental disorders. CT scanning does have its advantages with speed of testing (MRI requires the sedation of many young children) and the resolution to see disorders related to bone, blood, air, or foreign bodies quite well. CT scanning is the preferred imaging modality in any emergent neurological situation due to these advantages and, in most cases, can determine the difference between a neurosurgical evaluation or a neurological consultation. Contrast enhancement may also be used to improve sensitivity in both imaging modalities; however, it is not recommended as a standard approach due to potential complications from the contrast agents.

MRI and CT can also be used for imaging the spinal cord (MRI) or spine (CT) to look for abnormalities of development, acquired deformities and/or injuries. In infants, ultrasound is an additional imaging modality to evaluate brain structures via imaging through the anterior fontanelle or to assess for spinal cord syndromes such as spina bifida.

Outside neuroimaging, other neurodiagnostic testing may be ordered to go beyond the evaluation of neuroanatomy and attempt to measure neurophysiology. These tests are specific to the potential etiologies of the patient's symptoms derived from the history and physical examination and are used not in isolation, but to aid in the understanding of the suspected disorder. Neurodiagnostic studies all tend to measure electrical activity of the brain, spinal cord, or peripheral nerves. The two most commonly performed in the neurologically compromised child are the electroencephalogram (EEG) and the polysomnogram (PSG, sleep study).

EEG is a very frequently used test to evaluate an individual's cortical and subcortical activity, looking for abnormally high and orchestrated activity. One such example is seizure, or slowed and/or diminished activity, which can represent an encephalopathy or brain lesion. EEGs have limitations in sensitivity due to restraints on testing duration and neuroanatomical restrictions on seeing all areas of the brain equally.

A polysomnogram (PSG), which is considered the "gold standard" for diagnosing obstructive sleep apnea (OSA) (Lumeng & Chervin, 2008, p. 243), is an often underutilized neurodiagnostic test relative to EEG due to the increased challenge of access in the pediatric population. Sleep studies can be very helpful for patients with obstructive or restrictive airflow during sleep, which can be more common in children with genetic causes of developmental delay (Angriman, Caravale, Novelli, Ferri, & Bruni, 2015). Appropriate diagnosis of a breathing-related sleep disorder can make a dramatic difference in treating any child, as it can potentially be cured through appropriate intervention.

At times, chemical, genetic, or metabolic studies may be ordered. These may include simple and straightforward testing such as basic electrolyte levels, liver function, thyroid function, blood counts, and toxin levels (lead) to detect derangements in metabolic function or potential metabolic injury. Often, these tests will be nondiagnostic unless there is suspicion of an abnormality based on history and/or examination. More specialized testing is often needed to help establish a cause or diagnosis.

There are two approaches to these more specialized tests based on if you have historical or physical evidence toward a specific cause or diagnosis (think Down syndrome, neurofibromatosis, tuberous sclerosis) versus if you believe there is a metabolic or genetic cause for the symptoms but are not sure of a specific etiology. Because testing for specific disorders relates directly to tests associated with the suspected anomaly, we will focus more on the options for the nonsyndromic or potentially genetic/metabolic disorder evaluation with two genetic tests, metabolic testing and mitochondrial testing.

Recent advances in genetic testing have helped to shed new light into genetic causes of many disorders that would have historically been very difficult, if possible at all, to diagnose. The two most common genetic tests you may see from a pediatric neurologist are a chromosomal microarray or exome sequencing. There are various versions of each of these tests based on the lab and the desired detail of testing for the patient.

Chromosome microarrays (CMA) work by detecting increases (duplications) or decreases (deletions) in genetic material when compared to pieces of DNA from a control sample. Based on the genetic material lost or gained, you can identify the affected genes and determine if they may be the cause of your patients symptoms. Loss of genetic material has a greater chance to cause clinical features than gains of genetic material overall (Brewer, Holloway, Zawalnyski, Schinzel, & FitzPatrick, 1998). However, a simple loss or gain of genetic material will not always result in a clinical or developmental disorder. Ordering a microarray for patients with a neurodevelopmental order is well supported and is considered a first-tier diagnostic test recommended by the American College of Medical Genetics (ACMG), the American Academy of Neurology (AAN), the Child Neurology Society (CNS), the American Academy of Pediatrics (AAP), and the International Standard Cytogenomic Array (ISCA) Consortium (baylorgenetics.com/cma).

Whole exome sequencing has become the next level of common testing when you need to find more detail than what a CMA can provide. The exome is all of the exons your DNA produces that serve as the protein coding instructions for your body. Sequencing is a technology that screens a person's DNA at its smallest components in the exome, allowing scientists to compare the child's exons to the exons from a person without known disorders. Additionally, there are now whole genome testing options as well, which function in many ways as a combination of whole exome sequencing and a CMA. Frequent clinical use of both of these sophisticated tests is often limited by cost.

Metabolic testing for neurologically compromised children focuses on disorders of breaking down carbohydrates, fats, or proteins for energy; changing excess nitrogen into waste products; or altering other chemicals for use, clearance, or storage. Some of these disorders may initially present with nonspecific abnormalities on electrolyte panels as well as blood glucose or liver function testing. The clinical history and physical examination can further help direct testing for the suspected functional area of metabolic dysfunction. Metabolic testing can be performed on urine, blood/serum or even biopsies of affected organs; however, the details of the potential tests exceed the scope of our discussion.

The last common area of testing you may see from a neurologist is mitochondrial testing. Mitochondria are the energy-producing organelles inside all our cells, and they maintain their own mitochondrial DNA. Mitochondria depend on the mitochondria DNA as well as the nuclear DNA in each cell to work normally. Mitochondrial disorders often impact multiple organ systems such as the brain, eyes, muscles, or liver, and are suspected more often when there are multiple organ systems involved in one patient. Mitochondrial DNA contains 37 genes, with 13 of these genes providing instructions for making enzymes that use oxygen and simple sugars to create adenosine triphosphate (ATP), the cell's main energy source (https://ghr.nlm.nih.gov/mitochondrial-dna). Damage or dysfunction of the mitochondrial DNA can result in severe disorders affecting multiple organs. Disorders of nuclear DNA that affect the mitochondrial function can range from very mild to severe, depending on which of the hundreds of genes is affected. Information on these disorders can be found through the Genetics Home Reference webpage of the National Institute of Health's US National Library of Medicine at https://ghr.nlm.nih.gov.

Often, neuropsychological studies may be requested. If there are school-related issues regarding the child's learning, affect, and/or behavior, the neurologist may also request educational studies as a part of this evaluation. For many neurologically compromised children, neuropsychological evaluation may be the key step in determining the direction of further neurodiagnostic testing or potential medical intervention for the pediatric neurologist.

The process

When a child and his/her parents arrive for a neuropsychoeducational evaluation, the first thing that must be done is to verify the reason for the consultation.

If the parents (either biological or adoptive) are divorced or never married, both parents must allow the examination to commence. If the parents are married, only one parent needs to give written permission to proceed. In the case of guardianship, legal proof must be offered.

Then, the examination may begin. When referred by the pediatric neurologist, typically medical information has been received before the initial clinical family interview. If this information has not been received, a written request to receive the child's file and referral information must be completed. In America, this request is usually sent by fax to the pediatric neurologist's office.

Before the initial clinical family interview, the following vital signs are taken: height, weight, blood pressure, and pulse. Then, a mental status examination is conducted, addressing the following variables (Table 1):

The child's parents have also been asked to complete a checklist reviewing any significant psychological and physical symptoms (Fig. 1, Williams, 2019):

Afterward, the reason for the referral is addressed. Careful behavioral observations are made and the desired outcome of this evaluation is discussed. For example, clarification of the following questions may be included:

1. What is the child's brain-behavior functioning?
2. What is the child's intellectual functioning?
3. What is the child's educational functioning?
4. What is the child's emotional functioning?
5. Does the child have any learning disabilities?
6. Does the child have autism or Asperger's disorder?
7. Does the child have a bipolar disorder (BD) or a serious mental illness (SMI)?
8. Does the child have an attentional deficit hyperactivity disorder (ADHD)?

Although these questions are typically the most common ones, there may be other concerns as well.

TABLE 1 Example of mental status examination form.

	(Normal) YES	NO			(Normal) YES	NO	
General appearance	☐	☐	______	Thought content	☐	☐	______
Attitude	☐	☐	______	Preoccupations	☐	☐	______
Gait	☐	☐	______	Hallucination/delusion	☐	☐	______
Health	☐	☐	______	Suicidality/homicidality	☐	☐	______
Activity level	☐	☐	______	Cognition/thinking	☐	☐	______
Speech	☐	☐	______	Memory	☐	☐	______
Level of consciousness	☐	☐	______	Intoxication	☐	☐	______
Affect and mood	☐	☐	______	Confidence in MSE	☐	☐	______

Risk level: High Medium Low No risk
Risk management:
(if needed)

PLEASE CHECK SYMPTOMS THAT APPLY TO YOU (FRONT AND BACK).

PSYCHOLOGICAL SYMPTOMS

MOOD

- ☐ Excessive sadness
- ☐ No interest in things
- ☐ Moving slowly
- ☐ Feeling hopeless /worthless
- ☐ Feeling guilty
- ☐ Can't make decisions
- ☐ Social withdrawal
- ☐ Less talkative
- ☐ Thoughts of suicide
- ☐ Intensely happy or angry
- ☐ More talkative
- ☐ Racing thoughts
- ☐ Risky behaviors
- ☐ Cutting/self-harm
- ☐ Thoughts of suicide
- ☐ Suicide attempt

ANXIETY

- ☐ Excessive worry
- ☐ Feeling tense/"on-edge"
- ☐ Afraid of future
- ☐ Panic attacks
- ☐ Fears
- ☐ Unwelcome thoughts
- ☐ Obsessions / compulsions
- ☐ Social anxiety
- ☐ Phobias
- ☐ Nightmares
- ☐ Disturbing memories of past
- ☐ Feeling detached
- ☐ Avoiding reminders of past
- ☐ Jumpy/Easily Startled
- ☐ Feeling numb
- ☐ Avoiding situations

THOUGHT SYMPTOMS

- ☐ I am being conspired against
- ☐ I am being followed or recorded
- ☐ People hear my thoughts
- ☐ People put thoughts in my head
- ☐ People steal my thoughts
- ☐ Someone I know was replaced by an imposter
- ☐ A celebrity loves me
- ☐ My thoughts influence world events
- ☐ I have special powers
- ☐ Excessive jealousy
- ☐ Reality does not exist
- ☐ I receive special messages from media sources
- ☐ I see things others can't
- ☐ I hear things others can't

MEMORY/NEUROPSYCH

- ☐ Problems remembering recent events
- ☐ Problems remembering past events
- ☐ Problems keeping things in mind
- ☐ Word finding problems

EXECUTIVE FUNCTIONS

- ☐ Problems planning
- ☐ Problems starting tasks
- ☐ Problems keeping track of things
- ☐ Poor impulse control
- ☐ Poor time management
- ☐ Problems shifting from one thing to another
- ☐ Difficulty keeping up with conversation
- ☐ Problem controlling emotion

ADHD / CONDUCT

- ☐ Poor attention
- ☐ Not appearing to listen
- ☐ Not completing tasks
- ☐ Poor organization
- ☐ Avoid thinking
- ☐ Losing things
- ☐ Easily distracted
- ☐ Forgetful
- ☐ Fidgeting
- ☐ Act or feel like driven by a motor
- ☐ Blurting out
- ☐ Impatient
- ☐ Hot temper
- ☐ Argumentative
- ☐ Defiant
- ☐ Blame others
- ☐ Spiteful
- ☐ Aggression

ADAPTIVE FUNCTIONS

- ☐ Hygiene problems
- ☐ Toileting problems
- ☐ Money management problems
- ☐ Can't perform daily activities

SUBSTANCE USE

- ☐ Tobacco use
- ☐ Alcohol use
- ☐ Drug use
- ☐ Relapse

LIFE STRESS PROBLEMS

- ☐ Loss of loved one
- ☐ Marriage problems
- ☐ Custody problems
- ☐ Child management issues
- ☐ Problems with friends
- ☐ Excessive job stress
- ☐ Poor job satisfaction
- ☐ Unemployment
- ☐ Financial problems
- ☐ Access to care problems
- ☐ Criminal legal problems
- ☐ Civil legal problems
- ☐ Housing problems
- ☐ Hunger
- ☐ Poverty
- ☐ Natural disaster survivor
- ☐ Abuse survivor

FIG. 1 Example of symptom checklist presented to patients at the initial clinical interview.

PHYSICAL SYMPTOMS

CONSTITUTIONAL
- ☐ Weight loss/gain
- ☐ Fatigue
- ☐ Fever/chills
- ☐ Weakness
- ☐ Sleep disturbance
- ☐ Pain all over

EARS/NOSE/MOUTH/THROAT
- ☐ Hearing problems
- ☐ Sinus issues / runny nose
- ☐ Ringing in the ears
- ☐ Nosebleeds
- ☐ Sore throat
- ☐ Mouth sores

SKIN
- ☐ Rash
- ☐ Itching
- ☐ Dryness
- ☐ Color changes
- ☐ Hair/nail changes
- ☐ Breast Lumps
- ☐ Nipple discharge
- ☐ Breast pain
- ☐ Hair loss

CARDIOVASCULAR
- ☐ Skipping heartbeats
- ☐ Irregular heartbeats
- ☐ Racing heart
- ☐ Chest pain
- ☐ Swelling in feet/legs
- ☐ High blood pressure
- ☐ Leg pain while walking
- ☐ Nightsweats

RESPIRATORY
- ☐ Short of breath
- ☐ Cough
- ☐ Cough up blood
- ☐ Wheezing
- ☐ Blue fingers/toes
- ☐ Sleep apnea

GASTROINTESTINAL
- ☐ Heartburn
- ☐ Constipation
- ☐ Diarrhea
- ☐ Abdominal pain
- ☐ Nausea / Vomiting
- ☐ Bright red blood in stool
- ☐ Dark blood in stool
- ☐ Change in bowel habits

GENITOURINARY
- ☐ Painful urination
- ☐ Frequent urination
- ☐ Urinary urgency
- ☐ Incomplete bladder emptying
- ☐ Dribbling
- ☐ Erectile dysfunction
- ☐ Genital pain
- ☐ Bladder problems
- ☐ Testicular pain or swelling
- ☐ Discharge from genitals
- ☐ STD / STI

MUSCULOSKELATAL
- ☐ Joint pain
- ☐ Joint swelling
- ☐ Muscle pain
- ☐ Neck pain
- ☐ Shoulder pain
- ☐ Low back pain
- ☐ Muscle stiffness
- ☐ Arthritis
- ☐ Gout

NEUROLOGICAL
- ☐ Headaches
- ☐ Double vision
- ☐ Weakness
- ☐ Change in sensation
- ☐ Dizziness-Room spinning
- ☐ Dizziness-Fainting
- ☐ Dizziness-Imbalance
- ☐ Tremor
- ☐ Muscle spasms
- ☐ Loss of consciousness
- ☐ Involuntary movements
- ☐ Numbness
- ☐ Tingling (pins and needles)
- ☐ Seizures
- ☐ Memory loss
- ☐ Tics

ENDOCRINE
- ☐ Intolerance to heat/cold
- ☐ Menstrual irregularities
- ☐ Frequent hunger/thirst/urination
- ☐ Changes in sex drive
- ☐ Excessive sweating
- ☐ Thyroid problems

HEMATOLOGIC
- ☐ Easy Bleeding
- ☐ Easy Bruising
- ☐ Anemia
- ☐ Enlarged lymph nodes
- ☐ Recent transfusion

IMMUNOLOGIC
- ☐ Hives
- ☐ Seasonal allergies
- ☐ Environmental allergies
- ☐ Food sensitivities
- ☐ HIV exposure

MEDICATION CHANGES

____
____
____
____
____
____
____
____

RECENT MEDICAL PROCEDURES OR MEDICAL STATUS CHANGES

____
____
____
____
____
____
____
____

FIG. 1, CONT'D

Frequently used measures

In America, the pediatric neuropsychologist may choose from the following noninclusive list of tests to answer the referral questions. For young children ages 5–8, the Reitan-Indiana Neuropsychological Test Battery (RINB) may be included in the examination. For older children ages 9–14, the Halstead-Reitan Neuropsychological Test Battery for Older Children (HRNB-OC) is often used. Over age 14, the adult Halstead-Reitan Neuropsychological Test Battery (HRNB) may be utilized.

Intellectual functioning:
- SIT (ages 2 +)
- PPVT (ages 2–90)
- RIAS-II (ages 3 +)
- WPPSI-III (ages 4–7.3)
- WASI (ages 6 +)
- WISC-V (ages 6–16)
- WAIS-IV (ages 16 +)
- Shipley-2 (ages 14 +)

Education/achievement:
- Bracken (ages 2–7)
- WJ-A (ages 5 +)
- WRAT-4 (ages 5 +)
- WIAT (ages 5 +)
- PIAT-R (ages 5–21)

Cognitive functioning:
- WJ-C (ages 5 +)

Attentional functioning:
- Brown (SR, PR, TR)
- Conners (PR, TR)
- TOVA (ages 4 +)
- TEACH (ages 6–15)
- Marching (ages 5–8)
- Trail Making Test, Parts A and B (ages 9–14; age 15 +)

Adaptive behavioral/development:
- Vineland-II
- ABAS

Autism/Asperger's:
- CARS
- GARS
- GADS (age 3–22)

Affective functioning:
- CDI-2 (ages 7–17)
- CAS (ages 5–13)
- MDI-C (ages 8–17)
- TSC-children (ages 8–16)
- MDI (ages 14 +)
- SCL-90-R (ages 13–17)

Language/reading functioning:
- GORT (grades 2–12)
- WJ-Oral Language (grades Pre-K—adult)
- CTOPP (ages 5–24)
- ITPA-3 (ages 5–12)
- PPVT (ages 2–90)
- WRMT (ages 5 +)
- SORT (ages 2 +)
- TLC-E (ages 5–16)
- Nelson Denny (grades 9 +)

Neuropsychological functioning:
- RINB (ages 5–8)
- HRNB-OC (ages 9–14)
- HRNB (ages 15 +)
- NEPSY-II (ages 3–16)
- DKEFS (ages 8–80)
- Stroop (ages 7 +)
- Melendez
- CNS Vital Signs (ages 8–90)

Executive functioning:
- Category Test—YC (ages 5–8)
- HCT-OC (ages 9–14)
- HCT (ages 15 +)
- Tower of London (ages 7 +)
- BRIEF-2 (SR, PR, TR; ages 11–18)
- TVCF

The IEP meeting

When children have school-related issues, a formal neuropsychoeducational evaluation is conducted to help them receive special educational services.

Although these services are guaranteed by law in America, the parents must formally request an individualized educational plan (IEP) meeting in writing. At the time of the IEP meeting, the parents usually present a copy of the child's comprehensive, independently obtained neuropsychoeducational evaluation, which includes the pediatric neurologist's request and the child's medical records. Among the most frequently required special services are accommodations for seizure disorders, learning disabilities, autism spectrum disorders, bipolar disorders, and attention deficit hyperactivity disorders (ADHD).

Are medications needed?

When the neuropsychoeducational report is received by the pediatric neurologist, usually there is a phone consultation regarding medication management. The pediatric neurologist will take the lead on medically and metabolically based problems. For example, seizure disorders are typically regulated by the pediatric neurologist. In the state of Louisiana in America, there are pediatric neuropsychologists who are trained to prescribe medications for several of these disorders, such as ADHD. This, however, is usually done in collaboration with the pediatric neurologist, pediatric cardiologist, or pediatrician.

Should there be a decision to medicate, the pediatric neurologist typically explores the child's symptom presentation and the results of the child's neuropsychological or neuropsychoeducational evaluation before choosing specific medications. This pharmacotherapy is done in collaboration with the parents, who will typically be administering these drugs. If a school nurse is involved, both the parents and the physician must give written permission to dispense these medications at school.

What medications for what symptoms?

When the decision to initiate a pharmacotherapeutic intervention for a neurologically compromised child is made between the providers and the patient/patient's family or caregivers, commonly it is due to the desire to remove a symptom-based obstacle for the child that is preventing the full benefit of therapeutic interventions from a cognitive, academic, psychological, and/or physical standpoint. Therefore, the medication is chosen to alleviate a specific obstacle or, for some children, multiple obstacles and thus allow for a greater impact to the core disorder or dysfunction by the therapeutic intervention or academic regimen. Alternatively, some children undergo medication programs to help with the daily care provided by the family. The burden carried by some families can be great. Having the family maintain a good quality of life where the parents can focus their energy on therapeutic reinforcement and developing a good parent-child relationship is invaluable. Lastly, there are symptoms that require treatment for the safety of the child, for example, seizures, pica, or severe impulse control disorders.

Symptom-based approaches

In the following sections, a symptom-based approach to nine common neurological or neuropsychological disorders that may present to the pediatric neurologist and their potential pharmacologic interventions will be presented. We will not explore more common psychiatric symptoms such as depression, bipolar disorder, or anxiety, as those would be less likely to present to or be addressed by a pediatric neurologist. Recommendations will be evidence-based, unless noted otherwise, and are not intended to be a supplement to clinical training and/or collaboration with an experienced prescribing provider. The medical treatments are not meant to be exhaustive and will focus on medications with indications for use in pediatric patients or that have gained common clinical use in this specific population. Some medications or medication types may be presented under multiple sections.

Attention deficit and hyperactivity disorders

Although the classic diagnosis of ADHD gets much of the attention, there are a number of children who do not yet fit the criteria established by the American Academy of Pediatrics for an ADHD diagnosis (Subcommittee on Attention Deficit/Hyperactivity Disorder, Steering Committee on Quality Improvement and Management, 2011) who still struggle with severe hyperactivity, which limits developmental attainment and is commonly classified as a behavioral/emotional problem (Lavigne et al., 1993). In children younger than 4 who demonstrate severe hyperactivity and who have failed behavioral interventions, there are fewer medication options than in the older age groups. Stimulants do not have an indication in this age range and therefore off-label interventions must be utilized.

There is a small amount of literature to support alpha-2 adrenergic agonist use for these patients (Black, Soden, Kearns, & Jones, 2016); thus, the main focus of discussion is on guanfacine. Guanfacine can be useful to help decrease the degree of hyperactivity and allow the child to respond better to behavioral intervention. It can also help after school to improve working memory. Doses can range from 0.25 mg once daily and higher as needed and can be tolerated up to three times daily. In patients where guanfacine could not be tolerated due to somnolence or ineffectiveness, oxcarbazepine can be used successfully. This medication has been researched down to 1 month of age for epilepsy (Piña-Garza et al., 2005) with somnolence and pyrexia (elevated body temperature) as the most common side effects in this young age group. Given its off-label use as a mood stabilizer (Emrich, Dose, & Von Zerssen, 1985; Muller & Stoll, 1984), it can confer some stabilization of the hyperactivity, in combination with its common side effect of somnolence or fatigue, to decrease the child's hyperactivity. Doses tend to start at 10 mg/kg/day divided into two doses and titrated up to 20–30 mg/kg/day as needed and tolerated for behavioral impact.

In children 6 years of age and up with diagnosed ADHD, stimulants in the methylphenidate or amphetamine categories may be used (Stahl, 2017). A select few of the short-acting stimulants are approved and can be used in children ages 4–5 years of age; however, some providers try to utilize some of the newer long-acting liquid formulations. With the two basic types of stimulants, methylphenidates and amphetamines, there is no clear evidence to support one over the other based on potential efficacy. Providers tend to develop their own approach to prescribing these medications, but if prescribers treat a lot of ADHD, they should have a wide array of methods with many different indicated medications in play for patients.

One approach involves using medications based on the timing of symptoms that are most prevalent for each individual patient by juxtaposing the pharmacological properties of the medication with the timing of the most problematic symptom. For example, considering a medication with a 50-50 extended release format for someone with higher morning symptoms due to the requirements of the start of the day and possible higher concentration of intellectual needs at school in the morning. Compare that situation to a child with sustained intellectual needs throughout the day who may do better with a more distributed release format such as a 30-70 release, prodrug limited absorption, or even a newer triphasic option. A second approach involves looking at comorbidities and the potential for worsening or improving them with the various stimulant agents. For example, issues with insomnia are a common concern for longer-acting stimulant medications and can influence choices to help prevent worsening of any preexisting insomnia. The third approach, and perhaps the most important, is finding a stimulant the child can routinely take without a high risk of noncompliance. The less frequent a dose is required (Srivastava et al., 2013) and an easier route of administration (less medication manipulation) can improve compliance for many medications, although no formal studies on compliance have been performed within the ADHD population.

A combination of the three approaches will help bring a provider to the best initial option for the patient. Rapid feedback is important with the initiation of a stimulant medication and adjustments can be made every few days based on response and tolerability until the correct dose or medication is identified for each patient. Common stimulant medication side effects include sleep problems, weight loss, decreased appetite, rebound hyperactivity and irritability, and headaches. Please find in Table 2 each medication's specific list of adverse effects for specific concerns for each compound and formulation.

Nonstimulants can also be used in ADHD patients and may be preferable in certain populations, including those with comorbid sleep disorders or tic disorders or those who may be underweight. The aforementioned guanfacine can be used in this population. There is the additional option of Intuniv (guanfacine ER), which can confer better tolerance of the guanfacine molecule by giving a lower maximum concentration and slower time to maximum concentration in a milligram-to-milligram dose comparison (Intuniv package insert).

TABLE 2 **ADHD stimulant medications (available in the United States).**

Category	Short/intermediate-acting	Long-acting
Methylphenidate	Methylphenidate HCl, Methylin[a], Ritalin[a]	Adhansia XR, Aptensio XR, Concerta[a], Contempla XR ODT, Daytrana, Jornay PM, Metadate CD[a], Quillichew ER, Quillivant XR, Ritalin LA[a], Ritalin SR[a]
Dexmethyphenidate	Focalin[a]	Focalin XR[a]
Amphetamine		Adzenys ER, Adzenys XR-ODT, Dynavel XR
Dextroamphetamine	Dexedrine, ProCentra[a], Zenzedi	Dexedrine ER
Methamphetamine	Desoxyn	
Mixed amphetamine salts	Adderall[a]	Adderall XR[a], Mydayis
Amphetamine sulfate	Evekeo	
Lisdexamphetamine		Vyvanse

[a]*Available generic product.*

Typically, the hyperactive symptoms tend to respond better to guanfacine in its various forms compared to inattentive symptoms. Another alpha-2 adrenergic agonist that may be used in the older ADHD patients is Kapvay (clonidine ER). Whereas the immediate-release clonidine tends to be too sedating for ADHD use, the extended-release version decreases the pharmacokinetic properties (similar to the way guanfacine ER compares to guanfacine), creating diminished levels of a comparative equal dose of clonidine (Kapvay package insert) that result in a clinically observed decrease in side effect prominence. Both medications still have sedation/somnolence as the most common side effect, even in the extended-release versions.

Another nonstimulant medication with an on-label indication for ADHD is Strattera (atomoxetine). Atomoxetine is a selective norepinephrine reuptake inhibitor indicated for the treatment of ADHD (Strattera package insert) in children and adults. Preventing use by some providers is the boxed warning of suicidal ideation in children and adolescents. In the studies for atomoxetine, ADHD symptoms improved on the ADHDRS scale; nevertheless, clinically there has been the discovery of more potency in the inattentiveness categories of ADHD with lower efficacy in hyperactivity. Additionally, it can take a few weeks on therapy to see the maximal benefit of atomoxetine through titration and a few weeks on the initial goal dose (Cascade, Kalali, & Feifel, 2007). In children, the slow titration improves tolerability; however, providers need to watch for gastrointestinal side effects and fatigue.

Wellbutrin XL (bupropion) has an off-label use for ADHD for patients with comorbid mood disorders or with substance use disorders (Bond et al., 2012). This medication is anecdotally used less by neurologists in general because of the concern for lowering the seizure threshold and creating abnormalities in the EEG (Wellbutrin XL package insert).

Sleep disorders

Sleep is an area that tends to be overlooked or minimized in clinical practice due to a high prevalence of the problem. Estimates are around 30% of all children may have sleep abnormalities at some point in childhood; understanding what normal sleep is for the age of the child is important to start the evaluation. The American Academy of Sleep Medicine (*assm.org*) produced a consensus statement in 2016 for the amount of sleep various age groups of children should be expected to attain per night or 24-h period. Behavioral and environmental issues are the cause of many sleep issues and can be corrected without medication intervention. Occasionally, there will be children with sleep issues that go beyond behavioral or environmental causes and require medical or even surgical interventions.

Insomnia is the most common pediatric sleep problem that would require medical intervention. Clinically, insomnia can be divided between sleep onset, sleep maintenance, or a combination of onset and maintenance issues to help direct intervention, as medications tend to have pharmacokinetic and pharmacodynamic properties that may be advantageous for different types of insomnia. Without question, cognitive behavioral therapy for insomnia (CBIT) is recommended as a first-line therapy in adults and adolescents (Trauer, Qian, Doyle, Rajaratnam, & Cunnington, 2015). However, younger children may struggle to implement the needed understanding and actions to make it as effective as it can be in older children and adults. For children who do not achieve full benefit with nonmedical interventions, short-term medication interventions should be considered. The use of medications commonly associated with adult insomnia treatments do not have any studies noting clear benefits in pediatric patients, although some have studies showing tolerability (e.g., eszopiclone). Zolpidem had studies showing both tolerability and neuropsychiatric adverse effects (Anand et al., 2017).

With a lack of quality studies, the following chart outlines a possible approach to off-label use of medications and supplements based on the timing of the patient's insomnia from my clinical practice (Table 3):

Additionally, the side effects of other medications being prescribed for epilepsy, behavioral disorder, headaches, and other CNS disorders can be used to strategically augment any behavioral or medical intervention for insomnia.

TABLE 3 Possible approaches to off-label use of medications and supplements in treating insomnia.

Insomnia	Agent	Dosing	Articles
Sleep onset	Clonidine	0.05–0.3 mg QHS	Hunt, Minderaa, and Cohen (1985)
	Melatonin	0.5–10 mg QHS	Numerous, see Schwichtenberg and Malow (2015)
Sleep maintenance	Clonazepam	<30 kg: 0.005–0.01 mg/kg QPM >30 kg: 0.25–1 mg QPM	
	Amitriptyline	>30 kg: 10–50 mg QPM (max 1 mg/kg)	
Mixed	Gabapentin	<20 kg: 5 mg/kg QPM >20 kg: 100–300 mg QPM	
	Trazodone	25–200 mg QPM	Hollway and Aman (2011)
	Pregabalin	25–100 mg QPM	

Some children may report insomnias related to a restless leg-like phenomenon. In this specific population, it is very important to check serum iron and ferritin levels. Low ferritin levels can cause these symptoms in children and adults, and there is a very good response to iron supplementation (Rulong, Dye, & Simakajornboon, 2018).

Obstructive sleep apnea, or the broader terminology of sleep disordered breathing, is not a disorder that will respond to medication interventions outside severe allergy disorders causing airflow restriction. As noted earlier in this chapter, it can play a role in complicating development with even typical children suffering from daytime sleepiness, hyperactivity, trouble with learning, and behavior and personality function at an almost threefold increase over children with normal sleep. Apply these same effects to the neurologically compromised child and you will see the inherent challenges increase (Bonuck & Grant, 2012). Additionally, children with neurological syndromes or injuries may have higher risk factors for symptoms that predispose to sleep disordered breathing such as obesity, a low airway tone, a smaller airway size, or an enlarged tongue size. If patients have any of these predisposing risk factors, a much higher sensitivity to ordering a polysomnogram to determine the presence or absence of hypopneas (not moving enough air) or apneas (not moving any air) in a neurologically compromised child must be maintained. Subsequent surgical correction, appliance use, or airway assistance through mechanical positive airway pressure systems can diminish the disruption of airflow and limit the developmental impact of the sleep disordered breathing, although clinical research has not shown the benefits of a specific intervention as being superior (Kuhle, Urschitz, Eitner, & Poets, 2009).

Seizures and epilepsy

The presence of seizures that lead to a diagnosis of epilepsy is a big problem in the neurologically compromised child, beginning with the initial diagnosis. Children can present with a myriad of abnormal behaviors that may or may not be epileptic in nature. Careful history and evaluation with an electroencephalogram are the most important steps, but they can still leave an unclear picture as to the etiology of some events. Prevalence rates specific to children with neurodevelopment disorders are not easily available, as some disorders may rarely have seizures and other disorders have seizures as a dominant feature. Furthermore, some epilepsies can cause epileptic encephalopathies, whereas the neurodevelopmental symptoms are potentially secondary to the seizures or the underlying defect that manifests as seizure activity.

Once the child is thought to have an epileptic process, the diagnosis will be categorized by the International League Against Epilepsy's classification scheme as a focal, generalized, combined generalized and focal, or unknown epilepsy (Scheffer et al., 2017). These classifications are important as they help dictate treatment choice, as the indications of different anticonvulsant medications are studied and indicated for use based on epilepsy type. The following replace "chart" with "table" to be consistent with labelingchart lists medications by the generic name that are available in the United States and their indications for use in epilepsy. Not all these medications will have pediatric indications; however, off-label use is commonplace in pediatric epilepsy. Additionally, some of the older medications did not go through the same clinical trials as medications from the 1990s and later, and therefore their indication is based on clinical use data in place of clinical trial data (Table 4).

The choice of anticonvulsant medication is a very complex process and will vary from provider to provider. We do not yet have enough genetic data aligned with clinical pharmacology to have a specific global intervention algorithm for individuals with epilepsy. Therefore, treatment is based on clinical data, electroencephalogram features, and indications for epilepsy type. The route of administration also becomes a major issue in pediatric patients, in addition to choosing medications that have pediatric indications over medications where use would be off-label. Comorbid disorders can help a provider choose an anticonvulsant from the list, as select anticonvulsants have additional indications for treating headaches, behavioral disorders, sleep disorders, pain disorders, and movement disorders (discussed in the relevant sections).

TABLE 4 Anticonvulsant medications.

Medication	Indication(s)	Notes
Brivaracetam	Focal (M,A)	
Cannabidiol oral solution		Seizures associated with Lennox-Gastaut syndrome and Dravet syndrome
Carbamazepine (ER)	Focal, Generalized, Mixed (M,A)	
Clobazam		Seizures associated with Lennox-Gastaut syndrome
Clonazepam[a]	Focal, Generalized, Mixed (M,A)	
Diazepam[a]	Focal, Generalized, Mixed (M,A)	
Divalproex sodium (ER)	Focal, Generalized, Mixed (M,A)	
Eslicarbazepine	Focal (M,A)	
Ethosuximide	Generalized (M,A)	
Ezogabine	Focal (A)	No longer available in the United States
Felbamate	Focal (M,A)	Seizures associated with Lennox-Gastaut syndrome
Gabapentin	Focal (A)	
Lacosamide	Focal (M,A)	
Lamotrigine (ER)	Focal, Generalized, Mixed (M,A)	Generalized seizures associated with Lennox-Gastaut syndrome
Levetiracetam (XR)	Focal, Generalized, Mixed (A)	Accepted as monotherapy
Lorazepam[a]	Focal, Generalized, Mixed (M,A)	
Oxcarbapezine (XR)	Focal (M,A)	
Perampanel	Focal, Generalized, Mixed (M,A)	Monotherapy only with focal
Phenobarbital[a]	Focal, Generalized, Mixed (M,A)	
Phenytoin[a]	Focal, Generalized, Mixed (M,A)	

TABLE 4 Anticonvulsant medications—cont'd

Medication	Indication(s)	Notes
Pregabalin	Focal (A)	
Primidone[a]	Focal, Generalized, Mixed (M,A)	
Rufinamide		Adjunctive therapy for seizures associated with Lennox-Gastaut syndrome
Tiagabine	Focal (A)	
Topiramate (XR)	Focal, Generalized, Mixed (M,A)	Seizures associated with Lennox-Gastaut syndrome
Valproic acid	Focal, Generalized, Mixed (M,A)	
Vigabatrin	Focal (A)—*refractory only*	Monotherapy in infantile spasms
Zonisamide	Focal (A)	Accepted as monotherapy and for use in generalized or mixed epilepsies

M, monotherapy, *A*, adjunctive therapy.
[a] *Older anticonvulsant with indications based on historical use.*
Adapted from Seizure Medication List, Epilepsy Foundation.

The side effects of anticonvulsant medications vary from agent to agent; however, there are some common adverse reactions that providers need to monitor closely due to the potential worsening of neurocognitive function in typically developing children and with even greater impact in neurologically compromised children. The presence of somnolence, fatigue, dizziness, headaches, nausea and vomiting, cognitive slowing, and vision changes all can potentially be seen with the use of anticonvulsant medications, even when they provide good control of the seizures. Education of the possible side effects of each specific medication is important for the patient and any caregivers to help improve the sensitivity for detecting negative impacts in neurocognitive functioning.

Headaches

Headaches are a very common problem in adults and pediatric patients, with around 33%–40% of school-aged children having headaches once per week (Straube, Heinen, Ebinger, & von Kries, 2013). Headaches are reactive to nonmedical risk factors such as a dysfunctional family situation, caffeine ingestion, smoking, obesity, a low level of physical activity, physical or emotional abuse, bullying by peers, unfair treatment in school, and insufficient leisure time (Russo, Bruno, Trojsi, Tessitore, & Tedeschi, 2016; Straube et al., 2013). Mild acute headaches can be treated with nonmedication intervention (rest, eating, cold/warn compress); normal doses of nonprescriptive medications such as acetaminophen, ibuprofen, and naproxen; or with supplements containing magnesium, caffeine, B-vitamins, feverfew, or butterbur. Occasionally, strong prescriptive medications will be needed to help abort headaches; however, because of their intermittent use and limited duration of side effects, the focus will be more on those patients whose chronic headache burden requires preventative treatments, as those daily medications may have a greater impact on function in the neurologically compromised child.

It is important to understand the types of headaches commonly seen in children. The first step is always to rule out any underlying dangerous secondary causes of headaches such as tumors, infection, or increased intracranial pressure, to name a few (Gelfand, 2018). Once this child's headaches have been established as a primary headache syndrome, clinicians will find that migraine headaches and tension-type headaches prevail as the most common two that warrant prevention treatment. Other less-common primary headache syndromes in children are posttraumatic headache, daily persistent headache, and stabbing headache, which in some circumstances may also warrant preventative care.

Migraine headaches in the pediatric population have been well studied for both abortive and prevention therapies. Prevention therapies are aimed not only at medications, but lifestyle changes alone or in combination with medication. Having patients try to prevent unnecessary changes in daily schedules and transitions, work toward adequate sleep, avoid skipping meals, maintain good hydration, control caffeine intake, and exercise can be very helpful in reducing headache frequency. Cognitive-behavioral therapy has also been shown to help reduce migraines in adolescents when combined with medication, even more than medication and lifestyle advice (Gelfand, 2018). From a medication standpoint, the only medication with an indication for migraine prevention in children ages 12–17 is topiramate; however, that option is not the only medication used. The following chart (Table 5) presents other options for headache prevention in the pediatric population that have not been shown in any placebo-controlled clinical trials, but have common use in clinical practice.

New migraine prevention therapies are recently coming to use, including calcitonin gene-related peptide manipulators, but they are without any evidence of safety or efficacy in children below 18 years of age.

Tension-type headaches may also need prevention therapies if they are burdensome with a frequency of more than 4–6 per month. Many of the same prevention treatments used for migraine headache prevention can also be used for tension-type headache prevention with a higher prevalence of nonmedical or nonprescriptive treatments in these patients. If needed, the same prescriptive options can also be utilized.

TABLE 5 Options for headache prevention in the pediatric population.

Category	Agent	
Antidepressant	Amitriptyline	> 30 kg: 10–50 mg QPM (max 1 mg/kg/day)
	Sertraline	These agents work best with comorbid stress, anxiety, or depressive orders; no large studies in children with migraine; no established doses
	Fluoxetine	
	Venlafaxine	
Antihypertensive	Propranolol	Beta-blocker, avoid in asthmatics; no established doses
	Verapamil	Calcium-channel blocker; no established doses
	Candesartan	Angiotensin II receptor blocker; teratogenicity risk; no established doses
Anticonvulsant	Topiramate	Approved for 12–17 year olds; can be used in very young children with migraine (studied down to 3 months of age in epilepsy)
	Valproic acid	Teratogenicity risk
	Zonisamide	Fewer cognitive and paraesthesia side effects than topiramate
	Gabapentin	More effective if symptoms of cervical nerve irritability with headache
Other	Riboflavin	400 mg/day in adult study
	Melatonin	3 mg dose in adult trial showed efficacy even to amitriptyline at 25 mg
	Butterbur	Adult evidence for Petadolex version specifically, some caution against use due to possible presence of pyrrolizide alkaloids in butterbur products (hepatotoxic); none found in Petadolex
	Riboflavin, magnesium, fevefew	Compound sold as Children's Migrelief
	Botulinum toxin A	Injection

Adapted from Gelfand, A. A. (2018). Pediatric and adolescent headache. *CONTINUUM: Lifelong learning in Neurology, 24*(4), 1108–1136. https://doi.org/10.1212/CON.0000000000000638; Bravo, T. P., & Vargas, B. B. (2015). Migraine preventative butterbur has safety concerns. *Neurology Times;* migrelief.com; Tajti, J., Szok, D., Csáti, A., & Vécsei, L. (2016). Prophylactic drug treatment of migraine in children and adolescents: An update. *Current Pain and Headache Reports, 20*(1), 1. https://doi.org/10.1007/s11916-015-0536-6.

Tic disorders

Abnormal movements are a common presenting symptom that will be referred to a pediatric neurologist. A number of these cases will turn out to be tics. Education and treatment can begin within the first visit. Tics can range from transient tics of childhood on the mild end of the spectrum to the commonly misperceived Tourette syndrome on the more severe end of the spectrum. Fortunately, after educating the patient and family, most children will not need any medication to treat their tics. A two-stage approach to evaluate the need for medication is recommended:

1. Do the tics bother you? Do the tics get attention placed on you that bothers you? Are the tics causing a disruption or distraction when trying to do schoolwork or activities? Do the tics cause physical pain?
2. If yes to any of the above questions, is it bad enough to take a medication every day?

Many children would answer positive to one of the initial four questions; however, most would answer in the negative about taking a daily medication. In patients who would answer in the affirmative about taking a daily medication, generally, the presenting pain related to the tics is the most common reason in preadolescents. Also, the social impacts of the first two questions typically drove medication decisions for adolescent patients.

In patients who present with a tic disorder, it is also important to screen them for ADHD and obsessive-compulsive symptoms or disorder (Tagwerker Gloor & Walitza, 2016). This triad of symptoms is a common finding and in cases where the full triad is not present, two of the three symptoms may be active in the patient. These comorbidities with tic disorder can heavily influence treatment decisions in trying to improve tics (treating OCD) or attempting to not provoke tics (treating ADHD), even when the provider is not initiating a therapy for the tics. Also, it may be that these symptoms need to be treated first and that the tics may improve following better control of ADHD or OCD (Shprecher & Kurlan, 2009).

When choosing to start a treatment for tics, there are generally first-line agents in the form of an alpha-2 agonist, second-line agents that are dopamine-blocking antipsychotic agents, and then many alternative medications with limited studies, case reports, or small case series data only. Common tic treatments are noted in the following chart (Table 6) with comments specific to each agent relative to dosing or side effects.

The alpha-2 agonists as a group are milder in potency compared to the dopamine-acting medications and are each limited by sedation side effects; however, the more extended release versions may have improved tolerability and allow for more effective dosing compared to the immediate release versions. The dopamine-acting medications fall into the antipsychotic classes of atypical antipsychotics and classical neuroleptics. The atypical antipsychotics

TABLE 6 Common tic treatments.

Category	Agent	Notes
Alpha-2 agonist	Clonidine	May be too sedating for daytime use
	Clonidine ER	Must be able to swallow whole
	Clonidine transdermal	Option for children who cannot swallow or are adverse to medication
	Guanfacine	Must balance efficacy with sedation, can be dosed QAM to TID
	Guanfacine ER	Must be able to swallow whole
Dopaminergic	Risperidone	Tablets or oral solution
	Aripiprazole	Tablets or oral solution
	Olanzapine	Tablets or orally disintegrating tablets
	Haloperidol	Tablets or oral solution, higher risk of extrapyramidal symptoms
	Pimozide	Tablets only, worse side effect profile
	Fluphenazine	Tablets only, worse side effect profile
Other	Topiramate	Can be used alone or as adjunctive
	Clonazepam	May be too sedating for daytime use, but can be helpful if concurrent anxiety
	Tetrabenazine	Dosed BID to TID, about 1/5th of patients with side effects
	Botulinum toxin	May help if tics have some dystonic features

Adapted from Shprecher, D., & Kurlan, R. (2009). The management of tics. *Movement Disorders, 24*(1), 15–24. https://doi.org/10.1002/mds.22378.

of risperidone, olanzapine, and aripiprazole are preferred over the classical neuroleptics due to decreased side effects; these three have been shown to be superior to clozapine and quetiapine in treating tics (Shprecher & Kurlan, 2009). In some patients, combination therapy may be needed. If a patient is not completely controlled on a single agent, switching to a more potent option or adding a second agent can be considered. Topiramate can be very helpful as an add-on therapy; however, it can be very effective as a monotherapy treatment as well.

Obsessive-compulsive disorders

Obsessive-compulsiveness as a spectrum stretching from personality traits to a severe disorder is common in the child neurology clinic, but it often goes undetected or attributed to some other etiology. Obsessive-compulsive disorder itself is a moderately prevalent neurodevelopmental disorder at 0.25%–4% in children and adolescents (Krebs & Heyman, 2015), and many children suffer from subclinical obsessive-compulsive symptoms (Zijlmans et al., 2017). The biggest challenge in bringing obsessive-compulsiveness to light is the strong misperception by the public on how obsessive-compulsiveness may manifest. When exploring the topic with families, statements like "but his room is a mess" or "she never washes her hands" would often be stated by the parents. The first challenge, therefore, in treating obsessive-compulsiveness with any intervention is education for the patient and caregivers.

Obsessive-compulsive disorder (OCD) is defined as a disorder in which a person has uncontrollable, reoccurring thoughts (obsessions) and behaviors (compulsions) that he or she feels the urge to repeat over and over (National Institute of Mental Health, 2016). Perhaps this definition can be considered to be a rule-setting disorder in which the patient will think or say things in an all-or-none fashion like "I have to…," "I must…," or even "it should…" as examples. Broadening of the terminology does decrease the specificity of the history gathering; however, the approach can have a tremendous positive impact on the sensitivity to detect those with OCD versus those with obsessive-compulsive personality or behaviors. By utilizing this broader definition, many children referred for behavioral problems actually end up having obsessive-compulsive symptoms as the etiology of their behavioral concerns.

As with many psychological disorders, psychotherapy is recommended as the first line of intervention. Some patients, however, who may be severe enough at the time of diagnosis or who may be refractory to psychotherapy alone, will need medication management. Use of an SSRI is often the first option for OCD. There is good evidence that fluoxetine, sertraline, paroxetine, fluvoxamine, and citalopram are effective, but there have been few head-to-head trials to suggest the superiority of one agent over another (Krebs & Heyman, 2015). If a patient is not responsive to these treatments, clomipramine or an atypical antipsychotic such as risperidone can be considered (risperidone may be a first option in a child with comorbid tic disorder).

Comorbid conditions may impact the responsiveness to medications. Patients with depression or anxiety seem to benefit from SSRIs, but those with OCD, oppositional defiant disorder, and conduct disorder show diminished responses to SSRI use (Krebs & Heyman, 2015).

Aggressive behavior

The complaint of "behavioral problems" is a common but very nonspecific reason for a referral to child neurology and/or child psychology/psychiatry. It is important to evaluate the cause of the behavioral problem as a construct of social or educational struggles or one independent of psychosocial dysfunction. Elucidating a specific or singular etiology may be difficult, especially in neurologically compromised children. A 2002 study in the Netherlands showed about 18% of children with intelligence quotients above 80 scored in the deviant range on the Child Behavior Checklist compared to almost 50% in children with intelligence quotients less than 80 (Dekker, Koot, Ende, & Verhulst, 2002). In the same study, there was more noted aggressive behavior in the higher functioning intellectual disability group (IQs of 60-80). It is the aggressive behavior that may need medical intervention as part of the overall therapeutic program.

The goal of treating aggressive behavior is to improve the safety of the patient and the patient's caregivers. Common aggressive behaviors in developmentally delayed children are reactive in nature and present with hitting, biting, pinching, and spitting. In more functional patients, verbally aggressive behaviors can also be seen. Proactive aggression can occur as well and may be difficult to differentiate from reactive aggression. Typically, aggressive behavior in neurologically compromised children has been one of the most difficult areas to achieve satisfactory success over time. The challenge comes from balancing the desired level of ideal behavior with the side effects of medical interventions. It is helpful to establish a way of tracking the unwanted aggressive behaviors to help measure the efficacy of any treatment. The medication choice is drawn from a wide spectrum of classes of medications. Choosing specific medications is still more of an art than a science, as research data is limited (Table 7).

The chart of medications for aggression is nowhere near an exhaustive list of options, as there are many off-label studies of numerous medications looking to help this challenging symptom of aggressive behavior. The medications listed are chosen due to evidence of use in children either for aggression or for other indications such as seizures or hypertension that can establish some safety information. Numerous studies point to stimulant use as a first-line agent; however, there are not enough clinical trial data to suggest that it would be the first treatment for all individuals with aggressive behavior. When a case is very complicated, a child neurologist will often seek the professional help of a child psychiatrist or a medical psychologist to help manage these patients.

Drooling

Excessive drooling, known as sialorrhea, is a major issue in children with cerebral palsy as well as children with other neurodegenerative or neuromuscular disorders. Regardless of the cause, drooling is problematic, leading to complications such as impairment in social functioning (embarrassment and isolation), aspiration, skin breakdown, bad odor, infection (Lakraj, Moghimi, & Jabbari, 2013), and impairment of speech through trying to control the volume of saliva. These children will often present clinically with either wet clothing or commonly with towels that have been turned into bibs to capture the saliva that falls from the mouth.

Sialorrhea can be from increased production of saliva or related to failure of mechanisms that clear the saliva from the oral cavity. In children with neurologic

TABLE 7 Examples of possible medications for treating aggression.

Category	Agent	Notes
Antipsychotic	Risperidone	Most broadly studied atypical antipsychotic in children
	Aripiprazole	Approved for children with autism and bipolar I disorder
	Olanzapine	Approved for children with bipolar I disorder
	Quetiapine	Approved for children with bipolar I disorder
Stimulant	Amphetamine-based	Use if hyperactivity and impulsivity are prominent features of the aggression
	Methylphenidate-based	
Antidepressant	SSRI	May serve as a class to regulate response to provocation-based aggression
Mood stabilizer	Lithium	Studied initially with aggressive behavior in conduct disorder; needs lab monitoring
	Valproic acid	Good with explosive temper and mood lability; needs lab monitoring
	Oxcarbazepine	Off-label psych use, similar to carbamazepine in mechanism of action with less enzyme induction
	Lamotrigine	Approved for adults with bipolar I disorder
	Carbamazepine	Mixed evidence on efficacy, enzyme induction
Adrenergic agent	Clondine, clonidine ER	Use if hyperactivity and impulsivity are prominent features of the aggression
	Guanfacine, guanfacine ER	
Other agents	Amantadine/propranolol	Both have been studied to help with aggression following brain injury, with propranolol having a clearer benefit; the combination tends to aid in patients with frontal lobe dysfunction due to the amantadine impact on dopamine

Adapted from Farmer, C. A., Arnold, L. E., Bukstein, O. G., Findling, R. L., Gadow, K. D., Li, X., et al. (2011). The treatment of severe child aggression (TOSCA) study: Design challenges. *Child and Adolescent Psychiatry and Mental Health, 5*(1), 36. https://doi.org/10.1186/1753-2000-5-36; Berman, M. E., McCloskey, M. S., Fanning, J. R., Schumacher, J. A., & Coccaro, E. F. (2009). Serotonin augmentation reduces response to attack in aggressive individuals. *Psychological Science, 20*(6), 714–720. https://doi.org/10.1111/j.1467-9280.2009.02355.x; Lexicomp Drug Database 5.0.0; Levy, M., Berson, A., Cook, T., Bollegala, N., Seto, E., Tursanski, S., et al. (2005). Treatment of agitation following traumatic brain injury: A review of the literature. *NeuroRehabilitation, 20*(4), 279–306.

TABLE 8 Sialorrhea treatments.

Treatment	Agent	Notes
Oral	Glycopyrrolate	Solution or tablets
	Benztropine	Off-label use, solution or tablets
Topical (oral)	Tropicamide	Off-label use, optic drop
	Atropine ophthalmic 1%	Off-label use, optic drop
Topical (skin)	Scopolamine patch	Off-label use
Toxin	Botulinum toxin A	Level B evidence in adults
	Botulinum toxin B	Level A evidence in adults
Surgical	Gland excision	
	Denervation of the gland	
	Ligation of salivary ducts	

Adapted from Lakraj, A. A., Moghimi, N., & Jabbari, B. (2013). Sialorrhea: Anatomy, pathophysiology and treatment with emphasis on the role of botulinum toxins. *Toxins (Basel), 5*(5), 1010–1031. https://doi.org/10.3390/toxins5051010 and Norderyd, J., Graf, J., Marcusson, A., Nilsson, K., Sjöstrand, E., Steinwall, G., et al. (2017). Sublingual administration of atropine eyedrops in children with excessive drooling—A pilot study. *International Journal of Paediatric Dentistry 27*(1), 22–29. https://doi.org/10.1111/ipd.12219.

disorders, drooling appears to be an effect of inefficient tongue and/or bulbar control, rather than increased salivary secretion. Ultimately, muscle incoordination inhibits the reflexive swallow mechanism due to decreased voluntary control or the first phase of swallowing (Lakraj et al., 2013). Management of sialorrhea can be aimed at improving function with oral-motor exercises or palatal training devices; however, much of the treatment is aimed at decreasing the amount of saliva produced from the salivary glands. Treatments can be divided into oral, topical, toxin, or surgical (Table 8).

The oral and topical medications are all anticholinergics and therefore have the common risk factors of those medications, including dry mouth, constipation, urinary retention, bowel obstruction, dilated pupils, blurred vision, increased heart rate, and decreased sweating as well as more central effects causing impaired concentration, confusion, attention deficit, and memory impairment (Lieberman, 2004). Monitoring for side effects is important in the neurologically compromised child as they may already have some of these side effects as preexisting symptoms. There is some belief that topical treatments would create less systemic side effects, but there is no research in children to prove this thought true or false.

Toxin injection has undergone multiple studies in adult patients with sialorrhea and has shown good evidence. There are still variables that warrant further study, including the concentration of toxin, the method used to locate injection sites, and the method of injection (Lakraj et al., 2013). From a pediatric standpoint, there is limited evidence to comment on broad efficacy; however, there is a single paper on patients with cerebral palsy that demonstrated botulinum toxin to be an effective, temporary treatment for sialorrhea (Rodwell, Edwards, Ware, & Boyd, 2012).

Surgical treatments are reserved for more severe cases of sialorrhea. There is an increased risk of nerve damage, especially when removing the parotid gland in the upper jaw region due to the course of the facial nerve.

Constipation

Compared to typically developing children, children with developmental disorders have higher rates of gastrointestinal complaints with constipation being reported as one of the most common across the combination of developmental disorders (15%–16% in a three month period of time with typically developing children at 3.5% (Chaidez, Hansen, & Hertz-Picciotto, 2014)). Considering children with motor dysfunction in addition to cognitive delays, the prevalence of constipation can range up to 74%, depending on the diagnostic criteria being utilized (Veugelers et al., 2010). In the same article, Veugelers et al. noted that laxative use was frequent, but in a majority of patients fiber intake and hydration status were below required standards.

Constipation in neurologically compromised children can have all the severe physical impacts including bowel impaction, anal fissures, hemorrhoids, and rectal prolapse; however, the presence of abdominal pain, nausea/vomiting, and behavioral changes may be the more commonly observed symptoms in addition to a reduction in stool production from the baseline. In autistic patients, for example, the presence of constipation caused them to experience more irritability, social withdrawal, and hyperactivity parameters than autistic children without constipation (Chaidez et al., 2014). There is also developing evidence that constipation can cause a change in intestinal gut bacteria, which may have a negative impact on gut transit, helping create a potential bridge to chronic constipation (Zhao & Yu, 2016). Because decreased mobility is a risk factor noted in cerebral palsy or other motor disorders, getting patients moving though physical therapy can be beneficial, in addition to gentle abdominal massage. Acupuncture has also been used (Mayo Clinic, 2019).

In direct response to the information above, initial treatments for constipation involve dietary assessment, including hydration and fiber intake. Because many patients will be deficient in these two specific areas, increasing fiber through dietary or supplemental options and increasing water intake though fluids or more water-rich foods will be the first steps in therapy. For patients who do not respond to increased hydration and fiber, or who have adequate intake but continued constipation, various options exists for helping soften and/or mobilize the stool. Some patients may benefit from prebiotic or probiotic therapy, although the current research does not clarify how best to manipulate the intestinal microbiome to have a clear positive impact (Zhao & Yu, 2016).

TABLE 9 Acute disimpaction therapies.

Category	Type	Agent
Oral	Osmotics	Miralax (polyethylene glycol powder) Golytely (polyethylene glycol solution) Magnesium citrate
	Stimulants	Senekot (senna) Ducolax (bisacodyl)
	Lubricants	Mineral oil
Rectal	Enemas	Saline Mineral oil Phosphate soda
	Suppository	Bisacodyl Glycerin

Adapted from Nurko, S., & Zimmerman, L. A. (2014). Evaluation and treatment of constipation in children and adolescents. *American Family Physician, 90*(2), 82–90.

For patients requiring medical treatment for constipation, treatment can be divided into acute disimpaction modalities and maintenance therapy to prevent build-up of stool and aim for once-daily bowel movements. Agents aimed at acute disimpaction fall into oral and rectal categories, with oral polyethylene glycol being as efficacious as the rectal treatments. The oral option in many cases is considered a first-line therapy, even without evidence of superiority, due to ease of use and tolerability (Nurko & Zimmerman, 2014) (Table 9).

Options for children who are not impacted or have become disimpacted with the above treatments can then move onto maintenance therapy, utilizing oral options falling into either an osmotic, stimulant, or lubricant category (Table 10).

Once children have normal daily stools for a period of time (duration will vary from patient to patient), the maintenance therapies can be weaned off to see if the child can maintain a normal bowel routine with only continued monitoring of dietary intake and hydration status.

When pharmacogenomic studies help

In the United States, in order to reduce the trial-and-error approach toward medication management, it is possible to order a genetic study. The most common one is called the Genomind Genecept Assay. This is the one often used by pediatric neuropsychologists who prescribe. These results allow the prescriber to know if the child can metabolize medications normally or if he/she is an ultrarapid metabolizer. It also lists the medications to which the child is likely to have a good response. In this regard, the following categories of drugs as well as the specific drugs in those categories may be listed. For example, there are

TABLE 10 Maintenance therapies.

Category	Agent
Osmotics	Miralax (polyethylene glycol powder)
	Lactulose
	Magnesium hydroxide
	Sorbitol (e.g. prune juice)
Stimulants	Senekot (senna)
	Ducolax (bisacodyl)
Lubricants	Mineral oil

Adapted from Nurko, S., & Zimmerman, L. A. (2014). Evaluation and treatment of constipation in children and adolescents. *American Family Physician, 90*(2), 82–90.

categories for antidepressants, anxiolytics, stimulants, pain medications, bipolar medications, antipsychotic medications, sleep medications, etc. Of course, many of these medications are not approved for young children. But knowing the ones that are approved saves experimentation, time, and money. More information can be obtained from genomind.com.

Medicine versus behavior modification

In the United States, busy parents may be looking for a "quick fix" for their child's difficulties. Medication, however, is not the answer to bad behavior or absent/permissive parenting. All special needs children (SEN) require active parenting, good boundaries, reasonable expectations, and the opportunity to be successful. They desire secure attachment, attention, affection, acceptance, approval, and acknowledgment (Nemeth, Ray, & Schexnayder, 2003). Regardless of their abilities or disabilities, children need love. Most children desire to please. If they are rewarded for good behavior, more good behavior will follow. Medicine will not fix bad parenting.

Parents must learn to accept their child "as is" and appreciate his/her uniqueness. The goal of healthy parenting is to raise independent individuals who can function in society. Some children need more help than others to achieve this goal. Some may never achieve total independence. Regardless of their abilities or disabilities, the goal is to help children be the best they can be.

Good parenting is the first step in this process. For SEN, seeking out caring pediatric neurological and/or neuropsychological professionals is the second step. Securing competent educational opportunities and therapeutic intervention is the third step. In this regard, medication may help along the way, but it is not <u>the</u> answer. It is merely a part of the process.

References

Anand, S., Tong, H., Besag, F. M. C., Chan, E. W., Cortes, S., & Wong, I. C. K. (2017). Safety, tolerability and efficacy of drugs for treating behavioural insomnia in children with attention deficit/hyperactivity disorder: Systematic review with methodological quality assessment. *Pediatric Drugs, 19*(3), 235–250. https://doi.org/10.1007/s40272-017-0224-6.

Angriman, M., Caravale, B., Novelli, L., Ferri, R., & Bruni, O. (2015). Sleep in children with neurodevelopmental disabilities. *Neuropediatrics, 46*, 199–210. https://doi.org/10.1055/s-0035-1550151.

Black, B. T., Soden, S. E., Kearns, G. L., & Jones, B. L. (2016). Clinical and pharmacologic considerations for guanfacine use in very young children. *Journal of Child and Adolescent Psychopharmacology, 26*(6), 498–504. https://doi.org/10.1089/cap.2014.0159.

Bond, D. J., Hadjipavlou, G., Lam, R. W., McIntyre, R. S., Beaulieu, S., Schaffer, A., et al. (2012). The Canadian Network for Mood and Anxiety Treatments (CANMAT) task force recommendations for the management of patients with mood disorders and comorbid attention-deficit/hyperactivity disorder. *Annals of Clinical Psychiatry, 24*(1), 23–37.

Bonuck, K., & Grant, R. (2012). Sleep problems and early developmental delay: Implications for early intervention programs. *American Association on Intellectual and Developmental Disabilities, 50*(1), 41–52. https://doi.org/10.1352/1934-9556-50.1.41.

Brewer, C., Holloway, S., Zawalnyski, P., Schinzel, A., & FitzPatrick, D. (1998). A chromosomal deletion map of human malformations. *American Journal of Human Genetics, 63*, 1153–1159. https://doi.org/10.1086/302041.

Cascade, E. F., Kalali, A. H., & Feifel, D. (2007). Strattera: Ups, downs, and emerging uses. *Psychiatry (Edgmont), 4*(4), 23–25.

Chaidez, V., Hansen, R. L., & Hertz-Picciotto, I. (2014). Gastrointestinal problems in children with autism, developmental delays or typical development. *Journal of Autism and Developmental Disorders, 44*(5), 1117–1127. https://doi.org/10.1007/s10803-013-1973-x.

Dekker, M. C., Koot, H. M., Ende, J.v., & Verhulst, F. C. (2002). Emotional and behavioral problems in children and adolescents with and without intellectual disability. *Journal of Child Psychology and Psychiatry, 43*, 1087–1098. https://doi.org/10.1111/1469-7610.00235.

Emrich, H. M., Dose, M., & Von Zerssen, D. (1985). The use of sodium valproate, carbamazepine and oxcarbazepine in patients with affective disorder. *Journal of Affective Disorders, 8*, 243–250.

Gelfand, A. A. (2018). Pediatric and adolescent headache. *CONTINUUM: Lifelong learning in Neurology, 24*(4), 1108–1136. https://doi.org/10.1212/CON.0000000000000638.

Hollway, J. A., & Aman, M. G. (2011). Pharmacological treatment of sleep disturbance in developmental disabilities: A review of the literature. *Research in Developmental Disabilities, 32*(3), 939–962. https://doi.org/10.1016/j.ridd.2010.12.035. [Epub 2011 Feb 5]. 21296553.

Hunt, R. D., Minderaa, R. B., & Cohen, D. J. (1985). Clonidine benefits children with attention deficit disorder and hyperactivity: Report of a double-blind placebo-crossover therapeutic trial. *Journal of the American Academy of Child and Adolescent Psychiatry, 24*(5), 617–629.

Krebs, G., & Heyman, I. (2015). Obsessive-compulsive disorder in children and adolescents. *Archives of Disease in Childhood, 100*(5), 495–499. https://doi.org/10.1136/archdischild-2014-306934.

Kuhle, S., Urschitz, M. S., Eitner, S., & Poets, C. F. (2009). Interventions for obstructive sleep apnea in children: A systematic review. *Sleep Medicine Reviews, 13*(2), 123–131. https://doi.org/10.1016/j.smrv.2008.07.006.

Lakraj, A. A., Moghimi, N., & Jabbari, B. (2013). Sialorrhea: Anatomy, pathophysiology and treatment with emphasis on the role of botulinum toxins. *Toxins (Basel), 5*(5), 1010–1031. https://doi.org/10.3390/toxins5051010.

Lavigne, J. V., Binns, H. J., Christoffel, K. K., Rosenbaum, D., Arend, R., Smith, K., et al. (1993). Behavioral and emotional problems among preschool children in pediatric primary care: Prevalence and pediatricians' recognition. *Pediatrics*, *91*(3), 649–655.

Lieberman, J. A., 3rd. (2004). Managing anticholinergic side effects. *Primary Care Companion to The Journal of Clinical Psychiatry*, *6*(Suppl 2), 20–23. Erratum in: *Primary Care Companion to The Journal of Clinical Psychiatry*, 2012, *14*(1):PCC.12lcx01362. PMID: 16001097; PMCID: PMC487008.

Lumeng, J. C., & Chervin, R. D. (2008). Epidemiology of pediatric obstructive sleep apnea. *ATS Journals*, *5*, 242–252. https://doi.org/10.1513/pats.200708-135MG.

Mayo Clinic. (2019). *Constipation in children*. https://www.mayoclinic.org/diseases-conditions/constipation-in-children/diagnosis-treatment/drc-20354248.

Muller, A. A., & Stoll, K. D. (1984). Carbamazepine and oxcarbazepine in the treatment of manic syndromes: Studies in Germany. In H. M. Emrich, T. Okuma, & A. A. Muller (Eds.), *Anticonvulsants in Affective Disorders* (pp. 139–147). Amsterdam, Netherlands: Excerpta Medica.

National Institute of Mental Health. (2016). *Obsessive-compulsive disorder*. https://www.nimh.nih.gov/health/topics/obsessive-compulsive-disorder-ocd/index.shtml.

Nemeth, D. G., Ray, K. P., & Schexnayder, M. M. (2003). *Helping your angry child*. Oakland: New Harbinger Publications.

Nurko, S., & Zimmerman, L. A. (2014). Evaluation and treatment of constipation in children and adolescents. *American Family Physician*, *90*(2), 82–90.

Piña-Garza, J. E., Espinoza, R., Nordli, D., Bennett, D. A., Spirito, S., Stites, T. E., et al. (2005). Oxcarbazepine adjunctive therapy in infants and young children with partial seizures. *Neurology*, *65*(9), 1370–1375. https://doi.org/10.1212/01.wnl.0000186800.18456.72.

Rodwell, K., Edwards, P., Ware, R. S., & Boyd, R. (2012). Salivary gland botulinum toxin injections for drooling in children with cerebral palsy and neurodevelopmental disability: A systematic review. *Developmental Medicine and Child Neurology*, *54*(11), 977–987. https://doi.org/10.1111/j.1469-8749.2012.04370.x.

Rulong, G., Dye, T., & Simakajornboon, N. (2018). Pharmacological management of restless legs syndrome and periodic limb movement disorder in children. *Pediatric Drugs*, *20*(1), 9.

Russo, A., Bruno, A., Trojsi, F., Tessitore, A., & Tedeschi, G. (2016). Lifestyle factors and migraine in childhood. *Current Pain and Headache Reports*, *20*(2), 9. https://doi.org/10.1007/s11916-016-0539-y.

Scheffer, I. E., Berkovic, S., Capovilla, G., Connolly, M. B., French, J., Guilhoto, L., et al. (2017). ILAE classification of the epilepsies: Position paper of the ILAE Commission for Classification and Terminology. *Epilepsia*, *58*(4), 512–521. https://doi.org/10.1111/epi.13709.

Schwichtenberg, A. J., & Malow, B. A. (2015). Melatonin treatment in children with developmental disabilities. *Sleep Medicine Clinics*, *10*(2), 181–187. https://doi.org/10.1016/j.jsmc.2015.02.008.

Shprecher, D., & Kurlan, R. (2009). The management of tics. *Movement Disorders*, *24*(1), 15–24. https://doi.org/10.1002/mds.22378.

Srivastava, K., Arora, A., Kataria, A., Cappelleri, J. C., Sadosky, A., & Peterson, A. M. (2013). Impact of reducing dosing frequency on adherence to oral therapies: A literature review and meta-analysis. *Patient Preference and Adherence*, *7*, 419–434. https://doi.org/10.2147/PPA.S44646.

Stahl, S. M. (2017). *Stahl's essential psychopharmacology prescriber's guide* (6th ed.). New York, NY: Cambridge University Press.

Straube, A., Heinen, F., Ebinger, F., & von Kries, R. (2013). Headache in school children: Prevalence and risk factors. *Deutsches Ärzteblatt International*, *110*(48), 811–818. https://doi.org/10.3238/arztebl.2013.0811.

Subcommittee on Attention-Deficit/Hyperactivity Disorder, Steering Committee on Quality Improvement and Management. (2011). ADHD: Clinical practice guideline for the diagnosis, evaluation, and treatment of attention-deficit/hyperactivity disorder in children and adolescents. *Pediatrics*, *128*(5), 1007–1022. https://doi.org/10.1542/peds.2011-2654.

Tagwerker Gloor, F., & Walitza, S. (2016). Tic disorders and Tourette syndrome: Current concepts of etiology and treatment in children and adolescents. *Neuropediatrics*, *47*(2), 84–96. https://doi.org/10.1055/s-0035-1570492.

Trauer, J. M., Qian, M. Y., Doyle, J. S., Rajaratnam, S. M., & Cunnington, D. (2015). Cognitive behavioral therapy for chronic insomnia: A systematic review and meta-analysis. *Annals of Internal Medicine*, *163*(3), 191–204. https://doi.org/10.7326/M14-2841.

Veugelers, R., Benninga, M. A., Calis, E. A., Willemsen, S. P., Evenhuis, H., Tibboel, D., et al. (2010). Prevalence and clinical presentation of constipation in children with severe generalized cerebral palsy. *Developmental Medicine & Child Neurology*, *52*, e216–e221. https://doi.org/10.1111/j.1469-8749.2010.03701.

Williams, D. (2019). Personal Communication.

Zhao, Y., & Yu, Y. (2016). Intestinal microbiota and chronic constipation. *Springerplus*, *5*(1), 1130. https://doi.org/10.1186/s40064-016-2821-1.

Zijlmans, J., Marhe, R., van der Ende, J., Verhulst, F. C., Popma, A., Tiemeier, H., et al. (2017). Children with obsessive-compulsive symptomology in the general population: Different subtypes? *Journal of Developmental & Behavioral Pediatrics*, *38*(7), 476–482. https://doi.org/10.1097/DBP.0000000000000467.

Further reading

Berman, M. E., McCloskey, M. S., Fanning, J. R., Schumacher, J. A., & Coccaro, E. F. (2009). Serotonin augmentation reduces response to attack in aggressive individuals. *Psychological Science*, *20*(6), 714–720. https://doi.org/10.1111/j.1467-9280.2009.02355.x.

Bravo, T. P., & Vargas, B. B. (2015). Migraine preventative butterbur has safety concerns. *Neurology Times*.

Epilepsy Foundation. (2014). *Seizure Medication List*. https://www.epilepsy.com/learn/treating-seizures-and-epilepsy/seizure-medication-list.

Farmer, C. A., Arnold, L. E., Bukstein, O. G., Findling, R. L., Gadow, K. D., Li, X., et al. (2011). The treatment of severe child aggression (TOSCA) study: Design challenges. *Child and Adolescent Psychiatry and Mental Health*, *5*(1), 36. https://doi.org/10.1186/1753-2000-5-36.

Levy, M., Berson, A., Cook, T., Bollegala, N., Seto, E., Tursanski, S., et al. (2005). Treatment of agitation following traumatic brain injury: A review of the literature. *NeuroRehabilitation*, *20*(4), 279–306.

Norderyd, J., Graf, J., Marcusson, A., Nilsson, K., Sjöstrand, E., Steinwall, G., et al. (2017). Sublingual administration of atropine eyedrops in children with excessive drooling—A pilot study. *International Journal of Paediatric Dentistry*, *27*(1), 22–29. https://doi.org/10.1111/ipd.12219.

Tajti, J., Szok, D., Csáti, A., & Vécsei, L. (2016). Prophylactic drug treatment of migraine in children and adolescents: An update. *Current Pain and Headache Reports*, *20*(1), 1. https://doi.org/10.1007/s11916-015-0536-6.

Chapter 15

Implications for the future

Darlyne G. Nemeth[a], Janna Glozman[b]
[a]*The Neuropsychology Center of Louisiana, LLC, Baton Rouge, LA, United States,*
[b]*M. V. Lomonosov Moscow State University, Moscow, Russia*

By understanding our rich cultural-historical heritage, we can become more aware of the implementation of developmental neuropsychology programs throughout the world. In order to pave the way for an exciting tomorrow, understanding Luria's and Reitan's ideas will help us move forward.

How are Luria and Reitan seen by the academic community?

- As the "fathers" of neuropsychology.
- As the creators of comprehensive methods (batteries) of neuropsychological assessment (Luria, 1965, 1973, 1999; Reitan & Wolfson, 1986, 1993).
- As major contributors to theories of mental disturbances and methods for remediation (Luria, 1973; Reitan, 1955a, 1955b).

For Luria we should add two more points:

- A pioneer cross-cultural psychologist. His neuropsychology is the application of a general theory of the human mind, of the cultural-historical school. "For Luria the brain was an instrument for making culture accessible to mind. … for him the 'internalization of culture' was a mastering of possible worlds of a certain kind. The shape of those possible worlds was in large measure determined by the culture in which one grew up and in which one interacted with others" (Bruner, 2005, p. XII).
- The classic expression of romantic science, studying each human as a whole.

This cross-fertilization of Luria's and Reitan's ideas, as presented in many chapters in this volume, is just the beginning. It is bound to prepare new pathways for the future—more programs and more discoveries, all of which will make a better world possible for our neuropsychologically compromised children.

Throughout this volume, all chapter authors have emphasized the importance of a thorough evaluation process. Certainly, Luria and Reitan would agree. Although Luria was the primary advocate of qualitative neuropsychological analysis and Reitan was the primary advocate of quantitative neuropsychological

Evaluation and Treatment of Neuropsychologically Compromised Children
https://doi.org/10.1016/B978-0-12-819545-1.00015-1

analysis, both approaches are needed. Thus, combining the two creates the best approach to neuropsychological evaluation and efficient remediation of neuropsychologically compromised children.

This is especially true in the evaluation of children with attentional issues. All too often, mere symptom checklists are used to diagnose attention deficit hyperactivity disorder (ADHD) in children. Yet these checklists are not enough! A thorough evaluation based on syndrome analysis is needed, especially for intervention planning, which must be specific to the child's brain functions, needs, and interests.

The modern orientation of both medicine and neuropsychology is the *prevention of possible disturbances*:

- Learning disabilities;
- Behavior troubles;
- Emotional imbalance;
- Maladjustment at school or kindergarten; and
- Difficult child-parent interrelationships.

Three main possibilities of prevention derive from the Luria-Reitan heritage:

1. An early thorough neuropsychological evaluation and consequently an early intervention. The first autistic symptoms appear at the first months of a baby's life. A motor underdevelopment during the first year provokes cognitive underdevelopment, namely a missed crawl stage provokes bad orientation in space—an important cause of future problems in grammar and in math. Delayed drawing skills very often correlate with dysgraphia at school. A delay in speech development interferes with the whole cognitive development, and intervention should start as early as 2 years old. Underdeveloped communication abilities in preschoolers result in behavioral and emotional problems at school. This list can be continued.
2. A team approach to intervention, including the common work of a neuropsychologist, speech therapist, pediatric neurologist, psychotherapist, and family psychologist for overcoming problems revealed at the neuropsychological assessment.
3. Neuropsychological education of the future and actual parents to optimize the baby's development, to be sensitive for developmental milestones and possible disturbances, to support and encourage the child in overcoming problems, and to consolidate his/her self-appraisal and respect.
   Each child must be accepted, protected, and respected in his/her own family. This is an important principle of culturally oriented developmental neuropsychology, created by Luria and Reitan.

One of the most important issues for school-aged children is that of executive functions. Many consider these skills as making people uniquely human. They allow us to regulate our thinking, manage our feelings, control our behaviors, and adjust them to social requirements. As these skills involve attention, working memory, and processing speed—among others—they are essential for children to learn. Play and social interactions help preschool children to develop these skills. Play also encourages logical thinking and planning.

Executive functions can be influenced by "cold" (logical) and "hot" (emotional) factors. When logical thinking prevails, children can be quite successful in school; however, when emotional thinking prevails, children can become quite disruptive. Integrating thinking and feelings is essential in order to produce adaptive behavior.

The sooner children learn to recognize, label, and share their feelings, the easier it will be to teach them to think logically, to manage their feelings, and to behave appropriately. This process must begin at home. Promoting parent/caregiver awareness and enhancing children's age-appropriate zone of proximal development are so important. Early intervention for babies and their parents/caregivers is key.

This is especially true for the development of speech. Teaching children to speak at an early age facilitates brain development, for building brain functions is not *rehabilitation* (correction), it is *creation* (Glozman, 2013).

Speech development requires socialization. If there is no need to speak, children will not learn to speak. Instead, they will merely point. Including children, regardless of their intellectual abilities, in playful, problem-solving activities will facilitate their speech. Each functional system is a result of the interaction of social, cultural, and biological factors.

Building children's brain functions requires interpersonal learning. When children learn together in small groups, they thrive. They experience both qualitative and quantitative growth, which can then translate to the academic arena. Frequently, emotional distress interferes with learning, especially in mathematics. When children learn to manage their performance anxiety, they can excel to the level that their innate abilities will allow.

Some children have a more difficult time than others in this regard. Frequently, their medical problems dominate. This is often seen in childhood cancer, epilepsy, or spina bifida, for example. These children must not only deal with their medical issues, but also their neuropsychological development. Careful evaluations must precede interventions. For these children, an integrated approach to care is essential. Their parents/caregivers must be intricately involved at every stage of their journey.

Integrated medication management is often an essential component of a child's care. Collaboration is essential. When an inpatient multidisciplinary team works together, the outcome is more productive. On an outpatient basis, this process may be more difficult but still possible to arrange. At the very least, the child's primary care physician (e.g., pediatrician, pediatric neurologist, pediatric oncologist, pediatric cardiologist) and the neuropsychologist must work together for the best results possible. In most cases, as in Louisiana in the United States and Moscow in Russia, the neuropsychologist might be a prescriber. This often facilitates effective medication management; however, medication is only

one of many interventions. Multiple interventions are usually needed. They typically include, but are not limited to, good parenting, caring physicians, meaningful educational opportunities, and appropriate therapeutic interventions. Medication alone is not a substitute for the above.

Environmental traumatization is another source of anxiety for children. No child expects to be exposed to hurricanes, floods, earthquakes, abuse, etc. Yet, few children are spared from one or more of these events. These experiences lead to hot emotions, which typically interfere with children's executive functions. When children have no home, no food, no family, no sense of safety, how can they learn? Yes, children are incredibly resilient, but how much can they take? When children are traumatized, they need to have their sense of attachment and security reestablished. Workshops to assist children in processing their pain and fear are essential. Via play, songs, games, and group interactions, traumatized children can, once again, learn not only to survive, but also to thrive. Excellent interventions built upon the works of Luria and Reitan can help restore children's coping and adaptive skills.

In Luria's words, "We need to step outside the organism to discover the sources of specifically human forms of psychological activity and the way natural processes such as physical maturation and sensory mechanisms become intertwined with culturally determined processes to produce the psychological functions of adults" (Luria, 1979, p. 43).

With the rich heritages of Luria and Reitan, the foundations have been laid for meaningful neuropsychological evaluation and intervention processes. Now that there is a growing cross-cultural fertilization of these founding fathers' ideas, there is no need for separate pyramids. Their ideas can be combined in unique ways to enhance the rich field of developmental neuropsychology to the benefit of all.

Let us summarize the recommendations for the future

Assessment

1. All neuropsychologically compromised children should receive a comprehensive evaluation using both qualitative and quantitative methods before intervention begins.
2. The assessment is always oriented on both the child's weak and strong functions.
3. The main task of child neuropsychological assessment should not be to evaluate him or her among other children of this age, but rather to work out an efficient multidisciplinary program of remediation for weak (delayed) mental functions and for ways to prevent learning disabilities and/or social and intrafamily maladjustment.
4. Luria's principle of dialogue interaction during assessment permits the understanding of the zone of proximal development (amelioration of test achievements with the help of the neuropsychologist), which is primordial for intervention plans.

5. The assessment should consider, among others, the ecological value of tests, age, gender, and cultural differences in test performances as well as the emotional state and communication skills of the assessed child. Therefore, the neuropsychological evaluation should be an individualized assessment of disturbances as well as strengths.
6. ADHD questionnaires should be used for symptom reporting, not diagnosis.

Intervention

1. Early intervention should be utilized, especially in the area of speech.
2. Babies suspected of developmental issues should be followed from birth until they can be mainstreamed into a school setting, wherein the school neuropsychologist can take over this responsibility.
3. Professionals should work together as a multidisciplinary team in both inpatient and outpatient settings.
4. All parents/caregivers should be involved in a holistic approach to intervention.
5. Children should be included in the intervention planning and modification process.
6. The interventions should not only be scientifically appropriate (i.e., evidence-based), but also fun (games) and meaningful for the child.
7. Intervention opportunities should be close to the child's home.
8. Intervention times should be convenient for the parents/caregivers. These may often occur after school.
9. Ongoing feedback should be given to the children and their families, and home exercises should be encouraged.
10. Medication management should be used as only **one** component of a comprehensive intervention program.

Research

1. More cross-cultural/international research should be encouraged.
2. Qualitative as well as quantitative data should be gathered.
3. Behavioral observations should be considered to be as meaningful as numerical data.
4. Data should be gathered in small, rather than large, group settings where interaction can facilitate growth.
5. Because this process can obfuscate the value of the interventions, metaanalysis should be avoided.
6. Practicing neuropsychologists should be included in research endeavors.
7. Neuroimaging and/or metabolic studies should be conducted where/when appropriate.
8. Excluding academic assignments, screens (i.e., video, computer, games, etc.) should be viewed by children for no more than one hour per day.

To conclude, we must recognize, that Luria and Reitan left us all richer for their having been amongst us. Luria's (1979) words explain it best:

> *"People come and go, but the creative sources of great historical events and the important ideas and deeds remain."*

References

Bruner, J. (2005). Preface. In T. V. Akhutina, J. M. Glozman, L. I. Moskovich, & D. Robbins (Eds.), *A.R. Luria and contemporary psychology: Festschrift celebrating the centennial of his birth* (pp. XI–XIII). New York: Nova Publishers.

Glozman, J. M. (2013). *Developmental neuropsychology*. London/New York: Psychology Press/ Taylor and Francis group.

Luria, A. R. (1965). Neuropsychological analysis of focal brain lesions. In B. B. Wolman (Ed.), *Handbook of clinical psychology* (pp. 689–754). New York: McGraw-Hill.

Luria, A. R. (1973). *The working brain. An introduction to neuropsychology*. London: Penguin Books.

Luria, A. R. (1979). *The making of mind*. Cambridge, MA: Harvard University Press.

Luria, A. R. (1999). Outline for the neuropsychological examination of patients with local brain lesions. *Neuropsychology Review*, *9*(1), 9–22.

Reitan, R. M. (1955a). Certain differential effects of left and right cerebral lesions in human adults. *Journal of Comparative and Physiological Psychology*, *48*, 474–477.

Reitan, R. M. (1955b). Investigation of the validity of Halstead's measures of biological intelligence. *Archives of Neurology and Psychiatry*, *73*, 28–35.

Reitan, R. M., & Wolfson, D. (1986). The Halstead-Reitan neuropsychological test battery. In D. Wedding, Horton, A. M.Jr., & J. Webster (Eds.), *The neuropsychology handbook: Behavioral and clinical perspectives* (pp. 134–160). New York: Springer.

Reitan, R. M., & Wolfson, D. (1993). *The Halstead–Reitan neuropsychological test battery; Theory and clinical interpretation* (2nd ed.). Tucson, AZ: Neuropsychology Press.

Further reading

Reitan, R. M. (1964). Psychological deficits resulting from cerebral lesions in men. In J. M. Warren & K. Akert (Eds.), *The frontal granular cortex and behavior* (pp. 295–312). New York: McGraw-Hill.

Epilogue

A.R. Luria and R.M. Reitan have independently built outstanding pyramids of neuropsychological knowledge, to the point where they are considered by many to be the fathers of international developmental neuropsychology. The purpose of this volume has been to integrate Luria's qualitative and Reitan's quantitative approaches to the evaluation and treatment of neuropsychologically compromised children.

Although separated by time and space, Luria and Reitan have offered solid foundations for the understanding of children's brain-behavior development.

As editors and disciples of these two distinguished individuals, we have invited chapter authors from many parts of the world to ignite the spark with new ideas to build upon Luria's and Reitan's rich legacies. We therefore encourage all who read these chapters to create new tomorrows for our neuropsychologically compromised children.

Darlyne G. Nemeth
Janna Glozman

Index

Note: Page numbers followed by *f* indicate figures and *t* indicate tables.

A

Abnormal child development, 5
Absolute threshold, 126
Acquired Brain Injury (ABI), 113–114, 123
Acute disimpaction therapies, 293, 293*t*
ADHD. *See* Attention deficit hyperactivity disorder (ADHD)
Agenesis of the corpus callosum (ACC), 20
Aggressive behavior, 288–289
Alcohol-related neurodevelopmental disorder (ARND), 7, 11
Alternative Impairment Index (AII), 101
Alternative Impairment Index-Children's Version (AII-CV), 101–102
Alternative Impairment Index-Revised (AII-R), 101
Amphetamines, 277
Anokhin, P.K., 36
Anticonvulsant medications, 281, 282–283t, 283
Anxiety, 126
Apgar scores, 255–257
Aphasia Screening Test, 6, 8–10*t*, 68
Asperger's Syndrome, 20
Atomoxetine, 278–279
Attention deficit hyperactivity disorder (ADHD), 276–279, 278*t*, 300, 303
  Conners' Scale, 75, 78–79, 83
  family hyperactivity, 18
  frequency of, 73
  frontal-subcortical relationships, immaturity of, 19
  hyperactive-impulsive ADHD, 74
  impulsivity, 19
  inattentive, 74
  inattentive-hyperactive-impulsive combined ADHD, 74
  learning disabilities, 19–20
  Luria's neuropsychological assessment
    child's mental functioning, general characteristics of, 76
    gnostic functions, assessment of, 77
    intellectual functions, assessment of, 78
    memory assessment, 77
    mental activity, assessment of, 76
    motor functions, assessment of, 76–77
    penalty point system, 75
    results, 83–86
    verbal functions, assessment of, 77
  medications, 274–279
  oppositional and deviant behavior, 18
  psychometric assessment methods
    Daily Planning Test, 75, 81
    Hayling Test, 75, 79–80, 88
    Iowa Gambling Task (IGT), 75, 82–83, 86–87, 87*f*
    Numeric Stroop Test, 75, 80–81
  questionnaire of early child development, 79
  reduced sensitivity to weak stimuli, 18
  risky behavior, involvement in, 73
  symptoms, 19
  voluntary attention, 18
Attention system, 37–38
Auditory learners, 232–233
Auditory memory, 77, 98
Autism spectrum disorder, 20–22

B

Barcelona Test, 59–60
Behavioral activity model, 35
Behavioral Regulation Index (BRI), 112
Behavior Assessment System for Children (3rd Edition) (BASC-3), 204, 213, 214*t*
Behavior Rating Inventory of Executive Function, Second Edition (BRIEF-2), 111, 204, 212–213
  behavioral manifestations, 111–112
  Teacher Rating Scales, 111–112
Bibliotherapeutic tasks, 170
Bibliotherapy, 168, 170
Bigler, E.D., 111
Biological intelligence, 93–94
Biosocial synthesis, 4–5
Bipolar disorder (BD), 23, 128
Birthweight classifications, 256
Blind interpretation approach, 27–28, 32, 49
Block Design Test, 21, 37, 62–63, 63*f*

Boston process approach, 59–60
Brain-behavior relationships, 5–6, 55, 95, 100
Bronchopulmonary dysplasia (BPD), 256
Brown Attention-Deficit Disorder Scales, 204, 212
Build-A-Brain (BAB) program
  emotional reactivity, 197–198
  experiential learning techniques, 198
  historical perspective, 198–199
  hold harmless agreement, 198, 201*f*
  information sheet, 198, 199*f*, 203
  logical thinking, 197–198
  Luria and Reitan models of intervention, integration of, 200–202
  measures/materials, utilization of, 204–205
  methods, 211
  "no confidentiality" agreements, 198, 200*f*
  online math training software, 210
  outline
    attention, importance of, 207
    audio compact discs, 206
    auditory learners, 208–209
    basic emotions, 207
    basic feelings, 206
    behavioral control, 207
    body language, 206
    communication techniques, 206–207
    components, 208
    creation*vs.* education, 207
    effective communication and offered strategies, 206
    emotional functioning, 206
    healthy*vs.* unhealthy coping mechanisms, 207
    introduction, 205–206
    learned communication techniques, 207
    mood rings, 209
    play games, 209
    pretests, 206
    proximal development, zone of, 209
    Pyramid Game, 207
    Rey-Ostereith Complex Figure, 208
    "RILEE Relaxation Exercise", 208
    Seashore Rhythm Test, 209
    somatic symptoms, 206
    spatial and speech control, 207
    Tinker Toy activity, 207
    TOVA, 207
    visual learners, 208–209
    visual memory, 208
    widgets, 208
    working memory, 208
    wrap-up, 209–210
  participant demographics, 210
  program description, 202–204
  results
    behavioral observations, 216
    Behavior Assessment System for Children (3rd Edition) (BASC-3), 213, 214*t*
    Behavior Rating Inventory of Executive Function, Second Edition (BRIEF-2), 212–213
    Brown Attention-Deficit Disorder Scales, 212
    Halstead Category Test (HCT), 215
    questionnaires, 211–212
    Repeatable Battery for the Assessment of Neuropsychological Status (RBANS), 215
    TOVA (visual version), 216
    Trail Making Test, Parts A and B, 216
    Wide Range Achievement Test (4th Edition) (WRAT-4), 214–215, 215*t*
  technology agreements, 198, 202*f*

C

California Verbal Learning Test (CVLT), 66–67
Case-by-case approach, 30, 32, 49
Category Test, 31, 97, 100, 134
Cerebral Palsy (CP), 22
Chromosome microarrays (CMA), 269
Cinema therapy, 168
Clinical case analysis, 30–31
Cognitive Behavioral Therapy, 7, 284
Cognitive Behavioral Therapy for Insomnia (CBIT), 279
Cognitive disorder, 22
Cognitive neuropsychology, 30
Cognitive Regulation Index (CRI)
  initiate, 113
  organization of materials, 113
  plan/organize, 113
  task-monitor, 113
  working memory, 113
Cognitive switching task, 31
Color Form Test, 31
Color Piano activity, 46–47
Color-Word Interference Test, 116
Complex functional systems, 36, 133
Comprehensive Test of Nonverbal Intelligence, Second Edition (CTONI-2), 261
Computed tomography (CT), 268
Conners' Scale, 75, 78–79, 113
Constipation, 292–293

CRI. *See* Cognitive Regulation Index (CRI)
Crystallized intelligence, 124
Cultural-historical psychology, 1–2, 33–34, 132
Cummings, J.L., 110

D

Daily Planning Test, 75, 81
Dawson, P., 110
Delis-Kaplan Executive Function System (D-KEFS), 116
  Color-Word Interference Test, 116
  Sorting Test, 116
  Tower Test, 116
  Trail Making Test, 117
  Twenty Questions Test, 116
  Verbal Fluency Test, 117
  Word Context Test, 116
Dementia, 30
Denver Developmental Screening Test (Denver II), 267–268
Depression, 127–128
Deterioration quotient, 95–96
Developmental dyslexia, 4
Developmental Neuropsychology
  agenesis of the corpus callosum (ACC), 20
  in America, 4–5
  Asperger's Syndrome, 20
  Attention Deficit Hyperactivity Disorder (ADHD), 18–20
  Autism Spectrum Disorder, 20–22
  Bipolar Disorder, 23
  cognitive, affective, and behavioral dyscontrol, global developmental delay with, 23
  Cognitive Disorder, 22
  Luria, contributions of (*see* Luria, Alexander R.)
  neuropsychologically compromised children, 6–7
  Reitan, contributions of (*see* Reitan, Ralph M.)
  in Russia (*see* Russian developmental neuropsychology)
  Traumatic Brain Injury (TBI), 23
Diagnostic and Statistical Manual of Mental Disorders (DSM-IV-TR), 19
Diamond, 111
Dichotic testing, 158
Differential Ability Scales, Second Edition (DAS-II), 261
Digital Praxis Test, 76
Dizygotic twins, 2
D-KEFS. *See* Delis-Kaplan Executive Function System (D-KEFS)
Double development law, 34–35
Drooling, 289–292
Dynamic Praxis Test, 77
Dyscalculia, 16
Dysgraphia, 6–7, 17–18
Dyslexia, 16–17

E

Early intervention, 153–154
  child development
    attachment and brain development, 142–146
    early stimulation, 151
    extreme vulnerability, 153
    interactive activities, 152
    low birth weight, 150–151
    Luria's functional system, 148–150
  importance of, 153
  prenatal orientations, 134–138
  SGSII, orientations to caregivers, 138
    active postural control, 139
    auditory and language, 140
    cognitive, 142
    locomotor, 139
    manipulatives, 139–140
    passive postural control, 138
    personal autonomy, 141–142
    social interaction, 141
    speech and language, 141
    visual, 140
Electroencephalogram (EEG), 268
Emotional intelligence (EI), 124–125
Emotion Regulation Index (ERI), 112
Environmental trauma, in children and adolescents
  American neuropsychology, 224–225
  attention, assurance of, 231
  community identification, 223
  cultures and settings, wellness workshops in, 237–238
  empowerment, 223
  executive functions, 224
  impaired functioning, 221–222
  insuring safety, 230–231
  learning styles, 232–233
  major policy agreements, 238
  moving energy, 231–232
  multisensory approach, 227
  natural disasters, neurocognitive impacts of, 238
  neurocognitive functioning, 221–222
    acknowledgment, value of, 234
    assessment, 237

Environmental trauma, in children and adolescents *(Continued)*
disaster recovery interventions, 235
group format, value of, 234–235
long-lasting trauma, 235
posttraumatic growth, 235
processing anniversary reactions, value of, 234
recovery stages, 236
REHABIT system (*see* REHABIT system)
resilience, 223
Russian neuropsychology, 224
self-esteem, 232
social reengagement, 223
storytelling, 232
"tracks", 225
trust restoration, 230
workshop activities, neurocognitive aspects of, 227–232
Epilepsy, 281–283
Episodic memory, 127
Erdogan, F., 181
ERI. *See* Emotion Regulation Index (ERI)
Eslinger, P.J., 110
Executive disturbances, 16
Executive Functions (EFs)
American perspective
measures, 115–117
questionnaires, 111–113
definition
American clinicians and researchers, 109–111
Russian style, 115
dysregulation profile, 113–115
emotional regulation via play, 107, 109
environmental trauma, in children and adolescents (*see* Environmental trauma, in children and adolescents)
Hot and Cold (*see* Hot and Cold Executive Functions)
Luria's approach, 117–118
Russian perspective, 117
tweens' with learning disabilities (*see* Tweens' with learning disabilities, executive functions in)
value of play in, 108

F

Factor Analysis, 103–104
10 Finger Attention activity, 47–48
Finger Tapping Test, 62–63, 98–99, 102–103
Fitch, E.F., 181
Fluid intelligence, 124
Four score rating system, 60
Functional diagnostics, 5
Functional Nuclear Magnetic Resonance Imaging (fMRI), 160, 163–164
Functional systems, 36–37, 133
Anokhin, P.K., 36
childhood intervention, 148–150
reorganization of, 42
Functional Transcranial Dopplerography, 159

G

Galperin's theory, 43–44
Genealogical method, 2
General Law of Psychology, 34–35
General Neuropsychological Deficit Scale (GNDS), 60, 100–102
General Neuropsychological Deficit Scale for Older Children (GNDS-OC), 101–102
General neuropsychology, 1–2
Genomind Genecept Assay, 293–294
Genotype/environment relations, 2–3, 3*f*
Gestational age classifications, 256
Global Executive Composite (GEC), 113, 204, 213
Guanfacine, 276–278
Guare, R., 110

H

Hall, J.K., 181
Halstead Category Test (HCT), 115–116, 205, 215
Halstead Impairment Index (HII), 100–101
Halstead-Reitan Neuropsychological Battery for Older Children (HRNB-OC), 205, 215, 216*t*, 274
Halstead-Reitan Neuropsychological Test Battery (HRNB), 5, 7, 8*t*, 31, 133, 274
for children and adults with brain injuries, 55–56
additional tests, 99
Alternative Impairment Index (AII), 101
Alternative Impairment Index-Children's Version (AII-CV), 101–102
biological intelligence, 93–94
Category Test, 97
children's versions, 100
clinical interpretation, 102–103
experimental psychology procedures, 93–94
factor analysis, 103–104
Finger Tapping Test, 98–99

General Neuropsychological Deficit Scale (GNDS), 100–101
Halstead Reitan Neuropsychological Test Battery for Older Children (HRNB-OC), 97
level-of-performance strategy, 95–96
motor *vs.* sensory-perceptual performances, 95–96
neuropsychological abilities, four factor model of, 93–94
pathognomonic signs, 95–96
patterns of performance, 95–96
Reitan-Indiana Aphasia Screening Test, 99
Reitan-Indiana Neuropsychological Test Battery (RINB) for children, 97
Reitan-Klove Lateral Dominance Examination, 99
Reitan-Klove Sensory-Perceptual Examination, 99
research status, 94–95
Rhythm Test, 98
screening procedures, 103
specific deficits on simple tasks, identification of, 95–96
Speech Sounds Perception Test, 98
Strength of Grip Test, 99
Tactual Performance Test (TPT), 97–98
test categories, 95
Trail Making Test, 98
Halstead Reitan Neuropsychological Test Battery for Older Children (HRNB-OC), 6–7, 8*t*, 97, 101
Hayling Test, 75, 79–80, 88
Headaches, 283–284, 285*t*
Higher Cortical Functions (HCFs), 34–42
bottom-up development, 38–39
brain regions, 34
dynamic organization, 37–38
interpsychological function, 34
intrapsychological function, 34
law of double development, 34–35
Luria, Alexander R.
clinical-psychological investigation, 41–42
functional blocks, 39–41
regulatory role of language, on behavior, 35
symptom and syndrome analysis, 41–42
systemic organization, 36–37
Higher Mental Functions (HMFs), 17, 22
Cerebral Palsy, children with, 22
children with SEN and ND
child-adult communities, 180
cooperative learning, 181
critical thinking skills, 181
cultural-historical psychology, 179–180
dialogic learning, 181
group discussion strategy, 181
joint problem solving, 181, 186–192
language skills, second language acquisition, 181
metacooperative type of "community" ("obstchnost"), 191
physical defect, 179
Piaget's concept, 182
reflective thinking activities, 181
research and methods, 182–186
shared meaning, 181
social deprivation, 179–180
social interactions, 179–180
underdevelopment of, 179–180
dynamic organization and localization, principle of, 1–2
primary defect (immaturity), 17
social genesis, principle of, 1–2
system organization, principle of, 1–2
Holarchical, Multidimensional Functional Model of Executive Functions (HMEF), 114
Hooper Visual Organization Test, 64–65
Hot and Cold Executive Functions
anxiety, 126
children's adaptive functioning and well-being, 121
cognition, 126–128
definition of, 122–123
depression, 127–128
dysregulation profile, 123–124
"IQ" *vs.* "EQ (EI)" concept, 124–125
problem solving, 121, 128–129
Hot (emotion-dependent) cognition, 126–127
Howieson, D.B., 111
HRNB. *See* Halstead-Reitan Neuropsychological Test Battery (HRNB)
Hulgin, K.M., 181
Hunt-Minnesota Test for Organic Brain Damage, 29
Hyperactive-impulsive ADHD, 74

I

Inattentive-hyperactive-impulsive combined ADHD, 74
Individualized Educational Plan (IEP) meeting, 274–275
Infantile Cerebral Palsy, 22
Insomnia, 277, 279–280, 280*t*
Integrative multidisciplinary approach, 5

Intellectual assessment batteries, 261–262
Intellectual Quotient (IQ), 7, 124–125
Interindividual inferential model, 95–96
International Classification of Diseases, Tenth Revision, Clinical Modification (ICD-10-CM), 19
Interpsychological process, 34
Intrapsychological process, 34
Intraventricular hemorrhage (IVH), 256
Inverted U-Model, 126
Iowa Gambling Task (IGT), 75, 82–83, 86–87, 87*f*

J

Johnstone, B., 109
Joint problem solving
  cooperative type, 190
  metacooperative type, 191
  precooperative type, 186
  pseudocooperative type of, 188
Just Noticeable Difference (JND), 126

K

Kapvay, 277–278
Karpova, N.L., 162–163
Kaufman-Brief Intelligence Test (K-BIT), 64–67
Kinesitherapy, 168
Kinesthetic learners, 232–233
Kinetic memory, 66
Kohs's cubes, 37

L

Learning Disabilities (LD), children with, 12–18, 134
  difficulties at school, 12–16, 14–16*t*
    mathematics (dyscalculia), 11–12, 16
    preschoolers, 6–7
    reading (dyslexia), 11–12, 16–17
    written language (dysgraphia), 6–7, 17–18
  emotional and behavioral difficulties, 11–12
  Selz-Reitan study, 7, 11*f*
  speech rehabilitation, family's role in (*see* Speech rehabilitation of children)
  speech remediation, Reitan and Luria's ideas (*see* Speech remediation, in children and adolescents)
Leiter International Performance Scale, Third Edition (Leiter-3), 262
Leontiev, A.N., 32–33
Level-of-performance approach, 95–96
Lezak, M.D., 111
Logical memory, 34, 36
Logopsychotherapy, 157
  motivational involvement, psychological mechanisms of
    adequacy, 171
    aspiration, 171
    co-participation, 171
    Pygmalion effect, 171
    realization of goal, in ideal image, 171
  neuropsychological, psychological and psychophysiological study, of participants
    communication assessment in stuttering, Luria battery in, 167–168
    results in 6th month, retention of, 166–167
    stutterers, lateral features in, 164–166
    stuttering brain mechanisms, system inter- and multidisciplinary study of, 163–164
  speech remediation in children and adolescents, Nekrasova and Karpova, 162–163
  verbal communication remediation, family members involvement in, 168–171
Low birth weight, 150–151, 254–257
Luria, Alexander R., 132–133
  in academic community, 299
  brain-injured patients, neuropsychological assessment of (*see* Neuropsychological assessment, of brain-injured patients)
  Build-A-Brain (BAB) program, 200–202
  childhood interventions (*see* Early intervention)
  children with ADHD, neuropsychological assessment of (*see* Attention deficit hyperactivity disorder (ADHD))
  clinical neuropsychology, in Portugal, 27
  communication assessment in stuttering, Luria battery in, 167–168
  cross-cultural psychologist, 299
  cultural-historical psychology, 132
  developmental neuropsychology
    children with learning disabilities, 6–7, 13, 14–16*t*, 17
    mental development, in childhood, 3
    neuropsychological education (habilitation), 43–44
    principles, 1–2
    psychogenic studies, 2–4
    syndrome of frontal lobe action control disorder, 44–49
  Executive Functions (EFs), definition, 117–118

Higher Cortical Functions (HCFs)
clinical-psychological investigation, 41–42
functional blocks, 39–41
regulatory role of language, on behavior, 35
'internalization of culture,', 299
neuropsychological clinical practice, 32–34
SEN and ND, children with (*see* Higher mental functions (HMFs))
speech remediation in children and adolescents, learning disabilities, 161–163
Luria-Nebraska Neuropsychological Battery, 33

M

Magnetic Resonance Imaging (MRI), 268
Maintenance therapy, 293, 294*t*
"Make-believe" play, 109
Mann's decisional conflict model, 127–128
Mateer, C.A., 109–110
Mathematics (dyscalculia), 16
"Mature play", 108
Mayor-Salovey-Caruso Emotional Intelligence Test (MSCEIT), 125
MBD. *See* Minimal Brain Dysfunction (MBD)
McCloskey Executive Functions Scale (MEFS), 114
Medical complexity, pediatric medical conditions
acquired and traumatic brain injuries, 260
challenges, 254
neurocognitive functioning, 254
pediatric cancer, 257–260
prematurity/low birth weight, 254–257
Medications
vs. behavior modification, 294
Individualized Educational Plan (IEP) meeting, 274–275
measures, 274
need for, 275
neuroimaging studies and neurodiagnostic testing, 268–270
pharmacogenomic studies, 293–294
process, 270–271
symptom-based approaches
aggressive behavior, 288–289
Attention Deficit and Hyperactivity Disorders, 276–279
constipation, 292–293
drooling, 289–292
headaches, 283–284, 285*t*
Obsessive-Compulsive Disorders, 287–288
seizures and epilepsy, 281–283
sleep disorders, 279–281
tic disorders, 286–287, 287*t*
for symptom types, 275
trial-and-error approach, 293–294
Mega, M.S., 110
Memory Validity Profile (MVP), 262
Mental development, 2–4
Metabolic testing, 270
Methylphenidates, 277
Migraine headaches, 284, 285*t*
Miller, B.L., 110
Minimal Brain Dysfunction (MBD), 4, 12
Mitochondrial testing, 270
MobyMax, 198–199, 202*f*, 205–206, 210
Monozygotic twins, 2, 4
Motor memory, 77
Moving energy, 231–232

N

Narrative speech, 48–49
NCCEA Sentence Repetition Subtest, 66
NCCEA Word Fluency Subtest, 65–66
Nekrasova, Y.B., 162–163
Neonatal Intensive Care Units (NICU), 254
NEPSY battery, 59–60
Neuropathology, 30
Neuropsychological assessment, of brain-injured patients, 61, 69
application, 54
combined qualitative and quantitative measures, 59–61
gnostic functions, evaluation of, 64–65
intellectual processes, evaluation of, 67–69
memory assessment, 66–67
motor activity, assessment of, 62–64
patient's general characteristics, 62
verbal functions, evaluation of, 65–66
diagnostic, remediative, preventive, and prognostic aspects, 54
Lurian qualitative analysis, 56–59, 59*f*
psychometric methods, 56, 58–59, 59*f*
Halstead-Reitan Neuropsychological Test Battery (HRNB) (*see* Halstead-Reitan Neuropsychological Test Battery (HRNB))
Reitan-Indiana Neuropsychological Test Battery for Children (RINB), 56
specificity and sensitivity, 55
Stroop Test, 55

Neuropsychological assessment, of brain-injured patients *(Continued)*
three-step procedure, for brain damage diagnostics, 56
Trail Making Test, 55
Wechsler Scale, 55
purposes, 53
task analysis, 57
Neuropsychological Deficit Scale (NDS), 9–10*t*
Neuropsychological Evaluation, 302–303
children's brain functions, 301
complex pediatric medical conditions
acquired and traumatic brain injuries, 260
challenges, 254
neurocognitive functioning, 254
pediatric cancer, 257–260
prematurity/low birth weight, 254–257
components of
feedback and follow-up/re-evaluation, 252–253
initial interview, 251
neuropsychological report, 252
records, reviewing of, 251–252
cross-cultural fertilization, 302
emotional distress, 301
environmental traumatization, 302
executive functions, 300–301
integrated medication management, 301–302
interpersonal learning, 301
intervention, 303
logical thinking and planning, 300–301
Pediatric Neuropsychological Evaluations
inpatient settings, 250
outpatient settings, 250
referral source and reason for referral, 249–250
rehabilitation settings, 250
Pediatric Neuropsychologists
intellectual assessment batteries, 261–262
in interdisciplinary care, 262–263
Performance Validity Tests, 262
resilience, in children and families, 263
play and social interactions, 300–301
prevention of disturbances, medicine and neuropsychology, 300
prevention possibilities, Luria-Reitan heritage, 300
research, 303–304
speech development, 301
Neuropsychological habilitation, 43–44
Neuropsychology Center of Louisiana (NCLA), 197–198
Nonstimulant medication, 277–279
Nonverbal communication, 159–160, 202–203
Normally developing children (ND), SEN and
child-adult communities, 180
cooperative learning, 181
critical thinking skills, 181
cultural-historical psychology, 179–180
dialogic learning, 181
group discussion strategy, 181
joint problem solving, 181, 186–192
language skills, second language acquisition, 181
metacooperative type of "community" ("obstchnost"), 191
physical defect, 179
Piaget's concept, 182
reflective thinking activities, 181
research and methods, 182–186
shared meaning, 181
social deprivation, 179–180
social interactions, 179–180
underdevelopment of, 179–180
Numeric Stroop Test, 75, 80–81

O

Obsessive-Compulsive Disorders (OCD), 287–288
Obstructive Sleep Apnea (OSA), 268–269
Occupational Therapy (OT), 18
Online math training software, 210
Openness, 125
Oral Praxis Test, 77
Oseretsky Test of Reciprocal Coordination, 62–63
Oxcarbazepine, 276

P

Parent counseling, 198
Parenting, special needs children, 294
Parkinson's disease, 38–39
Pearson Product-Moment Correlations, 100–101
Pediatric cancer, 257–260
Pediatric Neurologist
children's symptom presentation, 267
chromosomal microarray, 269
Denver Developmental Screening Test (Denver II), 267–268
exome sequencing, 269
general physical examination, 267
medical information, 271
seizure disorders, 275

Pediatric Neuropsychological Evaluations
  inpatient settings, 250
  outpatient settings, 250
  referral source and reason for referral, 249–250
  rehabilitation settings, 250
Pediatric Neuropsychologists
  Attention Deficit and Hyperactivity Disorders, 275
  intellectual assessment batteries, 261–262
  in interdisciplinary care, 262–263
  Performance Validity Tests, 262
  resilience, in children and families, 263
Pediatric Neuropsychology. *See* Developmental Neuropsychology
Performance Validity Tests (PVTs), 262
Periventricular Leukomalacia (PVL), 256
Personal autonomy, 141–142
Phraseological transition formula, 48–49
Pointing gesture, 189
Polysomnogram (PSG), 268–269
Prematurity/low birth weight, 254–257
Preschoolers, learning disabilities in, 6–7
Primary school maladjustment, 6–7, 19
Progressive Figures Test, 100
Proof-reading test, 76
Psychogenic studies, 2–4, 3*f*
Public health, 135
Pygmalion effect, 171

Q

Quantitative deficits, 6

R

Raskin, S.A., 110
Raven's Colored Progressive Matrices, 68
Reading (dyslexia), 16–17
Reflexive functioning, 153
REHABIT system, 202, 224–227
Reitan-Indiana Aphasia Screening Test, 65–66, 99, 102–103
Reitan-Indiana Neuropsychological Test Battery (RINB), 6–12, 8*t*, 31, 56–57, 97, 134, 274
Reitan-Indiana Sensory-Perceptual Examination, 65
Reitan-Klove Lateral Dominance Examination, 99
Reitan-Klove Sensory-Perceptual Examination, 99–100, 102–103
Reitan, Ralph M., 93, 133–134
  in academic community, 299
  brain-behavior functions, 108
  Build-A-Brain (BAB) program, 200–202
  clinical neuropsychology in Portugal, contribution to, 27–32
  Developmental Neuropsychology
    brain-behavior relationships, study of, 5–6
    children with learning disabilities, 11–16
    neuropsychological education (habilitation), 43–44
    neuropsychologically compromised children, 6–7
    quantitative and qualitative deficits, 6
    quantitative data analysis, 6
    syndrome of frontal lobe action control disorder, 44–49
  Halstead-Reitan Battery (*see* Halstead-Reitan Neuropsychological Test Battery (HRNB))
  quantitative neuropsychological analysis, 299–300
  REHABIT system, 225, 225*f*
  Reitan-Indiana Neuropsychological Test Battery (RINB) (*see* Reitan-Indiana Neuropsychological Test Battery (RINB))
  speech remediation in children and adolescents, learning disabilities, 161–163
Repeatable Battery for the Assessment of Neuropsychological Status (RBANS), 205, 215
Resilience and Empowerment Training and Workshop (RETAW) Child Ebola Version, 223, 237
Resilience, in children and families, 263
Retinopathy of prematurity (ROP), 256
Revised Children's Version of the Alternative Impairment Index (AII-CV-R), 101
Rey-Osterrieth Complex Figure Test, 63–64, 64*f*, 66
Rhythm Test, 98, 103
RINB. *See* Reitan-Indiana Neuropsychological Test Battery (RINB)
"Risk and Benefit" Test, 75, 82–83, 86–87, 87*f*
Risperidone, 288
Rizzo, M., 110
Rorschach-Exner examination, 46, 49
Rorschach Inkblot Test, 29
Rubtsov, V.V., 182–183
Russian developmental neuropsychology
  principles, 1–2
  psychogenic studies, 2–4

S

Safety, 230–231
Schedule of Growing Skills II (SGSII), 138
 active postural control, 139
 auditory and language, 140
 cognitive, 142
 locomotor, 139
 manipulatives, 139–140
 passive postural control, 138
 personal autonomy, 141–142
 social interaction, 141
 speech and language, 141
 visual, 140
Seizures, 281–283
Self-esteem, 232
Self-regulation, 108, 114
Serial Digit Learning Test, 66
Shifting, 112, 125, 230
Sialorrhea, 289–291, 291*t*
Six point scoring system, 60–61
Sleep disorders, 279–281
Social deficits, 212
Social rehabilitation
 general principles of
  different-age psychotherapeutic group, 173
  dynamic psychotherapeutic diagnosis and internal representation of health, 173
  as integral process, 172
  moral-psychological approach, problem of norm pathology, 172
  process, universal importance of, 172
  "psychological ground," preparation of, 173
  psychological-pedagogical and psychotherapeutic effects unity, 172
 motivational involvement, psychological mechanisms of
  adequacy, 171
  aspiration, 171
  coparticipation, 171
  Pygmalion effect, 171
  realization of goal, in ideal image, 171
Sohlberg, M.M., 109–110
Sorting Test, 116
Spatial memory, 66–67
Special Educational Needs (SEN), childrens with ND and
 child-adult communities, 180
 cooperative learning, 181
 critical thinking skills, 181
 cultural-historical psychology, 179–180
 dialogic learning, 181
 group discussion strategy, 181
 joint problem solving, 181, 186–192
 language skills, second language acquisition, 181
 physical defect, 179
 Piaget's concept, 182
 reflective thinking activities, 181
 research and methods, 182–186
 shared meaning, 181
 social deprivation, 179–180
 social interactions, 179–180
 underdevelopment of, 179–180
Special Needs Children (SEN), 294
Speech acquisition, 2–3
Speech rehabilitation of children
 family logopsychotherapy (*see* Logopsychotherapy)
 hemispheric interactions, 157
 lateralized function, 157
 logoneurosis, 157
 remediation process, psychological mechanisms of, 171–173
 social rehabilitation, general principles of
  different-age psychotherapeutic group, 173
  dynamic psychotherapeutic diagnosis and internal representation of health, 173
  as integral process, 172
  moral-psychological approach, problem of norm pathology, 172
  process, universal importance of, 172
  "psychological ground," preparation of, 173
  psychological-pedagogical and psychotherapeutic effects unity, 172
 stuttering (*see* Stuttering)
Speech remediation, in children and adolescents
 family group logopsychotherapy, Nekrasova and Karpova, 162–163
 family relations and speech disturbances, 161–162
Speech Sounds Perception Test, 6, 98, 100, 103
Speech Therapy, 3–4
Speech Unfolding task, 48–49
Stanford Binet Intelligence Scales, Fifth Edition (SB-5), 261
State anxiety, 126
Step-by-step method, 4
Stonnington, H.H., 109
Storytelling, 232
Strattera (atomoxetine), 278–279
Strength of Grip Test, 99, 102–103
Stroop Test, 55
Stuttering, 157
 brain mechanisms, system inter- and multidisciplinary study of, 163–164

communication assessment, Luria battery in, 167–168
communication problems and, 159–160
genetic and psychophysiological courses of, 158–159
sympathetic nervous system, logopsychotherapy, 166–167
Symbol therapy, 168, 170
Sympathetic nervous system, 166–167
Syndrome analysis, 45–46
brain-injured patients, neuropsychological assessment of, 56–58
clinical-psychological investigation, 41–42
Syndrome of frontal lobe action control disorder, 44–49
Syntagmatic analysis, 57

T

Tactile Form Recognition Test, 65
Tactile stimuli, 149
Tactual Performance Test (TPT), 57, 97–98, 100, 102–103
Task analysis, 57
Task-Monitor Scale, 113
Tension-type headaches, 284
Test of Memory Malingering (TOMM), 262
Tests of Variables of Attention (TOVAs), 205, 216
Tic disorders, 286–287, 287*t*
Topical diagnostics, 5
Topiramate, 286–287
Tower Test, 116
Trail Making Test, 55, 62, 98, 100, 103, 117, 216
Trait anxiety, 126
Tranel, D., 111
Traumatic Brain Injury (TBI), 23, 29, 132
Tweens' with learning disabilities, executive functions in
Build-A-Brain program (*see* Build-A-Brain (BAB) program)
emotional thinking, 197, 198*t*
language skills, 197
rational thinking, 197, 198*t*
Twenty Questions Test, 116
Twins model, 2–4, 3*f*

V

Verbal Fluency Test, 117
Verbal-Manual Interference Test, 158, 165
Verbal memory, 66–67
Verbal processing, 227–228
Verbal thinking, 34
Visual learners, 232–233
Visual memory, 66, 77
Visual reasoning, 4
Visual Search and Attention Test, 62
Visual stimuli, 149
Voice-activated writing, 18
Voluntary attention, 18, 34, 36
Vulnerability, 153
Vygotsky, L.S., 32–33
cultural-historical approach, 1–2, 115
executive functions, Luris's definition of, 115
Higher Cortical Functions (HCFs), 34, 36–38
Parkinson's disease, 38–39
SEN and ND, children with (*see* Higher mental functions (HMFs))

W

Wada Test, 158–159
WAIS-R
Block Design Subtest, 62–63, 63*f*
Picture Arrangement, 67
Picture Completion Subtest, 64–65
Weber-Fechner Law, 126
Wechsler Abbreviated Scale of Intelligence, Second Edition (WASI-II), 261
Wechsler Intelligence Scale for Children, Fifth Edition (WISC-V), 261
Wechsler Intelligence Scale for Children, Fifth Edition, Integrated (WISC-V-Integrated), 261
Wechsler Intelligence Scale for Children-Revised (WISC-R), 101–102
Wechsler Scale, 29–30, 55, 95–96
Wellbutrin XL (bupropion), 279
Whole exome sequencing, 269–270
Wide Range Achievement Test (4th Edition) (WRAT-4), 204, 214–215, 215*t*
Wisconsin Card Sorting Test (WCST), 21, 67, 117
Word Context Test, 116
Working memory
Build-A-Brain (BAB) program, 208
updating, 124
World Health Organization (WHO), 221

Y

Yerkes-Dodson Law, 126

Z

Zone of proximal development (ZPD), 34–35

FSC
www.fsc.org
MIX
Papier | Fördert
gute Waldnutzung
FSC® C083411

Kolibri 360 GmbH
Ferdinand-Jühlke-Straße 7
99095 Erfurt, Deutschland
produktsicherheit@kolibri360.de